EARTH REPORT 2000

EARTH REPORT 2000

Revisiting the True State of the Planet

RONALD BAILEY, EDITOR

McGraw-Hill
New York   San Francisco   Washington, D.C.   Auckland   Bogotá
Caracas   Lisbon   London   Madrid   Mexico City   Milan
Montreal   New Delhi   San Juan   Singapore
Sydney   Tokyo   Toronto

McGraw-Hill
A Division of The **McGraw·Hill** Companies

Copyright © 2000 by Ronald Bailey. All rights reserved. Printed in the United States of America. Except as permitted under the United States Copyright Act of 1976, no part of this publication may be reproduced or distributed in any form or by any means, or stored in a data base or retrieval system, without the prior written permission of the publisher.

1 2 3 4 5 6 7 8 9 0   DOC/DOC   9 0 9 8 7 6 5 4 3 2 1 0 9

ISBN 0-07-134260-5

This book was set in Goudy by North Market Street Graphics. Printed and bound by R. R. Donnelley & Sons Company

McGraw-Hill books are available at special quantity discounts to use as premiums and sales promotions, or for use in corporate training programs. For more information, please write to the Director of Special Sales, McGraw-Hill, 11 West 19th Street, New York, NY 10011. Or contact your local bookstore.

 This book is printed on recycled, acid-free paper containing a minimum of 50% recycled, de-inked fiber.

CONTENTS

Contributors   vii

Dedication: Julian Simon—An Appreciation   xiii
Fred L. Smith

Introduction: Thinking Clearly   xvii
Michael Novak

1. The Progress Explosion: Permanently Escaping the Malthusian Trap   1
Ronald Bailey

2. How Do We Know the Temperature of The Earth? Global Warming and Global Temperatures   23
Roy Spencer

3. Doing More with Less: Dematerialization—Unsung Environmental Triumph?   41
Lynn Scarlett

4. World Population Prospects for the Twenty-First Century: The Specter of "Depopulation"?   63
Nicholas Eberstadt

5. Fishing for Solutions: The State of the World's Fisheries   85
Michael De Alessi

6. Soft Energy Versus Hard Facts: Powering the Twenty-First Century   115
Jerry Taylor and Peter VanDoren

7. Richer Is More Resilient: Dealing with Climate Change and More Urgent Environmental Problems   155
Indur M. Goklany

8. Endocrine Disruptors: New Toxic Menace? 189
Stephen H. Safe

9. Biological Diversity: Divergent Views on Its Status and Diverging Approaches to Its Conservation 203
Rowan B. Martin

Benchmarks: The Global Trends That Are Shaping Our World 237
Paul Georgia, Indur Goklany, and the Competitive Enterprise Institute Staff

Endnotes 311

Index 351

Acknowledgments 363

CONTRIBUTORS

Ronald Bailey is the science correspondent for *Reason* magazine. He is the author of *ECO-SCAM: The False Prophets of Ecological Apocalypse* (St. Martins Press, 1993). In 1995, he edited *The True State of the Planet* (The Free Press). He has produced several series and documentaries for PBS television and ABC News. Mr. Bailey was the 1993 Warren T. Brookes Fellow in Environmental Journalism at the Competitive Enterprise Institute. His articles and reviews have appeared in *The Wall Street Journal, The Washington Post, Commentary, The New York Times Book Review, The Public Interest, Smithsonian* magazine, *National Review, Reason, Forbes, The Washington Times, Newsday,* and *Readers Digest*. He has lectured at Harvard University, Rutgers University, McGill University, University of Alaska, Université de Québec à Montréal, the Cato Institute, the Instituto de Libertad y Desarrollo (Chile), and the American Enterprise Institute. He is a member of the Society of Environmental Journalists.

Michael De Alessi is director of the Center for Private Conservation, and a research associate at the Competitive Enterprise Institute, specializing in marine conservation issues. He received a B.A. in economics and an M.S. in engineering economic systems from Stanford University, and an M.A. in marine policy from the Rosenstiel School of Marine and Atmospheric Science at the University of Miami. He is the author of *Fishing for Solutions* (IEA, 1997), and the Center for Private Conservation study, entitled *Emerging Technologies and the Private Stewardship of Marine Resources*. His writings on marine issues have appeared in the *International Herald Tribune, New Scientist, The Wall Street Journal, Journal of Commerce,* and *Scientific American,* among other publications.

Nicholas Eberstadt is a researcher with the American Enterprise Institute and the Harvard Center for Population and Development Studies. He has written widely, in both professional journals and mass media, about issues in population and development, and serves as a consultant to the U.S. Bureau of the Census. Mr. Eberstadt's books include *Fertility Decline in the Less Developed Countries* (editor, 1981), *The Population of North Korea* (coauthor, 1992), and *The Tyranny of Numbers: Mismeasurement and Misrule* (1995). A graduate of

Harvard College, Mr. Eberstadt earned master's degrees from both the Kennedy School of Government and the London School of Economics, and a Ph.D. from Harvard University.

Indur M. Goklany is manager of science and engineering in the U.S. Department of the Interior's Office of Policy Analysis. He has over 25 years' experience dealing with energy and environmental issues working for various state and federal environmental agencies, and as a consultant to government and industry. Between 1988 and 1992, he represented the United States at the Intergovernmental Negotiating Committee, which formulated the Framework Convention on Climate Change, and the Intergovernmental Panel on Climate Change (IPCC) and a number of its working groups and subsidiary bodies dealing with impacts, adaptation, and mitigation. He also led the U.S. delegation to the IPCC's Resource Use and Management Subgroup. As rapporteur to that Subgroup, he was the prime author of its report on strategies to adapt to climate change for the agricultural, water resources, forestry, land use, and other resource management sectors. As Executive Director of the Departmental Working Group on Climate Change, he conceived, organized, and managed the development of the Department of the Interior's portion of the Federal Global Change Research Program during its first year of existence. In addition to climate change, his most recent publications have dealt with long-term trends in habitat loss, biodiversity, and air and water quality; how these trends have been affected by technological change and economic growth; and whether and how future global food needs can be met while conserving habitat, forests, and biodiversity. He is currently working on a book, to be published by the Cato Institute, on the trends in U.S. air quality over the last century and the social, economic, and technological factors driving those trends. He contributed the chapter on adaptation to climate change as an independent scholar, and it reflects solely his views and not those of the Department of the Interior or of the federal government.

Rowan Martin was born in Harare in 1942 and is a Zimbabwe citizen. He attended school in Zimbabwe and university in England, where he graduated as an electrical engineer and also obtained a master's degree in solid-state physics with a thesis on superconductivity. Much later in his career, he obtained a diploma in field ecology from the University of Zimbabwe, where he is still registered as a Ph.D. researcher on a part-time basis.

From 1966 to 1969, he worked for the Anglo American Corporation in South Africa as an electronic engineer, and his projects included automation of mining processes for gold, diamond, and iron ore mines in South Africa, optimization of underground railway systems, and marine diamond mining off the coast of Namibia where he carried out oceanographic surveys, research in mining methods, and design of equipment for sea mining.

He spent 1970 on a 1-year bush safari in Southern Africa, and in 1971 he sailed across the Indian Ocean. He specialized in wildlife and bird sound recordings during these 2 years.

He began his career with the Zimbabwe Department of National Parks and Wildlife Management in 1972 working on biotelemetry projects and retired as deputy director of that organization in 1997. His first 7 years in the Department were spent at Sengwa Wildlife Research Institute where he designed and constructed radio collars for a variety of large mammal species and carried out field research on elephant home ranges and movement patterns. This research was registered for a doctoral thesis and has become internationally recognized (*National Geographic* magazine, August 1989).

His career experience has covered activities ranging from regional land use planning to representing Zimbabwe in international environmental treaties. He is perhaps best known for the development of one of the first community-based wildlife management programs in Africa: Zimbabwe's CAMPFIRE program, under which local people have assumed full responsibilities for managing wildlife and forest resources and created a land use revolution that genuinely achieves "conservation with development." CAMPFIRE has now become well known internationally, and the model is being adopted by many other countries.

He is now retired and working as an independent environmental consultant.

Michael Novak is the George Frederick Jewett Scholar in Religion, Philosophy, and Public Policy and the Director of Social and Political Studies at the American Enterprise Institute in Washington, D.C.

He has served as U.S. Delegate to the Conference on Security and Cooperation in Europe, 1986; U.S. Ambassador to the U.N. Human Rights Commission in Geneva, 1981–1982; Adviser in the White House Office of Ethnic Affairs, 1974–1980; and as faculty at Harvard University, the State University of New York at Old Westbury, Syracuse University, and the University of Notre Dame.

He is the author of numerous books, including *On Cultivating Liberty: Reflections on Moral Ecology* (1999), *To Empower People: From State to Civil Society* (editor, 1996), *The Spirit of Democratic Capitalism* (revised edition, 1991), and *This Hemisphere of Liberty: A Philosophy of the Americas* (1990). His articles have appeared in a wide range of journals, including *The New Republic*, *The American Spectator*, *First Things*, *Commentary*, *National Review*, *Yale Law Journal*, *The Atlantic Monthly*, *The Weekly Standard*, *The Public Interest*, *Crisis*, and *Harpers*.

His work has been widely recognized and he received many awards, including The Francis Boyer Award, 1999; Twenty-fourth Templeton Prize for Progress in Religion, 1994; and the Anthony Fisher Prize for *The Spirit of Democratic Capitalism*, 1992.

He received an M.A. in history and philosophy of religion from Harvard University, a B.A., *cum laude*, from the Gregorian University in Rome, and a B.A., *summa cum laude*, from Stonehill College.

Stephen Safe is a Distinguished Professor of Toxicology in the College of Veterinary Medicine, Chair of the Faculty of Toxicology, and Director of the National Institute of Health Sciences (NIEHS) Center at Texas A&M University. He has served on a number of committees, including the National Research Council, Committee on Hormonally Active Agents in the Environment, the advisory council for the NIEHS, and has been chair of the Education Committee and Councilor of the Society of Toxicology. He was a Burroughs Wellcome Toxicology Scholar (1989–1994), and he currently serves on the Program Advisory Committee of the Burroughs Wellcome Fund. His research is focused on molecular mechanisms of estrogen receptor and growth factor action, crosstalk between the aryl hydrocarbon (Ah) receptor and mitogen-induced responses in breast cancer cells and the development of new Ah receptor-based drugs for treatment of breast cancer. He is coauthor of over 450 refereed publications and five books.

Lynn Scarlett is executive director of Reason Public Policy Institute in Los Angeles, where her primary research focus is on environmental issues. She was appointed by California's Governor Pete Wilson in 1994 to serve as Chair of the state's Inspection and Maintenance Review Committee, which evaluates the state's automobile emission-testing program. She also chairs the "How Clean Is Clean" Working Group of the National Environmental Policy Institute. She has served as an expert panelist for the U.S. Environmental Protection Agency on two satellite video programs on solid waste management. She also served as Technical Advisor to the Solid Waste Association of North America's Integrated Waste Management Project. Scarlett has published numerous articles on solid waste, recycling, and resource use in both popular media and academic journals.

Fred L. Smith, Jr., is the founder and president of the Competitive Enterprise Institute (CEI), a public-policy research group studying how to apply the principles of free enterprise and limited government to a wide range of economic and environmental public-policy issues. Based in Washington, D.C., CEI works to educate and inform policymakers, journalists, and other opinion leaders on market-based alternatives to regulatory initiatives, ranging from antitrust and insurance to energy and environmental protection, and engages in public interest litigation to protect property rights and economic liberty. Mr. Smith is a frequent contributor to leading newspapers and journals, such as *The Wall Street Journal, National Review, Economic Affairs,* and the *Washington Times*. Mr. Smith is also a columnist for the journal *Regulation,* and a contributing editor to *Liberty*. Mr. Smith is coeditor (with Michael Greve) of the book, *Environmental Politics: Public Costs, Private Rewards,* and has contributed chapters to over one dozen books, including *The True State of the Planet; Market Liberalism: A Paradigm for the 21st Century;* and *Assessing the Reagan Years.*

Before founding CEI, Mr. Smith served as the director of government relations for the Council for a Competitive Economy, as a senior economist for the Association of American Railroads, and for 5 years as a senior policy analyst at the Environmental Protection Agency. Mr. Smith has a degree in mathematics and political science from Tulane University, where he earned the Arts and Sciences Medal. He has also done graduate work at Harvard, SUNY at Buffalo, and the University of Pennsylvania.

Dr. Roy W. Spencer is senior scientist for climate studies at NASA's Marshall Space Flight Center in Huntsville, Alabama. He received his Ph.D. in meteorology from the University of Wisconsin in 1981. At NASA, Dr. Spencer directs research into the development and application of satellite-passive microwave remote sensing techniques for measuring global temperature, water vapor, and precipitation. Dr. Spencer received the American Meteorological Society's 1996 Special Award for his satellite-based temperature-monitoring work, and is a recipient of NASA's Exceptional Scientific Achievement Medal. He is the author of numerous scientific articles, which have appeared in *Science, Nature, Journal of Climate, Monthly Weather Review, Journal of Atmospheric and Oceanic Technology, Journal of Climate and Applied Meteorology, Remote Sensing Reviews, Advances in Space Research,* and *Climatic Change.* He has testified in the House and Senate on the subject of global warming.

Jerry Taylor is the director of natural resource studies at the Cato Institute and senior editor of *Regulation* magazine. Mr. Taylor has authored studies on energy conservation, trade, and the environment; sustainable development; electric utility restructuring; Superfund; and solid waste management. He has testified frequently on these and other issues before the United States Congress and had the distinction of appearing on former Energy Secretary Hazel O'Leary's "enemies list." Taylor has also contributed to several anthologies, including *Market Liberalism: A New Paradigm for the 21st Century, The Cato Handbook for Congress,* and most recently, *China as a Global Economic Power: Market Reforms and the New Millennium.* He is also the author of *A Natural Resources Policy Agenda for the 1990s.*

Mr. Taylor is an adjunct scholar at the Institute for Energy Research in Houston. He is a member of numerous professional societies, including the International Society for Ecological Economics, the American Association for the Advancement of Science, the Air and Waste Management Association, and the International Association for Energy Economics. He is a graduate of the University of Iowa, where he received a B.A. in political science.

Peter VanDoren is the editor of *Regulation* magazine. He received his bachelor of science degree from the Massachusetts Institute of Technology (1977), and his master's (1980) and Ph.D. degrees (1985) from Yale. He taught at the Woodrow Wilson School of Public and International Affairs, Princeton University, from 1984 until 1991, at the School of Organization and Management, Yale University, from 1991 until 1993, and in the Public Administration Program at the University of North Carolina at Chapel Hill from 1993 until 1997. In 1987–1988, he was a postdoctoral fellow in political economy at Carnegie Mellon University.

His research examines positive and normative issues in the political regulation of markets, including banking, housing, land, energy, transportation, health, environment, and labor markets. His publications include *Politics, Markets, and Congressional Policy Choices*, "Should Congress Listen to Economists?", in *Journal of Politics*; "Do Legislators Vote Their Constituents' Wallets (And How Would We Know If They Did?)," in *Southern Economic Journal*; "The Effects of Exposure to Synthetic Chemicals on Human Health: A Review," in *Risk Analysis*; *The Deregulation of the Electricity Industry: A Primer*; and the recently published Cato book, *Cancer, Chemicals, and Choices: Risk Reduction Through Markets*.

DEDICATION
Julian Simon—An Appreciation

Fred L. Smith

This volume is dedicated to the memory of Julian Simon.

Julian Simon was the first—and for many years almost the only—academic to challenge the Malthusian belief that progress is illusory, that mankind faces an increasingly bleak future. His route to that position was somewhat unusual. Prior to becoming an economist, he was a direct marketer and advertising specialist. He began his academic career in the field of population studies. To Julian and others of that era, overpopulation seemed *the* problem of civilization. Each person, it was commonly observed, consumed resources and occupied space, thereby diminishing the prospects for others. If mankind's blind biological urges were left unchecked, the population growth would soon exhaust the finite resources of the earth. Julian initially accepted this conventional wisdom; however, unlike his more ideological brethren, he examined the facts, found they did not support pessimism, and soon rejected the Malthusian thesis.

Julian's rejection of Malthusianism was, in fact, a rebuke of pessimism in general, an antidote to the poisonous theories he encountered throughout the academic world. That widespread pessimism has been documented by Arthur Herman in his recent book, *The Idea of Decline in Western History*, where he identifies two distinct wings of this gloomy philosophy: the Historic Pessimists (largely conservatives) and the Cultural Pessimists (largely left liberal). Pessimists of the first type see civilization as inevitably overwhelmed by attacks from malign and destructive forces that develop over time. Joseph Schumpeter is perhaps the most typical representative of this view. In contrast, the cultural pessimist sees civilization itself as the destructive force that threatens man's existence. The collapse of civilization, some of them suggest, might not be a bad thing. Although Julian did not explicitly tackle these scholastic naysayers, his work was a universal solvent dissolving away the negativism of both schools.

Although in his personal life Julian sometimes experienced bouts of despair, his optimism about the ultimate outcome of man's struggle for a better world never varied. In large part that optimism was aesthetic. To Julian, life is the ultimate experience, a rapturous opportunity for the individual to contribute positively to a challenging, but increasingly hospitable, world. Although his arguments were often utilitarian in detail, they remained profoundly aesthetic and moral in structure. Every human life, Julian insisted, was a unique creative experience. How dare anyone judge that some lives are not worth living? Thus, although his work consistently demonstrated the true bounty and resiliency of the earth, his most enthusiastic praise was always reserved for the true *Ultimate Resource, humanity*.

My interactions with Julian were infrequent, but they were always stimulating, despite his soft demeanor. Julian did not like conflict and was reluctant to partake in the vicious rhetorical attacks typical of the political world; however, Julian cared and responded accordingly. One example: he was our keynote speaker at an Earth Day Alternative Conference some years ago. Softly, he announced that even though he had always hoped that intellectual error accounted for the policies of the environmental establishment, he would no longer accept such excuses. These people, he concluded, were enemies of humanity. Julian was soft spoken, but passionate about humanity and its potential. That persistence and competence made him impossible to ignore. Indeed, Julian's talk at that Earth Day event led later to a major *New York Times Magazine* article surveying his work.

Julian was eclectic. Beyond his work on population and resource economics, he wrote on statistics, research methods, the economics of advertising, managerial economics, and even on depression. The diversity of Julian's interests was something to which his critics (always favorable to diversity in other guises) were hostile. What right did a former ad man have to expose the fallacies of the ecocatastrophists? Julian was frustrated by the difficulty of gaining a hearing for his contrarian views, but his training in marketing led him to innovate. In his book, *Ultimate Resource Two*, he noted, "I have decided that the only way to deal adequately with the subject of [pollution] . . . may be satire . . ." His flair at marketing was perhaps best demonstrated by his famous wager with Paul Ehrlich over whether scarcity or abundance best characterized man's future. Ehrlich picked the commodities—and still lost overwhelmingly. That wager transformed an abstract policy dispute into a major news story and will remain a thorn in the side of Green activism for years to come.

Simon was eclectic in another way, also. There are many academics who reject the pessimistic "we're running out of everything" views, advanced by Lester Brown and his colleagues at the Worldwatch Institute, whose view is that somehow reducing material use is good and necessary. Few of these resource economists, however, extend their criticisms to those calling for population control, who view reducing the number of people on this planet as a "good thing." Julian is one of the few scholars who worked in both areas and who rejected both Malthusian beliefs, emphasizing the similarity of the biases and errors behind each of these neo-Malthusian prongs. Julian noted that babies, like other investments, involve up-front costs for later benefits, both of which are necessary for a positive tomorrow. Julian thought it was wrong to view mankind as a plague on this earth; he also thought it was wrong to view subsistence poverty as inevitable. Julian bridged the gap between the economic and social wings of the conservative intellectual movement, making possible an alliance needed to offset the Malthusian forces in society.

As a fighter within academia, Julian understood, earlier and more painfully than most, the academy's resistance to dissent. He experienced what has now become obvious to us all: the attempt to choke off the intellectual debate by systematically discrediting all non-establishment views. Only his persistence and brilliance forced people to listen. Julian recognized that the intellectual battlefield was not level—that efforts to distort his views would be all too frequent. He also knew, however, that the battle must be waged. To Julian, the world remains bright only by individuals lighting again and again the flame of truth.

Julian had an almost eschatological faith: Regardless of the evils that man (especially man operating through the coercive instruments of government) might embrace, mankind's positive spirit, he believed, would still triumph. Elitist prejudices and political power might deflect, censor, hinder, hamstring and restrict—but humanity would ultimately prevail. Wrong ideas, Julian believed, could not prevail against the creative power of mankind. After all, he noted, "markets are not driven by grand ideas, but by human desires and economic incentives." Julian, of course, realized that reversals were unavoidable (pointing to the 70-year tragedy of communism), but he hoped that "in a world where people can move ever more freely, these reversions will be of shorter duration and of lesser magnitude."

I sometimes was critical of Julian for spending too little time discussing the institutions and social arrangements critical for man's creative spirit to flourish. To me, Julian seemed often to take such freedom-enhancing institutions (private property, a rule of law, voluntary contracts, tolerance)—all too rare both historically and geographically—for granted. Julian never explicitly addressed my concern that if the institutions of freedom were to wither away, mankind might very well be faced with a true Malthusian tragedy.

Yet, as time goes by, I've come to think that perhaps Julian was right. He realized, of course, that progress would vary greatly, depending on the prevailing institutional framework. Certainly, Julian fully understood that oppressive institutions would oppress. Yet, he remained convinced that mankind would surmount the limits of the present institutions, that the Iron Curtains that restrict mankind would be forced open by man's unconquerable spirit.

Julian's work has been very important in the crusade to liberate the human spirit. This book is intended to further that project, to clarify ways in which the institutional framework that exists liberates more or less of man's creative powers, allowing more or fewer of us to contribute to mankind's future, to enjoy even more the full rapture of life. This book is one step in the struggle to advance Julian's vision of human progress and a healthy natural environment.

Julian did not survive to see the end of this struggle, and many of us may not either. He did not slay the doomsayers—and perhaps that is an impossibility. Pessimists are likely always to be with us. Julian did, however, strike some of the first blows in the effort to free man from the Malthusian miasma, and his efforts encouraged me and others to continue that work in this volume. I do believe that his work will continue to influence this debate and that his optimism will ultimately prevail.

INTRODUCTION

Our first moral obligation, Pascal wrote, is to think clearly. Meeting that obligation is the purpose of this book.

Of all the creatures known to us, the human being is the only one who is free to obey, or not to obey, the laws of his or her own nature. Of all creatures, the human being is the only one with the capacity to reflect (to deliberate upon alternatives) and to choose (to make commitments on which others can rely). Of course, we do not always heed these possibilities of our nature. Instead of reflecting first, we sometimes rush into thoughtless action. Instead of making a reflective, seriously intended, self-committing choice, we sometimes prefer to follow the line of least resistance and to drift lazily along, long-term consequences be damned.

The entire environmental movement is based on these propositions. If it is not constituted by study groups, inquiries, data collection, publications, warnings and alarms, consciousness raising, propaganda, education, and political action campaigns designed, at a minimum, to raise public awareness, what is the environmental movement? If it is not concerned with depicting the possible or probable consequences of current behaviors (usually consequences predicted to be disastrous) and if it is not concerned with proposing alternatives (whose consequences are portrayed as more benevolent) on what, exactly, is it spending considerable human energies and resources?

The environmental movement is either a serious moral and intellectual inquiry or it is not. If it is not serious, it is not worth our energies. If it is serious, it must consider arguments on all sides of a question—it is not enough to jump to preloved and predesired conclusions. It must give evidence of having thought clearly, of having made all necessary and useful distinctions, of having examined all assumptions (including those at first well hidden), and of having entertained all arguments contrary to its own initial conclusions. The last thing it can afford to offer is a rush to judgment, for that is precisely the fault it finds in the status quo. Its primal cry is: "Wake up! Inquire! Study! Think! Become responsible!" The environmental movement, therefore, must heed its own advice.

That is why, more than most political movements, the environmental movement needs to foster a thorough and dramatic competition of ideas. What it cannot afford is a single smelly orthodoxy to which all must conform. That would be as stale as a crowded room without ventilation. That would create an atmosphere of great danger to the future of this planet. That would be as toxic to the "moral ecology" of reflection and choice as an invisible poison gas in a subway car.

This book, therefore, is a great gift to the environmental movement. It opens up room in which individuals may exercise the crucial faculty of critical thinking. It presents data in abundance, data often widely neglected in the press and picked up only in the most alert and thoughtful quarters. It also presents turns of argument and original conceptions that the chief voices of Official Environmentalism seem never to have sufficiently considered. This book is, for that reason alone, exhilarating to read. It does not ask one to conform. It does not ask one to shout "Amen!" This book invites its readers to think—to think critically for themselves, in the light of more than one way of thinking, with more than one set of data, more than one set of hypotheses, more than one Big Picture of the way things stand at the end of the twentieth century.

Finally, I want to say a few words about the concept of "moral ecology." Just as there is an environment for our living, breathing bodies (and a rare environment it is in this vast cold cosmos), so also there is an environment for human reflecting and choosing. The ancient word for this environment is *ethos*. That is, the full and complicated set of narratives, expectations, fears, symbols, concepts, tendencies, symbols, memories that constitute "the spirit of the age," the context that bears in upon our reflections and choices, the context that dates us, the context that makes it difficult for truly independent minds and spirits to transcend their age. The ethos may be imagined as the ocean in which we swim, or even the thin band of air around planet Earth within which we are able to breathe. However, it is actually more penetrating than either of those, because the ethos of our time enters into our very spirits and our minds, our vocabulary of words and images, our turns of thought and feeling and speech.

Keeping this ethos pure—that is, favorable to serious reflection and deliberate choosing—is a task crucial to human health of soul. For the term *soul* means reflecting and choosing, just as a great-souled person is one unusually wise, generous, and penetrating in judgment and brave and longsuffering in fidelity to commitments made. Put it this way: What good would it be for us to have clean water, clean food, clean air, sanitary homes, and purified workplaces, if our moral ecology reduced us to living the life of cows in clean, well-lighted barns? For human beings, the moral ecology of Earth is even more important than its physical ecology—not in all respects primary, but of weightier final worth.

Why is that? Because at the end of the day we cannot help wishing to live as human beings ought to live—that is, as far as possible out of generous and accurate reflection and deliberate, wholehearted choice. We blame ourselves when we do not, when we have not done so—when we were not careful in our reflections, but stupid, and when we are forced to recognize that many of our choices have been bad.

There is another reason, too, having to do with a word frequently used but seldom clearly defined: *integrity*. "Purity of soul," Kierkegaard learned from pain, "is to will one thing." That is what *integrity*—wholeheartedness—means. People who say what they mean and mean what they say, who, as it were, stand fully behind every word and every deed, are the most precious resources the human race possesses.

To maintain an ecology of the spirit in which acts of reflection and choice, and the experience of meeting integrity in others, are frequent everyday occurrences is exceedingly important to human happiness. However, it is also important, instrumentally, to every serious political and moral movement. An environmental movement without serious reflection, and deliberate choice among clearly considered alternatives, is not worth having.

That is why this book is vital to the health of the environmental movement. The competition of ideas is as necessary for a healthy environmental movement as it is for any society that wishes to be free. To promote such competition is to commit oneself to counterthinking, to thinking against the grain of what most people of the age are saying, to lean against prevailing winds. For myself, I have always found the most exciting thinking to arise from just such struggles.

The reader who enjoys the vigorous competition of ideas and a shaking up of accepted but premature conclusions will find sustained excitement in this book. Even those who in the end disagree with parts of what is presented here will be grateful to have at hand clear statements of arguments they will now have to face head-on, and show others how to surmount. That, too, to any serious thinker is a gift.

I extend my thanks to the publisher, the editor, and the writers of the research papers that have afforded me much pleasure and much intellectual sustenance. This is the sort of book from which one comes away, agree or disagree, a better citizen.

Michael Novak
Washington, D.C.

Chapter 1

THE PROGRESS EXPLOSION
Permanently Escaping the Malthusian Trap

Ronald Bailey

HIGHLIGHTS

- *Two hundred years ago, Thomas Robert Malthus, in his* An Essay on the Principle of Population, *argued that the human population would increase at an exponential rate, always outstripping available food supplies, which could only grow at an arithmetic rate. This mismatch guaranteed that some portion of humanity would always suffer starvation and misery.*

- *In the second half of the twentieth century, modern Malthusians, including Stanford University biologist Paul Ehrlich, Worldwatch Institute founder Lester Brown, and researchers for* The Limits to Growth *report to the Club of Rome, expanded Malthus' theory to apply it to a far greater range of resources. They too claimed that exponential growth rates in population and economic growth would cause imminent resource depletion, starvation, and increasing death rates.*

- *Human population has tripled in this century, yet, contrary to Malthusian theory, food supplies and real wealth have grown at an even faster pace. As a result, global life expectancy has more than doubled since 1900.*

- *Recent developments in economic theory, called New Growth Theory, have shed considerable light on how humanity has avoided the Malthusian trap. The wellsprings of economic growth are new ideas. People actually improve their lives not through simply using more physical resources, like land, timber, or oil, but by discovering better ways of doing things and novel inventions. Humanity cannot deplete the supply of new ideas, designs, and recipes.*

- *The potency of ideas is shown by the fact that although the world's population has nearly doubled since the 1960s, the amount of land devoted to agriculture has not increased.*

- *Increased wealth makes it possible for people to demand and to pay for environmental improvements, like safe drinking water and cleaner air. For example, since the 1970s, the U.S. gross domestic product (GDP) has doubled while air and water pollution levels have fallen. This is a worldwide phenomenon.*

- *On the basis of the so-called I = PAT equation—environmental Impact equals Population, multiplied by consumption (Affluence), and further multiplied by Technology—modern Malthusians claim that people in developed countries overconsume and create even more environmental problems than poor people living in developing countries. The I = PAT formula actually gets it backward—Greater affluence and technological sophistication mean an improving natural environment, not a worsening one. The average American worker's output today is 10 times more valuable than 100 years ago, making it possible for Americans to devote resources to protecting and restoring the natural environment. In short, the average Westerner creates more resources, especially knowledge and technology, than she or he consumes. That's why they live in countries where both their economies and their environments are improving.*

In 1798, Malthus proposed one of the central doctrines of modern environmentalism: He asserted that human population always grows faster than food supplies, leading to misery and the destruction of nature.
(Credit: Mary Evans Picture Library.)

- *Open markets and democratic governance seem to be indispensable institutions for the prevention of famine in modern times. Nobel Prize–winning economist Amartya Sen notes "that in the terrible history of famines in the world, there is hardly any case in which a famine has occurred in a country that is independent and democratic with an uncensored press."*

- *Two centuries after Malthus, it is now clear that the exponential growth of knowledge, not population, is the real key to understanding the future of humanity and the earth.*

Two hundred years after Thomas Robert Malthus first published his *An Essay on the Principle of Population*, demographers, ecologists, economists, biologists, and policymakers are still hotly debating his theory of population. Leading foundations spend scores of millions of dollars on population programs, and the United Nations holds international conferences on the topic and has a specialized agency, the United Nations Population Fund, devoted to the issue. Every year, scores of weighty studies and books pour from the universities and think tanks discussing what is to be done about population.

Malthus made two propositions that he regarded as completely self-evident: First, "food is necessary for the existence of man"; second, "the passion between the sexes is necessary and will remain nearly in its present state."[1] Based on these propositions, Malthus famously concluded that "the power of population is indefinitely greater than the power in the earth to produce subsistence for man. Population, when unchecked, increases in a geometrical ratio. Subsistence increases only in an arithmetical ratio. A slight acquaintance with numbers will show the immensity of the first power in comparison with the second . . . This implies a strong and constantly operating check on population from the difficulty of subsistence."[2] Malthus' dismal summary of the situation in which humanity finds itself is "that the superior power of population cannot be checked without producing misery or vice. . . ."[3] In other words, some portion of humanity must forever be starving to death. In addition, trying to help those who are starving will only lead to further misery later as those initially spared from famine bear too many children and food supplies are no longer adequate to feed the new mouths.

Malthus illustrated his hypothesis using two series of numbers: "The human species would increase in the ratio of—1, 2, 4, 8, 16, 32, 64, 128, 256, 512, &c. and subsistence as—1, 2, 3, 4, 5, 6, 7, 8, 9, 10, &c."[4] He further asserted, "That population does invariably increase where there are the means of subsistence, the history of every people that have ever existed will abundantly prove."[5] In his first edition of the *Essay,* Malthus argued that there were two "checks" on population: *preventive* and *positive.* Preventive checks (those that prevent births) include abortion, infanticide, prostitution, and so forth, whereas positive checks include war, pestilence, and famine. In later editions, he added a third check, which he called *moral restraint,* which includes voluntary celibacy, late marriage, and so on. Moral restraint is basically just a milder version of the earlier preventive check.

If all else fails to keep human numbers in check, Malthus chillingly concludes:

> Famine seems to be the last, the most dreadful resource of nature. The power of population is so superior to the power in the earth to produce subsistence for man, that premature death must in some shape or other visit the human race. The vices of mankind are active and able ministers of depopulation. They are the precursors in the great army of destruction, and often finish the dreadful work themselves. But should they fail in this war of extermination, sickly seasons, epidemics, pestilence, and plague, advance in terrific array, and sweep off their thousands and ten thousands. Should success be still incomplete, gigantic inevitable famine stalks in the rear, and with one mighty blow, levels the population with the food of the world.[6]

Clearly, economics rightly deserved the "dismal science" moniker that Carlyle put on the fledgling field after reading Malthus.

Malthus' principle of population has been one of the most influential and most contested theories in history. For example, the principle of population provided a crucial insight for Charles Darwin as he was developing his theory of natural selection. In his autobiography Darwin wrote that in October 1838: "I happened to read for amusement Malthus on Population, and being well prepared to appreciate the struggle for existence which everywhere goes on, from long-continued observation of the habits of animals and plants, it at once struck me that under these circumstances favourable variations would tend to be preserved, and unfavourable ones would be destroyed. The result of this would be the formation of a new species. Here, then, I had at last got a theory by which to work."[7] Darwin knew that most plants and animals produced far more offspring than would survive to adulthood owing to predation and limits on food supplies. The differential rates of survival among the offspring are the driving forces behind most natural selection and, thus, of biological evolution.

Ever since Darwin, naturalists, biologists, and ecologists have been the leading champions of Malthus' theory, applying it not only to animals and plants, but to human societies as well. Undeniably, Malthusian theory has an appealing simplicity that purports to explain a lot of complicated data. In fact, Malthus' principle of population has been a very fruitful hypothesis for ecology and population biology. It undergirds such biological concepts as carrying capacity (which is a measure of the population of, for instance, deer or buffalo) that a given ecosystem can support. The Kaibab Plateau deer is a famous case of an animal population outstripping its food supply. In the 1920s, the deer population expanded dramatically in the absence of predators, leading to a forage shortage that resulted in a massive die-off.

Surely, if Malthus' theory is so successful in biology, reasoned some intellectuals in the second half of the twentieth century, it should apply equally to human populations. "To ecologists who study animals, food and population often seem like sides of the same coin. If too many animals are devouring it, the food supply declines; too little food, the supply of animals declines. . . . Homo sapiens is no exception to that rule, and at the moment it seems likely that food will be our limiting resource,"[8] succinctly explains Stanford University entomologist Paul Ehrlich.

In the late 1960s, Ehrlich was one of the biologists and agronomists who began issuing dire warnings about human *overpopulation*. His most famous prediction appeared in his book, *The Population Bomb*, published in 1968: "The battle to feed all of humanity is over. In the 1970s, the world will undergo famines—hundreds of millions of people are going to starve to death in spite of any crash programs embarked on now."[9] Later, in an article for the first Earth Day in 1970, Ehrlich outlined a horrific scenario in which 65 million Americans and 4 billion other people would die of starvation in the "Great Die-Off" between 1980 and 1989.[10] Ever loyal to Malthusian theory, Ehrlich and his wife Anne published

The Population Explosion in 1990. They once again asserted: "One thing seems safe to predict: starvation and epidemic disease will raise the death rates over most of the planet"[11] near the beginning of the twenty-first century.

Ehrlich, however, was far from alone in the modern revival of Malthusian population theory. In 1967, the Paddock brothers asserted in *Famine 1975!*: "The famines which are now approaching... are for a surety, inevitable.... In fifteen years the famines will be catastrophic...."[12] Today, the Worldwatch Institute, a Washington, D.C.–based environmentalist advocacy group headed by Lester Brown, has a solid Malthusian focus. A former U.S. Department of Agriculture analyst, Brown declared in 1981, "The period of global food security is over." In 1994, Brown wrote: "The world's farmers can no longer be counted on to feed the projected additions to our numbers,"[13] and in 1997, "Food scarcity will be the defining issue of the new era now unfolding, much as ideological conflict was the defining issue of the historical era that recently ended." He continued: "Rising food prices will be the first major economic indicator to show that the world economy is on an environmentally unsustainable path."[14]

Shortly after the revival of Malthusian concerns about overpopulation in the 1960s, others began to focus on the availability of resources other than food. In 1972, the Club of Rome (a group of politicians, businessmen, and high international bureaucrats) commissioned the famous *The Limits to Growth* report. The report was devised by a team using a computer model of the world developed initially by Jay Forrester at the Massachusetts Institute of Technology. The report concluded: "If the present growth trends in world population, industrialization, pollution, food production, and resource depletion continue unchanged, the limits to growth on this planet will be reached sometime in the next one hundred years. The probable result will be a rather sudden and uncontrollable decline in both population and industrial capacity."[15] In 1976, Paul and Anne Ehrlich projected in their book, *The End of Affluence*, that "before 1985 mankind will enter a genuine age of scarcity... in which the accessible supplies of many key minerals will be facing depletion."[16]

The Limits to Growth tried to define other limits that the natural environment would set on the growth of human economies as well as on human populations. This is Malthus writ large. Not only would humanity run out of food, but we would also run out of places to put our wastes and out of nonrenewable resources like minerals and fossil fuels. If humanity didn't suffer a massive famine, then our factories would grind to a halt as oil and iron ran out and/or clouds of pollution would strangle an overcrowded humanity. More recently, neo-Malthusians have raised concerns that humanity is rapidly depleting biodiversity, freshwater supplies, oceanic fisheries, and topsoil. Two hundred years after Malthus first proposed it, the principle of population has been applied to nearly any activity involving the human use of resources, both renewable and nonrenewable.

It's an interesting fact of intellectual history that biologists and ecologists have so completely embraced a theory of population devised by an economist. Malthus' theory is one of the first formulations of the theory of *diminishing marginal returns*. As one analyst explains it:

> While he argued that the quantity of arable land was fixed and someday might be completely occupied by farms, Malthus also recognized that land could be made more productive through intensive cultivation. With greater effort, farmers could gradually squeeze more produce from the same fixed amount of land—and herein lies the rub—at decreasing rates per each additional laborer. Thus each new worker sent to the field produces incrementally fewer crops or, as later economists would say, with diminishing marginal returns. . . . Malthus predicted diminishing marginal returns as farmers sought ways to feed the ever-increasing masses. The economic scarcity would arise because society would have to sacrifice increasingly more to obtain less on the margin. Whether measured by the number of field hands and their hoes, or by the money required to pay for that labor and equipment, the cost of extracting agricultural produce would increase.[17]

The idea is that as more and more farm laborers work on an acre of land, additions to output will diminish. If one worker produces 2 tons of wheat, two might produce 4 tons of wheat. Three laborers, however, might produce only 5 tons, whereas 10 or 20 laborers would get in each other's way, trampling the wheat.

The law of diminishing returns clearly operates in the natural world. As the effort to gain resources like food or sunlight becomes harder, the less chance the weakest or less favorably situated individual members of a species have to survive in an ever more crowded ecosystem. The Malthusian model of diminishing marginal returns does accurately describe the experience of every other species on earth. The idea of diminishing marginal returns is what prompts many ecologists and biologists to argue that continued human population growth may bring catastrophe.

The law of diminishing returns applies to many activities in which human beings engage, including such ordinary activities as the declining benefits that a person gains from extra hours of going to the gym, the pleasure obtained from eating the 20th chocolate chip cookie, or the medical advantages stemming from one's fifth prostate exam of the month.

How has Malthus' principle fared empirically with regard to the population whose behavior it was devised to explain—human beings? Historically, it is interesting to note that just as Malthus was writing, France became the first country in the world in which fertility began to decline. Malthus had concluded that in many countries, humanity had already reached its limits to growth, which is why England and Europe experienced so much poverty, misery, and vice. "The principle he enunciated with such force was a uni-

Contrary to Malthus and his modern disciples, Lester Brown and Paul Ehrlich, global crop yields have greatly outstripped population growth making food ever more available to the poor. (*Credit:* USDA.)

versal one, capable of explaining the past, present, and future condition of mankind, wherever it was to be found,"[18] writes Malthus biographer Donald Winch.

However, just as Malthus was formulating his theory, we now know that the world was on the brink of the largest surge in economic and population growth ever experienced by humanity. In the century between the publication of his *Essay* and the beginning of the twentieth century, per capita income in England rose sixfold, despite a sixfold increase in population. Taking even a longer time period, between 1820 and 1992, world population quintupled even as the world's economies grew 40-fold.[19]

In his *Essay*, Malthus claimed that he had proved "that population does invariably increase when the means of subsistence increase."[20] His modern-day intellectual heirs insist that Malthus was right. "Making food still cheaper and more available for more people will encourage more population growth and thus ensure that life will, in many important respects, become worse," wrote Garret Hardin,[21] emeritus professor of human ecology at the University of California at Santa Barbara. "The Malthusian thesis has been true and at work at all times. Population is regulated to food supply,"[22] wrote the father of *The Limits to Growth* study, Jay Forrester, in his book, *World Dynamics*. Forrester adds that in his computer model "an abundance of food is assumed to raise the birth rate by a factor of 2."[23] Thus, the race is on between food and population, and famine is the ultimate winner.

Given this grim calculus, modern Malthusians often adopt Malthus' own prescription that aid should be withheld from the poorest because it will only increase misery and vice later. Garrett Hardin argues for *lifeboat ethics*, by which he analogizes countries to lifeboats that would sink if, in a fit of misdirected compassion, the occupants allowed drowning people in the water around them to come on board. Adopting a similar cruel logic, Maurice King, a professor of medicine at the University of Leeds in Britain, wants to judiciously ration *mortality controls*. Just as birth control prevents births, mortality control prevents deaths. King argues that modern mortality controls, like simple oral rehydration therapy, which has saved countless millions of children from dying of diarrheal diseases, should not be taught to poor people in the developing world unless they adopt stiff birth control measures first. "If no adequately sustaining complementary measures [e.g., family planning] are possible, such desustaining measures as oral rehydration should not be introduced on a public health scale, since they increase the man-years of human misery, ultimately from starvation," writes King.[24]

Still, other modern Malthusians believe that such draconian measures will not be limited to the developing countries. Ecologist Michael Tobias says, "I foresee that we are going to probably have to counter a severely deteriorated environment with a severe loss of democratic principles in the sense that we will have to initiate laws and regulations that a lot of people are going to be very unhappy with. Limitations on basic freedoms will have to be drastically reduced because there will not be enough clean air and water to do whatever you want to do."[25]

Are the human and environmental situations, however, really so dire? Contrary to the predictions of Malthus and his intellectual heirs, we find that the countries that are the wealthiest and have the greatest access to food—the United States, Germany, Italy, Spain, Japan, France—are precisely those countries that have the lowest birth rates, all of them below replacement levels (see Eberstadt in this book, Chapter 4). It turns out that for developed countries, more food doesn't mean more children; instead, it means more fat, old people.

In the past half-century, demographers have found that economic growth and steep declines in fertility rates go hand-in-hand. Brown University demographer Robert Kates identifies four reasons for fertility declines:[26]

1. Less need for child labor, more need for educated children
2. Less need for more births because more children survive
3. Less time for childbearing and -rearing, more time and need for education and work
4. More access to birth control technology to achieve fewer births

"Of course, changing needs of labor, greater child survival, improved opportunities for women, and access to birth control all seem to proceed together in the course of development," concludes Kates.[27] Development goes hand-in-hand with economic growth. Kates adds, "Several cross-cultural studies, covering 94 or more countries, have found that increases in development are strongly associated with a decline in the birthrate and in fact account for about two-thirds of the decline."[28] In addition, access to effective family planning accounts for between 15 and 20 percent, though some analysts say it accounts for as little as 5 percent of the decline.[29] Increasing people's choices, especially with regard to their family sizes, is itself a good thing and comes as a result of economic growth.

Over the past two centuries, the law of diminishing returns appears somehow to have been violated, given the enormous increase in wealth and food supplies. Since Malthus wrote, the fixed physical resources of the earth have not increased—for example, land area remains the same; there is no more iron or copper in the earth's crust; and freshwater supplies have not increased. Yet, a much larger human population lives better than ever, and a significant portion lives in material conditions—cars, vaccines, computers, airplanes, antibiotics, and winter fruits and vegetables—that would seem unimaginably luxurious to even the wealthiest inhabitants of Malthus' England. Given that Malthus believed that the effective limits to economic and population growth had already been reached for many countries and that he viewed his principle of population as the explanation for the miseries of humanity during his and all other times, how did humanity get around the iron law of diminishing returns? This question puzzled economists for nearly two centuries. Now, new theoretical developments are shedding light on this issue, and perhaps are pointing the way to a permanent escape from the Malthusian trap.

For decades, economists essentially used a two-factor model in which growth was accounted for by adding more labor and more capital to create more goods. The problem in this model is that, over time, growth must stop when the marginal value of the goods produced equals the cost of the labor and capital used to produce the goods. This neoclassical model of economic growth was elaborated in the 1950s by Nobelist Robert Solow and his colleagues.

"Solow focused attention on the process of capital formation. Aggregate savings, he argued, finance additions to the national capital stock. An economy with an initially low capital-labor ratio will have a high marginal product of capital. Then, if a constant fraction of the income generated by a new piece of equipment is saved, the gross investment in new capital goods may exceed the amount needed to offset depreciation and to equip new members of the workforce. Over time, capital per worker will rise, which (with constant returns to scale and a fixed technology) will generate a decline in the marginal product of capital. But if the marginal product continues to fall, the savings generated by the income accruing to new capital also will fall, and will eventually be only just sufficient to replace worn-out machines and equip new workers. At this point the economy enters a stationary state with an unchanging standard of living."[30]

In other words, when some factory workers are first equipped with drill presses for shaping metal parts for engines, they can build many more engines than they could when they had to shape the parts using hand tools. Their productivity greatly increases and boosts the profits of the factory owners. The factory owners can sell the engines and use some of their profits to buy more drill presses to equip more workers who, in turn, can build even more engines. Of course, the original drill presses suffer some wear and tear, so the owners also have to set aside some of their profits to pay for repairs for the older drill presses. As more engines are produced, it becomes harder and harder to sell them, so the owners lower the price to attract more customers. As prices spiral downward in pursuit of more customers, it eventually costs more to pay the workers and to repair the drill presses than additional customers will pay for the engines. At this point, the growth in engine production comes to a halt: The factory owners stop buying drill presses and hire no more workers.

Paul Romer, Stanford University economist, describes the situation as follows: "We now know that the classical suggestion that we can grow rich by accumulating more and more pieces of physical capital like fork lifts is simply wrong. The problem an economy faces . . . is what economists call 'diminishing returns.' In handling heavy objects, a fork lift is a very useful piece of equipment. When there were few fork lifts in the economy, the return on an investment in an additional fork lift drops rapidly. Eventually, additional fork lifts would have no value and become a nuisance. The return on investment in an additional fork lift diminishes and eventually becomes negative. As a result, an economy cannot grow merely by accumulating more and more of the same kind of capital goods."[31]

This neoclassical model of economic growth was incorporated into *The Limits to Growth* computer model and accounts for why the MIT researchers predicted eventual collapse as the inevitable result of continued economic and population growth.

In the last two decades, economists, following the lead of Paul Romer, have made a conceptual breakthrough that has given them a way to rigorously and accurately describe how economic growth occurs and how, with the proper social institutions, it can go on for the foreseeable future.

"New Growth theorists now start by dividing the world into two fundamentally different types of productive inputs that can be called 'ideas' and 'things.' Ideas are nonrival goods that could be stored in a bit string. Things are rival goods with mass (or energy). With ideas and things, one can explain how economic growth works. Nonrival ideas can be used to rearrange things, for example, when one follows a recipe and transforms noxious olives into tasty and healthful olive oil. Economic growth arises from the discovery of new recipes and the transformation of things from low to high value configurations,"[32] explains Romer.

Decoding the clunky economic terminology, *rival* goods are simply things that cannot be used by two or more persons at once—for instance, cars, drill presses, computers, even human bodies and brains—hence, *rivalry* to use them. *Nonrival* goods can be used by any number of people simultaneously—including recipes for bread, blueprints for houses, techniques for growing corn, formulas for pharmaceuticals, scientific principles like the law of gravity, and computer programs.

To understand the potency of ideas, just consider that a few decades ago, the only thing humanity could use iron oxide (ordinary rust) for was as pigment in paintings. Now, scientists and engineers have developed an elaborate set of instructions telling manufacturers how to apply iron oxide to plastic tapes to store video and audio information, and to computer diskettes to preserve digital information. Fifty years ago, silicon was used to make glass; now, we have created designs that also show us how to use silicon to make very complicated and high-valued microchips to run our computers, and optical fibers to transmit vast amounts of data over the Internet. In fact, the Internet is a perfect example of how technology permits very rapid exponential growth—the number of people using the Internet is doubling every 100 days. Another earlier example is petroleum. Before the 1870s, petroleum was a major nuisance for people drilling water wells. Then, it was transformed from a nuisance into kerosene, which served as a cheap lighting replacement for increasingly scarce whale oil.

Ideas are a different kind of resource—they are immaterial and can be shared at nearly no cost among a great many people. Once a new technique or a new discovery is made, it can be passed along to other people without much effort. It is easy to see how this works. Take the situation 10,000 years ago when some neolithic woman noticed that delicious grass seeds could be collected and covered in soil, and that she could come back later to more easily harvest the concentrated numbers of nutritious seeds. With this new knowledge, she greatly increased the capacity of the ecosystem to feed more people than hunting and gathering could support. The finite resources of the earth were not increased, just rearranged. The breakthrough was not the seeds—human beings had been gathering and eating grass seeds for tens of thousands of years—rather, it was the idea that they could be deliberately increased by planting them. Thus, farming grass seeds resulted in increasing returns, whereas simply gathering and eating them immediately led to diminishing returns. As one wag put it, "both jayhawks and men eat chickens, but whilst more jayhawks mean fewer chickens, more men mean more chickens."

Romer explains it this way: "Economic growth occurs whenever people take resources and rearrange them in ways that are more valuable. A useful metaphor for production in an economy comes from the kitchen. To create valuable products, we mix inexpensive ingredients together according to a recipe. The cooking one can do is limited by the supply of ingredients, and most cooking in the economy produces undesirable side effects. If economic growth could be achieved only by doing more and more of the same kind of cooking, we would eventually run out of raw materials and suffer from unacceptable levels of pollution and nuisance. Human history teaches us, however, that economic growth springs from better recipes, not just from more cooking. New recipes generally produce fewer unpleasant side effects and generate more economic value per unit of raw material."[33]

We make ourselves better off not by increasing the amount of stuff on planet earth—that is, of course, fixed—but by rearranging the stuff we have available so that it provides us with more of what we want—food, clothing, shelter, and entertainment. As we become cleverer about rearranging material, the more goods and services we can get from relatively less stuff. This process of improvement has been going on ever since the first members of our species walked the earth. We have moved from heavy earthenware pots to protect our food and drink to more effective and safer ultrathin plastics and lightweight aluminum cans. We have shifted from smoky, dangerous wood-intensive campfires to clean, efficient natural gas to cook our food. If our technologies had remained stuck in the past and if somehow the world's population had nevertheless been able to grow to its current level, the impact of humanity on the natural environment would have been calamitous.

By using better and better recipes, though, humanity has avoided the Malthusian trap while, at the same time, making the world safer, more comfortable, and more pleasant for both larger numbers of people as well as for a larger proportion of the world's people.

In fact, New Growth theorists point out that today many economic activities can be better characterized by *increasing returns* rather than diminishing returns. For example, it may cost $150 million in research and development to make the first vial of a new vaccine against Lyme disease. However, every vial after that is essentially free because the value of the vaccine is not the cost of manufacturing it, but in the cost of devising the recipe for making it. The same is true for computer programs—it may cost Microsoft $500 million for the first copy of Windows 98, but each subsequent copy is the cost of the CD-ROM disks on which it is stored. In the case of telecommunications, laying a fiber-optic network may cost billions; however, once it is operational, it can carry millions of messages at essentially no added costs. As every new vial of Lyme vaccine, every Windows program, or every phone call costs its inventors/owners nothing additional, they can therefore offer it at progressively cheaper prices to consumers. In addition, the low costs of each of these inventions make it possible for the people who buy them to be even more productive in their own activities (such as avoiding illness, speeding up word processing, and facilitating information exchange).

What modern Malthusians who worry about the depletion of resources miss is that people don't want oil, they want to cool and heat their homes; they don't want copper telephone lines, they want to communicate quickly and easily with friends, family, and businesses; they don't want paper, they want a convenient and cheap way to store written information. If oil, copper, and paper become scarce, humanity will turn to other sources of energy, other methods of communication, and other ways to store information.

Brown University demographer Robert Kates notes that technological discoveries have "each transformed the meaning of resources and increased the carrying capacity of the Earth."[34] History has clearly confirmed that "no exhaustible resource is essential or irreplaceable," adds economist Gale Johnson.[35] Economist Dwight Lee points out, "The relevant resource base is defined by knowledge, rather than by physical deposits of existing resources."[36] In other words, even the richest deposit of copper ore is just a bunch of rocks without the know-how to mine, mill, refine, shape, ship, and market it.

Romer sums it up this way: "Every generation has perceived the limits to growth that finite resources and undesirable side effects would pose if no new recipes or ideas were discovered. And every generation has underestimated the potential for finding new recipes and ideas. We consistently fail to grasp how many ideas remain to be discovered. The difficulty is the same one we have with compounding. Possibilities do not add up. They multiply."[37] This is the mirror image of Malthus' argument about exponential growth. In this case, ideas grow much faster than population.

Romer illustrates the point that the number of possible discoveries and inventions is almost incomprehensibly vast by using a number of simple calculations. Take, for example, the chemical combinations one can derive from the periodic table of elements. There are about 100 different elements, and if one serially combined any four different elements ($100 \times 99 \times 98 \times 97$), one would get about 94 million combinations. Then, for simplicity, Romer assumes that the elements could be combined in differing proportions ranging from 1 to 10, no fractions allowed. This yields 3500 proportions $\times$ 94 million combinations and provides 330 billion different recipes in total. At the rate of 1000 recipes per day, it would take scientists nearly 1 million years to evaluate them all. Of course, this vastly underestimates the actual number of combinations available, because one could combine more than four elements, in different proportions, at different temperatures and pressures, and so on.[38]

Consider the number of computer programs that could be installed on a single computer hard-disk drive. Romer calculates that the number of distinct software programs (sequences of zeros and ones) that can be put on a 1-gigabyte hard disk is roughly 1 followed by 2.7 billion zeros. By comparison, the total number of seconds that have elapsed since the beginning of the universe is only about 1 followed by 17 zeroes; the total number of atoms in the universe is equal to about 1 followed by 100 zeros.[39]

Take the case of assembling a machine that has 20 parts. A worker could start with part number 1, go on to connect part number 2, then part number 3, and so on, proceeding in sequence. Or, she could start with part number 13, connect part number 11, then part number 17, and so on. The number of different ways to assemble even this simple machine is equal to about 1 followed by 18 zeros, more than the number of seconds since the big bang.[40]

As these examples make clear, people possess a nearly infinite capacity to rearrange physical objects by creating new recipes for their use. "On the ideas side you have combinatorial explosion. There's essentially no scarcity to deal with," concludes Romer.[41]

Some committed Malthusians object that Romer and others who hold that economic growth is potentially limitless, are not only violating the law of diminishing returns, but they are transgressing an even more fundamental physical law—the second law of thermodynamics.[42] According to the second law, in a closed system, entropy tends to increase. Entropy is a measure of disorder. Think of a droplet of ink as a highly ordered pigment, which is diluted into invisibility when it is then dropped into a 10-gallon aquarium. When the pigment molecules are spread evenly through the water in the aquarium, disorder is at a maximum. It would take a considerable amount of effort to reconstitute the droplet. The idea is that to increase order in one part of the system (heating a house) requires an increase of disorder elsewhere (burning oil to run an electric generator). You can't burn the same barrel of oil twice; it is dissipated into the atmosphere as carbon dioxide and water and is unavailable for reuse.

Life itself would appear to be a violation of the second law, because living things are highly ordered complex entities that are continually using and dissipating energy to maintain themselves. The solution to the puzzle of life and of a growing economy is that the earth is not a closed system—the energy that drives it comes principally from the sun. It is true that the sun's energy is being dissipated and, as a consequence, it will burn out in another 4 to 5 billion years, but it seems premature to worry about that eventuality now. What about that burned barrel of oil, though? Recall that what people want is to heat their houses, not to burn oil. The recipes that humans could devise for obtaining and using energy are nearly limitless. Until medieval times, people inefficiently heated and cooked with open flames in their homes; then, someone in Europe invented the chimney, which dramatically increased the efficiency of heating and cooking. Next, in the eighteenth century, Benjamin Franklin invented the cast-iron stove, which again boosted efficiency, and so on, to today's modern electric heat pumps, gas furnaces, and so forth. Over time, these ideas and designs have dramatically increased the services that people get from various sources of energy, and more ideas and designs are being developed all the time [for example, passive solar homes, solar cells, fuel cells, nuclear power plants, and so on (see "Benchmarks," Consumption of Energy per Unit of GDP)]. It seems safe to conclude that as long as the sun shines, the second law of thermodynamics isn't relevant at the local level of planet earth, so both natural and human systems can become increasingly complex and more highly ordered.

Many people believe that oil/natural gas/coal are the "bridge fuels" to the solar/hydrogen energy economy of the future. On closer inspection, this kind of thinking is little more than a truism. Just as whale oil was a bridge fuel from beeswax candles to kerosene, and as kerosene was a bridge fuel from whale oil to electric lights, today's fossil fuels are by definition bridge fuels to some other kind of fuel in the future. Fossil fuels clearly are bridge fuels to some future energy mix. It is very unlikely that the world's current mix of energy sources will be the same as the energy mix at the dawn of the twenty-second century.

One implication of this type of analysis is that trying to plan now, on a global scale, the energy mix for the next 100 years is as silly as someone in 1900 trying to plan for our current energy mix. A person in 1900 would simply not have been able to plan for scores of millions of automobiles and trucks, electric lighting in hundreds of millions of houses and office buildings, fuel for thousands of jet planes, scores of millions of refrigerators, air conditioners, and so forth. None of the devices on this nearly endless list had been invented. We are undoubtedly in an even worse situation with respect to trying to foresee the developments in the next 100 years, given the current rate of technological innovation, than the person in 1900 would have been with respect to our world. It is clear that no person or centralized agency can possibly anticipate the energy or other needs of the next 100 years. Therefore, the wisest course is for humanity to support institutions and incentive systems that will encourage future scientists, inventors, and entrepreneurs to mobilize their decentralized, special knowledge, allowing them to discover, finance, and build the technologies that will supply human needs and protect the natural world in the coming century.

Insights from New Growth Theory reframe many environmental problems and suggest some surprising solutions. For example, one of the global environmental problems often attributed to population and economic growth is the loss of tropical forests and the biodiversity that they harbor. Is this really the case, though? Consider that Brazil has only two-thirds the population density of the United States, yet the area being cleared from agriculture in Brazil continues to grow. Why? According to the Consultative Group on International Agricultural Research, the chief factor that drives deforestation in developing countries is not commercial logging, but "poor farmers who have no other option to feeding their families other than slashing and burning a patch of forest. . . . Slash-and-burn agriculture results in the loss or degradation of some 25 million acres of land per year."[43]

By contrast, the United States uses less than half of the land for farming in the 1990s than it used in the 1920s, but it produces far more food now than it did then.[44] This reduction in land devoted to agriculture has resulted in the regrowth of forests, the protection of rivers from runoff, and has been a great boon for wildlife.

Farming technology is available from the developed countries, which could prevent and, in many cases, reverse the loss of tropical forests and other wildlife habitat around the globe. "If during the next sixty to seventy years the world farmer reaches the average yield of today's U.S. corn grower, the ten billion [in projected population] will need only half of today's cropland while they eat today's American calories," concludes Paul Waggoner, a distinguished scientist at the Connecticut Agricultural Experiment Station.[45] Poor people in developing countries could improve both their lives and their natural environments if they could expeditiously get access to modern methods.

Unfortunately, it is neither technology nor economic growth that stands in the way of environmental restoration; it is more often pernicious institutional barriers, including a lack of secure property rights, corrupt governments, and a lack of education.

Another environmental problem often attributed to population growth is pollution. In 1972, *The Limits to Growth* computer model projected that pollution would skyrocket as population increased: "Virtually every pollutant that has been measured as a function of time appears to be increasing exponentially."[46] Let's take the case of the world's largest economy. Since 1972, U.S. population has risen 26 percent, and the economy has grown by more than 100 percent. Similar improvements have been made in Western Europe and Japan. Yet, instead of increasing as predicted, air pollutants have dramatically declined.

For example, sulfur dioxide emissions are down 53 percent, carbon monoxide is down 57 percent, and volatile organic compounds—chief contributors to smog formation—have been reduced by 39 percent. Total particulates like smoke, soot, and dust have fallen by 59 percent. Even smog dropped by 50 percent in Los Angeles over the last decade. In other words, economic growth leads to less pollution, not more.

In fact, Department of Interior analyst Indur Goklany has found that for most pollutants there is a threshold of wealth at which the amount of a pollutant begins to decline. He calls these thresholds the *environmental transition*. What this means is that when people rise above mere subsistence, they start demanding environmental amenities like clean air and water. The first environmental transition is clean drinking water. Goklany found that fecal coliform bacteria in rivers, which is a good measure of water pollution, peaks when average per capita incomes reach $1,400 per year. The next transition is particulates, like smoke and soot, which peak when average per capita incomes reach $3,200 and sulfur dioxide peaks at $3,700.[47] This is less certain, but the income threshold for reducing nitrogen oxide is probably around $15,000 annual per capita income.

Committed Malthusians continue to reject the new scientific understanding of how economic growth occurs and the scope it offers for improving both human life and the natural world. For instance, Paul Ehrlich stubbornly insists: "*Most people do not recognize that, at least in rich nations, economic growth is the disease, not the cure*" (emphasis Ehrlich's).[48] Ehrlich and energy analyst John Holdren summarized this view in their I = PAT equation: environmental *impact* equals *population*, multiplied by consumption (*affluence*), then multiplied by *technology*. According to Ehrlich, this formula proves that people in developed countries overconsume and create even more environmental problems than poor people living in developing countries.

To counteract the disease of economic growth, Maurice King recommends *consumption control*, including "intensive energy conservation, fewer unnecessary journeys, more public transport; fewer, smaller, slower cars, warmer clothes, and colder rooms." According to King, this means that people in the "privileged North" should engage in "the deliberate quest of poverty" to curb their "luxurious resource consumption."[49]

Americans are supposedly consuming more than their fair share of the world's goods and are causing more of the world's bads. Supposedly, there is only so much of the world's finite resources to go around, and they should be shared more equally. However, as we have seen, the average American is not only a consumer, but also a producer of both goods and ideas. The average American lives and works in a society and an economy that enable him or her to increase the availability of the resources he or she uses. Americans and Europeans get more done with relatively less because of their higher levels of education, and greater access to productive tools (including a better infrastructure) and more open social institutions (including democratic governments and free markets). As a consequence, output per hour worked in the United States today is 10 times as valuable as output per hour worked 100 years ago.[50] In every sense of the word, the average Westerner has created more resources, especially knowledge and technology, than she or he consumes. That's why they live in countries where both their economies and environments are improving. The facts show that the I = PAT formula gets it backward: Greater affluence and technological sophistication mean an improving natural environment, not a worsening one.

However, if the right social institutions are lacking—democratic governance, secure private property, free markets—it is possible for some portion of the world's people to fall into the classic Malthusian trap of rising poverty and increasing environmental degradation. Some historians have plausibly speculated that the collapses of some civilizations resulted from environmental degradation that occurred because they lacked the proper social institutions to encourage the discovery and the implementation of knowledge that would have prevented the environmental damage. Perhaps the Mayan civilization in Central America suffered such a collapse. Today, the economies of many countries in Africa are declining—not because of high population growth rates or lack of resources—but because they have failed to implement even the most minimal policies for encouraging economic growth, including the development of human capital through widespread education, secure property rights, and democratic governments.

In comparing the performance of economies across time, economists can show that countries that have a larger total stock of human capital grow faster than those with less human capital. Free international trade acts to speed up growth in all economies. The fostering of human capital by developed economies, along with the adoption of free markets and democratic governments, explains how they have experienced rates of growth in per capita income that are unprecedented in human history. Low levels of human capital account for the negligible economic growth in the underdeveloped economies that are also closed to trade and, thus, cannot benefit from technologies developed elsewhere.[51] "[F]or the poorest countries today, if the stock of human capital is too low, growth may not take place at all,"[52] concludes Romer.

Even if social institutions are not as open as they should be, as in much of Asia, the development of human capital alone seems to go a long way toward boosting economic growth. In 1968, Paul Ehrlich agreed with an expert who predicted India couldn't "possibly feed two hundred million more people by 1980." He further claimed, "I have yet to meet anyone familiar with the situation who thinks that India will be self-sufficient in food by 1971." In the revised *The Population Bomb* in 1971, Ehrlich evidently recognized that his predictions about India had already proven wrong because he discreetly omitted them. In fact, India became more than self-sufficient, exporting surplus grain in the early 1980s to the Soviet Union.

India was in fact open enough to modern technology and its markets operated freely enough that its farmers could take advantage of the new much more highly productive varieties of wheat and rice developed by "Green Revolution" plant breeders in the 1960s. Recent years have seen China's economy boom, despite its far-from-open social institutions. However, China has done at least two things right: (1) it has opened itself to foreign investors who have brought modern technologies with them, and (2) it has had a relatively successful educational system, which has boosted human capital so that, when given the chance, the Chinese people took rapid advantage of new opportunities and developments.

Democratic governance and open markets seem to be indispensable institutions for the prevention of famine in modern times. Nobel Prize–winning economist Amartya Sen notes, "that in the terrible history of famines in the world, there is hardly any case in which a famine has occurred in a country that is independent and democratic with an uncensored press."[53] The widely reported famines in the past decade in Sudan, Somalia, and Ethiopia occurred in countries that are neither democratic nor that have free presses. "So long as famines are relatively costless for the government, with no threat to its survival or credibility, effective actions to prevent famines do not have the urgency to make them inescapable imperatives for the government," writes Sen. "The persistence of severe famines in many of the sub-Saharan African countries—both with 'left-wing' and 'right-wing' governments—relates closely to the lack of democratic political systems and practice."[54] Sen also points out that lack of democracy and the absence of an uncensored press were responsible for the massive Communist Chinese famine in the 1950s during "the Great Leap Forward," in which 30 million people may have starved to death. Along with Romer and other theorists, Sen also argues that economic growth, not just growth in food output, is crucial to ending the threat of famine in Africa. He calls "for measures to encourage and enhance technical change, skill formation and productivity—both in agriculture and in other fields."[55] Sen points out that economic growth makes it possible for people to earn the income that allows them to purchase food in international markets, even if there is a shortfall in local markets.

Now, we know how to keep the Malthusian trap from closing. Humanity, represented by our governments and international agencies, must make sure that individuals, corporations, and research institutions have strong incentives to explore, discover, and invent the innovations that will supply our future energy, agricultural, medical, and materials needs. Contrary to the I = PAT formula's original interpretation, technological innovation and wealth creation also help humanity lighten its footprint on the earth, thus preserving the natural world and helping to restore those areas that have been damaged.

Contemporary Malthusians often liken modern human society to a car going 100 miles per hour on a foggy road. They ask if it wouldn't be better if we slowed down, so that we don't crash into a wall hidden in the fog? However, if we take the Malthusians' advice and adopt institutions that slow the pace of innovation, humanity runs the risk of perhaps depleting our current energy supplies before they can be replaced by new innovations. This failure could result in considerable harm to our societies and to the natural world. New Growth Theory suggests that a better analogy might be that human society is in an airplane going 600 miles per hour. If the plane slows down too much, it will lose airspeed and crash before arriving safely at its destination.

"Of course, humans could make a mess of things. The Chinese had cast iron fifteen centuries before Westerners did and movable type four hundred years before Gutenberg. Nevertheless, the political and social system in China eventually stifled the incentives for additional discovery, and progress there virtually came to a halt. It is always possible that the same thing could happen for the human race as a whole. Technological determinists would then tell us that the technology did it to us. In truth, for progress to come to an end, we will have to do it to ourselves," writes Romer.[56] Sadly, as we have seen, a lack of open social institutions, including representative government, a free press, legally protected property rights and free markets, still leaves far too many of our fellow human beings caught in local versions of the Malthusian trap. However, we must not mistake their situation as representing the future of humanity and the earth: It is, instead, a dwindling remnant of the unhappy past.

As New Growth Theory demonstrates, we cannot deplete the supply of ideas, designs, and recipes. These are immaterial and limitless; therefore, they aren't bound in any meaningful sense by the second law of thermodynamics. Surely, no one believes that humanity has already thought of all the ways to conserve, to find, and to make use of new sources of energy, much less that people have run out of ideas to improve houses, transportation, communications, medicine, and farming. As we have seen, as humanity discovers these new recipes and ideas, the opportunities for protecting and improving the natural world also grow.

Misery and vice are not the inevitable lot of humanity, nor is the ruin of the natural world a foregone conclusion. Two centuries after Malthus, we now know that the exponential growth of knowledge, not of our numbers, is the real key to understanding the promising future that lies ahead for humanity and for the earth.

Chapter 2

HOW DO WE KNOW THE TEMPERATURE OF THE EARTH?

Global Warming and Global Temperatures

Roy W. Spencer

HIGHLIGHTS

- *The popular perception of global warming as an environmental catastrophe cannot be supported with measurements or current climate change theory. As scientific understanding of the climate system improves, estimates of future warming continue to fall. Even if warming does prove to be substantial, the time required for it to occur (many decades) will allow humanity considerable time to better understand the problem, and formulate any policy changes that might be deemed necessary.*

- *Concerns about possible catastrophic global warming are based largely on computer model predictions that the atmosphere will respond by amplifying the initial warming tendency.*

- *As computer models of the climate system have been improved in recent years, their projections of the magnitude of global warming by 2100 continue to be revised downward (3.3°C in 1990, 2.6°C in 1992, and 2.2°C in 1995). The warming of 0.6°C (1°F) in the last century is only about one-half of what current global warming theory predicts should have occurred.*

- *Climatologists compute from measured greenhouse gas increases that the atmosphere's ability to trap infrared radiation has increased by about 1 percent compared with preindustrial times. This should have caused an imbalance in the earth's energy balance, resulting in a warming tendency. What they don't know, however, is how the atmosphere is responding to either limit or amplify this small warming tendency.*

- *All weather processes act, directly or indirectly, to cool the surface of the earth. Although the earth's natural greenhouse effect would like to warm the average surface temperature to near 130°F, evaporation of water and heat transport from the surface to the upper atmosphere reduces this to a much more comfortable 55°F. Computer climate models do not simulate weather processes well.*

- *Weather systems are the atmosphere's way of removing excess heat. This is a consequence of the second law of thermodynamics: A fluid system like the atmosphere acts to remove differences in temperature between different locations. Water in the oceans and in the atmosphere is an extremely important part of the earth's heat removal process, acting in many ways like freon does in an air conditioner or heat pump, moving heat from one location to another.*

- *Detecting any global warming increase of 0.2 or 0.35°C per decade is difficult. The rate of temperature change associated with daily weather is about 100,000 times larger than the widely predicted 0.35°F-per-decade global warming signal.*

- *It has been estimated that the earth has warmed by about 1°F in the last 100 years. However, studies have shown that most of that warming has occurred at night and during the coldest winter months.*

- *The surface temperature data using land- and ocean-based thermometers show a warming trend of 0.15°C per decade. By contrast, weather balloon temperature data show a cooling trend of –0.07, –0.04, or –0.02°C/decade, depending on which research group is analyzing which weather balloon data. Recently corrected satellite data has produced a slight warming trend of +0.01°C/decade for the period of 1979 through 1997.*

- *All measurement systems agree that 1998 was the warmest year on record. The most recent satellite measurements, through 1998, give an average warming trend of +0.06°C/decade for the 20-year period 1979 through 1998. Even though this period ends with a very warm El Niño event, the resulting trend is still only one-fourth of model-predicted average global warming for the next 100 years for the layer measured by the satellite.*

- *Global surface air temperatures were widely reported to reach record warm levels in 1997 and 1998. What wasn't mentioned was that most of this warmth occurred over the tropical oceans, where a strong El Niño was occurring.*

While politicians and policymakers at the 1997 Kyoto climate treaty meeting debated the terms for reducing greenhouse gas emissions, climate scientists continued to debate the evidence for global warming. How much warming has occurred in the last 100 years? How much of this warming was due to natural climate variability? to spurious instrumental problems? How much warming does global warming theory predict we will experience in the future? How reliable is that theory? Are hurricanes becoming more destructive? Is our weather getting worse?

News reports have claimed widespread scientific consensus on global warming. About the only thing that climate scientists actually agree on, however, is that increasing atmospheric concentrations of greenhouse gases will probably cause some amount of future warming, though just how much is in considerable dispute.

Before addressing the possible impact of global warming on weather, first it is useful to understand why some scientists are concerned.

Carbon Dioxide, the Greenhouse Effect, and Global Warming

Global warming theory is based on a predicted change in the earth's energy balance due to mankind's activities, primarily the emission of carbon dioxide (CO_2) from fossil fuel use. *Global warming* is the widely expected response of globally averaged temperatures to the continued increase in atmospheric greenhouse gas concentrations. The concentration of CO_2 in the atmosphere is only about 360 parts per million, making CO_2 a *trace gas*. Atmospheric concentrations of CO_2 are currently increasing at a rate of about 0.5 percent per year (Figure 2-1). This rate of increase would be about twice as large if it were not for vegetation (which uses CO_2 as food and stores the carbon), as well as storage by ocean biota. Thus, the biosphere is absorbing about half of the carbon we emit as CO_2.[1] The concentration of atmospheric carbon dioxide is expected to double late in the twenty-first century when compared with preindustrial levels.[2] However, there are now new reports of uncertainty about these projections based on CO_2 alone. Other human-induced influences that cause cooling, thus offsetting CO_2-induced warming, include pollution aerosols, stratospheric ozone depletion, forced cloud changes, and vegetation and other land use changes. This has led one leading climate scientist to state that "the forcings that drive long-term climate change are not known with an accuracy sufficient to determine future climate change."[3] Furthermore, there is still considerable uncertainty about how much of the CO_2 we produce will be absorbed by the biosphere.[4] It is possible that we have underestimated the ability of the earth to absorb the excess carbon, which would then reduce the magnitude of future warming.

To understand global warming, it is necessary to know how temperature is related to the earth's energy balance.[5] For the earth (or anything else) to remain at a constant temperature, there must be a balance between incoming energy (sunlight that warms the earth) and outgoing energy (infrared radiation that cools the earth). Warming occurs when there is more energy coming in than is going out; cooling happens if more energy goes out than is coming in. There are many complex processes that determine how much sunlight is let in, and how much infrared radiation escapes. The average temperature of the earth is the

FIGURE 2-1 Monthly atmospheric concentrations of carbon dioxide from the top of Mauna Loa, Hawaii. This remote site is believed to be representative of globally averaged conditions.

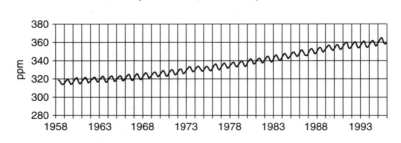

(*Source:* Data courtesy of C. Keeling.)

result of these myriad processes. For instance, for most cloud types, a cloudier earth would be a cooler earth because clouds reflect sunlight back out to space.[6,7]

In contrast to sunlight, the role of infrared radiation is a little more complex. Infrared radiation is the radiant heat you feel at a distance from a fire. Objects, however, do not have to be as hot as a fire to emit this type of radiation. It is continually being emitted by everything—the atmosphere, the ground, clouds, even your body. Even though the surface of the earth cools (partly) by infrared radiation flowing outward toward space, it is at the same time warmed by infrared radiation being emitted downward from the atmosphere and clouds above it. This is the so-called *greenhouse effect*. It is a natural process whereby the gases (primarily water vapor and CO_2) that absorb and emit infrared radiation cause the surface of the earth to be considerably warmer than it would otherwise be without those gases. There would probably be little or no life on earth if it were not for the warming provided by the natural greenhouse effect.

We can compute from measured greenhouse gas increases that the atmosphere's ability to trap infrared radiation has increased by about 1 percent compared with preindustrial times. This should have caused an imbalance in the earth's energy balance, resulting in a warming tendency. What we don't know, however, is how the atmosphere is responding to either limit or amplify this small warming tendency.

Limits to the Greenhouse Effect

It is often stated that the natural greenhouse effect causes the surface to be about 50°F warmer than it would otherwise be. Actually, this is only half of the story, and it neglects the cooling processes that also keep the earth habitable.[8] If the natural greenhouse effect were allowed to act alone, the average surface temperature of the earth would be about 130°F, rather than the observed 55°F.[9] Instead, heat is removed from the surface by evaporation of water and other weather processes. Because these natural cooling processes are an integral part of the climate system, any discussion of global warming theory must include them. In other words, the natural greenhouse effect cannot be considered in isolation as a process warming the earth, without at the same time accounting for cooling processes that actually keep the greenhouse effect from scorching us all (see Figure 2-2).

Because these cooling processes are very complex and difficult to include in computer models of the climate system, there is still considerable uncertainty whether mankind's small contribution to the greenhouse effect will cause significant warming.

Feedbacks: The Climate System's Response to Forcing

Fears of catastrophic global warming are based largely on computer model predictions that the atmosphere will respond by amplifying the initial warming tendency. Any process that

FIGURE 2-2 All weather processes act, directly or indirectly, to cool the surface of the earth. Although the earth's natural greenhouse effect would like to warm the average surface temperature to near 130°F, evaporation of water and heat transport from the surface to the upper atmosphere reduce this to a much more comfortable 55°F.

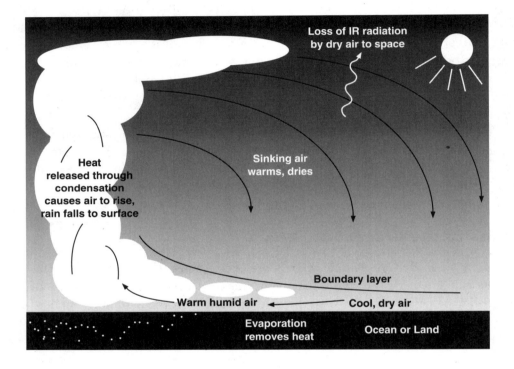

amplifies the initial warming tendency is called a *positive feedback,* whereas a process that reduces the warming is termed a *negative feedback.* The issue of feedbacks, especially those related to clouds, is still an area of active research. Feedbacks lie at the heart of most disagreements over the magnitude of future global warming, and they will determine the eventual intensity of global warming.

Can we believe computer predictions of global warming? One test would be whether the models can reproduce the current climate. There is wide disagreement about whether models have yet reached this point. When the physics that we believe are controlling these processes are put into computer models, the resulting climate simulation is almost always quite different than what is observed on the earth. Most models must be "fudged" to produce a climate that looks like the real one.[10] To accomplish this, fictitious energy "flux adjustments" are imposed at the surface of the earth in the model, where huge amounts of energy are absorbed (sunlight) and lost (evaporation, infrared radiation, and so on). The fudge factors are invoked to produce a more realistic climate simulation. Of course, if the model already had the proper physics and feedbacks, these adjustments would not be necessary. These fudge factors turn out to be much larger than the anticipated forcing from an expected doubling of CO_2 levels in the next 100 years.[8]

Even convective clouds (thunderstorms and other rain systems), which have a profound effect on the climate system, are not explicitly included in these models. This is because computers are still not nearly fast enough to run global climate models at a resolution at which clouds operate (less than 1 mile). Therefore, the cloud effects must be represented in a crude fashion to match the climate model's smallest scale, which is closer to 100 miles. There is still much uncertainty about how clouds act to amplify or offset global warming.[11]

Positive or Negative Feedbacks?

Ultimately, the magnitude of global warming will depend on whether the climate system's response to forcing (for instance, greenhouse gas increases) is dominated by either positive or negative feedbacks. If we examine weather systems in terms of their most fundamental role in the climate system, we find they are the atmosphere's way of removing excess heat. Every cloud that forms and every gust of wind that blows has occurred, either directly or indirectly, as part of a cooling process that moves excess heat from one region to another, or from the earth's surface to a higher altitude in the atmosphere. This is a consequence of the second law of thermodynamics: A fluid system like the atmosphere acts to remove differences in temperature between different locations. For instance, the sun will not be allowed to warm the surface of the earth without the atmosphere responding in such a way that reduces that warming.

Water is an extremely important part of this whole heat removal process. Surface water absorbs huge quantities of heat when it evaporates. This heat is later released higher in the atmosphere when a cloud forms. The ocean also acts to transport excess heat from the tropics to higher latitudes. This cools the tropics, and warms the higher latitudes. In many ways, water functions like freon does in an air conditioner or heat pump, moving heat from one location to another.

Water vapor deserves special mention. It is estimated that water vapor accounts for about 95 percent of the earth's natural greenhouse effect, whereas carbon dioxide contributes most of the remaining 5 percent. Global warming projections assume that water vapor will increase along with any warming resulting from the increases in carbon dioxide concentrations. The magnitude of this positive water vapor feedback is such that it doubles the amount of global warming within computer models. Although it is likely that moistening would occur for the lowest (boundary) layer of the atmosphere (see Figure 2-2), it is much less certain whether the air above the boundary layer, called the *free troposphere*, will moisten.[12] The boundary layer is the lowest layer of the atmosphere, about 1 mile thick, where turbulent air currents carry evaporated moisture away from the surface. Warming of the surface will very likely cause more evaporation and a more humid boundary layer, contributing to positive water vapor feedback. However, the humidity of the free troposphere, extending from above the boundary layer up to about 6 to 10 miles in altitude, is controlled by complex processes within clouds. The water vapor response of this layer is potentially more important to global warming estimates than is the boundary layer's response.[12] Some portion of the clouds that form in this layer reevaporates to humidify the surrounding air, whereas the rest falls out as rain.[13,14] We do not even have a very good conceptual understanding of the physics controlling the balance between clouds and rainfall, let alone have them included in today's computer climate models.[15] In my view, this introduces considerable uncertainty about the supposed factor-of-2 magnification of global warming by positive water vapor feedback.

If we know that the atmosphere acts, on the whole, to rid itself of excess heat, would it not be plausible that a 1 to 2 percent increase in total greenhouse trapping of infrared radiation might have a minimal warming effect? I believe so. It is for this reason that I believe that computer models of the climate system do not yet contain all of the negative feedback processes that the real atmosphere possesses. In support of this view, the continual improvement of climate models in the last 30 years has seen a gradual reduction in the positive feedbacks contained in those models. Combined with other improvements in our knowledge of how the climate system works, the U.N.'s Intergovernmental Panel on Climate Change (IPCC) best estimate of global warming by the year 2100 has decreased as well, from 3.3°C (5.9°F) in 1990, to 2.6°C (4.7°F) in 1992, to 2.2°C (4.0°F) in 1995.[2] At some point, we might well see this estimate reduced to such a small value that it is not much different from the range of natural climate variability.

Do We See Global Warming at the Surface?

The identification of a human-induced warming signal in global temperature records continues to be a difficult task. The size of the expected warming signal at the surface [0.2°C (0.35°F) per decade] is so small that it presents a couple of problems. First, our existing temperature monitoring systems were never designed to identify such a small signal with any certainty. Note that the rate of temperature change associated with daily weather is about 100,000 times larger than the widely predicted 0.35°F per decade global warming signal. Surface thermometer records are plagued by poor coverage over much of the earth (especially 100 years ago), changing instrumentation and site placement, and natural and man-made changes in the local environment around the thermometer site. Debate continues on the last issue, the so-called urban warming bias that results from an average increase in man-made structures around thermometer sites.[16–18] Over the ocean, a continually varying mixture of water bucket temperatures (including issues concerning what those buckets are made of), ship engine intake water temperatures, buoy measurements, and satellite measurements make up our temperature record.[19] It is not well known how these various changes have corrupted global warming surface estimates of 0.6°C (1.0°F) in the last 100 years (Figure 2-3).

FIGURE 2-3 Yearly surface air temperature anomalies for the period 1855 through 1998 as estimated from a mixture of land, air, and seawater thermometer measurements.

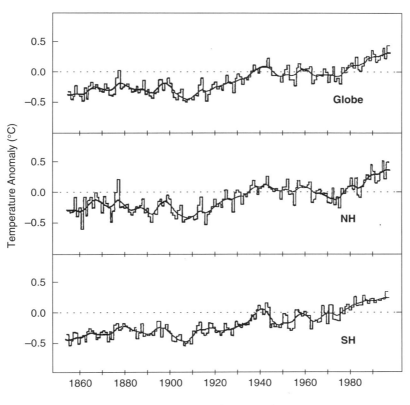

(*Source:* Courtesy of P. D. Jones.)

Weather balloon data collected around the world do not find the large increases in global temperatures predicted by computer climate models. (*Credit:* NOAA.)

Second, we still do not have a good understanding of what causes natural climate variability on decadal-to-century-scale timescales. For us to identify a global warming signal, we must be able to identify the temperature changes related to natural fluctuations in the climate system. For instance, what caused the cool period during the 1970s that resulted in fears of another ice age? Why was the period around 1940 so warm? Is the recent warmth we have been experiencing since the 1980s of largely natural origin, or is it due to the increasing concentrations of greenhouse gases from mankind's activities? Is the net warming of near 1°F in the last 100 years a sign of global warming, or is it just a natural result of coming out of the "Little Ice Age" in the nineteenth century? These questions do not have definitive answers, and they evoke strong debate between scientists.

Even if this surface warming has indeed occurred, studies have shown that most of it has occurred at night and during the coldest winter months.[20,21] Some scientists argue that warming at these times might actually be beneficial, or at least benign. Also, the largest amount of global warming is supposed to occur at high latitudes, where sea ice is supposed to melt. Because this warming has not materialized, the cooling effect of air pollution aerosols from industrialized countries has been invoked to explain why the poles have not seen significant warming.[2] However, using two competing man-made influences to explain why polar temperatures have not changed significantly is not very satisfying—are we possibly giving ourselves too much credit for our influence on climate?

What About the Sun?

New research is shedding more light (literally) on the warming that has been measured in the last 100 years. Although we assume that the sun shines just as brightly this year as it always has, new research suggests that as much as one-half of the warming in the last 100 years might have been caused by a brightening sun.[22] This issue is extremely difficult to study because estimates of the sun's increasing brightness in the last century depend on assumed relationships between brightness and sunspot activity, as well as other factors. It is likely that more research into the variable sun's influence on climate will be performed in the coming years.

The Surface Versus Deep-Layer Temperature Controversy

Computerized climate models all predict that any surface warming that occurs will be amplified with height, up to 5 or 6 miles in altitude, where a maximum warming should occur. Therefore, monitoring of a deep layer of air should give a stronger global warming signal. There are only two systems that have produced decadal timescale measurements of this deep layer of the atmosphere: radiosondes (weather balloons) and satellites. Whereas radiosonde data have existed since the 1950s, satellite data have existed for only the last 20 years, since 1979 (Figure 2-4).[23]

Much controversy has surrounded the satellite measurements, which have suggested a slight globally averaged cooling trend during 1979 through 1997, a period when the surface measurements showed warming. Some have remarked that the deep-layer measurements aren't that relevant, because it is the surface where people live. However, model predictions that warming should increase with height do not agree with the surface and

FIGURE 2-4 Monthly global temperature anomalies in the lower troposphere between 1979 and December 1998. A linear trend of +0.06°C is about one-fourth of what would be expected from current best estimates of global warming in the next 100 years. These data contain the latest adjustments for satellite orbit decay and instrument temperature cross talk.

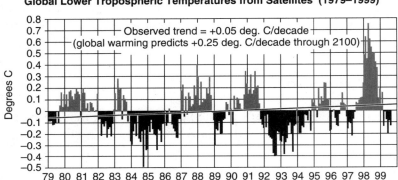

deep-layer measurements over the last 20 years. This calls into question the utility of the models for global warming predictions. One theory is that stratospheric ozone depletion has caused the global warming signal to be reduced, and has caused the deep layer to not warm as rapidly as the surface.[24]

The controversy was further fueled when researchers reported that the satellite temperature record needed an adjustment for decay of the satellites' orbits.[25] Their estimated correction to the satellite temperature record resulted in a small warming trend (+0.08°C/decade) during the period 1979 through 1997, in closer agreement to the surface measurements of 0.15°C/decade. The radiosondes for the same period, in contrast, showed a cooling trend of −0.07, −0.04, or −0.02°C/decade, depending on which research group is analyzing which weather balloon data. Reanalysis of the raw satellite measurements, including an additional consequence of the decay of the satellite orbits, as well as new calibration adjustments, has produced a trend of +0.01°C/decade for the same period.[26] This falls between the surface measurements and the radiosonde measurements, and so has reduced the discrepancy between the satellite and surface measurements—although the discrepancy remains for the radiosondes and the surface measurements. Because neither radiosondes nor satellites reveal the expected warming signal, true believers in global warming typically dismiss both the radiosondes and satellites as being wrong.

Then, 1998 came along. Finally, all measurement systems agreed that 1998 was the warmest year on record (Figure 2-4). The most recent satellite measurements through 1998 give an average warming trend of +0.06°C/decade for the 20-year period 1979 through 1998. Even though this period ends with a very warm El Niño event, the resulting trend is still only one-fourth of model-predicted-average global warming for the next 100 years for the layer measured by the satellite. As is often pointed out, however, 20 years is not sufficient to say much about climate temperature trends. This is because of the large amount of year-to-year variability, also seen in Figure 2-4. Volcanic eruptions, which cool the surface of the earth, and El Niño (warming) and La Niña (cooling) are responsible for most of the temperature changes seen in the last 20 years.

The 1997–1998 El Niño

Global surface air temperatures were widely reported to reach record warm levels in 1997 and 1998. What wasn't mentioned was that most of this warmth occurred over the tropical oceans, where a strong El Niño was occurring. El Niño is a natural climate fluctuation that occurs when the easterly trade winds over the Pacific Ocean weaken.[27] This slackening of the trade winds causes reduced upwelling of cool ocean water along the western coasts of North and South America, and sea surface temperatures warm above their average level over much of the tropical Pacific. This changes atmospheric circulation patterns over the Pacific, which then impact weather patterns around the world. Were it not for El Niño, 1997 and 1998 would not have been record warm years. Still, global warming effects might have contributed to some of the record warmth.

In a new twist, at least one scientist is now suggesting that global warming might be causing El Niño to be more severe and more frequent.[28] Although it is not out of the realm of possibility, such a relationship is mostly conjecture at this point. There are historical records of past events that suggest even more severe El Niños in previous centuries. Therefore, it will be difficult to ever have observational evidence to support such a claim, unless El Niño changes substantially.

Is Our Weather Changing?

Many people are tempted to blame any change in regional weather on global warming. It is well known, however, that the chaotic nature of weather has always caused floods, droughts, and blizzards. It seems to be human nature to believe that recent weather events are more unusual than in past years. One difficulty in determining whether recent events are unusual from a climate perspective is that our measurements are often not good enough, over a long enough period of time, to know what "unusual" weather would look

Twenty years of data from satellites like this one are used by the author to show that the Earth's atmosphere appears to be warming much more slowly than originally predicted by climate models. (*Credit:* NASA.)

like. Misunderstandings often occur when we talk about "record" events. For instance, it would not be unusual for "hundred-year" floods to occur every year, as long as they occur in different places. Similarly, record-high and -low temperatures are routinely reported every month of every year . . . again, for different locations. Record temperature, rainfall, and flooding events are always stated for the specific location where they occur. The news media seem to give preference to record-high temperature reports while giving less play to events such as the all-time state record-low temperatures in Illinois (−36°F at Congerville) and in Maine (−55°F at Allagash) during the winter of 1998–1999.

Increased hurricane damage in recent years, such as that from Hurricane Andrew in 1992, has many people wondering whether mankind's activities have caused these tropical maelstroms to worsen. However, researchers who study the long-term trends in hurricane activity have found that fewer hurricanes have struck the U.S. East Coast in recent decades.[29] The same researchers warn, though, that recent changes in the circulation of the Atlantic Ocean, which regularly occur about every 30 years, portend increased hurricane activity for the United States in the coming years. On a more global scale, one study claims that the frequency of intense hurricanes in the tropics has increased in the last 30 years.[30] Although some theoretical studies have concluded that global warming should lead to an average increase in hurricane intensity,[31,32] other work has suggested just the opposite.[31–34] One thing seems certain, however: Continued construction in hurricane-prone areas has resulted in increased susceptibility to damage, leading to larger insurance claims and the perception that hurricanes are becoming more dangerous.[35]

There have also been reports of an increase in intense rain events in the United States over the last century.[36] Streamflow measurements in the United States, however, do not suggest any average increase in streamflow that would result if heavier rainfall is causing more runoff.[37] Therefore, the unusual devastation caused by floods in Grand Forks, North Dakota, in April 1997, which were widely attributed to global warming by some scientists, can instead be traced to man-made changes in the landscape. These changes have made settled areas more prone to extreme flooding events.

Increased media coverage in this information age makes weather disasters more widely known than ever before. Ratings-driven sensationalization of weather coverage by the media gives the public a false impression of the severity of many weather events.

Despite all this uncertainty, it is widely agreed among climate scientists that increases in greenhouse gas concentrations must have some effect on weather. The important question is, Will we ever recognize it as such? Weather and climate change without any help from humans. As discussed previously, negative feedbacks might limit the amount of surface warming we see. However, even negative feedbacks must be accompanied by real changes in weather and climate (for example, more cloudiness, which acts to limit warming).

One possibility is that global warming won't manifest itself as a large change in surface temperature. Instead, we might experience the effects of the atmospheric adjustments that will occur to limit surface warming. For instance, small increases in cloudiness and precipitation are a distinct possibility. Climate model investigations suggest that for every 1°C (1.8°F) rise in global temperatures, there should be about a 4 percent increase in globally averaged rainfall.[38] An increase as small as this will be difficult to observe, because it is so difficult to measure globally averaged changes in clouds or precipitation. As discussed earlier, natural weather patterns are so variable on a regional basis that the fingerprint of global warming has been very difficult to identify. Instead, global warming might only be evident in globally averaged data. Because the earth's surface is mostly covered by oceans, we must rely on satellites to provide global observations, and it is not yet obvious whether our satellites are stable enough to observe such small changes over such long periods of time.

Summary and Conclusions

We have seen that the earth's natural greenhouse effect is limited in its ability to warm the surface. The evaporation of water and the transport of excess heat away from the surface to the upper troposphere by cloud and rainfall systems drastically cools the earth's surface to an average temperature of 55°F, compared with what the natural greenhouse effect wants it to be (130°F).

Increasing atmospheric concentrations of carbon dioxide, primarily due to the burning of fossil fuels, are slowly augmenting the natural greenhouse effect. If all other aspects of the climate system remained unchanged (which they won't), a doubling of atmospheric CO_2 concentrations near the end of the next century would increase the atmospheric greenhouse trapping of infrared radiation by about 2 percent. How the climate system will respond to this small forcing is very uncertain, due to the myriad and complex ways in which weather systems act to rid the earth of excess heat. The response of clouds and free tropospheric water vapor remain sources of substantial uncertainty in global warming predictions. As computer models of the climate system have been improved in recent years, their projections of the magnitude of global warming by 2100 continue to be revised downward (3.3°C in 1990, 2.6°C in 1992, and 2.2°C in 1995). The warming of 0.6°C (1°F) in the last century is only about one-half of what current global warming theory predicts. Computers are still not fast enough to include the physics of clouds and rain systems, of which we have some understanding, in computer climate models. In addition, there are still some critical aspects of clouds, vegetation, sea ice, and the oceans that we don't yet understand well enough to put into the models.

Uncertainties about how variable the climate system was in past centuries translate directly into uncertainty about whether the current climate is unusual in any way. It does seem that the 1980s and 1990s have been unusually warm in the context of the last 100 years. However, because that period started with the end of the "Little Ice Age," we might merely be seeing more normal conditions now. In any case, much of the warming in the last 100 years occurred before 1940, which preceded the bulk of greenhouse gas increases. There is now evidence that about one-half of that warming might have been the result of a brightening of the sun. The record warmth of 1997 and 1998 would not have occurred if not for the El Niño event during those two years. Nevertheless, some of the warming in the last century could well be from increasing atmospheric concentrations of carbon dioxide.

The seeming tendency toward more severe weather events in recent times can usually be explained in terms of modern building and land use practices, and more frequent and sensationalized reporting by the media. Although climate models suggest that warming should be accompanied by slight increases in precipitation, attributing any storm or flood event to the effects of global warming is seriously misleading. Natural fluctuations in the climate system have, so far, provided much larger sources of variability.

The last 20 years have seen our most complete observational coverage of the climate system. During this period, satellite, thermometer, and weather balloon measurements reveal warming trends that decrease with height, in opposition to predictions from current computer models. The reasons for this discrepancy are not yet known, although depletion of stratospheric ozone is one possibility.

In conclusion, there remain substantial uncertainties in our understanding of how the climate system will respond to increasing concentrations of carbon dioxide and other greenhouse gases. The popular perception of global warming as an environmental catastrophe cannot be supported with measurements or current climate change theory. As our understanding of the climate system improves, estimates of future warming continue to fall. I believe that any warming will likely be more modest and benign than had originally been feared. Even if warming does prove to be substantial, the time required for it to occur (many decades) will allow us considerable time to better understand the problem, and to formulate any policy changes that might be deemed necessary.

Chapter 3

DOING MORE WITH LESS
Dematerialization—Unsung Environmental Triumph?

Lynn Scarlett

HIGHLIGHTS

- *American households generate over 200 million tons of solid waste each year. Add in industrial wastes and the figure exceeds an estimated 11 billion tons per year.*

- *In 1900, New York City's 120,000 horses produced over 200 tons of manure per day. The average New Yorker produced more garbage in 1900 than does today's New Yorker.*

- *Dematerialization, put simply, means using fewer raw materials and less energy per unit of output. As Vice President Al Gore has observed, "In the past 50 years the value of our economy has tripled, while the physical weight of our economy as whole has barely increased at all."*

- *Total consumption is rising, though the mix of resources consumed has changed over time. However, resource consumption per unit of output is declining. This dematerialization means a defined level of consumption is occurring with less resource use, less accompanying waste, and a "lighter" footprint on the earth.*

- *For example, despite population growth, increased size of homes, and more furniture per household, total per capita consumption of wood in the United States has declined to less than half what it was in 1900, partly through decline in use of wood for fuel, partly through substitutions of other materials, and partly as a consequence of more efficient use of wood materials.*

- *In many cases, developing countries are able to take advantage of dematerialization technologies from industrial countries and leapfrog over resource-intensive stages of development.*

- *Materials used for basic infrastructure and construction account for some 70 percent of total materials consumed, excluding fuels. Hence, using less stuff per construction project can have dramatic, long-term environmental benefits. A skyscraper built today requires 35 percent less steel than the same building would have required just a few decades ago. Less steel per building translates into less energy use, less mining, and fewer emissions associated with creating that building.*

- *A single fiber-optic cable, requiring 65 kilograms of silica, can carry many times the number of messages carried by a cable made from 1 ton of copper.*

- *A basket of typical U.S. grocery items fell from over 2750 pounds of packaging per gross production unit in 1989 to approximately 2100 pounds in 1993–1994. With these dematerializing trends, grocery packaging as a percentage of total municipal solid waste actually declined between 1980 and 1993 from 15.3 percent to 12.1 percent, despite a population increase of around 14 percent over the same time.*

- *A report to the U.S. Environmental Protection Agency found in 1997 that the rate of growth of municipal solid waste (MSW) had begun to slow by the mid-1990s, apparently as a result of source reduction, increased recycling, and yard waste composting.*

- *In market economies, innovations—finding ways to do more with less—are rewarded with higher returns on investment. Finding ways to use fewer resources to make a product or provide a service translates into cost savings. Pick-the-winner strategies that use the political process to anoint specific technologies as "better" or "best" undermine the constant, competitive discovery process of the market and could perversely lead to more, rather than less, waste.*

- *Ecologist Michael Edesses suggests that instead of being overdeveloped, perhaps the human economy is underdeveloped. Perhaps it still has many empty niches that should be occupied by agents passing materials and energy efficiently along to the next compartment in the cycle. Perhaps future development of the economy can continue to fill those niches, essentially turning what was once waste into raw materials for another product or service.*

People, Prosperity, and the Consumption Conundrum

Nineteenth-century British economist Thomas Malthus cautioned that prosperity would create its own destruction. Booming populations would accompany increased production until, at some point, available land and resources would be insufficient to feed, house, and clothe all these people. Ultimately, in this constrained world, incomes would drop.

Fast-forward nearly 200 years to the 1970s. Selling some 4 million copies, a modern Malthusian depiction of world conditions, *The Limits to Growth*, reiterated this thesis and appealed, as its title suggests, for controls on consumption and economic growth.[1] Twenty years later, concern over human populations and human consumption persists, but with a twist.

By the 1990s, the concern was less on the impending impoverishment that overpopulation might generate, though that worry still troubled some observers. Instead, concern turned to our environmental footprint. Surely, a human population of 5.7 billion must weigh heavily on Earth's ecosystems, and still higher projected populations by the mid-twenty-first century must be catastrophic.[2] This 1990s Malthusian picture has three prongs:

1. There are too many people.
2. These people, through modernization and industrialization, consume more and more resources.
3. This consumption produces prodigious amounts of waste—into the air, water, and soils.

We measure emissions into the atmosphere and effluent into waters in millions of tons. American households alone generate over 200 million tons of solid waste each year.[3] Add in industrial wastes and the figure exceeds an estimated 11 billion tons.

The Dynamic Vision: Technology and Conservation

This snapshot of present conditions is misleading. A snapshot focus blinds us to past ills that have been surmounted through human action so that people can enjoy a better world.[4] A snapshot view is a static view. It prevents an examination of change that a longer time horizon permits. The moving picture of human history shows a progression from a Stone Age to a Bronze Age to an Iron Age and, by the late twentieth century, an Information Age. This cinematic vision invites two key observations.

First, people seek the attributes of particular raw materials, not each stone, chemical, drop of oil, or organic compound per se. Humans need fuel, not necessarily oil; material that can be woven, not just cotton or wool; materials that are malleable, conductive, or strong, not just silver, copper, or steel. Because people seek particular attributes, not specific resources, to satisfy their needs and desires, the production and consumption process holds near-endless opportunities for invention, exploration, substitution, and conserving technologies that, in effect, expand the potential resource base. This process is not mere speculation. As Harvard economist Robert Stavins pointed out in 1993, "reserves have increased; demand has changed; substitution has occurred; and recycling has been stimulated."[5] Human innovations—through sequential scientific and technological revolutions—have "each transformed the meaning of resources and increased the carrying capacity of the Earth."[6]

Second, changing circumstances give rise to changing priorities. When requirements for basic food and shelter absorbed the total attention of most of humankind, many environmental values were neglected. However, as fundamental survival needs begin to be met by some societies, consumers have revised their hierarchy of values to include environmental amenities, conservation, and long-term health concerns as high priorities.

Our industrial practices reflect those changing priorities. The late nineteenth century was a time of mass production in the West—the mechanical era—in which large amounts of materials were assembled using machines to produce look-alike products that could be sold (relatively) cheaply to large numbers of people. Minimizing waste and the release of production residuals into what seemed a capacious environment was deemed less important than making many products widely available.[7]

Later, quality and product improvements became more and more important. We entered what might be called the "era of chemistry," in which manufacturers disassembled and reassembled molecules into new materials with more and more refined characteristics that opened up new possibilities for softer, wrinkle-free clothes; safer and better-preserved foods; contact lenses; new medicines; home computers; and easy-to-use household cleansers.

By the late twentieth century, we had begun to enter a new era—call it the "era of biology"—in which many manufacturers were looking for closed-loop opportunities to recycle on-site plant wastes and dematerialize their products—by using less and less stuff to meet each individual need.

This new era of biology is new only in its deliberate focus on reducing environmental impacts from manufacturing processes and final products. The actual trend of dematerialization is evident in an uninterrupted progression since before the dawn of the Industrial Revolution. Competitive markets have pushed entrepreneurs on farms and in factories to look for new ways to "do more with less"—to use fewer resources and less energy in producing goods and services.

Alongside this trend toward closed-loop manufacturing has come a gradual shift toward achieving value through providing information and services rather than simply materials. Value added comes increasingly from sophisticated new service sectors centered on immaterial factors, such as design, image, quality, flexibility, safety, reliability, public relations and environmental compatibility. Interface Flooring Systems, for example, leases rather than sells carpets to commercial building owners. When portions of the carpet are worn, Interface replaces those portions through techniques that permit integrating new carpet pieces into the old carpet. Building owners are, in effect, buying an ongoing service rather than carpets. The result is a reduction in materials usage.

Xerox Corporation had traditionally relied on one-way packaging to receive parts shipments from its suppliers. The company created a Supplier Packaging Program to develop reusable or recyclable shipment packaging. The program saves the firm $20 million in packaging costs while substantially reducing materials use. Nortel, a telecommunications equipment manufacturer, now pays chemical suppliers a fixed price for chemical services, rather than simply paying for chemicals consumed. Under the fixed fee, Nortel purchases technical assistance, and chemical storage and disposal services. The fixed fee for service gives the supplier an incentive to find efficiency improvements in how the chemicals are handled, used, and disposed, and also to provide less-hazardous chemicals.

As Jesse Ausubel, director of the Program for the Human Environment at Rockefeller University, points out, all human production and consumption activities modify and have an impact on our natural environment. There is no "golden age" in which mankind's touch upon the earth was not evident.[8]

We are getting better, though, at lightening the impact of individual products and practices.[9] Ausubel reminds us that a neolithic home used up 13 tons of firewood just to make the plaster for the walls and floor. By the time of Alexander the Great, forests had been cleared from the eastern Mediterranean region. It was not until Benjamin Franklin's stove that efficient indoor wood burning for heating and cooking was possible. The ratio of weight to power in industrial boilers is now one-hundredth what it was in the early 1800s through changes in metallurgy, thin casting, ion-beam implantation, drop and cold forging, and other advances.[10]

In the early twentieth century, New Yorkers' horses left as much as 200 tons of excrement in city soils each day.[11] By 1900, New York City was home to some 120,000 horses, each producing some "twenty pounds of manure and gallons of urine daily, most of which ended up in the streets."[12] That was not all. Citizens of Manhattan, Brooklyn, and the Bronx produced some 160 pounds of garbage, 1231 pounds of ashes, and another 97 pounds of rubbish in the early 1900s, an amount that exceeds total personal municipal waste generation today, even though the composition of waste today has dramatically changed.[13]

Waste, residuals from production, and other environmental impacts are not a consequence of modernization and industrialization. "Humans have," as Ausubel comments, "always exploited the territories within reach. The question is whether the technology that has extended our reach can now also liberate the environment from human impact—and perhaps even transform it for the better."[14] This question invites yet a larger one: What institutional arrangements are most likely to assure that technological advances and dematerializing innovations occur?

Dematerialization is one step in the journey toward reducing our environmental impacts while still achieving other human ends. Dematerialization, put simply, means using fewer raw materials and less energy per unit of output.[15] As Vice President Al Gore has observed, "in the past 50 years the value of our economy has tripled, while the physical weight of our economy as whole has barely increased at all."[16] This increasingly efficient use of resources need not result from deliberate pursuit of environmental goals. Indeed, most such achievements may simply accompany innovations spawned by competitive marketplace searches for ways to cut costs and improve productivity.

Complexity of Consumption Trends

Before turning to dematerialization trends, a word of caution is in order. Although innovations have delivered individual products and services that use less energy and fewer materials per unit of output, total resource consumption—and accompanying waste—in many cases continues to grow. The reasons are simple.

First, world (including U.S.) population is still growing. More people mean more demand for food, clothing, transportation, and shelter.

Second, at least up to some point, "wealth appears to be a materializer."[17] As incomes increase, most people expand the universe of what they consume. Habits and consumer cultures change. Consumers seek larger homes, more clothing, a broad array of appliances, and more goods not tied to simple survival. With greater societal wealth comes an *individuation* of products—different soaps for different people and different occasions, special shoes for special activities; in short, a proliferation of product choices. For example, in 1960, on average, a grocery store stocked some 6,000 stock-keeping units, which had climbed to over 30,000 by 1992.[18] So, although the energy and raw material inputs for each product may decline, the total number of products consumed has generally increased as per capita income increases.

There is a third confounding factor: Technology makes possible new activities. The much discussed increase in paper use that accompanied the widespread use of personal computers in homes and offices highlights the complex interrelationship between new and old technologies. Computers—so far—have not ushered in paperless offices. (Americans consumed about 1 kilogram of paper per day on average in the 1990s compared with half that amount in 1950.)[19] Computers have, instead, made it easier to generate reports, memos, and other paper-using products, though still-newer technologies—e-mail, better image resolution, higher electronic transmission speeds, and so on—could alter this trend.

These observations, however, are snapshot observations. Population growth rates peaked in 1970 and have now dropped—worldwide—more than halfway toward the zero growth rate of 2.1 children per woman. Many nations have already reached the point of near-zero growth rates.

Increasing wealth per capita may be a materializer up to a point. However, beyond some threshold a saturation point for automobiles, appliances, telephones, and so on may be reached. The percent of household incomes spent on physical "stuff" may decline, as more disposable income is spent on services and other nonmaterial consumption. Similarly, new technologies may initially spark increased consumption of other goods—as in the case of computers and paper—but, over time, still newer technologies may revolutionize consumption patterns in dematerializing ways. Compact discs, for example, are replacing phone books at phone companies that offer information services, with dramatic dematerializing results: A single disc carries 90 million phone numbers that would once have been displayed in 5 tons of phone books.[20]

Even individuation may have its limits. Shelf space in stores is at a premium. Manufacturers face a trade-off between placing more and more products that sell only a few units per week on shelves, or concentrating on a smaller number of products with high-volume sales.[21] Internet shopping may overcome shelf space limitations, but manufacturers may still moderate the trend toward individuation to maintain economies of scale in production.

Still, at least to date, the claim for dematerialization is not made in absolute terms. Total consumption is rising, though the mix of resources consumed has changed over time. However, resource consumption per unit of output is declining. This dematerialization means a defined level of consumption is occurring with less resource use, less accompanying waste, and a "lighter" footprint on the earth. In some instances, the dematerialization is so dramatic that absolute reductions have occurred in use of material across a total economic activity, even in the face of population growth and increased wealth.

Dematerialization Trends

The big-picture trend toward ever more efficient use of materials is unequivocal. A 1997 report on materials use in the United States concludes that "an assessment of consumption per unit of economic activity shows a dematerialization in physical materials of about one-third since 1970."[22]

Use of some materials, such as steel, copper, lead, and cement, has declined by weight per dollar of gross domestic product (GDP). Other materials, such as plastics, have increased their share of consumption per dollar of GDP.[23] Despite population growth, increased size of homes, and more furniture per household, total per capita consumption of wood in the United States has declined to less than one-half of what it was in 1900, partly through decline in use of wood for fuel, partly through substitutions of other materials, and partly as a consequence of more efficient use of wood materials.[24] Put another way, total consumption for wood grew 70 percent between 1900 and 1993, with especially large increases in consumption of pulp for paper and paperboard (in part due to increased literacy and the shift of economic activity toward services).[25]

This absolute increase obscures several important factors. During the same time period, U.S. population increased 300 percent and increasing GDP per capita meant total GDP grew 16-fold. On an annual basis, wood consumption increased 0.5 percent, whereas GDP grew 3 percent. Examining these trends, a 1997 study on timber consumption concludes that "intensity of use"—use as a portion of total consumption—declined. Americans, in effect, become "more efficient in terms of timber products, annually making their GDP with 2.5% less wood."[26] Improved efficiencies meant that increases in total timber use were actually accompanied by increases in forested land and the volume of timber available by some 30 percent since the turn of the century.

These improved efficiencies have enormous implications for the human environmental footprint. Without the efficiency gains in how forests were managed, timber was harvested, and products were made between 1970 and 1993, large additional amounts of timber would have been required to meet wood and pulp demand. Had harvesting and production practices remained static, U.S. consumers would have used 252 million cubic meters of lumber in 1993, rather than the 84 million cubic meters actually consumed.[27] Efficiency improvements also meant dramatic reductions in production losses—from 26 percent in 1970 to a loss of less than 2 percent of the residues from lumber manufacture in 1993 (see Figure 3-1).[28] Effluent and atmospheric emissions also plummeted—from 64 million cubic meters, or 14 percent, in 1970, to 9 million cubic meters, or 1.5 percent, in 1993.[29]

Material substitutions have also affected the amount and the mix of materials used per dollar spent in the U.S. economy, with the trend toward lighter materials accompanied by more efficient use of traditional materials (see Figure 3-2).

FIGURE 3-1 Volume of unused residues at primary manufacturing plants: United States, 1952–1991.

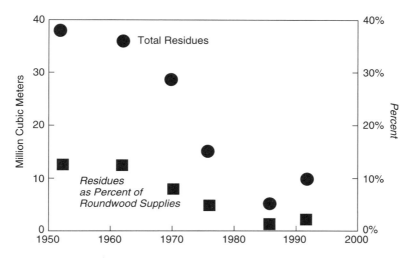

Source: Iddo Wernick et al., "Searching for leverage to conserve forests," *Journal of Industrial Ecology* (Summer 1997).

In a 1978 study on materials use, W. Malenbaum introduced the idea of *intensity of use*, which measured the ratio of material consumption to gross domestic product.[30] Malenbaum observed a bell-shaped pattern in intensity of use for individual materials, with intensity first increasing as GDP rises, then peaking, and then declining. These patterns are repeated over time for different materials and across economies, with peak intensity of usage occurring "in different countries or regions at about the same level of per capita GDP."[31] Although the bell-shaped pattern is remarkably similar across materials, time, and nations, "the maximum in the intensity of use attained by different countries declines substantially over time."[32] In other words, later entrants into the industrialized world economy appear to leapfrog some technology steps.

Total consumption figures obscure many efficiency trends because growing wealth and population have meant growth in absolute consumption, even while materials consumption per unit of output has declined. It is the stories of individual products that show how innovation is enabling manufacturers to accomplish the same tasks with much less stuff. These trends appear in products, large and small, and include basic infrastructure, buildings, and daily household items.

Materials used for basic infrastructure and construction account for some 70 percent of total materials consumed, excluding fuels.[33] Hence, using less stuff per construction project

FIGURE 3-2 Changing weight of materials.

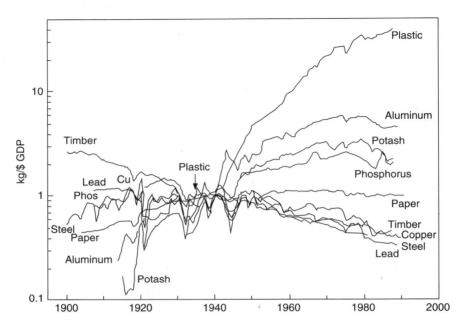

Source: Iddo Wernick et al., "Materialization and dematerialization," in *Technological Trajectories and the Human Environment* (Washington, D.C.: National Academy Press, 1997), p. 140.

can have dramatic, long-term environmental benefits. A skyscraper built today requires 35 percent less steel than the same building would have required just a few decades ago.[34] Less steel per building translates into less energy use, less mining, and fewer emissions associated with creating that building.

Similar trends have occurred with the ubiquitous automobile, which has lost weight through a combination of materials substitution and efficiency improvements in traditional materials. Lightweight plastics and composite materials have replaced some steel parts (see Figure 3-3). The steel itself has undergone a transformation toward lighter-weight, but higher-strength, steel. According to the American Iron and Steel Institute, steel parts in the 1990s were more dent-resistant and as much as 30 percent stronger than earlier types of steel.[35] By 1998, joint steel industry development of a new ultralight steel auto body (ULSAB) was under way. The new steel allows a midsize sedan to reduce its body-in-white weight (vehicle weight without doors and engine) by 24 percent without compromising performance and safety.[36] Recycling of the steel components of autos further reduces the net materials usage for vehicles. In 1996, over 12 million tons of steel was recycled, a recovery rate of nearly 98 percent.

Doing More with Less 51

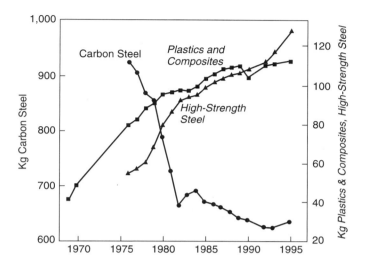

FIGURE 3-3 Changing weight of selected materials in the average U.S. automobile.

Source: Iddo Wernick et al., "Materialization and Dematerialization," in *Technological Trajectories and the Human Environment* (Washington, D.C.: National Academy Press, 1997), p. 144.

Even more dramatic than trends in construction and automobiles have been the reductions in resource use made possible by the invention of fiber-optic cable. A single fiber-optic cable, requiring 65 kilograms of silica, can carry many times the number of messages carried by a cable made from 1 ton of copper.[37] This substitution of abundant silica for less-abundant and less-efficient copper over time results in substantially less mining and materials used to supply telecommunications services. Wireless communication, over time, may further reduce the environmental impact from telecommunications if wireless substantially replaces, rather than merely supplements, wired communication. Telephony may already be headed toward the Internet, which will run almost exclusively on fiber optics. Moreover, cheap, easily available video telephony is anticipated as we move into the twenty-first century, possibly cutting into the need or desire to travel.

Appliances, too, continue to dematerialize. Between 1972 and 1987, the average stove became more compact, with a 17 percent decline in weight from 245.67 pounds per unit to 203.29 pounds per unit.[38] Water heaters, washers, dryers, air conditioners, and freezers all saw a drop in the average weight per unit. Among appliances, only refrigerators and dishwashers gained weight and size during this time frame. On a per-unit basis, manufac-

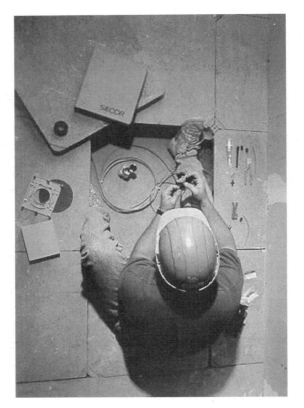

Optical fibers, like those being installed here, are made of abundant silicon and transmit thousands more calls than the bulky copper wires they replace. (*Credit:* Corning Glass.)

turers were achieving more with less. In absolute terms, increased numbers of households and other demographic trends translated into rising total consumption and an increase in the weight of appliance discards (see Table 3-1).

Perhaps no set of consumer products has received more scrutiny in recent years than packaging. Despite claims of wasteful packaging, dematerializing trends have actually been persistent and, sometimes, dramatic. A basket of typical U.S. grocery items fell from over 2750 pounds of packaging per gross production unit in 1989 to approximately 2100 pounds in 1993–1994 (see Figure 3-4).[39]

With these dematerializing trends, grocery packaging as a percentage of total MSW actually declined between 1980 and 1993 from 15.3 percent to 12.1 percent, despite a pop-

TABLE 3-1 Average Weight per Appliance Unit Discarded

	1972		1987		% Weight Change/Unit
	Avg. Size	Avg. Lb./Unit	Avg. Size	Avg. Lb./Unit	
Range	36 in	245.47	30 in	203.29	−17.18
Refrigerator	7.5–8.4 ft^3	299.67	11.5–14.4 ft^3	373.63	24.68
Freezer	12.5–16.4 ft^3	380.00	14.5–19.4 ft^3	342.22	−9.94
Washer	12-lb load	245.57	Std. size	207.36	−15.56
Dryer	10-lb load	191.22	Std. size	150.71	−21.19
Water heater	38-gal avg.	169.18*	48-gal avg.	155.17*	−8.28
Dishwasher	Standard size	136.88	Std. size	142.50	4.11
Microwave	—	—	1.3 ft^3	79.80	—
Air conditioner, Room	Standard size	200.20	Std. size	143.18	−28.48

Source: Franklin Associates, *Analysis of Trends in Municipal Solid Waste Generation: 1972–1987*, pp. 2–4.
*For water heaters, the lbs/unit represents the weight of gas and electric appliances averaged.

ulation increase of around 14 percent over the same time.[40] Put a different way, grocery packaging discards declined 26 percent between 1980 and 1993 in absolute terms, due to a combination of recycling and dematerialization. This trend was especially dramatic for some specific types of items. For example, snack-food consumption in the United States climbed some 43 percent between the early 1970s and 1987. Despite this jump in con-

FIGURE 3-4 Material use per production unit in North America.

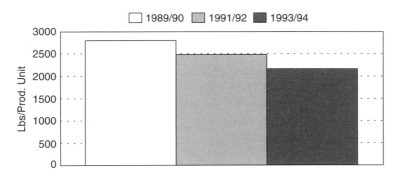

Source: Lynn Scarlett et al., *Packaging, Recycling, and Solid Waste* (Los Angeles: Reason Foundation, 1997), p. 86.

Due to modern materials, the average car weighs less than it did 30 years ago, thus reducing the use of metals and improving gas mileage. (*Credit:* Ford Motor Company.)

sumption, snack-food packaging decreased in weight by 9 percent over the same time frame.[41] That is, the decreases in packaging through dematerialization and recycling were sufficiently large to counteract increases in consumption.

Each package has its own unique tale that combines with others to make up the total dematerialization picture. Consider a few examples:[42]

- Upon its first appearance in 1963, the aluminum soda can required 54.8 pounds of metal per 1000 cans. By the early 1990s, only 33 pounds of metal were required per 1000 cans. For an individual firm, these reductions translate into substantial savings in material inputs. By reducing the weight of aluminum cans 32 percent over a 20-year period, Anheuser-Busch saved 200 million pounds of aluminum annually. Including more than 50 percent of recycled content in its cans generates additional reductions in net new material required.[43]

- Plastic milk jugs weighed 95 grams in the early 1970s; by 1990, the same jug weighed just 60 grams.

- Plastic grocery bags were 2.3 mils thick in 1976; by 1989, they were 0.7 mils thick.

- Between 1990 and 1993, Gillette reduced its packaging needs by more than 10 million pounds by eliminating the outer boxes on personal care products. Redesigning its hair products packaging reduced plastic consumption by 20 million pounds.

- Across a broad spectrum of packaging, Kraft reduced material consumption by 250 million pounds between 1992 and 1995.

- Through a combination of lightweighting and package redesign, Best Foods saved 4.8 million pounds of paper and 380,000 pounds of plastic in a single product, its Mazola Corn Oil, between 1989 and 1994. Additional changes led to 1.4 million pounds of additional savings in plastic in 1995.

- New materials, such as flexible packaging, made possible large reductions by weight in packaging for a number of products. For example, the plastic frozen food bag resulted in an 89 percent weight reduction and an 83 percent volume reduction for some frozen foods previously packaged in waxed wrap cartons. Flexible plastic diaper packages resulted in an 85 percent weight reduction over folding cartons for some manufacturers.[44]

Cumulatively, these incremental efforts to use less stuff to deliver each product to the consumer have finally reversed trends toward increased household waste generation. Other reductions in resource use accompany these packaging changes, and even small changes can unleash large spillover benefits. For example, one juice manufacturer reduced the cubic dimensions of a juice package by 16 percent and the size of the label by 10.7 percent. This change saved nearly 20,000 pounds of materials, more than 500 truckloads of outgoing freight, 20,000 shipping pallets, 7,000 pounds of stretch wrap, and 250,000 square feet of chilled warehouse space.[45]

Franklin Associates, which prepares for the U.S. Environmental Protection Agency regular updates on the composition, amount, and handling of MSW, reported in 1997 that the rate of growth of MSW had begun to slow by the mid-1990s, apparently as a result of source reduction, increased recycling, and yard waste composting.[46] In previous decades, as GDP grew, MSW grew at approximately the same rate. By the early 1990s, that had begun to break, with the rate of increase in waste leveling off to 1.3 percent per year, well below rates in growth of GDP, and also below previous rates of increase in waste of 3 to 5 percent per year (see Table 3-2). Franklin Associates points out that waste generation increased *less* than total product generation, suggesting that increased production to meet growing consumer demands is occurring alongside decreases in the amount of waste generated per product (see Figure 3-5).

TABLE 3-2 Growth Rates of MSW Generation and Other Factors*

	MSW Generation	Product Generation	Resident Population	GDP 1992$	No. of Households	Persons per Household
1960–1995	2.5%	3.2%	1.1%	3.2%	1.8%	−0.7%
1980–1995	2.0%	2.6%	1.1%	2.6%	1.7%	−0.7%
1990–1995	1.5%	2.8%	1.3%	1.9%	1.3%	0%

Source: EPA, *Characterization of Municipal Solid Waste: 1996 Update;* U.S. Bureau of the Census; Franklin Associates, Ltd.
*All values are percentages.

The Role of Recycling

Dematerialization actually results from different kinds of innovations that include:

- *Lightweighting.* Using less of the same material either by redesigning the product or by improving the material itself
- *Substitution.* Replacing a dense and less efficient material with a less dense and more efficient one, accomplishing the same task with lighter weight, though not necessarily smaller volume materials
- *Recycling.* Reprocessing plant scrap as well as postconsumer discards

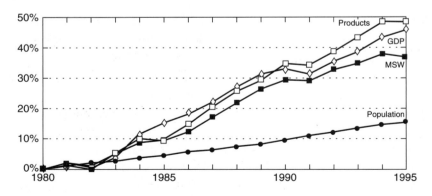

FIGURE 3-5 Growth of population, MSW generation, MSW product generation, and GDP (percentage increase since 1980).

Source: Franklin Associates, *Solid Waste Management at the Crossroads,* p. 1–15, Table 1-7.

Recycling is a form of dematerialization because it can reduce the net amount of materials needed to produce a set of products over time. Notwithstanding popular perceptions, recycling has a long history and has been primarily driven by economic dynamics within the marketplace rather than by politics. By 1992, some 44 percent of U.S. copper requirements were met by recycled copper scrap, half of which derives from plant scrap and half from postconsumer scrap.[47] High percentages of steel, lead, aluminum, and paper are also recycled (see Table 3-3).

TABLE 3-3   Amounts of Recycled Content for Selected Materials

	Amount Recycled*	% Recycled[†]
Aluminum	3,509,000	40.0
Aluminum packaging	1,036,000	51.8
Chromium	123,200	19.8
Copper	1,452,000	38.6
Glass	3,136,000	24.5
Glass containers	3,133,440	27.2
Iron and steel	79,200,000	40.0
Steel	70,672,000	68.5
Cans	1,505,100	55.9
Appliances	2,068,330	74.8
Automobiles	13,355,114	96.5
Lead	1,069,200	61.5
Magnesium	71,610	32.0
Nickel	70,950	35.6
Paper and paperboard	32,600,000	40.0
Plastic containers and packaging	1,729,000	9.7
Tin	12,760	27
Tires	665,000	17.5
Titanium	22,550	49
Wood materials (incl. packaging)	1,430,400	9.6
Yard trimmings	9,029,400	30.3
Zinc	388,300	24.2

Source: Lynn Scarlett et al., *Packaging, Recycling, and Solid Waste* (Los Angeles: Reason Foundation, 1997), p. 86.
*All values in this column are weight in tons.
[†]All values in this column are percent.

Although recycling can result in net material savings, its utility as a dematerializer varies by material and is linked to several key product attributes. Specifically, because recycling requires capturing materials from a waste stream and reprocessing those materials, its contribution as a net "dematerializer" typically will depend on three factors: (1) the ease with which the material can be isolated from the waste stream, (2) whether large quantities of material are available in relatively uniform quality, and (3) how much embedded value remains within the discarded material.

Many metals meet these criteria. Many metals are relatively easy to extract from the waste stream. Citing the ease-of-isolation criterion, authors of a 1996 study on materials usage note, "the ease of isolation explains why lead now enjoys a recovery rate exceeding 70 percent of its demand. Lead is used mainly for automobile batteries, which are readily separated from the general waste stream. Dissipative uses of lead (such as paint and gasoline) have been substantially curtailed over the last few decades."[48] The same authors point out that cadmium, by contrast, is difficult to isolate, possibly accounting for its minimal 7 percent recycling rate.

The three criteria that influence the recycling rates of specific materials also help explain why plastics are, to date, often not recycled in large quantities (with a few exceptions, such as plastic soda bottles). Plastics are often difficult to isolate from the waste stream, because they occur in many different, often difficult-to-distinguish resin forms; they often occur in composite form with other materials or in conjunction with other plastics. Moreover, plastics are an extremely efficient material—for many products, a little material goes a long way, so that only small amounts of any given resin are used per product. Thus, recovering that product does not yield much material for the effort undertaken.

There is another confounding factor. In many respects, plastics are themselves a result of a kind of recycling: They are often made from what had once been considered "waste" gases burned off in petroleum refining processes. One study thus notes, "as long as cars run on oil, new plastic resin will be cheaply available."[49] Plastics result from the very efficient transformation of gases into usable materials, with little residual materials remaining. This contrasts starkly to the mining of metals, which often requires extracting large amounts of materials and applying large amounts of energy in the transformation process to achieve a much smaller amount of usable material. Recycling is a means of avoiding this waste-generating, energy-consuming process. Because plastics often derive from a very efficient, residual gas–using process, there are fewer "avoided costs" achieved through recycling than is the case with many metals, glass, and paper.

Ironically, some forms of dematerialization may work against recycling. Many of the efficiencies in materials use that have allowed lightweighting have been achieved by using composites, laminates, or chemical and other additives to the base material. These technologies introduce complexity into the material profile and make isolation of such materials from the waste stream more difficult. On the other hand, other technology developments—long-life tires, for example—may widen recycling opportunities and prevent "dissipative" uses of materials.[50] Moreover, the additives and laminates often result in such substantial materials savings that even very high rates of recycling traditional noncomplex materials fail to achieve the same levels of resource conservation achieved by using the high-technology, complex materials.

Achieving net reductions in materials usage thus involves information specific to each product and material—in short, there is no one-size-fits-all recipe for conservation. A 1997 Reason Public Policy Institute report found that the marketplace "likely is producing efficient levels of recycling and that attempts to force specific levels of recycling—either directly through recycled-content mandates or indirectly through various taxes and fees—will not uniformly generate hoped-for benefits."[51] Recycling can and often does reduce energy and material needs per product compared with a nonrecycled product made of the same material. Over time, however, resource conservation has often come about through substituting one very efficient material for more traditional, energy- and resource-intensive materials. Recycling of these very efficient materials is often not cost-effective for reasons already stated. Nor will recycling always bring environmental benefits when "avoided" manufacturing costs are low.

Efforts in the 1990s to mandate the use of recycled content in products overlook the potential trade-offs between some recycling and dematerialization. Mandatory recycled-content requirements, if widely promoted, could slow material-reducing innovations and even reverse trends toward use of less material per unit of output in some cases. For example, the state of California mandated that certain plastic bags must contain, over time, 30 percent recycled content. Over the last decade, manufacturers had trimmed down these bags from 2.5 mils in thickness to .75 mils; adding recycled content to these trimmer bags requires increasing their thickness to maintain overall strength requirements. Each product has its own resource "tale"; what brings about greatest opportunities for resource savings will depend on the material and the product.

A Word on Decision-Making Institutions

In an essay on sustainability of the human environment, Chauncey Starr, president emeritus of the Electric Power Research Institute, points out that major new technologies now appear every 20 years.[52] Though technology change is rapid, as Starr notes, it does not occur by magic. The pace and direction of change are affected by the shape of institutions within which people make decisions.

Economist Paul Romer has noted the importance of competition within a market context in spurring innovation. Where resources are owned and traded, as in market economies, innovations—finding ways to "do more with less"—are rewarded with higher returns on investment. Put simply, finding ways to use fewer resources to make a product or provide a service that people want translates into cost savings.

However, Romer also cautions that just as there are countless possible "better mousetraps" that innovators may discover, so, too, are there many innovations that turn out to be less effective, less desirable, or less efficient than other alternatives. The prospect that any individual innovator might settle on one of these less attractive options makes the case for open-ended market discovery, in which ideas and innovations compete, with less successful ones giving way to those that are more resource conserving, more energy conserving, and better at supplying the bundle of values people are looking for when they buy a particular product or service, or undertake a particular activity. Pick-the-winner strategies that use the political process to anoint specific technologies as "better" or "best" undermine this constant, competitive discovery process.

Markets also reward those who discern what values people hold dear and how to meet those values. As environmental values loom larger in the lifestyle and consumption choices people make, entrepreneurs will (and are) innovating in ways that address those values. Sometimes, these innovations are institutional rather than technological. For example, many cities that once offered trash service for free (paid out of property taxes) now use pay-as-you-throw trash fees, whereby households pay a trash collection fee that varies depending on how much trash they discard. This fee system is an institutional innovation that puts trash on people's "radar screen," so that when they buy, use, and discard goods, they consider the costs of the waste associated with that decision. Economist Lisa Skumatz has shown in numerous studies of these fees that they result in less trash generation and more recycling of household waste.

Industrial Ecology: Deliberate Dematerialization

Dematerialization is reducing the amount of material consumed per unit of output; however, many opportunities for further efficiencies exist. Ecologist Michael Edesses sums up this view:

> Instead of being overdeveloped, perhaps the human economy is underdeveloped. Perhaps it still has many empty niches that should be occupied by agents passing materials and energy efficiently along to the next compartment in the cycle. Perhaps future development of the economy can continue to fill those niches.[53]

The search for these niches is now under way, as we move into the "age of biology" in human economic production and consumption patterns. Whereas competition has always impelled a search for "doing more with less," new gains in materials efficiency are also now motivated by efforts to reduce environmental impacts and the costs associated with waste-handling and pollution management. Robert Frosch, writing of industrial ecology, claims that the "emerging field of industrial ecology shifts our perspective away from the choosing of product designs and manufacturing processes independent of the problems of waste. [In this view], the product and process designers try to incorporate the prevention of potential waste problems into the design process."[54]

Many companies have already moved in this direction. The 3M Company, for example, initiated its 3P (*pollution prevention pays*) program in 1975, in which it encouraged product and process designers to seek opportunities to minimize waste and other manufacturing residuals. By 1990, the company had undertaken over 2700 projects, resulting in a 50 percent reduction in pollution per unit of production and some $500 million in materials and other pollution-control savings. Releases into the air, water, and soil have declined by one-half million tons.[55]

The systematic incorporation of environmental values into industrial decisions about processes and products has translated into some opportunities to turn "waste" into saleable products. In Kalundborg, Denmark, in the 1980s, Asnaes, a large coal-fired electricity-generating plant, began providing process steam to a refinery and a pharmaceutical plant located nearby. The refinery, in turn, provides cooling water and purified wastewater to Asnaes. A wallboard producer, Gyproc, had long been buying surplus gas from the refinery; Asnaes joined in the purchase of surplus gas in 1991, absorbing all the refinery's surplus and reducing its need for coal by 30,000 tons per year. Purchase of the surplus gas by Asnaes became possible when the refinery began removing excess sulfur in the gas. The "waste" sulfur was, in turn, sold to a sulfuric acid plant. Asnaes also uses surplus heat to warm a seawater fish farm, which produces trout and turbot primarily for French markets. Sludge generated at the fish farm becomes fertilizer for local farmers.

These efforts did not spring from regulations. Exchanges occur through private market transactions, though some of the trades involve installation of infrastructure by one party in exchange for a competitive price offered by the other.

A 1995 study concluded that pursuit of both radical and incremental technological innovations in products and processes creates significant opportunities for pollution prevention and reductions in residuals.[56] This perspective, as Richard Florida points out in a 1996 article on industrial ecology, should not be confused with the win-win notion that environmental regulations are "good" for economic productivity.[57] Rather, this research points to the evidence that companies that aggressively make product and process improvements to enhance productivity often also achieve reductions in environmental impact simultaneously. In a survey of why manufacturers introduce waste-reducing (environmentally conscious) manufacturing efforts, improving overall industrial performance and productivity was found to be almost as important as environmental regulations.[58]

The Bottom Line: Dematerialization of the Future

Jesse Ausubel, director of the Program for the Human Environment at The Rockefeller University, is optimistic about the prospects for dematerializing trends to reduce our environmental footprint. Observing centuries of technology trends, he writes, "well-established trajectories raising the efficiency with which people use energy, land, water, and materials, can cut pollution and leave much more soil unturned."[59] The relatively high cost of materials processing—from mining and harvesting through final production—motivates a search for ways to make each unit of material more productive. Competition from newly invented materials also forces improvements in traditional materials. The advent of plastics was, for example, a major factor behind lightweighting of glass and steel packaging.

These market forces have persistently propelled more efficient use of resources. With environmental values now holding an increasingly important place among other values, market forces are now reinforced by deliberate efforts to include environmental impact variables among other design variables in product and process development, a trend that will likely accelerate dematerialization and reduction of production and consumption residuals. This process is an unsung environmental triumph, because it reduces environmental impacts associated with resource extraction and processing to make individual products, and may also reduce the "transport intensity" of economic growth.[60]

Chapter 4

WORLD POPULATION PROSPECTS FOR THE TWENTY-FIRST CENTURY
The Specter of "Depopulation"?

Nicholas Eberstadt[1]

HIGHLIGHTS

- World population rose from 1.65 billion in 1900 to 6.08 billion in 2000.

- The world population growth rate peaked in the 1960s at 2.2 percent per year and has now dropped to 1.3 percent per year.

- Plunging death rates, not soaring birth rates, are the main reason for rapid population increases in the last century. World average life expectancy more than doubled, rising from 30 years in 1900 to 63 years now. "World population increased not because people were breeding like rabbits, but because they stopped dying like flies."

- Today, almost one-half of the world's population lives in 79 countries where the total fertility rates are below replacement (an average of 2.1 children per woman over her lifetime).

- The average total fertility rate (TFR) for Western Europe is 1.4 children per woman. Eastern Europe's TFR is even lower at 1.3 children per woman. China's TFR is 1.8 and Japan's is 1.46. The United States' TFR is 2.07 children per woman.

- The TFRs in countries with above-replacement rates are beginning to fall. For all Asia, TFRs have dropped by over one-half from 5.7 children per woman in the 1960s to 2.8 today. Similarly, Latin America's average TFRs fell from 5.6 in the 1960s to 2.7 today.

- If U.N. median-variant projections of world population turn out to be correct, world population will be 7.5 billion in 2025 and 8.9 billion in 2050.

- If present global demographic trends continue, the U.N. low-variant projections are likely. That would mean that world population would top out at 7.5 billion in 2040 and begin to decline.

- In the low-variant scenario, the average age of the world's population would rise from 26 years old now to 44 years old by 2050. The aging of the world's people would push to the fore issues of health care and income security for the elderly in the twenty-first century.

The Twentieth-Century "Population Explosion": Reaching a Turning Point

The year 2000 will conclude a century of amazing, and utterly unprecedented, global population change—a period of abrupt and dramatic departure from all previous trends. It is all but a foregone conclusion that population trends in the next century will be very different from those of the era we have just lived through. Even so, it is possible that demographic developments in the twenty-first century may unfold in ways that would surprise even well-informed observers today.

Although total human numbers at any given moment cannot be estimated with pinpoint precision, demographers now expect that the world's population will exceed 6 billion in the year 1999, and will amount to something like 6.08 billion persons (give or take a few tens of millions) by midyear 2000.[2] Records for the year 1900 are naturally much spottier, but reasonable guesses for total world population for that year center near the number 1.65 billion.[3] Thus, in the course of our century, world population is believed to have come close to quadrupling; over the course of our century, the net number of inhabitants of the globe has risen by almost 4.5 billion. No previous stretch of history could have witnessed anything near to our century's pace of population growth, let alone our increments in absolute numbers.

By any historical yardstick, moreover, global population growth continues at an extraordinary tempo. For the world as a whole, both of today's premier demographic agencies—the U.S. Bureau of the Census and the U.N. Population Division—project a rate of natural increase of about 1.3 percent per year for the year 2000. That would be over twice the estimated pace for the nineteenth century, and something like four times the overall pace ascribed to the millennium now ending. In absolute terms, global population, by these reckonings, is thought to be increasing by almost 80 million persons a year—over twice as many as just half a century earlier, and perhaps 10 times as many as the average annual nineteenth-century increment.

Yet, at the same time, global population trends appear to have reached a monumental turning point: As the twenty-first century commences, the tempo of population growth looks to be in unmistakable decline.

Rapid as the current estimated rate of natural increase for the world as a whole may appear against the backdrop of history, it is nonetheless considerably slower than in the more immediate past. Calculations by the U.S. Census Bureau, for example, put the pace of global population growth in the very early 1960s at over 2.2 percent per year—nearly a full percentage point higher than the rate anticipated for the year 2000—and indicate that the tempo of global demographic growth has been steadily slowing over the past 4 decades. The absolute growth of global population, for its part, is now estimated to have hit its peak in the late 1980s at about 85 million per year, and to have been declining (albeit very gradually) over the past decade.

To attempt to anticipate population trends in the coming century, it is necessary first to recognize, and distinguish, the forces that have brought about the explosive acceleration, the peaking, and now the (at least temporary) decline in world population growth during our own century.

The Longevity Explosion

The twentieth-century "population explosion" was *entirely* the result of health improvements and the expansion of life expectancy. Between 1900 and the year 2000, human life expectancy at birth may have doubled or more, shooting up from something like 30 years to a year-2000 projection of over 63 years.[4] Population growth rates accelerated radically, thanks to that health progress and the concomitant plunge in death rates. Indeed, all other things being equal, that "health explosion" would have resulted in an *even greater* growth of human numbers than has actually been witnessed. Rough calculations, in fact, suggest that the world's population would be *over 50 percent larger today* if our century's recorded revolution in survival chances had unfolded in the absence of any other demographic changes![5]

Secular Fertility Decline

The reason the world population currently totals about 6 billion—rather than 9 billion or more—is that fertility patterns were also changing over the twentieth century. Of all the diverse changes in fertility trends registered over the past 100 years, without question the most significant change has been *secular fertility decline*—that is to say, sustained and progressive reductions in family size due to deliberate birth control practices by prospective parents.

In historic terms, secular fertility decline is very new: It apparently had not occurred in any human society until about 2 centuries ago. France was the first country to embark on secular fertility decline (unambiguously underway there by the early nineteenth century).[6] Since that beginning, secular fertility decline has spread steadily, if unevenly, across the planet, embracing an ever rising fraction of the global population, and depressing voluntary childbearing in the affected societies to successive new lows.

A milestone in the process was passed during the era between the two world wars. For the first time, fertility rates in industrialized countries during peacetime dropped below the net-replacement level: that is to say, below the level that would be necessary for long-term population stability.[7]

In the event, those subreplacement fertility levels proved to be just temporary dips, neither sufficiently prolonged nor sufficiently deep to bring on actual population decline in the countries affected. In the last quarter of the twentieth century, however, subreplacement fertility has made a commanding follow-up on its earlier debut: Subreplacement fertility has descended to previously unimaginable peacetime levels in a number of prosperous societies; it has now been experienced in uninterrupted bouts extending over more than a generation by a growing number of countries; and it has suddenly come amazingly close to describing the norm for childbearing the world over. *Indeed, at the end of the twentieth century, almost half of the world's population is thought to live in countries characterized by subreplacement fertility.*

Secular fertility decline has already had a powerful aggregate impact on global fertility levels. In the early 1950s, the planetary total fertility rates (TFRs)—that is to say, the average number of children per woman per lifetime—was thought to have stood at about 5.[8] For the year 2000, the global TFR is projected to average about 2.7 or 2.8—which would represent a decline of over two-fifths.[9] Those reductions have already brought about a curbing of the relative and absolute pace of world population growth. It is possible, however, that even more dramatic changes in world population trends lie ahead—albeit, the sort of changes not ordinarily contemplated by contemporary commentators on world population problems.

As we shall see in more detail in a moment, the past generation has demonstrated that it is now possible for fertility levels to fall with startling speed, even in low-income societies. Furthermore, although we now know—thanks to recent experience—that country-wide fertility levels can plunge well below replacement, and remain there for decade after decade, we do not actually know how far below replacement national fertility can go, or how long it can stay below the replacement level.

Demographers still lack any reliable method of forecasting long-range fertility trends. However, in reviewing the particulars of the current world population situation, it would appear only reasonable to begin entertaining the possibility that, contrary to even quite recent expectations, the subreplacement fertility regimen may come to typify not only particular regions of the world, but the world as a whole. If that were to occur, the twenty-first century could turn out to be a time in which world population peaked, and thereafter diminished.

World population, of course, is thought to have fallen before—over the course of the fourteenth century, for example.[10] Those earlier reductions, however, were the consequence of catastrophe—in the particular case of the fourteenth century, a repercussion of the terrible bubonic plague epidemic that decimated populations across Asia, Europe, and North Africa between 1333 and 1355.[11] A hypothetical twenty-first century "depopulation," by contrast, could be envisioned as taking place entirely in the absence of disaster—indeed, under conditions of steadily improving survival schedules and living standards for all humanity.

Even so, such a depopulation would pose its own socioeconomic challenges—possibly formidable ones—to the peoples of the world. Unaccustomed though we may be to contemplating such population problems today, we must now recognize that it is (at the very least) possible that these—rather than variants of the perennial Malthusian *problematik*—will emerge as great demographic issues of the coming century.

Fertility Trends at Century's End

Most general readers, and even some students of population affairs, do not appreciate just how far the spread of low-fertility regimens has already progressed. We may better understand the current situation if we divide the world into three categories: countries where fertility levels are currently believed to be below replacement; countries where fertility is above replacement but rapidly declining; and countries where fertility levels apparently remain high and resistant to secular fertility declines.

Subreplacement Fertility

Table 4-1 catalogs the countries and territories around the globe characterized in 1998 by subreplacement fertility levels, according to U.S. Census Bureau projections. Because those figures are *projections*—extrapolations based on earlier data—it is possible that they may exaggerate the dimensions of fertility decline to some degree. On the other hand, the population data for most of the countries and territories in Table 4-1 are both relatively up-to-date and reasonably good; therefore, any exaggerations would not likely be great. (For what it is worth, the U.S. Census Bureau's roster of subreplacement fertility societies is slightly more conservative than the U.N. Population Division's list, in the sense that the latter classifies as *subreplacement* several countries that the Census Bureau believes to be still slightly above the replacement level.)

In all, 79 countries and territories are thought to exhibit below-replacement fertility patterns today. The total number of persons inhabiting those countries is estimated at over 2.5 billion—roughly 44 percent of the world's total population. Moreover, the countries and territories included in Table 4-1 are striking in their geographic, cultural, and economic diversity.

Virtually every advanced industrial democracy, to begin, is on that list. In fact, 27 of the 29 members of the Organization for Economic Cooperation and Development (OECD) are given total fertility rates (TFRs) of less than 2.1—roughly speaking, the level required for long-term population replacement.[12,13] (The two exceptions, Mexico and Turkey, are highly uncharacteristic OECD states.) Within the regular OECD grouping, the highest TFRs are reportedly generated by the United States (2.07) and Iceland (2.04)—levels just shy of replacement; at the other end, Germany and Spain's current TFRs are said to be just over 1.2, and Italy's is currently thought to be *under* 1.2!

Most OECD members are Western European countries; Western Europe's TFR, according to the Census Bureau, averaged about 1.4 in 1998. However, overall fertility levels appear to be even lower in Eastern Europe—by Census Bureau reckoning, about 1.3. Bulgaria, in fact, is ascribed the lowest fertility level ever witnessed in a modern nation that is not at war: an estimated 1.14. (If such a pattern were maintained over the long run, each new generation in a population would be only half as large as the one before.) In all of Europe, only remote Albania and the tiny outposts of Gibraltar and the Faeroe Islands are thought to be above-replacement enclaves—and in those cases, only barely so.

Within the territory of the former Soviet Union, overall fertility levels have fallen far below replacement since the collapse of the Soviet state. While fertility rates in the six former Soviet republics peopled largely by citizens of Muslim heritage all appear to be above the net replacement level (from Kazakhstan's projected TFR of 2.12 to Tajikistan's 3.5), the other nine states are far below replacement. In the Russian Federation, by far the

TABLE 4-1 Countries and Territories with Subreplacement Fertility in 1998: U.S. Census Bureau Projections

	Total Fertility Rate	Population (million)*
OECD Countries		
Australia	1.82	18.6
Austria	1.37	8.1
Belgium	1.49	10.2
Canada	1.65	30.7
Czech Republic	1.17	10.3
Denmark	1.68	5.3
Finland	1.73	5.1
France	1.63	58.8
Germany	1.25	82.1
Greece	1.31	10.7
Hungary	1.45	10.2
Iceland	2.04	0.3
Ireland	1.82	3.6
Italy	1.19	56.8
Japan	1.46	125.9
South Korea	1.79	46.4
Luxembourg	1.63	0.4
The Netherlands	1.49	15.7
New Zealand	1.91	3.6
Norway	1.8	4.4
Poland	1.36	38.6
Portugal	1.35	9.9
Spain	1.21	39.1
Sweden	1.76	8.9
Switzerland	1.46	7.3
United Kingdom	1.64	59.0
United States	2.07	270.3
Eastern Europe and the former Soviet Union		
Bosnia and Herzegovina	1.14	3.4
Bulgaria	1.14	8.2
Croatia	1.54	4.7
Macedonia (former Yugoslavia)	2.06	2.0

TABLE 4-1 Countries and Territories with Subreplacement Fertility in 1998: U.S. Census Bureau Projections (*Continued*)

	Total Fertility Rate	Population (million)*
Montenegro	1.76	0.7
Romania	1.17	22.4
Serbia	1.75	10.5
Slovakia	1.27	5.4
Slovenia	1.17	2.0
Estonia	1.29	1.4
Latvia	1.2	2.4
Lithuania	1.46	3.6
Armenia	1.69	3.4
Belarus	1.34	10.4
Georgia	1.54	5.1
Moldova	1.88	4.5
Russia	1.34	146.9
Ukraine	1.35	50.1
Non-OECD East Asia		
China	1.8	1236.91
Hong Kong S.A.R.	1.36	6.71
Taiwan	1.77	21.9
Macau	1.55	0.4
Singapore	1.46	3.5
North Korea	1.8	21.2
Thailand	1.84	60.0
Latin America and the Carribean		
Anguilla	1.98	0.0
Antigua and Barbuda	1.74	0.1
Aruba	1.81	0.0
Barbados	1.85	0.3
Cayman Islands	1.34	0.0
Cuba	1.56	11.1
Dominica	1.9	0.1
Guadeloupe	1.84	0.4
Martinique	1.8	0.4
Montserrat	1.83	0.0

	Total Fertility Rate	Population (million)*
Netherlands Antilles	1.84	0.2
Puerto Rico	2.03	3.9
Saint Vincent and the Grenadines	1.97	0.1
Trinidad and Tobago	2.09	1.1
Turks and Caicos Islands	1.71	0.0
Africa		
Saint Helena	1.5	0.0
Seychelles	1.98	0.1
Other North America		
Bermuda	1.78	0.1
Saint Pierre and Miquelon	1.6	0.0
Other Europe		
Andorra	1.23	0.1
Guernsey	1.68	0.06
Jersey	1.5	0.1
Liechtenstein	1.61	0.0
Malta	1.73	0.4
Man, Isle of	1.67	0.1
Monaco	1.7	0.0
San Marino	1.51	0.02
Total population		2597
Total world population		5926
Total world population of subreplacement fertility		44%

*Based on 1998 midyear population taken to the 100,000.
Source: International Data Base, U.S. Bureau of the Census.

most populous of those countries, current TFRs are put at just over 1.3. In the next largest country, Ukraine, current TFRs are also thought to hover just over 1.3—as in Belarus, and in the three Baltic states taken together. Fertility levels appear to be only slightly higher in Georgia and Armenia, with projected TFRs of 1.5 and 1.7, respectively. With a projected TFR of 1.88, Moldova would rank as distinctly the most fertile European enclave within the former Soviet Union today.

Recent U.N. projections indicate that the world's population may well peak at around 8 billion people in the next generation and then begin to decline. (*Credit:* Uniphoto.)

Secular fertility decline, as already noted, happened to originate in Europe. Today, virtually every population in the world that can be described as being of European origin reports fertility rates below the replacement level. However, these countries and territories today account for only about 1 billion of the 2.5 billion people living in subreplacement regions. In that sense, subreplacement fertility is no longer an exclusively European phenomenon—nor is it now even a *predominantly* European one.

In the Western Hemisphere, subreplacement fertility now characterizes many of the populations of the Caribbean. Such diverse island societies as Barbados, Cuba, and Guadeloupe are among the Caribbean locales with fertility rates thought to be lower than the United States' own. Off the coast of Africa and in Micronesia, a few tiny territories have apparently also entered into subreplacement fertility. Today, the largest concentration of subreplacement populations, however, lies in East Asia. Japan was the first non-European society to report subreplacement fertility during times of peace and order. Japan's fertility rate fell below replacement in the late 1950s, and it has remained there almost continuously for the past 4 decades. The U.S. Census Bureau puts Japan's current TFR at 1.46.[14]

In addition to Japan, all four East Asian "tigers"—Hong Kong, the Republic of Korea, Singapore, and Taiwan—have reported subreplacement fertility levels since at least the early 1980s. According to the Census Bureau, South Korea has the highest fertility level of that group, with a TFR just under 1.8; Hong Kong, with a TFR of 1.36, is the lowest. Thailand's fertility rate also fell below replacement, after 1990; its current TFR is estimated at a bit over 1.8.

By far, the largest subreplacement population, however, is China's: TFRs on the Chinese Mainland are thought to have dropped below net replacement in the early 1990s, and are projected by the Census Bureau at 1.8 for 1998.[15] China's fertility profile, of course, has been the focus of Beijing's stringent antinatal population control campaign for 2 decades running. It is only reasonable to suppose that the Chinese State Family Planning Commission's strident, muscular, and not infrequently forcible interventions in the name of a one-child norm should have had a demographic impact. Unfortunately, it is currently impossible to quantify reliably just how great that impact has been—or what would happen to Chinese fertility levels if that program were moderated or altogether remanded.[16]

Above-Replacement but Rapidly Declining Fertility

Another large portion of humanity today lives in countries where fertility rates are still above the net replacement level, but where secular fertility decline is proceeding at a rapid pace. Just how large a fraction of humanity this grouping encompasses, of course, depends on one's definition of "rapid."

According to the U.N. Population Division's most recent estimates and projections, total fertility rates for the less developed regions dropped fully by one-half between the late 1960s and the late 1990s: from an average of six births per woman per lifetime, down to three.[17] Of course, those averages were strongly affected by trends in China, and China's circumstances were quite arguably anomalous. However, the singularity of the recent Chinese experience should not divert attention from the breadth and scale of fertility declines that have actually been taking place in other low-income settings.

Table 4-2 illustrates the point. It presents U.N. Population Division estimates of fertility change between the late 1960s and the late 1990s in the 15 most populous developing countries—countries estimated to account for over three-quarters of the entire current population of the less developed regions. During those 3 decades, fertility levels fell by over one-half in 7 of those 15 countries—that is to say, in 5 countries besides China and Thailand, both of which qualified for this table. Of those 5 countries, interestingly enough, 2—Brazil and Mexico—are traditionally Catholic societies, whereas the other 3—Bangladesh, Iran, and Turkey—have Muslim religious traditions.

In relative terms, 12 of the 15 countries in Table 4-2 experienced fertility declines of two-fifths or more; in absolute terms, 10 of the 15 are thought to have registered TFR declines of over three births per woman! Only one of the 15 countries—Ethiopia—has yet to embark on appreciable secular reductions in fertility.

Given prevailing preconceptions about conditions under which rapid fertility decline can—and cannot—occur, it is perhaps worth pointing out that, of the four low-income countries in Table 4-2 in which fertility levels dropped by four births per woman or more during those 30 years, one is Latin American (Mexico), and another has been governed for most of the period under consideration by a militantly Islamic state (Iran).

Table 4-2, however, underscores a more general feature of the fertility decline process now underway in contemporary, low-income countries: its lack of obvious, identifiable socioeconomic "thresholds", preconditions, or even correlates.

We think of fertility levels as being inversely associated with income, and so, in some very general way, they may be. Yet, Vietnam's current fertility level is thought to be lower than the United States' was at the time of the Tet Offensive, even though necessarily rough estimates suggest the level of per capita GDP in the United States then was perhaps over a dozen times higher, in purchasing-power-parity- (PPP)-adjusted terms, than it is in Vietnam today.[18] Rates of income growth are an equally problematic indicator of fertility decline: Although Indonesia's dramatic fertility reductions coincided with relatively rapid long-term (1960–1995) per capita GDP growth, Iran's per capita GDP growth was reportedly *negative* over those same years—and yet Iran's fertility declines were apparently even steeper than Indonesia's.[19]

We often hear that education (or, particularly, female education) bears strong influence on prospects for fertility change. Unfortunately, Table 4-2 (and other available data, for that matter) fails to illuminate any strong international patterns. According to the World Bank's estimates, for example, Nigeria's 1995 adult literacy rate is estimated to be higher than Egypt's—but so is its current TFR (by almost two births per woman).[20] Conversely, the World Bank estimates that adult literacy rates are currently more than 50 points lower today in Bangladesh than in the Philippines, and the gap in female literacy rates is closer to 70 percentage points.[21] Fertility levels today, however, are lower for Bangladesh than

TABLE 4-2 U.N. Population Division Estimated and Projected Fertility Change for Today's Fifteen Most Populous Low-Income Countries: 1965/1970 to 1995/2000

Country	Projected Population Midyear 1998 (millions)	Estimated Total Fertility Rate, 1965/1970*	Projected Total Fertility Rate, 1995/2000*	Percentage Change	Absolute Change
China	1256	6.1	1.8	−70	−4.3
India	982	5.7	3.1	−45	−2.6
Indonesia	206	5.6	2.6	−54	−3.0
Brazil	165	5.4	2.3	−58	−3.1
Pakistan	148	7.0	5.0	−29	−2.0
Bangladesh	125	6.9	3.1	−55	−3.7
Nigeria	106	6.9	5.2	−25	−1.2
Mexico	96	6.8	2.8	−60	−4.0
Vietnam	76	6.0	2.6	−56	−3.4
Philippines	73	6.0	3.6	−40	−2.4
Egypt	66	6.6	3.4	−48	−3.2
Iran	66	7.0	2.8	−60	−4.2
Turkey	65	5.6	2.5	−56	−3.1
Thailand	60	6.1	1.7	−72	−4.4
Ethiopia	60	6.8	6.3	−7	−0.5

Source: United Nations, *World Population Prospects: The 1998 Revisions* (New York: U.N. Department of Economic and Social Affairs, forthcoming).

*Note: Total fertility rate (TFR) is a measure of average births per woman per lifetime. TFRs are rounded to the nearest tenth.

the Philippines, and Bangladeshi fertility declines over the past 3 decades have been distinctly greater in magnitude.

What of family planning programs? It has become a tenet of faith for many that a national population program is instrumental, if not indispensable, for fertility decline in a low-income setting. It is true that most of the developing countries reporting major fertility declines in recent decades *did* have national birth control programs in place. (Some of these programs, like China's and Vietnam's, rely on pressure, intimidation, and even coercion to promote their particular "targets.") On the other hand, Brazil has *never* adopted a national family planning program—yet its percentage fertility decline over the past 3 decades has been almost identical to Mexico's, where a strong national program operates.[22] Although today Brazil is (according to World Bank and UNDP data) both poorer and more poorly educated than Mexico, its fertility level is thought to be lower as well.[23]

Reviewing these and other available data, it is all too clear that there are exceedingly few robust structural or developmental predictors of fertility differences between countries at any given point in time—and even fewer with any lasting value for trends over stretches of historical time. Indeed, reviewing the record of the past half-century, one is tempted to suggest that for any given low-income country, practically the strongest predictor of its fertility level may be the *calendar year*: The later its date in our century, the lower the fertility level is likely to be!

High and Resistant Fertility Levels

The final share of humanity demarcated by this tripartite fertility schema lives in countries where TFRs are very high (say, six or more) and for whom convincing evidence of secular fertility decline has yet to be reported.

In current commentary on the current world population situation, it is often implied that such countries typify the developing regions. However, because fertility levels in the less developed regions as a whole are thought to have fallen by one-half over the past 30 years, this clearly cannot be the case. For the entire Asian landmass, TFRs are thought to have fallen by more than one-half between the late 1960s and the late 1990s: from about 5.7 to about 2.8. For the entire Latin America/Caribbean area, TFRs are also thought to have fallen by more than one-half, from about 5.6 to about 2.7.

The regions where fertility levels remain highest, and where fertility declines to date have been most modest, are sub-Saharan Africa and the Islamic expanse to its north and east—more specifically, the Arab Middle East. (These are the areas the Census Bureau terms "sub-Saharan Africa," "North Africa," and "the Near East.") These areas encompassed a total projected population of about 930 million in 1998—a little less than one-fifth of the total for less-developed regions, and a bit under one-sixth of the world total.[24]

Fertility levels are, by all indications, much higher today within this agglomeration of countries than in any other comparably sized amalgam of nations. For this grouping, however, the image of uniformly high, persistently "traditional" fertility regimens is already badly outdated. A revolution in family formation patterns has begun to pass through the region—and has already impressed itself on some countries in the grouping quite profoundly.

Table 4-3 outlines the dimensions of some of these changes. It is no longer accurate to describe the "Arab world" as a place unfamiliar with major secular fertility declines. Over the past 30 years, in fact, TFRs for Northern Africa—the territory stretching from Western Sahara to Egypt—is believed to have dropped by almost one-half (or by an average of 3.3 births per woman). There remain Arab outposts in the late 1990s where fertility is thought to remain high and nearly unyielding: the Gaza Strip (projected TFR: 7.3), Oman (5.9), Saudi Arabia (5.8), and Yemen (7.6). These four spots, however, account for barely 40 million of the Arab Middle East's current quarter of a billion people. Elsewhere, relatively rapid fertility decline is currently underway; in some Arab countries, the pace of fer-

TABLE 4-3 Fertility Decline in "Resistant" Regions: Estimates and Projections for Selected Countries, 1975/1980 to 1995/2000

Region or Country	Estimated TFR, 1975/1980*	Projected TFR, 1995/2000*	TFR Change*	
			Percentage	Absolute
Middle East				
Algeria	7.2	3.8	−47	−3.5
Jordan	7.4	4.9	−34	−2.6
Libya	7.4	3.8	−49	−3.6
Morocco	5.9	3.1	−47	−2.8
Syria	7.4	4.0	−46	−3.4
Sub-Saharan Africa				
Botswana	6.4	4.4	−32	−2.0
Côte d'Ivoire	7.4	5.1	−31	−2.3
Kenya	8.1	4.5	−45	−3.7
Sudan	6.7	4.6	−31	−2.1
Zimbabwe	6.6	3.8	−42	−2.8

Source: United Nations, *World Population Prospects: The 1998 Revisions* (New York: U.N. Department of Economic and Social Affairs, forthcoming).
*Note: TFRs are rounded to the nearest tenth.

tility decline can only be described as very rapid. In Algeria, Libya, Morocco, and Syria, for example, TFRs are thought to have dropped by nearly one-half in just the past 2 decades. There are now Arab countries where fertility levels may be approaching the net-replacement level. The U.S. Census Bureau projections place current TFRs in Tunisia and Lebanon at 2.4 and 2.3, respectively (although U.N. Population Division estimates for those countries are slightly higher).

Even less generally appreciated than the phenomenon of pronounced fertility reductions throughout the Arab world is the fact that secular fertility decline appears to be unambiguously in progress in a number of countries in sub-Saharan Africa. As Table 4-3 illustrates, such declines are thought to be underway in countries from all regions of the continent. Particularly noteworthy is the recent Kenyan experience: Over the past 2 decades, the country's TFR is thought to have fallen by 45 percentage points, or by an average of 3.7 births per woman.

The Kenyan example speaks to another facet of secular fertility decline in low-income countries that we should bear in mind: the inevitable lag time between its onset and the moment demographers confidently determine its dimensions (or even ascertain that it is really underway). Like all other sub-Saharan countries, Kenya lacks a comprehensive and reliable vital registration system; its population trends must therefore be divined from occasional censuses and episodic demographic surveys.

Kenya collects more demographic information than most other sub-Saharan states; even so, the pace of the country's recent fertility declines has surprised population experts. In 1994, the U.N. Population Division's very lowest projection (low-variant fertility) for Kenya for the early 1990s was a TFR of over 6.2. On the basis of findings over the past 4 years, however, the actual TFR for Kenya at that time has been calculated at 5.4—or by almost one birth per woman lower than the lowest contemporary U.N. projections had imagined.

Contemporary fertility estimates for some other sub-Saharan locales may analogously overestimate current levels—or may not detect extant secular declines until years from now.

Whither World Fertility Trends?

In the coming century, barring the contingency of utter cataclysm, world population trends will be dominated and, indeed, determined by trends in fertility (as population trends for convened human populations always are when death rates are relatively low and stable). However, what course will world fertility trends take?

The inescapable truth of the matter is this: We have no way of accurately predicting long-term fertility trends in advance. For better or worse, the social sciences lack any reliable basis for forecasting fertility change before it occurs—or even for explaining its precise determinants after the fact.

The U.N. Population Division's "Expert Group Meeting on Below Replacement Fertility" summarizes the state of knowledge in this area succinctly: "There exists no compelling and quantifiable theory of reproductive behavior in low fertility societies."[25] As much also might be said about reproductive behavior in contemporary societies with higher levels of fertility. In practical terms, this means there is no positive framework for anticipating the onset of secular fertility decline, or for assessing its likely pace or endpoint once it commences.

With respect to subreplacement fertility, the brute facts are that there is no way for us to tell just how low fertility levels may plunge under "conditions of orderly progress"—or how long spells of below-replacement fertility may ultimately last in stable, modern societies.

Some eminent demographers have advanced a homeostatic hypothesis, suggesting that subreplacement fertility regimens may be drawn upward to replacement as if by "a magnetic force"—but that remains a pure and unsupported speculation.[26] By the same token, some demographers have recently suggested that TFRs in a stable industrial society are unlikely to dip below 0.7—but that postulate simply follows on the observation that TFRs at that level have *already* been observed in such societies (cf. Eastern Germany after unification).[27,28] The simple reality is that today's subreplacement fertility patterns are a *terra incognita*—and demographers have no workable instruments for gauging trajectories or courses once a population enters it.

As for fertility prospects for countries still above the replacement rate, the situation is not much more certain. Although demographers have argued that "no country has been modernized without going through the demographic transition [that leads to low levels of both mortality and fertility]," the definition for *modernization* must now be sufficiently elastic to stretch around cases like Bangladesh and Iran—countries where extremely low levels of income, high incidences of extreme poverty, slow or negative rates of economic growth, mass illiteracy, relatively high levels of mortality, and other ostensibly nonmodern social or cultural features characterize the local norm, and where massive voluntary reductions on fertility have, nevertheless, already taken place.[29]

We now know, furthermore, the fertility decline can occur with great speed in low-income settings, even over extended periods of time. Table 4-4 attests to this. In Asia, Latin America, the Middle East, and even sub-Saharan Africa, there are now examples of countries in which fertility levels have declined by 1.5 births per woman per decade for a full quarter of a century. In sub-Saharan Africa, a pace of TFR reduction of over 20 percent per decade has been maintained in at least one instance for 25 years running. In Latin America and the Middle East, a pace of around 30 percent per decade has been observed; in East Asia, a pace of nearly 40 percent per decade has been sustained for two and a half successive decades.

TABLE 4-4 Rapid Fertility Decline in Low-Income Countries: Selected Examples of Twenty-Five-Year Changes in Estimated Total Fertility Rates

Region or Country	Period	Initial TFR*	Final TFR*	TFR Change per Decade*	
				Percentage	*Absolute*
East Asia					
China	1965/1970–1990/2000	6.1	1.9	−37	−1.7
Republic of Korea	1960/1965–1985/1990	5.6	1.8	−37	−1.5
Singapore	1950/1955–1975/1980	6.4	1.9	−39	−1.8
Thailand	1965/1970–1990/1995	6.1	1.9	−37	−1.7
Latin America					
Colombia	1960/1965–1985/1990	6.8	3.2	−26	−1.4
Guyana	1965/1970–1990/1995	6.1	2.6	−29	−1.4
Mexico	1970/1975–1995/2000	6.5	2.8	−29	−1.5
Middle East					
Tunisia	1970/1975–1995/2000	6.2	2.6	−30	−1.5
Sub-Saharan Africa					
Kenya	1970/1975–1995/2000	8.1	4.5	−21	−1.5

Source: United Nations, *World Population Prospects: The 1998 Revisions* (New York: U.N. Department of Economic and Social Affairs, forthcoming).
*Notes: TFRs are rounded to the nearest tenth.

Irrespective of what theory may indicate, "existence proofs" now demonstrate that fertility levels can fall by three-fifths in just 25 years in an Arab country, where upward of one-half of all women of childbearing ages have had no formal schooling—or by 45 percent over a quarter century in a sub-Saharan country with an incidence of extreme poverty estimated to be 20 percentage points higher than that of Bangladesh.[30,31]

In the coming century, in short, a multiplicity of prospective fertility trends would appear to be well within the realm of possibility for the world as a whole and its subsidiary regions.

"Median variant" U.N. fertility projections currently envision a world 30 years hence with an overall TFR of 2.23 (1.75 in more-developed regions, 2.31 in the less developed regions). That trajectory results in a hypothetical global population of 7.8 billion by 2025, and of 8.9 billion by 2050.

It is easily possible to imagine factors which could raise the pace of population growth in the decades ahead above these medium variant assumptions: For example, a slower-than-postulated pace of fertility decline in such major population groupings as the Indian subcontinent; a later-than-postulated advent of secular fertility decline in much of sub-Saharan Africa; or a resumption of above-replacement fertility in China.[32] It is also possible, however, to imagine very different alternatives—alternatives that lead to a cessation of population growth and a subsequent depopulation, despite simultaneously assumed steady improvements in worldwide levels of health.

One Scenario for a Global Depopulation Next Century

The U.N. Population Division's latest low-variant population projections, in fact, provide us with precisely such a vision of the future. In this scenario, global life expectancies—and life expectancies in every region of the world—rise steadily over the first half of the twenty-first century. The world population crests, however, in 2040 at 7.47 billion (growing by about 25 percent, or about 1.5 billion people, between now and then), drops by about 120 million between 2040 and 2050, and then continues to decline by close to 30 percent per generation.

It is, of course, assumptions about fertility that drive this model. The low-variant scenario imagines net-replacement fertility for the world as a whole by the years 2000 to 2005—less than a decade from now—and subreplacement fertility thereafter. We must, therefore, ask: Are such presumptions even remotely feasible, much less realistic?

One way of assessing the feasibility of those hypothetical projections is to compare them with the actual record of the recent historical past. This we do in Table 4-5. This examines the low-variant model's assumed fertility declines for the 3 decades between the early 1990s and the early 2020s, and compares them with the actual, recorded declines over the 3 previous decades.

For every area of the world, these low-variant projections imagine vastly lower fertility levels by the early 2020s than those registered today (or ever before). Some readers may regard that by itself as a sign of inherent implausibility on its very face. Yet, in terms of the assumed *pace* of fertility decline, these low-variant projections simply seem to imagine a *continuation* of already existing trends—and in fact, a slight *deceleration* for the world as a whole and most of its regions from the tempo set between the early 1960s and the early 1990s.

For the world, the more developed regions and the less developed regions, not only the absolute but also the relative pace of fertility decline posited by the low-variant model for the period 1990/1995 to 2020/2025 happens to be lower than what was actually recorded between 1960/1965 and 1990/1995. The pace of fertility decline presumed for both Asia

TABLE 4-5 Getting to Depopulation: U.N. Population Division 1998 Low-Variant Fertility Assumption in Historical Perspective

Estimated TFR, Region	Assumed TFR, 1990/1995	2020/2025	Assumed TFR Change, per Decade		Actual TFR Change 1960/1965–1990/1995 per Decade	
			Percent	Absolute	Percent	Absolute
World	2.93	1.78	–15	–0.4	–16	–0.7
More developed regions	1.68	1.39	–6	–0.1	–12	–0.3
Less developed regions	3.27	1.84	–17	–0.5	–18	–0.9
Asia	2.85	1.64	–17	–0.5	–20	–0.9
Latin America and the Caribbean	2.97	1.67	–17	–0.4	–21	–1.0
Africa	5.47	2.64	–22	–0.9	–7	–0.4

Source: Derived from United Nations, *World Populations Prospects: The 1998 Revisions* (New York: U.N. Department of Economic and Social Affairs, forthcoming).

and Latin America for this future are distinctly slower than those actually to be recorded in the recent past.

The only region of the world for which the low-variant projections imagine a more rapid-tempo, long-term fertility decline than the one already experienced within the area is the African continent: Northern Africa and the sub-Sahara. For Africa, indeed, fertility would have to fall as rapidly in absolute terms in the coming decades as it did in Asia from the early sixties through the early nineties—and in relative terms (i.e., percent per year), Africa would have to outpace the Asian experience. Just how likely such an outcome may be is, of course, open to debate.[33] However, in light of the Asian and Latin American examples of rapid change after the advent of secular fertility decline—and no less important, of the extremely rapid fertility declines recently witnessed in a number of impoverished, developmentally challenged countries—one can hardly maintain that these low-variant projections for Africa demand a special, extraordinary imaginative leap.

Whether the world will embark on a path toward the sort of depopulation contemplated by the U.N.'s current low-variant projections is impossible for us to know today. Given the limits of long-term demographic forecasting techniques, it would be heroic even to assign a probability to such an outcome.[34] From today's vantage point, however, the assumptions embodied in the model, which projects a peaking and subsequent decline of human numbers during the coming century, do not in themselves look to be especially heroic.

Population Issues for a Depopulating World

If the past generation's pace of global fertility decline continues for another generation—and the world consequently heads toward the point of zero, or negative, population growth—the population issues of the future would look very different from the concerns that have captured the attention of informed readers, activists, and policymakers over the past several decades.

In a world of long life expectancies, small families, and marginal or negative population growth, the Malthusian specter—in many varied manifestations—could not credibly be said to conform to problems at hand, or stand as a convincing justification for far-reaching public or collective action. On the other hand, pervasive and prolonged subreplacement fertility in the context of good and generally improving health levels would likely pose a number of social, political, and economic challenges of its own.

Some of these potential challenges have been contemplated elsewhere in greater detail.[35] It may suffice here simply to mention a few of these.

Under any noncatastrophic circumstances, current and prospective health improvements mean that the world's population will be aging in the coming century; in a world with low levels of fertility, it will age all the more rapidly. At the moment, the median age of the world's population is thought to be about 26 years. If the trajectory anticipated by the current U.N. low-variant projections were to come to pass, the median age for the world as a whole would be above 35 years—about the same, in fact, as the median age for the world's more developed regions in 1995. (By 2050, on this hypothetical trajectory, the planetary median age would be nearly 44—higher than those for even the most elderly populations of our contemporary world.)

Rapid global aging would have a number of ineluctable implications. For one thing, it would increase the salience of addressing the health care and income security needs of the elderly. In Western countries, current public programs for these purposes are coming under increasing actuarial (read: demographic) pressure, and may require far-reaching overhauls to maintain financial soundness.[36] In low-income countries, where coverage by public pension and health systems is today far more limited, the issue of how to take care of vulnerable older citizens could be all the more pressing.

Rapid global aging would also likely beg the question of how to educate and train the workforces of the future. Given the arithmetic of sustained below-replacement fertility, it is not difficult to imagine circumstances in which a majority of a country's workers were

Plummeting global fertility rates mean that the average age of the world's population will increase significantly in the twenty-first century. (*Credit:* Uniphoto.)

over the age of 50. The age-structure changes heralded by the combination of long lives and negative population growth would considerably intensify the mismatch between an educational system designed to train people when they are young and the desire of workers to enjoy a long and worthwhile career in an increasingly complex economy.

Finally, prolonged subreplacement fertility in a world of long lives would presage a radical change in the structure of the family. It could mean that, for the first time in the human experience, there could be societies in which the only biological relatives for many people—possibly most people—would be their ancestors. With sufficiently low fertility for just two generations, blood siblings and cousins would become anomalous—people who had them would be the exception rather than the rule. Exactly how a society would operate under such conditions (just how children would be socialized, to take an obvious example) is difficult to imagine from our present vantage point. The ramifications of a world largely without blood peers might be far-reaching, even if all those ramifications are not obvious to us today.

To imagine these challenges as real global issues, of course, is mere speculation today. In indulging in such speculation, however, we acknowledge plausible contingency—and, thereby, may be better prepared for the world that actually does arrive as the intrinsically unpredictable demographic trends of the next century unfold.

Chapter 5

FISHING FOR SOLUTIONS
The State of the World's Fisheries

Michael De Alessi

HIGHLIGHTS

- *The global fish catch continues to increase despite claims that it has reached its upper limit. The 1996 world fishery production was 115.9 million tons, an increase from 113 million tons in 1995.*

- *Despite large population increases, per capita fish consumption has grown modestly over the past quarter century, from about 10.5 kg in 1970 to slightly over 13 kg in the last 3 years.*

- *World fishery production is now over six times what it was in 1950, and fish destined for direct human consumption has increased almost three times over the past 37 years, rising from around 27 million tons in 1960 to 90 million tons by 1996.*

- *Recent increases in world production, however, have come primarily from aquaculture and newly discovered stocks—many of the world's depleted stocks are not recovering.*

- *There is hope that depleted stocks can recover, however, as fisheries have generally shown a remarkable resiliency when given the chance.*

- *In addition, when people are given the opportunity to conserve marine resources, they generally do.*

- *To give people that opportunity, however, there must be a dramatic shift in the way fisheries are managed, away from many current regimes that all too often encourage the profligate waste of resources, time, effort, and capital.*

- *As long as the incentives created by fishery management institutions favor rapacious extraction of fish from the sea, then the prospect for marine life will be bleak. If, on the other hand, these institutions provide incentives for conservation and stewardship, then the outlook for these fish stocks will be bright.*

- *The difference, in most cases, is between public and private management of the fisheries. Government regulation of resources previously controlled by local participants has invariably proved to be less effective and efficient, if not disastrous in its consequences.*

- *Until fishing rights are safeguarded from the vagaries of public management, the incentive to harvest stocks sustainably will remain weak.*

- *Government programs that are moving toward more private control of the fisheries, however, are proving to be more successful.*

- *One such program, although certainly not without its problems, is the development of a system of individual transferable quotas (ITQs) for fisheries, especially in New Zealand.*

- *The more an ITQ resembles a private right, the greater flexibility the system has to adapt and evolve into a system of real private rights with the strongest possible incentives for conservation.*

- *The greatest indicator of fishery health is a management regime that includes positive incentives for stewardship and conservation.*

- *Aquaculture is one of the world's fastest growing industries—It has grown at an annual rate of about 10 percent since 1984, compared with 3 percent for livestock meat and 1.6 percent for capture fisheries production.*

- *The aquaculture sector's contribution to total food fish and shellfish was 29 percent in 1996 (closer to 20 percent of total fish production, which includes what is rendered for fish meal and other products).*

Although there has been a significant and disturbing decline in many important fish stocks over the years, the news is hardly all bad. Many marine resources are healthy and well protected, and a growing number of conservation initiatives are shedding light on just how and why some resources are successfully protected and others are pillaged.

Although some species of fish have suffered serious declines in certain areas, extrapolating in a straight-line fashion from these examples is a mistake. The World Wildlife Fund's recent declarations, "Nearly everywhere fisheries have suffered catastrophic declines," and claimed "Without a doubt we have exceeded the limits of the seas," are too broad.[1] Greenpeace also goes too far when it says that due to overfishing, "nature's balance is being altered across vast areas of the world's oceanic ecosystems in ways that may be irreversible."[2]

If one considers only the plight of the Atlantic cod, it is tempting to agree with these sentiments. Cod are one of the world's most fecund fishes (an average female produces 1 million eggs) and have been a staple of many diets for centuries. Cod has even been called the "beef of the sea."[3] Today, however, the cod fishery in New England and Atlantic Canada is the prototypical example of catastrophic fishery decline. Once one of the world's richest fishing grounds, cod are so scarce there now that they are close to commercial extinction.[4] See Figure 5-1.

Although cod fishery is certainly not an isolated example, there is also a rosier view. Many fisheries are healthy, and recent evidence indicates that even those that have been stressed may be remarkably resilient.[5] Based on a slowed, but still increasing world fish catch, the late economist Julian Simon even went so far as to claim that "No limit to the harvest of wild varieties of seafood is in sight."[6] See Figure 5-2.

Proponents of the divergent views of such optimists as Julian Simon and such pessimists as Greenpeace are often referred to as the doomsayers and the cornucopians; surely they both go too far. The world harvest of marine species *has* risen slowly in the last few years, but the increase has come primarily from harvests of lower-value species and the discovery of new stocks.

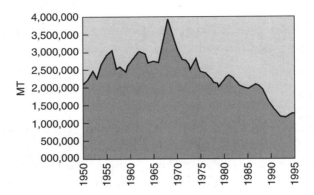

FIGURE 5-1 Atlantic cod (*Gadus morhua*)—total catches from 1950 through 1995.

(*Source:* Taken from Cohen, D. M., T. Inada, T. Iwamoto, and N. Scialabba, 1990, "Gadiform fishes of the world (Gadiformes), *FAO Species Catalogues, FAO Fisheries Synopsis*, 10, no. 125, 442 pp. The "Interest Fisheries" section has been updated by L. Garibaldi according to recent FAO fishery statistics) AND found at http://www.fao.org/waicent/faoinfo/fishery/sidp/htmls/species/ga_mo_ht.htm

What both sides ignore is fundamentally important: the role of institutions—the laws and social norms that constrain the behavior of individuals and groups. If the incentives created by these institutions favor unhampered extraction of fish from the sea, then the prospect for that targeted marine life will be bleak. If, on the other hand, these institutions provide incentives for conservation and stewardship, then the outlook for these fish stocks will be bright.

Searching for Solutions

There is no single answer as to how to conserve the ocean's resources. However, experience shows that when people are given the opportunity to conserve marine resources, they generally do. On the other hand, when leaving fish in the water simply means letting someone else catch them, far fewer fish get left in the water. Resource conservation is not happenstance; it is a rational response to a given situation.

Institutional constraints determine these responses, and are intrinsically bound to the question of who owns the rights to do what with a resource. Thus, property rights (rights to such things as the use of a resource, the income derived from a resource, and the ability

FIGURE 5-2 World marine production.

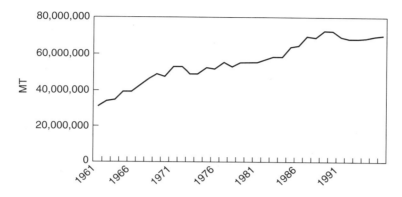

to transfer part or all of these rights) are a crucial element in any analysis of why some resources are conserved and others are not.[7] The structure of property rights affects behavior because it establishes different allocations of benefits and harms among individuals. Any attempt to exert control over a resource is an attempt to define property rights in that resource, whether through regulation, a group rule, or a form of exclusive ownership.

In the absence of any institutional constraints (a situation commonly referred to as *open access*), each user will tend to extract as much as possible, regardless of the consequences for the resource, because they bear only a fraction of the harms (for example, a degraded fishery for everyone) but reap all of the benefits (that is, the fish they haul up on deck).[8] Thus, a crucial element of conservation is that anyone depleting a resource bears the full consequences of that harm (or, conversely, captures the benefits of conserving the resource). In other words, both positive and negative effects must be internalized.

Responses to Depletion

Open access does not cause problems when fish are plentiful and catches are small, but as the pressure on a fishery grows, so does the potential for depletion. Thus, as pressures on resources increase, open-access regimes become rarer, and property rights wind up either held publicly by government or privately by groups or individuals.

Government Control

The most common response to open access and depletion has been government intervention, which normally results in restrictions on fishing gear, effort, and seasons. This relationship separates the steward (the state) from the exploiter (the fisher), who still benefits most from maximizing harvests instead of maximizing the value of the resource.

As the state takes responsibility for the fisheries, it also becomes responsible for taking care of those who depend on the resource. This creates a *moral hazard,* which means that generous government benefits to alleviate hardship today end up encouraging the very behavior that helped to create the misery in the first place. In this case, because of government intervention, fishers bear only a fraction of the consequences of their actions, and their impetus for continuing to deplete the fisheries remains. In fact, it is often stronger. Government regulation all too often encourages the profligate waste of resources, time, effort, and capital.

In the case of the U.S. and Canadian cod fisheries, calls to increase or maintain harvests levels were common, even in the face of drastic population declines. Responding to constituents, governments allowed overharvesting to continue, even encouraging investment in fishing capital as fish became more scarce, and, not surprisingly, resulting in the depletion of the fishery. When the fishery finally crashed, the government was on the hook and responded by pouring millions into communities that depended on fishing for a living (while steering clear of substantive reform and doing little to address the decline of the fishery). These efforts have included area closures, all manner of restrictions on fishing effort, boat buyout schemes, retraining programs, and simple handouts. All the while, harvests remain at all-time lows and stock recoveries have been minimal.

The problem is the politicization of fisheries management. The National Marine Fisheries Service in the United States routinely generates good science on the health of the fisheries, which is then just as routinely ignored in favor of conservation measures that lack teeth. Such ineffective reforms and bailouts are politically expedient because they obscure the need for drastic changes in the way fisheries are managed. Such has been and continues to be the case in New England, where the current situation was summed up nicely by an article from the *Bangor Daily News* in the summer of 1998. It reads: "For each of the last two years, the New England Fishery Management Council used a variety of mechanisms to reduce cod catches. But fishermen still brought to shore more than twice the target amounts the council's actions intended to reach—and roughly half of the total amount of cod in the Gulf of Maine."[9]

When efforts are made to restrict harvests, fishers are quite adept at staying one step ahead of restrictions imposed on them, often with ridiculous, and sometimes dangerous, results. So many variables influence harvest that regulators cannot hope to keep up. As seasons are shortened, fishers might respond with larger nets. As larger nets are restricted, more horsepower may take up the slack, and so on. One of the more extreme examples was the Alaskan halibut fishery, where the primary limitation was the length of the fishing season. As the season shortened, larger boats, larger nets, and technologies such as fish-finding sonar began to appear. Before long, a season that was once months long was down to 2 days, with no discernible reductions in the total harvests.

As a conservation measure, Maryland requires watermen to use decades old skipjacks making that oyster fishery the most technologically backward fishery in America. Even so, oyster production remains at only 1% of historic levels. (*Credit:* Marion E. Warren.)

Thus, even though government control may define who has the right to fish, it fails to make fishers pay for the damage they are causing to the resource.[10]

Public Oyster Beds

Much like the Atlantic cod of New England, the oyster fishery in Maryland was once a great source of industry and a staple of many diets. Oysters in the Chesapeake declined precipitously, despite warnings stretching back well into the last century. As stocks continued to decline over time, the Maryland government continued to increase its involvement in the fishery, presenting a dramatic case of regulatory failure. In fact, it has been said that Maryland has passed more legislation dealing with oysters than with any other issue.

In 1891, William Brooks, a scientist and Maryland Oyster Commissioner in the 1880s, writing about the public nature of the oyster fishery, declared even then that "all who are familiar with the subject have long been aware that out present system can have only one result—extermination."[11] Brooks recommended creating privately owned oyster beds to encourage oyster cultivation and stewardship, but regulation was chosen instead, resulting in all sorts of restrictions on harvesting, including when, where, by whom, and how. People who made their living from the Chesapeake waters fought over both these restrictions and the oysters themselves so ferociously that gunfights were not uncommon. These skirmishes that took place around the turn of the century are commonly referred to as the *Oyster Wars*.[12]

Today, oyster harvests in Maryland are only 1 percent of what they once were (the diseases Dermo and MSX have exacerbated the problem since the 1970s, but the fundamental damage was done long beforehand). See Figure 5-3.

Restrictions on technology were (and still are) so severe that the Maryland skipjacks that ply certain oyster beds are the last commercial fishing fleet in the United States still powered by sail. As if that weren't arcane enough, the boats are given an exemption on Mondays and Tuesdays when they are allowed to dredge for oysters with a *push*—a small motorized dinghy tied to the back of these large, wooden sailboats. This is all on top of restrictions on the oyster season, minimum size limits for harvestable oysters, specifics for

FIGURE 5-3 Oyster harvests in Maryland, 1870 through 1993.

Source: Maryland Department of Natural Resources, Fisheries Division, Annapolis, MD.

the types of dredges that may be used by different people in different places, and specific demarcations over certain areas that are open to harvesting. Nevertheless, and not surprisingly, the oyster beds remain severely depleted.

Private Ownership

Private ownership is the alternative to public management that *does* force people to bear the costs of their use of a resource. The crucial determinant for whether a resource is privately owned is whether the welfare of the decision makers is tied to the economic consequences of their decisions.[13] Private property rights must also be well defined, enforceable, and transferable.[14] As private property rights become more well defined, resource stewardship becomes more attractive and, equally, owners bear more of the costs of any rapacious behavior.

Unfortunately, clearly defined and readily enforceable private property rights to marine resources are rare. However, those few examples that do exist strongly support the arguments of theorists who have promoted private property rights in the oceans as a means to improve resource management.[15]

Private ownership institutions cover a wide spectrum ranging from communal to individual ownership. Both private communal and private individual property rights regimes create positive conservation incentives by allowing fishers to receive directly the benefits of conservation, and both allow owners to exclude others, decide how to manage resources, and bear the consequences of these actions. Private communal rights may not be so easily transferable, but in either case, the welfare of either the individual or group is tied directly to the health of the resource. There is no government agency standing ready to ameliorate resource deterioration, thus the fishers who own the resource intimately feel any effect, positive or negative.

Unfortunately, anthropologists, economists, and policy makers often promote either individual or group ownership at the expense of the other, even though the distinction is frequently muddled. Adding to the confusion are the varying definitions that different (and even often the same) schools of thought apply to terms like *the commons*, *common property*, and *private property*. For example, biologist Garret Hardin used the word *commons* to mean open access; anthropologists often use it to mean a strictly monitored form of group ownership; and economists frequently dismiss the concept entirely under the assumption that only individual ownership institutions are private.

Private individual property rights offer the greatest rewards for conservation to their owners, but are also the most costly to define and enforce. Thus, in some instances, private communal property may be optimal, depending on the resource and the costs of monitoring and enforcing rules and excluding outsiders. Private communal property rights may range from nearly open access to a strict system of controls and rules, but essentially they define the rights shared by the members of a group with exclusive access to a resource.[16]

Margaret McKean and Elinor Ostrom, for example, provide an explanation for the existence of private communal rights: "Common property regimes are a way of privatizing the rights to something without dividing it into pieces... Historically, common property regimes have evolved in places where the demand on a resource is too great to tolerate open access, so property rights in resources have to be created, but some other factor makes it impossible or undesirable to parcel the resource itself."[17] One such factor is uncertainty, and one advantage of common property arrangements may be risk sharing.[18] An example cited by McKean and Ostrom is a very large, forested area where edible flora and fauna are very patchily distributed.

Although similar in many ways, there remains a crucial difference between most communal and individual forms of ownership—transferability. Transferability is normally restricted in communal arrangements as they tend to rely on maintaining a closely knit group to monitor and enforce rules (by using sanctions such as social ostracism or even mere disapproval). This may lead to problems of transition for communal property owners, as transferability is crucial for owners to capitalize on the value of their assets, to use them as collateral, and to capture the future returns that stem from investments.

Transferability also bolsters resiliency in the face of pressure from outsiders. If out-transfers are not possible, pressure from outsiders for access often leads to expropriation, either of the resource itself or of the right of access to it. Legal recognition of communal rights would go a long way toward resolving this problem, but unfortunately, especially in developing countries, expropriation is the norm.

This may explain much of the current emphasis that many policy makers place on maintaining small fishing communities and their "cherished way of life." Barring legal recognition, sentiment seems to be the next best alternative. Unfortunately, this may do more harm than good, as it tends to work toward entrenching the status quo. Property rights institutions, including communal ones, are constantly evolving, and although some communities may choose to maintain a certain way of life, others may not. Legislating stasis is bad policy.

Private Oyster Beds

In marked contrast to public oyster beds in Maryland or unrecognized communal ownership arrangements, the oyster beds of Washington state are owned in fee simple—completely privately, and with a title to prove it. As a result, harvests of oysters in Washington state look very different from those in Maryland.[19] Additionally, the oysters are harvested by relatively modern means and the beds are often seeded from high-tech hatcheries financed by the oyster growers themselves. See Figure 5-4.

One of the few empirical studies of the effects of the private institutions on marine resources compared oyster beds managed by state regulators with those leased privately in the Chesapeake Bay and the Gulf of Mexico (in the Chesapeake, leased beds are common in Virginia).[20] This study found that the leased oyster beds were healthier, better maintained, and produced larger, better-quality oysters. Leaseholders invested in protecting their oysters and enhancing oyster habitat. One way they did this was by spreading old oyster shells on their beds, providing an ideal substrate for larval oysters to settle on. On public beds, no such steps were taken voluntarily. People who make their living on the water in Maryland were more interested in government-sponsored bailouts and subsidies for oyster bed maintenance than in taking steps on their own to improve harvests. It is possible to lease beds in Maryland, but there has been little interest—once the myriad state-sponsored programs were underway, water folk were loathe to give them up.

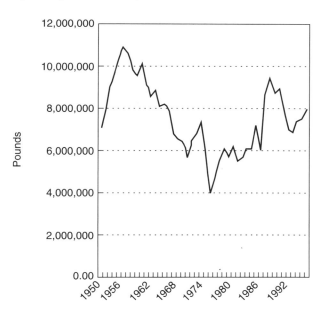

FIGURE 5-4 Washington state Pacific oyster production, 1950 to 1995.

A similar dichotomy of approaches and results occurred in England and France, where English oyster beds declined under public regulation, whereas those in France were nurtured by private cultivation.[21]

Individual Transferable Quotas

Although the benefits and feasibility of private ownership are most readily apparent for sedentary species like oysters, they may also be perfectly applicable to more far-ranging species as well. Of course, fisheries are rarely either wholly private or wholly public, but many countries are attempting to improve fisheries management by introducing some limited forms of private ownership into the fisheries, specifically by creating *individual transferable quotas* (ITQs).

Individual transferable quotas grant a right to harvest a certain percentage of the *total allowable catch* (TAC) of fish in a given year, and ITQs can be bought or sold. Over time, ITQs may also offer a real opportunity to move toward the private ownership of marine resources. Over the last few years they have been introduced most notably in New Zealand, Iceland, Australia, the United States, and Canada.

Although they are not really private rights, ITQs can be a tremendous step in the right direction. In contrast to regulation-based controls, they provide positive conservation incentives for those harvesting resources, in large part due to the fact that the health of the fishery is capitalized into the value of the quota. In other words, the brighter the prospects for future harvests, the more ITQs will be worth, allowing ITQ owners to gain now from steps they take to ensure the long-term future health of the fishery. Even some banks are beginning to accept ITQs as collateral, improving access to the fishery by making loans easier to secure for new entrants.

New Zealand

Until the introduction of ITQs, fisheries management in New Zealand followed a familiar pattern. Since 1960, the government had condoned free entry into the fisheries and subsidized development, producing a predictable result: falling fish stocks and rising investment in fishing boats, nets, and other technologies.[22] The deplorable state of many inshore fisheries led to the Fisheries Act of 1983, which consolidated all previous legislation and, most important, set out to both improve resource conservation and increase economic returns from the fisheries.[23] This led to the creation of tradable quotas for some of the deepwater fisheries and, in 1986, ITQs were introduced for all significant commercial finfish species with the creation of the *quota management system* (QMS). See Table 5-1 and Figure 5-5.

Today, following numerous improvements, the program appears to be tremendously suc-

TABLE 5-1 Total Marine Production in New Zealand, 1961 through 1995

Year	Production
1961	27,100
1962	28,400
1963	28,300
1964	29,900
1965	30,600
1966	33,600
1967	36,000
1968	33,900
1969	32,000
1970	40,100
1971	43,400
1972	38,000
1973	43,300
1974	47,772
1975	36,919
1976	47,025
1977	55,395
1978	75,978
1979	97,298
1980	135,326
1981	147,611
1982	150,031
1983	174,266
1984	177,173
1985	178,554
1986	179,863
1987	207,984
1988	243,329
1989	281,866
1990	310,044
1991	331,031
1992	395,157
1993	382,289
1994	377,552
1995	452,631

Source: FAOSTAT on Web.

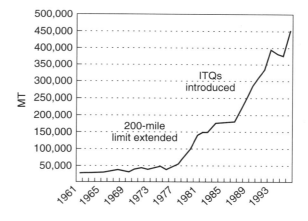

FIGURE 5-5 New Zealand total marine production, 1961 through 1995.

TABLE 5-2   New Zealand Exports: Quantity and Value, 1961 Through 1995

	Export (MT)	Exports (1000$)
1961	300	57
1962	400	76
1963	400	76
1964	300	57
1965	300	57
1966	200	38
1967	300	57
1968	300	57
1969	300	57
1970	400	157
1971	500	162
1972	1,400	513
1973	2,000	1,300
1974	2,100	1,366
1975	2,626	1,141
1979	4,360	7,110
1980	3,797	8,300
1981	4,265	9,391
1982	3,766	9,911
1983	3,852	10,093
1984	4,021	12,430
1985	4,394	14,555
1986	6,211	23,445
1987	4,070	23,462
1988	6,077	28,875
1989	5,539	27,895
1990	6,629	30,449
1991	7,722	32,682
1992	8,555	37,711
1993	8,188	39,473
1994	9,738	44,129
1995	8,070	45,116

Source: FAOSTAT on the Web.

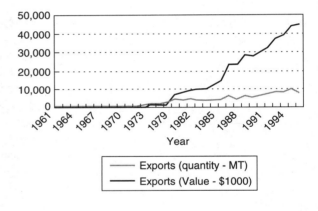

FIGURE 5-6   New Zealand exports: quantity and value, 1961 through 1995.

cessful. Fish stocks are generally healthy and ITQs have ended subsidies, reduced fishing capacity, and encouraged investment in scientific research.[24] The New Zealand Ministry of Agriculture's Philip Major described a remarkable transformation after the creation of the ITQ system: "It's the first group of fishers I've ever encountered who turned down the chance to take more fish."[25] See Table 5-2 and Figure 5-6.

It has been suggested that ITQs will result in the consolidation of the industry and the elimination of the small-scale fisher. Although there has been some consolidation, especially in the capital-intensive deepwater fisheries, the total numbers of vessels, full-time employees, and quota owners have all increased over the period from 1986 to 1996.[26] Limits do exist on the percentage of the overall quota any one fisher may own, ranging from a limit of 45 percent in a given area for species such as hoki and orange roughy to 10 percent for rock lobster.

The New Zealand quota system seems to be moving closer and closer to a real system of privately owned fisheries. In the orange roughy fishery, for example, quota owners got together in 1991 to form the Exploratory Fishing Company (ORH 3B) Ltd., in large part to fund management science and research.[27] Another example is the Challenger Scallop Enhancement Company Ltd., whose shareholders are the owners of scallop ITQs. These owners manage the fishery through contracts that allow the company to levy money for research, enhancement (a vigorous reseeding program), monitoring, and enforcement, which includes daily catch limits.[28] They have even contracted with fishers in other fleets to ameliorate the effects of other fisheries (in this case the oyster fishery) on the habitat and productivity of the whole environment.[29]

Fishers in New Zealand are taking on more and more responsibilities for fisheries management and scientific research, and it appears that the trend will continue, and the government's role in the fisheries will continue to shrink as the health of the fisheries improves.

Private Communal Rights—Coral Reefs in the South Pacific

Although New Zealand is striving to create private solutions where none existed before, other nations are turning back to existing, private communal conservation regimes. One such example occurs throughout the South Pacific in the form of village control over coral reefs.

Coral reefs in the South Pacific have suffered of late from destructive fishing practices, such as fishing with dynamite or cyanide. The World Wildlife Fund's Hong Kong office investigated the problem of cyanide fishing and found that reef fisheries in Southeast Asia "work in a sustainable way only in those few places where the rights to fish a particular reef are clearly established."[30]

Reef tenure typically takes the form of ownership by a clan, chief, or family, and marine tenure in these areas often extends from the beach to the outer edge of the reef, sometimes even miles out to sea.[31] Biologist Robert Johannes studied coral reef conservation throughout the Pacific and also found village control over local marine resources to be the surest indicator of reef health.[32] The reefs are valuable assets to the community and so are fiercely protected. In Fiji, some communities employ fish wardens to watch over the reefs. In Johannes' study of Palauan fishers, he found community-managed fisheries that employed closed seasons and areas, abided by size limits, and even imposed forms of quotas to ensure conservation.[33] These measures were particularly strict around spawning times for certain species, and sanctions ranged from mere disapproval to ostracism and, in the case of outsiders, even severe physical atonement.

Japanese Cooperatives

A much more formal communal arrangement exists in Japan, where fishery cooperative associations (FCAs) frequently hold the rights to coastal marine resources.[34] The FCAs impose strict conservation measures on their members, and coastal marine resources in Japan are generally healthy. Cooperative ownership in Japan is so strong that FCAs have even been able to block potentially harmful or polluting coastal development by asserting the primacy of their fishing rights.[35] As described by Kenneth Ruddle and Tomoya Akimichi, "Because fisheries rights have a legal status equal to land ownership under Japanese law, . . . a private developer must . . . either purchase all of the fisheries rights . . . or compensate for any reduction in the quality of the rights."[36]

These cooperatives are hardly private endeavors (they receive significant government subsidies as do most Japanese farmers), but they do demonstrate the emphatic link between exclusive control and the stewardship of marine resources.

Barriers to Private Solutions

Legal Recognition

One major reason the Japanese cooperatives have been so successful is that they have been recognized by law, which allows them both to defend their rights in court and develop ways of accommodating out-transfers. Unfortunately, in most places around the world, not only does the legal system not recognize private communal rights, it is often biased against them. Although some regimes may disappear naturally, in many instances they are simply legislated out of existence.[37] When resources that were previously controlled by local participants have been nationalized, state control has usually proved to be less effective and efficient, if not disastrous in its consequences, than control by those directly affected.[38]

This was certainly the case in the Pacific Northwest, where Native Americans had developed complicated arrangements, both within and between tribes, to manage their salmon fisheries.[39] They relied heavily on fixed nets and weirs along the riverbank, but were careful to allow plenty of fish to pass to maintain the spawning runs and ensure a future supply. According to Robert Higgs, "Indian regulation of the fishery, though varying from tribe to tribe, rested on the enforcement of clearly understood property rights. In some cases these rights rested in the tribe as a whole; in other cases in families or individuals."[40] However, as the numbers and power of settlers increased, these property rights were quickly expropriated by force. Ironically, intrasettler expropriation soon followed. Some of the new arrivals set up fish wheels (very effective fish-harvesting contraptions resembling waterwheels) and fish traps along the riverbanks whereas others used labor-intensive methods to chase down their prey at sea. Sensing their great superiority of numbers, the hook-and-line fishers went to the ballot box and were able to have all fixed fishing gear banned in 1934.

Allocation Problems

Once this cycle of expropriation has started, it is very difficult to return to a private system. In fact, more often than not, private conservation solutions are opposed not because of their effectiveness, but over how private rights might be allocated.

Individual transferable quotas have most often been allocated on the basis of historical catch, and so some of the most vehement opposition to ITQs has come from those whose historical catches have been low. For example, when ITQs were recently under consideration for some species in U.S. waters off of Alaska, any sort of fishing rights were vehemently opposed by the Alaskans in Congress out of fear that many of the new rights would be allocated to fishers in Washington state, who had historically fished off of Alaska.

Of course, it is rarely politically expedient to be so honestly direct, so many other objections are typically lodged against ITQs. One of the most common is the fear of consolidation. Some claim that the quota system in New Zealand has excluded "small-scale and independent fishers from fisheries, which fall increasingly under the control of large, profit-seeking corporations,"[41] but this is far from the case. Consolidation in New Zealand has occurred, but primarily in the offshore fisheries for orange roughy, hoki, and squid that have always involved large, capital-intensive efforts. The number of vessels (2768 in the 1994/1995 fishing season) in the domestic fleet, however, has remained relatively constant.[42] If it is accepted that there are too many boats chasing too few fish (and it generally

New Zealand fisheries are recovering after the adoption of individual transferable quotas (ITQs), which give fishers ownership rights and thus incentives to protect resources like the hoki fishery depicted here. (*Credits:* Wreford Hann Photography, Ltd. Timothy Hann, photographer.)

is), then some reduction of the fleet can only be expected. At least when everyone receives an initial quota, they leave the fishery by choice. (Consolidation may, however, be more likely if rights are auctioned rather than allocated based on historical involvement in the fisheries.)

Another objection often heard is the argument that fisheries are a public resource, and that any move in the direction of privatizing them will deny "the public" from benefiting from the resource. Surely, however, the greatest public benefit is derived from a healthy resource. Maintaining open access may appeal to egalitarian values, but in reality, a shift to private ownership is more likely to ensure access to a valuable, plentiful resource, as opposed to a depleted wasteland.

Additionally, the greater the formal recognition for private arrangements, the easier it becomes for new entrants to lease or buy their way into a fishery. If there is no collateral in the fishery, entry is much more difficult. When a form of private rights was instituted in New Zealand, researchers found almost immediately that "transferability . . . allowed fishers to enter and exit the fishery more easily."[43]

Political battles are inevitably fought over pieces of a pie that never gets bigger. Instead of investing in efforts to enlarge the pie, resources are devoted to attempts to grab a bigger share at someone else's expense.[44] Moving resource allocations out of the political arena turns a zero-sum game into a positive one. Of course, ITQs themselves are also a political solution. They do not confer a private right to the fish themselves, only to a percentage of an annual harvest determined by fisheries regulators. They are, however, a significant recognition of the importance of institutions, and in the case of New Zealand, offer the real potential to smooth the transition to self-management.

Overcoming These Obstacles

Francis Christy, a noted fisheries economist, believes that the transition to property rights regimes in fisheries is inexorable.[45] He also notes that the political feasibility of a move to private fishing rights is "inversely proportional to the degree of vested interests in the fishery."[46] The strongest resistance to change comes from those who have adapted and are doing relatively well under the current system, or who may have invested in the expectation that the status quo would continue.

Such was the case in the increasingly capital-intensive halibut fishery off of Alaska, where Christy notes that the theoretical arguments for limiting access to the fishery had been clearly laid out as early as 1961. Even so, reforms were minimal until the fishery endured a 2-day season that created a dangerous and expensive race for fish. As one fisher put it, the fishery was "flat ruined."[47] In the late 1980s, a concerted effort to introduce ITQs into the fishery began, and eventually succeeded. In 1995, the first year of the quota program, waste in the fishery (as defined by the International Pacific Halibut Commission) declined by 80 percent.[48] As further evidence of the change wrought by individual fishing quotas (IFQs)—a form of ITQ—processsors now grade halibut according to quality, whereas before there was always just one price. A recent letter from a small-boat halibut fisher to the *Alaska Fisherman's Journal* summed up some of the advantages of the ITQ program: "We fish better weather, deliver a better product, and have a better market. This is a better deal."[49]

The other major fishery under an ITQ program in the United States is the surf clam and ocean quahog fishery on the East Coast. These species are generally found in canned clam chowder. This fishery went through a series of booms and collapses as new stocks were discovered and boats rushed in and out of the fishery. Regulatory responses invariably lagged behind these cycles, often restricting harvests of plentiful stocks while acceding to harvests of depleted stocks. In the late 1980s, effort restrictions permitted only 6 hours of fishing every 2 weeks.[50] The surf clam and ocean quahog ITQ program, which began in 1990—the first in the United States—solved these problems, and has since been called the "best managed fishery" in the United States by a senior scientist at the National Marine Fisheries Service.[51]

Why, then, aren't more fisheries moving toward some kind of ITQ management? No matter how flawed a system is, changing it is difficult. The Maryland oyster and North American Atlantic cod fisheries are perfect examples. Someone will always do well under a given system or, at least, believe that they will not be better off under a new system, creating a vested interest in the status quo and vehement opposition to change. Even though these resources may be in dire straits, resistance to change has been strong enough to prevent any substantive reform.

Another example from the Chesapeake Bay bears this out. At one point not long ago, the striped bass (rockfish) was nearly gone from the Bay, and both Maryland and Virginia responded with a total moratorium on fishing the species (conservationwise, the only type of regulatory conservation to commonly succeed). As the fish came back, commercial fishers had already given up on the species, and so Virginia was able to devise an acceptable ITQ program for the fishery that should vastly improve the sense of stewardship among fishers.[52]

Still, when more is at stake, most fishers are quite savvy, and they know that getting access to the fisheries depends on political clout—if they do not have it, they will not trust any change in the current system. Additionally, creating rights to marine resources by definition results in a distribution of wealth, which creates real political problems and strong obstacles to substantive reform.[53]

Oyster beds in Washington state are private because their creation predated statehood. After the open-access fishery for the native Olympia oysters was cleaned out, ambitious oyster growers staked out territories and began both trying to revive the Olympias and introducing the Pacific oyster from Japan that still predominates today.

Well-established rights are also behind the recent creation of an exclusive lobster-fishing zone around the island of Monhegan in Maine.[54] Maine lobster fishers have long formed harbor gangs that mark territories and turn away outsiders. Even though these arrangements have always been extralegal, the gangs tend to have higher catches, larger lobsters, and larger incomes than lobster fishers who fish outside controlled areas.[55]

Unfortunately, the major impetus for a move to more private arrangements seems to be crisis. This was certainly the case in New Zealand where the deplorable state of many fisheries coincided with a governmental financial crisis, precluding the sorts of bailouts that have prevented meaningful reform elsewhere.

Along with New Zealand, Iceland has the most comprehensive ITQ system. The first transferable quotas appeared in 1979, and in 1990 a uniform program of ITQs was instituted for all commercial fisheries. Icelandic stocks have not suffered from catastrophic declines, but in a country where fishing is the island's principal industry, even a slight decline verges on a crisis. Thus, the will to move toward the ITQ system in Iceland was much more politically attractive than elsewhere.

Private alternatives improve resource management but are politically very difficult to establish. The above examples all indicate that private management systems are most likely to succeed either when they already exist (beating politicians to the punch) or in crisis (when politicians and vested interests have little to lose).

Overcoming the Political Nature of ITQs

The most notable aspect of the New Zealand ITQ system has been the evolution of ITQs. Through a series of upheavals, most notably the Maori claim to a significant portion of the fisheries based on their treaty rights, some ITQs seem to be evolving ever closer to real private rights. In the case of the Maoris, establishing even a limited form of right to the fisheries allowed them to settle their treaty claims to the fisheries with the government, which greatly strengthened the security of the ITQ system. Another notable incident resulted in a tradeoff where the government ceased compensating fishers for low harvests in return for strengthening ITQ rights and eliminating the threat of stiff taxes on the value of the quotas. The latest evolution is now taking place on the management level, where quota owners are banding together to invest in research-and-enhancement activities, drawing some of the fisheries closer self-management.

In other places and in many cases, however, ITQs are explicitly set up so that they cannot evolve into stronger rights. The IFQ program in Alaska, for example, specifically states that IFQs are not private property rights and that they can be taken away without compensation at any time, which strikes at the very reason why ITQs have had some measure of success in the first place.

Subjecting ITQs to bureaucratic whim severely limits the positive incentives that ITQs are created to mimic. As long as the system remains publicly managed, it will be susceptible to many of the pitfalls discussed earlier. It limits the impetus for innovation and resource enhancement, and also discourages the exploration of alternative resource uses.

For example, in some cases, it may be more efficient to own the rights to a particular area rather than the rights to particular species.

Thus, careful consideration is crucial before ITQs are implemented. In particular, the central lesson from the New Zealand experience should always be borne in mind: The closer an ITQ resembles a private right, the greater the flexibility there is to adapt and evolve into a system of real private rights with the strongest possible incentives for conservation. Unfortunately, real-world examples are few and far between, but those cases that have been mentioned, such as the Washington oyster industry, Japanese cooperatives, reef stewards in the South Pacific, and the New Zealand ITQ system, all bear this out, especially in comparison with their publicly managed counterparts.

The more that ITQs resemble government management as usual, the more ineffective the system becomes. There is also a real danger that ITQs will be used to tax the fishing industry, which would reduce the positive incentives created by ITQs to conserve resources, innovate new techniques, invest in research, and enhance the fishery. As economist Ron Johnson has pointed out, taxing away the value of an ITQ would also have a negative impact on cost-reducing activities, encourage government to meddle in the fisheries to increase tax revenue, create perverse incentives for industry to lower total catches, and impede collective action to try to raise the value of the quota.[56] Such was the case in New Zealand before the idea of capturing resource rents was finally abandoned, and it appears to be a growing issue in Iceland.[57]

Fear of taxation or redistribution also greatly reduces the efforts that fishers are willing to invest in substantive reform. One Maryland fisher recently agreed that a move to privately leased oyster beds was a good idea, but he personally was opposed to it because he'd hate to invest in enhancing and protecting an oyster bed only to have the state take it away again.

The real dangers that ITQs present all lie in failing to divorce politics from conservation. Creating ITQs addresses open-access problems, but rigidly and inappropriately defined ITQs may not be much of an improvement over the status quo. Until fishing rights are safeguarded from the vagaries of public management, the incentive to harvest stocks sustainably will remain weak.

What the Future Might Look Like

Of course, it is impossible to tell what the future will look like, except to say that a greater reliance on private solutions to marine conservation problems would certainly be a shift toward more effective stewardship of marine resources. Innovation would no longer be about finding ways to catch fish more quickly, but about protecting the value of the resource—by harvesting more economically, by treading more lightly on the resource and its surrounding environment, and by investing in scientific research and resource enhancement.

Of course, there is also no one answer as to what sort of private ownership schemes might develop in the long run. For example, in fisheries with greater uncertainty and catch fluctuations, there would no doubt be more risk sharing and group ownership, whereas in fisheries with more predictable harvests, individual ownership would be more likely.

The Evolution of Property Rights

How and why private rights develop depend on the value of resources and the costs of monitoring them. The process is circular: As resources become more valuable, owners invest more in monitoring and enforcing private ownership rights, which, in turn, make resources more valuable, and so on.

An exemplary case study is the American West at the end of the nineteenth century. Much like the oceans not so long ago, few could imagine depleting its vast resources. However, as the West was settled, its water and grassy lands became progressively more scarce and more valuable. Research by economists Terry Anderson and P. J. Hill has shown that, as the rights to these resources became more valuable, more effort went into enforcing private property rights, and therefore into innovation and resource conservation.[58]

Defining private property by physical barriers was desirable, but there were too few raw materials, so livestock intermingled and monitoring was difficult. However, frontier entrepreneurs soon developed branding systems to identify individual animals, and cattlemen's associations were formed to standardize and register these brands, allowing ranchers to define and enforce ownership over a valuable, roaming resource.

In the 1870s, another innovation came along that radically altered the frontier landscape: barbed wire. Barbed wire was an inexpensive and effective means of marking territory, excluding interlopers, and keeping in livestock. It made it easier to enclose property and exert private ownership, and it illustrates how private property rights encourage innovation.

Just as the Washington oyster growers staked their claims to the tidelands in the nineteenth century, the potential exists today to "homestead" the oceans. As rights are asserted, no doubt new innovations will help to make those rights more secure and to protect those resources.

Advanced Technologies

> The engineers who maintained the invisible fences of sound and electricity which now divided the mighty Pacific into manageable portions.... [held] at bay the specter of famine which had confronted all earlier ages, but which would never threaten the world again while the great plankton farms harvested their millions of tons of protein, and the whale herds

obeyed their new masters. Man had come back to the sea, his ancient home, after aeons of exile; until the oceans froze, he would never be hungry again."

—Arthur C. Clarke, *The Deep Range*, 1958[59]

"Sound will pen fish inside a sea ranch."

—headline in *Fish Farming International*, 1996[60]

Arthur C. Clarke specialized in imagining the future, but to see the potential for technology to revolutionize fishing and marine conservation, one need only look to the present. A host of advanced technologies already exists that could be used to define and protect resources in the oceans just as branding and barbed wire did in the frontier American West.

For example, each and every stream has a unique chemical signature, and a firm in British Columbia, called Elemental Research, can identify the exact origin of individual salmon by using a nonlethal technique involving lasers and mass spectrometry to analyze its scales. By analyzing fish scales in this way, it is possible to accurately identify even the smallest individual populations of salmon. Fish can also be identified using a bone in their inner ear, called an *otolith*, which produces daily rings much like those produced annually by trees. In a hatchery, distinctive patterns can be made in fish otoliths simply by altering water temperatures.

Large animals can also be tracked using satellites. Transmitters have been attached to manatees that use satellite telemetry to communicate the exact location, identity, water temperature, and which way a manatee appears to be headed.[61] Devices can also be placed on board a fishing vessel to constantly relay its exact location via satellite, to identify whether it belongs in a certain area, or to periodically record information in a black box. Heat-sensitive satellites cannot only monitor a ship's location, but can also use its heat profile to tell if it is towing nets or not. Heat profiles of the ocean's surface can be used to provide accurate clues to the whereabouts of certain species of fish commonly found at the interface of cool, nutrient-rich waters and warmer, higher-visibility waters.

Scientists at MIT are working on a "robo-tuna," which mimics the very efficient propulsion system of real tuna, that may one day allow it to stay at sea for up to 6 months patrolling spawning grounds or remote shellfish beds.[62] As one researcher in the lab said, "We herd cows. Why not fish?"[63]

These technologies may facilitate private conservation, but people often underestimate the extent to which marine resources are already parceled throughout the world, even without the advantage of advanced technologies.

> It is one thing to contemplate the inshore sea from land's end as a stranger, to observe an apparently empty, featureless, open-accessed expanse of water. The image in a fisherman's mind is something very different. Seascapes are blanketed with history and imbued with names, myths, and legends, and elaborate territories that sometimes become exclusive provinces partitioned with traditional rights and owners much like property on land.
>
> —John Cordell[64]

In the final analysis, the institutions and the incentives are what matter most and will determine the future of the world's fisheries.

Aquaculture

> A decade ago, a fish Malthusian might have predicted the end of salmon as a food. Human ingenuity seems to have beaten nature once again.
>
> —*Forbes*, 1990[65]

Although the world fish catch has stagnated in recent years, aquaculture production has grown dramatically. It is now responsible for nearly 20 percent of the world fish production, and it is one of the world's fastest-growing industries. In 1991, world aquaculture production was approximately 13 million metric tons, double what it was 7 years before.[66] By 1995, that number had jumped to over 21 million metric tons.[67] See Figure 5-7.

The reason for these increases is that aquaculture facilities have allowed entrepreneurs to set up private enclosures that fence parts of the sea (or even transport it onto land). A fish not harvested today will be there tomorrow, normal rates of mortality notwithstanding. Just as it did in the American West, private ownership has invigorated entrepreneurs to tinker, to experiment, and to innovate, and, even more important, it has encouraged others to innovate as well. It was not landowners in the West who invented barbed wire, but entrepreneurs looking to develop new markets and products.

Salmon is one of the most commonly farmed species, and fish farmers have developed ways to manage their fish in remarkable ways. Through genetic manipulations as well as environmental and dietary control, aquaculturalists increase the fat content for sushi chefs and reduce it for producers of smoked salmon. They can also increase a salmon's nutritional value, adjust its brilliant orange color, or set the flavor to bold or mild.[68]

One great advantage of aquaculture is the stability of supply. Farm-raised fish are often brought to market within a day of being harvested, whereas wild-caught fish sometimes take a week. Aquaculture facilities have fresh fish in holding tanks and can either slow or accel-

FIGURE 5-7 Global trends in aquaculture production.

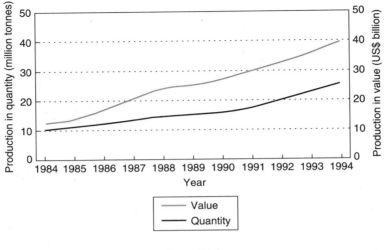

Source: FAO.

erate growth as they please. Markets and restaurants can count year-round on the availability of fresh fish of uniform quality and size. No wild fishery approaches that. See Figure 5-8.

Environmental Problems

Aquaculture is not without its problems. Most aquaculture (approximately two-thirds) occurs near the coast or in shallow estuaries where pollution from outside sources can cripple an aquaculture operation. In addition, intensive aquaculture in these areas can produce significant amounts of organic pollution, which can lead to reduced levels of oxygen in the water and an increase in quick-growing algae harmful to marine life. In some cases, there is also growing concern over the antibiotics used.

It is worth noting that when pollution does occur, it is generally because property rights have not been appropriately defined and/or are not readily enforceable. Government subsidies and incentives to expropriate coastal areas for aquaculture often further undermine nearshore private stewardship efforts. Unfortunately, critics of aquaculture tend to ignore these perverse government incentives, holding the aquaculture industry itself solely responsible for vast amounts of coastal habitat destruction in developing nations, particularly Thailand and Ecuador. The most extreme among them compare shrimp farming with slash-and-burn agriculture, and some have even gone so far as to hold mock trials for poor Thai shrimp farmers in New York, accusing them of "despoiling their country's coastal

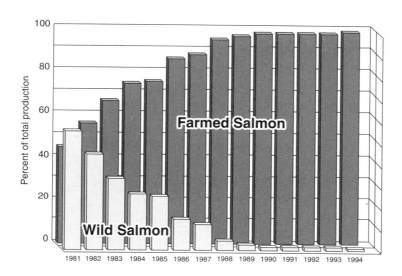

FIGURE 5-8 Production trend for Atlantic salmon, 1981 through 1994.

wetlands by raising shrimp."[69] In one sense, they are right. According to the United Nations' estimates, in Thailand only 40,000 acres of mangrove forest remain, down from nearly 1 million acres just 30 years ago.[70] Shrimp farming has certainly been a significant factor in this decline. Indeed, it is apparent that abandoned ponds can "saturate the surrounding soil with salt and pollute the land and water with a chemical sludge made up of fertilizer and antibiotics as well as larvicides, shrimp feed, and waste."[71] The root cause of this problem, however, is a lack of secure private rights to marine resources, which is the result of government intervention, *not* an inherent feature of aquaculturists (who are merely operating within the incentive structure defined by the extant institutions).

In Thailand, aquaculture is heavily subsidized, and, in many cases, farms are built in areas that were previously managed much more sustainably by a system of customary tenure.[72] In Malaysia, the Land Acquisition Act was amended in 1991 to allow the state to grab land for any reason deemed beneficial to economic development, including the construction of fishponds.[73] Similarly, in Ecuador, bribes, corrupt government partnerships, and landgrabs are common because "by law, coastal beaches, salt water marshes, and everything else below the high tide line is a national patrimony."[74] Not only shrimp farms but city slums regularly invade these areas, even in national ecological preserves.[75]

Alfredo Quarto, a director of the Mangrove Action Project, has pointed out that the main reason why shrimp farmers choose to clear mangrove forests is that they are usually government owned.[76] In other words, government-sanctioned open access and expropriation of common property rights are really to blame for coastal habitat destruction in places like Thailand. See Figures 5-9 and 5-10.

Moving operations offshore can often solve nearshore aquaculture problems, where water circulation is better and risks from pollution, both exogenous and endogenous, are limited. Offshore aquaculture is now beginning to move beyond the experimental stage.[77] The engineering problems of raising fish far from protected shores are substantial. Nevertheless, offshore net pens and cages are increasingly appearing off the coasts of places like Norway and Ireland.

Self-contained, indoor aquaculture facilities are another relatively new development, but one with tremendous potential. Aquafuture, a firm in Massachusetts, raises striped bass in a closed-tank system.[78] The process uses much less water and feed than conventional fish farms; produces fewer wastes (which can be converted to fertilizer); and, by changing the water temperature, fish can be grown to market size either faster or slower depending on the current market. The enclosed environment is also more sanitary, so Aquafuture's mortality rate (fish that die before they are ready to market) is half the industry average.

Conclusion

Attention to the world's oceans has been growing in recent years—1997 was the International Year of the Reef and 1998 the International Year of the Ocean. A number of environmental campaigns have also been launched to coincide with these events, aimed at drawing attention to some of the problems that plague the seas.

Unfortunately, although some of these problems are very real, little of this attention has been focused on the institutions that govern fisheries management or the benefits of private conservation and stewardship. From the extreme view of Greenpeace that "the financial captains of the global fishing . . . rush to vacuum the oceans and turn fish into cash,"[79] to a more moderate petition called "Troubled Water: A Call for Action" that still "paints a dismaying picture" of the destruction of the marine environment,[80] much of the environmental activism in this arena begs for more government involvement instead of less.

Some exceptions are the Marine Stewardship Council, set up by Unilever and the World Wildlife Fund to certify certain fish as caught sustainably, and the Environmental Defense Fund's (EDF) sponsorship of ITQs.[81] The EDF, however, recently strongly criticized the environmental effects of aquaculture, even though, as discussed earlier, that, too, is a result of ill-defined ownership and perverse government programs.[82]

FIGURE 5-9 Mangrove and shrimp farm area versus shrimp production, 1961 through 1993.

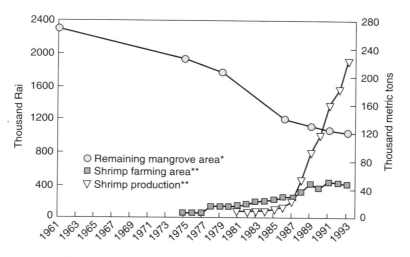

Sources: *Royal Forestry Department, **Department of Fisheries.

FIGURE 5-10 Growth of global cultured shrimp production, 1975 through 1992.

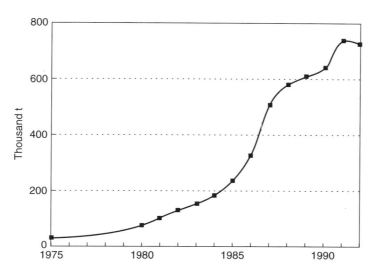

Sources: Data from Csavas, 1988; FAO, 1992; Rosenberry, 1991, 1992.

Entrepreneurs around the world are not nearly as hesitant to embrace the opportunities afforded by private stewardship. Ten years ago, the economist Elmer Keen envisaged vast increases in marine productivity with the extension of private rights into the seas.[83] Today, quota holders in New Zealand are moving in that direction, and an even more ambitious project is underway to fertilize the oceans—only made possible by exclusive access to the fisheries of a small island nation in the Pacific whose fisheries will, of course, benefit.[84]

These are the kinds of visionaries who will continue to offer real solutions to the problems of overfishing and marine habitat degradation. Their impressive results to date suggest that private conservation is the answer to protecting and enhancing the world's marine resources.

Chapter 6

SOFT ENERGY VERSUS HARD FACTS
Powering the Twenty-First Century

Jerry Taylor and Peter VanDoren

HIGHLIGHTS

- *The 25-year government campaign to promote renewable energy has cost consumers between $30 and $40 billion, but it resulted in only a 1.5 percent market share for favored fuels. Government subsidies and preferences have failed to make uncompetitive technologies competitive and are not likely to do so in the future.*

- *Energy markets are not infected by market failures that are serious enough to warrant government intervention. Energy markets are forward looking; are not prone to frequent, wild swings in price; and are not realistically vulnerable to embargo.*

- *Fossil fuels, rather than becoming more scarce, are becoming more abundant with time and will likely continue to dominate energy markets through the next century.*

- *Energy subsidies do not and have not significantly affected energy markets or consumer behavior.*

- *Government intervention in the energy marketplace has, over the course of the twentieth century, worked to the detriment of oil and gas technologies but to the benefit of nuclear, coal, and renewable energy.*

- *Renewable energy would have a decidedly mixed impact on the environment. Wind, solar, and biomass energy sources pose significant environmental problems that largely offset their advantages with regards to air emissions.*

- *Renewable energy facilities are so dependent on ideal sites for profitable operation that their ability to provide for America's electricity needs is limited, and largely confined to niche markets.*

- *Mandates, subsidies, and governmental preferences for energy-efficient technologies fail benefit/cost tests by a wide margin.*

- *Improvements in environmental quality have been and will continue to be compatible with a fossil fuel economy. Renewable energy preferences are unnecessary to achieve environmental goals.*

- *Consumers are demonstrably capable of making rational decisions about energy technologies and are not in need of government assistance to do so.*

- *Renewable energy technologies (save for hydropower) are so much more expensive than state-of-the-art fossil fuel technologies (typically, at least triple the price per kilowatt hour) that no realistic level of government subsidies or preferences will significantly change the market share of conventional energy sources.*

- *Private-sector investments in renewable energy are actually quite minuscule: less than 1 percent of total world energy investments. Notwithstanding flashy public-relations campaigns, the world's best energy minds are dismissive of renewable energy's ability to compete under any conceivable set of circumstances.*

- *Contrary to the administration's claims, there is no economic "free lunch" to be gained from restricting greenhouse gas emissions. Its own analyses concede that restricting greenhouse gas emissions comes with a price tag.*

- *The total costs associated with unconstrained global warming are quite minimal (no more than 2 percent of the economy at most) and almost certainly less than the costs of restricting greenhouse gas emissions.*

- *Even if every nation on earth complied with the terms of the Kyoto Protocol to reduce greenhouse gas emissions, the result would be only a 0.07°C reduction in projected temperatures by 2050.*

Ever since the 1970s, state and federal governments adopted the idea that fossil fuels were economically and environmentally detrimental and should be replaced by softer sources of energy. Renewable energy sources, such as solar, wind, and energy efficiency, were considered to be not only more environmentally benign than coal or oil but also nearly as attractive economically. Only a few stubborn market failures and the resistance of vested interests in the economy were preventing the acceptance of soft energy, it was thought, so only a moderate bit of government intervention was necessary to change the economy for the better.

The state and federal effort to replace fossil fuels, however, did not achieve the quick success that was expected. For over 25 years now, a total of between $30 and 40 billion has been spent to promote soft energy in a campaign employing a dizzying array of taxes, subsidies, preferences, and consumption orders including:[1,2]

- Tax code preferences for renewable energy generation

- Ratepayer cross-subsidies for renewable energy development

- Mandatory utility purchases of power generated by renewable energy sources at the utility's "avoided cost"

- Theoretical calculation of environmental costs when considering fossil fuel capacity versus soft energy choices

- Fuel diversity premiums to penalize reliance on fossil fuels

- Government payments for soft energy research, development, and commercialization far in excess of what is publicly spent on fossil fuels

- Forced utility purchases of soft energy as a condition for mergers, restructuring, and industry deregulation

- Taxpayer subsidies for energy efficiency programs
- Ratepayer subsidies for private energy efficiency investments
- Prohibition of energy-intensive building construction and consumer appliance purchases

Victory over fossil fuels, however, is nowhere in sight. Renewable energy—winds, solar, geothermal, and biomass—composes only 1.5 percent of the energy market,[3] and revolutionary advances in natural gas technology—not soft energy—promise to fundamentally reshape the energy industry.

The economic and environmental rationales for the ongoing campaign to promote soft energy, although superficially attractive at first, do not hold up well to scrutiny.

To begin: the contention that "market failures" are the reason that soft energy has yet to seriously penetrate the marketplace is without merit. The widespread belief that fossil fuels are in danger of disappearing in our lifetime, and that a "crash program" to promote alternatives is necessary, is wrong on both counts. The claim that government has long subsidized traditional energy sources to the detriment of the economy, and that promotion of soft energy merely "levels the playing field," is incorrect. The idea that promotion of soft energy is the best way to go about achieving environmental protection is unwarranted. The belief that soft energy is nearly competitive with traditional fossil fuels is contravened by the hard economic facts. The conviction that wind and solar power are more environmentally benign than fossil fuels is debatable. The argument that subsidies for energy conservation promise major energy savings and are economically efficient is completely baseless.

Government's record of intervention in energy markets is one instance after another of expensive and disastrous failure. There is no evidence to suggest that governmental agents are more capable of making energy technology choices than businesspeople or consumers.

The Intellectual Case for Intervention in Energy Production Reexamined

Soft energy advocates justify their call for governmental intervention in energy markets by relying on three sorts of arguments. First, it is often alleged that energy markets are riddled with "market failures" that lead to economic inefficiencies. Subsidies and preferences for soft energy, they claim, will correct the alleged market failures, eliminate the inefficiencies, and produce more robust and sustained economic growth. Second, it is argued that government has long subsidized fossil fuels and that the market is thus artificially tilted against soft energy. This, too, leads to economic inefficiency, and subsidizing soft energy provides the necessary corrective and results in a more efficient economy. Third, it is sometimes argued that soft energy policy experts have superior information and insights that market actors simply lack or choose to ignore. Government intervention is, therefore, supposedly the only way to achieve the best energy policies.

Market Failure 101

Despite its promiscuous use in public debate, remarkably few noneconomists understand the exact meaning of the term, or its companion term, *efficiency*. Steven Kelman, for instance, a professor of Public Policy at Harvard, interviewed staff members in congressional committees to determine their understanding of the terms *efficiency* and *market failure*. He found that neither Republican nor Democratic staff understood either term.[4] Consequently, the charge of market failure is used with little care or precision and is subject to extensive misuse. Nowhere is that more true than in the energy debate.

Market failures exist if not all transactions whose benefits exceed costs occur voluntarily. An example of a class of such transactions is *public goods*, defined as those commodities for which it is difficult to restrict the benefits of trade to those who participate in the transaction. The most common example of a public good is national defense. If an army defends a nation, it would be difficult to restrict the benefits that flow from an army's activities to those individuals that donated money to the army. Another common example is air pollution. If someone brought suit against a factory's pollution or negotiated a contract with the factory to reduce pollution, the benefits of the suit or contract could not be restricted to the person who did all the work. The others in the neighborhood, the free riders, also would benefit.[5]

Implicit in the charge of energy market failure, then, is the idea that fossil fuel markets do not make users pay for all the spillover costs imposed on others by their use, such as air and water pollution, and that the harmed third parties face public-good problems in organizing a solution. This view also implies that alternative soft energy sources have public-good characteristics that reduce their provision by entrepreneurs.

For market failure arguments to justify government promotion of soft energy, research would have to demonstrate that those failures result in fossil fuel prices that are too low and soft energy prices that are too high relative to their "optimal" prices. Some scholars make such arguments.[6] Other scholars, however, argue that although early pollution control efforts may have had total benefits that exceeded costs, they were inefficiently implemented.[7] Efficient pollution charges for tighter controls might not be very different from the costs of the current inefficient system. In addition, none of the analyses that we have reviewed recognizes that other nonenvironmental governmental actions have kept petroleum prices above, rather than below, an unregulated market price. The only fuel that government has consistently subsidized to any significant degree is nuclear power, but despite the subsidies, nuclear power has been a source of excessive electricity costs on both the East and West Coasts.[8] Thus, ironically, the use of expensive nuclear power has increased rather than decreased the viability of alternative fuel sources.

How Broken Are the Energy Markets?

Four characteristics of energy markets give rise to charges of energy market failure:[9]

- Petroleum is a nonrenewable resource. Are the preferences of future generations properly considered in the decisions of current owners to deplete petroleum stocks?

- The responsiveness of supply and demand to changes in price is very low in the short run. Thus, small changes in either produce large price changes. These price changes generate large political pressures for government intervention to ameliorate the threat of "price shocks."

- The production and consumption of fossil fuels generate emissions that impose tremendous burdens on the natural environment and, in turn, human health. Yet, consumers do not find the price of those substantial health and environmental costs reflected in energy prices. Thus, pricing signals are distorted and the market, in turn, is inefficient.

- Energy markets are inefficient because consumers are hobbled by poor information, lack adequate incentives to conserve, react sluggishly (if at all) to changes in the price of energy, have an unjustifiably jaundiced view of soft energy, lack access to the capital necessary for soft energy investments, and are unable to locate supply networks to support soft energy.

Let's examine the four charges of market failure a bit more closely.

Must Government Allocate Nonrenewable Resources?

A common theme in calls for government intervention in petroleum markets is the nonrenewable nature of petroleum. Because petroleum is exhaustible, it is sometimes argued, we need to ration production in ways that normal market forces would not to ensure that supplies exist for future generations. Another version of this argument does not emphasize the rights of future generations. Instead, it paints a picture of inevitable future oil shortages as production declines occur. These oil shortages will be accompanied by price hikes, recessions, and political struggle. These unpleasant effects can be avoided if government starts planning now.[10]

Reserve Estimates

If fossil fuels were being depleted at an alarming rate (or even at any consequential rate), the data would reflect such trends, but they do not. If present consumption levels were to hold steady, today's proven reserves of oil would last 44 years—a reserve 15 times larger than when record keeping began in 1948. Proven reserves of natural gas would last 70 years, a reserve almost 5 times larger than that of 30 years ago. Proven reserves of coal would last 221 years.[11]

Reserve estimates only reflect petroleum that "can be recovered under present and expected local economic conditions with existing available technology."[12] If relative scarcity of fossil fuels were actually to increase, prices would reflect that fact and those inventories would expand dramatically.[13] In addition, such figures presume no further advances in extraction or energy efficiency technology (more than offsetting the presumed lack of increasing annual consumption). Third, the world's stock of fossil fuels is far greater than traditional oil, natural gas, and coal. For example, "Orimulsion became the 'fourth fossil fuel' in the mid-1980s when technological improvements made Venezuela's reserves of the tar-like substance commercial," notes energy economist Robert L. Bradley, Jr. "Venezuela's reserve equivalent of 1.2 trillion barrels exceeds the world's known reserves of crude oil, and other countries' more modest supplies of natural bitumen add to this total."[14] Tar sands and oil shale also promise similar supplies of fuel if world petroleum prices were to reach $30 a barrel.

Thus, the U.S. Geological Survey did not attract criticism when it calculated 25 years ago that there are enough fossil fuels to last 520 years given projected rates of demand, whereas 10 years ago that figure was raised by some analysts to 650 years.[15] Today, one prominent study estimates that 6 trillion barrels of recoverable conventional petroleum exist today (a reserve of approximately 231 years given present consumption) and another 15 trillion barrels of unconventional petroleum is recoverable given favorable economics.[16] Given present consumption, that would give us 231 years of conventional petroleum and 808 years of petroleum resources of all kinds.[17]

All else being equal, the cheapest exploitable mineral deposits (including petroleum) are developed first, and costs, therefore, would seem to have to rise inevitably over time. However, technological improvements counteract the cost increases over time.[18] Consequently, proven economic reserves have expanded over time at real (inflation-adjusted) prices that have not, contrary to widespread warnings to the contrary, increased dramatically over time. In fact, gasoline prices in 1998 are substantially lower after adjusting for inflation than at any time since the late 1940s.[19]

A typical story is the Kern River field in California, discovered in 1899.[20] In 1942, known reserves were 54 million barrels. From 1942 through 1986, the field produced 736 million barrels, more than 13 times the known reserves of 1942, and reserves in 1986 were estimated to be 970 million barrels. In the Persian Gulf, estimated reserves in 1944 were 21 billion barrels. Cumulative production from 1944 to 1993 was 188 billion barrels, 9 times the 1944 estimate, and remaining reserves in 1993 were 633 billion barrels, 32 times the 1944 estimate.

Petroleum Prices Indicate Abundance, Not Scarcity

All this petroleum production has driven down prices steadily over time. For instance, the February 1998 domestic average price of $12.15 for a barrel of crude oil was about the same as the real price of oil in the 1966-through-1973 period, the lowest price during the post–World War II era. Coal prices are lower now in real terms than they were in the late 1950s.[21]

If and when the futures market suggests that petroleum is difficult to find at the current price, the price of futures will rise. This increase, in turn, will induce consumers to substitute away from petroleum-based fuels to other less expensive (hence, less scarce) fuels, and suppliers will have strong incentives to find alternatives. No one needs to decide centrally through government action whether or how this transition will take place. To subsidize alternatives to petroleum now to save petroleum for later use is perverse because it makes relatively poor people in the present use high-cost alternatives to save lower-cost alternatives for relatively richer people in the future.

Do Markets "Think" Ahead Far Enough?

There are limits to the time horizon of markets, but these limits are defensible and explicable. The first source of these limits is the effect of discounting future revenues. Everything else being equal, income now is better than income later. Market interest rates tell us the amount per year a given amount of money must increase to induce individuals to save money for later rather than current spending.

The effects of interest compound over time. Thus, to induce individuals to save for a long period rather than consume at any point along the way, the amount that an asset must increase in value is quite large. For example, at an interest rate of 5 percent, the value of an asset must increase 4.3 times (in real inflation-adjusted terms) to induce an individual to hold it for 30 years rather than consume it now. A 50-year time period requires an 11.5-fold increase in value, and a 100-year time period requires a 131.5-fold increase in value at an interest rate of 5 percent. Thus, to induce an individual to save a barrel of oil for use in the year 2098 would require the individual to believe that the price of oil in inflation-corrected dollars would be $1841 in 2098 instead of the current $14 a barrel. If you do not believe such a price increase is likely (and the trend in prices over the last 70 years is not encouraging in that regard), then saving oil for use 100 years from now is not economically prudent using a modest interest rate of 5 percent.

Are governments more forward-looking than markets? Any clear-eyed survey of government versus market decision making finds that market agents are far more likely to invest for the future than are governmental agents.[22] As the Tasman Institute, an Australian policy research organization, observes:

> Future generations do not take part in elections, but they are represented in the capital market. While many voters are concerned about future generations, democratically elected governments have a tendency to reflect the wishes of the marginal voter in the currently marginal electorate, so it is unreasonable to expect governments to be more conservation-minded than such a voter. Markets, on the other hand, can reflect more extreme views on the future value of a resource. Since the value of an asset hinges on expectations of what others may pay for access in the future, speculators become the representatives of future generations in today's markets.[23]

Economic growth also implies that the preservation of resources for use by future generations is probably unwise because such efforts are the equivalent of a regressive tax.[24] To see this, examine your own family history. Let us assume that your ancestors used whale oil to light their homes at some point in the early nineteenth century. Ignoring for the moment the wish to protect whales as a species preservation measure, what conservation measures would you have wanted your own poor ancestors (relative to you) to have taken 150 years ago so that you, who are enormously rich (relative to them), could use whale oil today to light your homes? Our guess is that almost all readers will answer that they would not have wanted their ancestors to save whale oil for use by them now. Similarly, our descendants in the year 2148 will look back with bemusement at the argument that we need to save petroleum for their use.

Petroleum Supply Shocks: Justification for Subsidy?

Another characteristic of petroleum markets that generates market failure discussion is the inflexibility of petroleum supply and demand in the short run. This inflexibility implies that small changes in supply or demand have very large effects on prices.[25] Over a longer time period, however, both supply and demand are very responsive to prices. For example, the price increases of the 1970s were followed by a 50 percent reduction in real oil prices after 1985.[26] Energy scholars have found through empirical research that for every 1 percent increase in energy prices, energy use, over the long run, will decrease by about 1 percent.[27]

Much misguided thinking exists in energy policy because analysts often fail to distinguish the long-term transition away from petroleum to other fuels from the short-run vulnerability of oil markets to supply shocks. Analysts incorrectly argue that the wrenching economic disruptions experienced during the 1970s oil shocks will occur as the world "runs out of oil." The disruptions, in turn, are used as a rationale for government support of alternatives to petroleum. Such reasoning is completely incorrect.

Wealth Fights and Oil Policy

The inflexibility of petroleum demand and supply in the short run is not a market failure. It does, however, lead to large transfers of wealth from consumers to firms in times of supply decreases (the Saudi and Texas booms of the 1970s) and from firms to consumers in times of supply increases (the Saudi and Texas busts of the 1980s). Both consumers and firms attempt to enlist the assistance of government to prevent these wealth transfers. The U.S. government aided the Texas oil cartel from 1935 until 1973 by making the shipment of oil across state lines in excess of state quotas a federal offense.[28] The Texas Railroad Commission set production quotas in Texas to match refinery needs at current prices and prevented excess production from lowering prices.

The market responded to the federally sanctioned Texas-production restrictions by importing oil. The government, once again, came to the aid of domestic producers by restricting imports from 1959 until 1973.[29] When the Organization of Petroleum Exporting Countries (OPEC)—itself a creation of U.S. foreign policy—reduced supplies after 1973, the government switched policies and allegedly came to the aid of consumers with an elaborate system of price controls on petroleum and subsidies for alternative fuels.[30]

The 1990 Iraqi oil shock illustrates how oil markets behave if government does nothing. After the Iraqi invasion of Kuwait in August 1990, the world market suffered a shortfall of about 4.5 million barrels per day (mbd) out of a total world supply of crude oil of approximately 61 mbd.[31] Prices rose from $16 a barrel in June 1990 to $30 in September of the same year. The shortfall in supply in this case was about 7.4 percent. Prices increased by 85 percent, but by the next year prices had returned to preshock levels.

The Gulf War oil shock was not without economic consequences, but the effects were much less than the effects of the shocks of the 1970s. This is particularly arresting because the shortfall generated in 1990 was larger than those generated in 1973 or 1979 (3 percent and 6 percent, respectively).[32] The main difference is that the government did not create an elaborate price-control system to take away the profits that come from the sudden increase in value of inventories. Once owners realized that the price control policies of the 1970s would not be reenacted, they sold inventory to the market and made money from the 85 percent price hike.[33]

Oil Shocks and Oil Imports

Soft energy subsidies are also rationalized as a method for reducing our use of imported oil, which, in turn, will reduce our vulnerability to the effects of oil shocks. Reducing dependence on imported oil may sound like a strategy to reduce the effect of oil shocks in the U.S. economy, but such beliefs do not have an economic basis. Changes in oil supplies anywhere in the world affect oil prices everywhere in the world as long as oil is freely traded in markets. The United States would have to isolate itself from world petroleum markets to eliminate the price effects of supply shocks elsewhere in the world, regardless of how much oil the United States imports.[34]

Likewise, the internationalization of the oil trade ensures that the United States will always have access to Persian Gulf oil whether OPEC members like it or not. As MIT's Thomas Lee, Ben Ball, Jr., and Richard Tabors observe regarding the 1973 embargo, "it was no more possible for OPEC to keep its oil out of U.S. supply lines than it was for the United States to keep its embargoed grain out of Soviet silos several years later. Simple rerouting through the international system circumvented the embargo. The significance of the embargo lay in its symbolism."[35] Granted, "there were short term supply disruptions," but "the only tangible effect of the embargo was to increase some transportation costs slightly, because of the diversions, reroutings, and transshipments necessitated."[36]

Must Government Intervene to Protect the Environment?

The argument that fossil fuel extraction and combustion foul the environment in ways that are incompatible with property rights and markets has some merit.[37] Air and water resources have been treated like a public commons rather than like private property. Soft energy advocates argue that the air and water exhibit classic market failure; fossil fuel consumers have not had to pay for the environmental damages caused by burning oil and coal, thus prices for fossil fuels are lower than their "true" prices. Consequently, society consumes "too much" fossil fuel. Soft energy subsidies, it is argued, would reduce fossil fuel consumption, increase economic efficiency, and, ultimately, produce more wealth.

Ends Versus Means

The idea that managing the energy marketplace is the best way to control pollution seems initially compelling. However, the belief that government agencies, not private businesspeople, know best how to achieve goals such as pollution reduction is dubious. As Adam Smith explained in *The Wealth of Nations*, when consumers seek various goods in the marketplace, market agents strive to deliver those goods at the lowest possible price. We seek various outputs at the lowest prices, and we let entrepreneurs, interacting spontaneously, worry about the inputs. As economists Daniel Klein and Pia Maria Koskenoja note:

When we go into a restaurant, for example, and order a crock of French onion soup, we specify only the desired output. We do not tell the chef how to slice the onions, grind the pepper, or grate the cheese. We do not tell the restaurant manager where to get the ingredients, how to store them, or how to train the employees. Customers merely specify the outputs, and, as Smith explained, entrepreneurs in the market attend to the inputs. Successful entrepreneurs are experts on local opportunities for effectively combining inputs, and they compete for customers by seeking to produce the outputs that customers desire.[38]

Thus, if technology permits, the government ought to address the problem of air pollution by focusing on goals, not on the means to arrive at those goals. This could be achieved most efficiently either by pollution taxes or emission trading regimes. Said Adam Smith, every individual can "in his local situation, judge much better than any statesman" what inputs are most appropriate to producing his desired output. "The statesman, who should attempt to direct private people . . . would . . . load himself with a most unnecessary attention."[39] Thus, even if soft energy advocates are correct about the need for further efforts against air pollution, their proposed remedy is not necessarily the proper prescription.

However, soft energy advocates are not necessarily correct about the need for further efforts to control pollution. Environmental regulation since the 1970s has imposed large costs on firms, particularly steel and coal-burning utilities, that probably have been passed on to consumers. Therefore, in a sense, energy consumers *have* had to pay a premium for the environmental consequences of the fossil fuels they consume. In fact, the costs of compliance with the Clean Air Act through the 1970s and 1980s (the "environmental tax" on fossil fuels) have been about $25 to $35 billion annually.[40] To be sure, these costs have been higher than necessary because the cheapest methods of emissions reduction have not been exploited by the EPA, but consumers certainly pay for environmental controls in the prices of products.[41] The relevant question, then, is whether the $25 to $35 billion paid annually by consumers already covers the environmental "cost" of fossil fuel consumption?

Benefits of Reduction in Pollution Exposure

Economic efficiency—the explicit goal of soft energy advocates who cite market failure as a rationale for government intervention—requires that the additional benefits obtained from pollution abatement expenditures exceed the additional costs. Estimating the benefits requires evidence about the effects of exposure to pollution on human health, on the productivity of agriculture, and on the amenity benefits of improved visibility.

All such benefit estimates are very controversial for four reasons. First, the statistical links between exposure and health are not definitive. Second, the estimates involve attributing prices to nonmarket goods, like visibility, an extremely problematical matter to say the least.[42] Third, the estimates require attributing a value to the lives saved and diseases prevented by pollution reduction, a highly contentious matter that constantly sparks controversy. Finally, the benefit estimates require analysts to separate the effect of policy on emissions reduction from other possible sources of pollution decline, which is itself a very uncertain undertaking.

This consideration of the costs and benefits of pollution control is important because subsidies to soft energy sources are necessary to correct for the costs of fossil fuel air pollution if, and only if, incremental net benefits would arise from reduced pollution relative to the current status quo. Even then, an economically justified subsidy would equal only the *difference* between the existing prices of fossil fuels (which include the cost of existing pollution controls as well as some taxes) and a price that included all pollution damages.[43] Because the prices of some fossil fuels (like gasoline) are already taxed, pollution policies already control emissions,[44] and a reasonable interpretation of the evidence suggests that the additional cost of further reducing exposures to fossil fuel emissions exceeds the additional health benefits,[45] the economically efficient subsidy of alternative power sources is, thus, probably zero.

Even if current regulatory costs do not fully reflect the true environmental costs, they are not so far off the mark as to significantly affect consumer decision making. For instance, when the U.S. General Accounting Office considered the issue of pollution costs versus the alleged benefits of renewable fuels as it relates to the electricity industry, it reported that:

> The consideration of externalities in the planning process for electricity has generally had no effect on the selection or acquisition of renewable energy sources [because] electricity from renewable energy usually costs so much more than electricity from fossil fuels that externality considerations do not overcome the difference.[46]

In other words, the cost of electricity produced using renewable fuels far outweighs the costs of any pollution produced by burning fossil fuels to make electricity.

Are Consumers Incompetent?

Advocates of energy conservation have succeeded in convincing many policymakers that energy consumers are either too ignorant or too incompetent to make energy consumption decisions. Let's briefly examine each of the major charges.

Limited Access to Capital
Individuals and corporations, it is argued, use irrationally high discount rates when they contemplate investment in technologies that use less energy than current equipment. According to soft energy advocate Amory Lovins, the clearest manifestation of pervasive

The amount of power produced by windmills is minuscule and costs much more than electricity produced by conventional means. (*Credit:* Northern States Power Co.)

market failure is that most customers require payback horizons of 1 to 2 years for energy savings, even as utilities cheerfully accept power plant payback periods ranging from decades to infinity. That disparity in discount rates means that society buys too many power plants and saves too little energy.[47] Thus, government must step in to ensure the adoption of energy-efficient technologies that have long-term benefits.

Economists are deeply skeptical about such arguments.[48] Studies of consumer behavior, which involve long-lasting investments in home heating and cooling rather than appliances such as refrigerators, find that the implicit rates of return used by consumers in making energy conservation investment decisions are consistent with returns available on other investments.[49]

Second, the up-and-down swings in energy prices over time creates consumer uncertainty about the return on energy conservation investments. Because such investments are essentially irreversible, consumers reasonably demand high returns on home conservation investments to compensate for the uncertainty.[50]

Third, the estimates of alleged energy savings that consumers pass up are based on engineering estimates rather than actual changes in use. For example, engineering models of energy use in California new homes significantly overestimated possible savings offered by new technology because the estimates erroneously assumed that consumers did not turn down the heat during the day when they were away from home.[51] A study based on changes in actual use of electricity, rather than engineering estimates, found that consumers invest sensibly in conservation measures, considering the cost of capital and the returns on alternative investments.[52]

Consumers are not generally averse to making other long-term investments incorporating low-discount rates. Thus, it's hard to believe that consumers are somehow "hardwired" to resist attractive, long-term energy investments but few others.

Limitations of the Supply Infrastructure

Soft energy advocates argue that that a chicken-and-egg problem exists with respect to new technologies and fuels that require an extensive investment in infrastructure. Automakers are reluctant to build methanol-fueled cars, for example, because few filling stations offer methanol fuel and there is no infrastructure to deliver or store methanol. Distributors and retailers of fuel are reluctant to invest in the expensive infrastructure necessary to provide retail methanol because few cars run on that fuel. Thus, unless government steps in, it is thought, the promise of methanol will be forever unrealized.

If that is true, how do we account for the fact that new technologies with similar problems—television, fax machines, compact disc players, and computer software, for example—developed without any help from the government? There is nothing that prevents an investor in methanol from providing both the vehicles and the infrastructure necessary to establish a market. Hardly any major technological advance would have occurred in the twentieth century if the chicken-and-egg problem were insurmountable in the free market.

Misplaced Incentives

Industrial buyers, writers of product specifications, architects, engineers, and builders, it is argued, have little incentive to provide energy efficiency because they are not paying the full life-cycle cost of inefficiency. Yet, if consumers truly demanded energy efficiency in products or homes, suppliers would have every incentive to provide it, and they would loudly advertise the energy-efficient attributes of their goods and services.[53] The fact that that is not happening to the extent desired by the energy conservationists proves, not that there is a failure in the market process, but that there is little demand for the kind of energy efficiencies preferred by the environmental activists.[54] As economist Albert Nichols explained:

> Profit-maximizing firms have strong incentives to take account of their customers' preferences. To the extent that they can provide a characteristic or feature at lower cost than the customer values it, they can earn profits (at least until competing firms also offer that feature). Problems can arise if the customer cannot judge the impacts of various characteristics, but those problems occur whether or not an "intermediary" is involved. Indeed, an important role of many intermediaries (particularly architects and engineers in the case of buildings) is to use their technical knowledge to better translate the customers' broader preferences (e.g., low operating costs) into action (e.g., the purchase of a more reliable or energy efficient heating system).[55]

The "Pocket Change" Problem

Finally, soft energy advocates point to what we might call the "pocket change" problem of consumer behavior. In an encounter at a forum hosted by the Alliance to Save Energy, one of the authors (Taylor) was challenged by soft energy advocate Amory Lovins to reveal the cost of running his refrigerator for an hour. The author admitted ignorance. Lovins then argued that here was an example of market failure: American consumers don't worry about such minor cost issues but, when such costs are aggregated, real losses to the economy—through unrealized energy savings—result. What amounts to unimportant "pocket change" to the average consumer amounts to significant uneconomic investments on a national scale.

The same argument, it should be noted, could be made to increase the efficiency of virtually any economic activity. Razor blades, for example, are cheaper at a major discount retailer, such as Wal-Mart, than they are at the corner 7-Eleven or even the supermarket. The difference in cost is too small for most consumers to spend the extra time necessary to get the better deal. However, if you add up the higher prices spent on razor blades (and every other product like it) throughout the economy, the aggregate "inefficiency" looks startling.

If it's a good idea to "maximize efficiency" by managing consumers' energy purchases, why not also "maximize efficiency" by managing consumers' razor blade, milk, clothing, ad infinitum purchases? Jerry Hausman, a professor of economics at MIT, argues rightly that such coercive paternalism is antithetical to a free society. "High discount rates [by consumers] aren't bad. There is no overriding reason to override people's preferences. [Even though the data tell us that the return on a college education is very large], we don't force people to stay in college even though they should."[56]

Efficiency doesn't mean doing everything in theoretically the most "optimal" way. Trade-offs must occur. A consumer may buy expensive razors at the 7-Eleven store, to spend more time at work where he is designing more energy-efficient engines.

Are Soft Energy Subsidies Necessary to "Level the Playing Field?"

Soft energy advocates also argue that subsidies to fossil fuels justify subsidies to renewables to "level the playing field." Let's consider the major subsidies alleged to exist for conventional fuels:

- Provisions in the tax code that treat oil, gas, and coal extraction differently than the activities of other industries and appropriations for research and development. The main tax privileges are the percentage depletion allowance and the expensing of intangible drilling costs.[57]
- Federal research and development expenditures for both nuclear and fossil fuels.
- Military protection of oil fields, shipping lanes, and the political stability of major oil-producing regions.

Tax Subsidies

Soft energy advocates assert that there is a plethora of preferences in the tax code that unfairly subsidize the fossil fuel industry. Those preferences are so extensive that the Alliance to Save Energy, a Washington-based soft energy advocacy group, concludes:

> There is currently no free market in energy. Given the size of federal energy subsidies, now and in the past, it is erroneous to speak of a "free market" in energy. Government intervention in energy markets has much to do with current market structure, in terms of dominant technologies, the established infrastructure, and even the expected viability of future alternatives.[58]

Such dramatic conclusions, however, are unwarranted. While past and present government interventions have certainly distorted the marketplace,[59] they are scarcely responsible for the major differences in prices and technological maturity between fossil-fueled energy and soft energy alternatives.

First, one must be careful to separate out those preferences in the code that deal specifically with the fossil fuel industry from those that apply to all businesses, energy and nonenergy alike. Although it's true that capital-intensive industries are more likely to benefit from tax credits than less capital-intensive industries, it is not at all clear that soft energy projects are any less capital-intensive than fossil fuel projects on a per-megawatt- or a per-barrel-of-oil-equivalent basis. As we shall see later, wind and solar power facilities, for example, are *the* most capital-intensive power projects on an installed capacity basis. Most of the alleged tax preferences for fossil fuels help the soft energy industry as much or even more so than they do their competitors.

Second, most of the tax preferences decried by the soft energy community are special exemptions, allowances, deductions, and credits designed to partially offset double—and sometimes triple—taxation of capital and capital returns. It is scarcely an unwarranted "preference" to relieve industry generally from onerous and excessive taxation.[60] Of the $58 billion of subsidies that one recent study assigned to the natural gas industry over the last 4 decades, for instance, $51 billion was that sort of tax relief.[61]

Third, the alleged size of the preferences is minuscule in relation to the energy industry as a whole. The Energy Information Administration reported that energy subsidies in 1990 totaled between $5 and $10 billion, only about 1 or 2 percent of the total energy economy.[62] Even the most liberal accounting of tax preferences—compiled by the Alliance to Save Energy (ASE)—finds only about $17 billion in energy subsidies, a figure that doesn't change the calculation of overall minimal effect on the economy very much.[63]

Finally, obsession with the tax code tends to blind analysts to the countervailing regulatory interventions that affect prices far more dramatically than do preferences or subsidies. The Energy Information Administration, for instance, concludes that regulatory interventions are far more likely to unbalance the energy playing field than are direct subsidies:

> It is regulation and not subsidization that has the greatest impact on energy markets. . . . The economic impact of just those energy regulatory programs considered in this [pre-1992 Energy Policy Act] report total at least 5 times that amount [of direct fiscal subsidy].[64]

Subsidy Effects Offset by Texas Cartel

A brief consideration of the oil industry tax preferences most often decried, the percentage depletion allowance and the expensing of intangible drilling costs, shows how unimportant tax preferences are.

First enacted in 1926, the percentage depletion allowance permits the producers of minerals to deduct a certain percentage of gross income before taxes are calculated rather than explicitly amortize exploration and development costs over a certain time period.

The percentage depletion deduction can be greater than the actual development costs. From 1926 to 1969 the rate was 27.5 percent of gross income.

The oil shocks of the 1970s and the high oil producer incomes that resulted reduced the political acceptability of the depletion allowance. The rate is now only 15 percent and limited since 1975 to so-called independent (nonvertically integrated) producers whose aggregate output is less than 1000 barrels a day.[65]

The expensing of intangible drilling costs allows the immediate expensing rather than amortization of expenses for labor, fuel, and other nondurable assets related to the extraction of oil and gas. The cost of derricks, pipes, tanks, and other durable assets used in extraction are amortized according to normal tax schedules. Vertically integrated producers may expense 70 percent of their successful domestic well expenses (and 100 percent of their unsuccessful well expenses). The remaining 30 percent must be amortized over 5 years. Independent producers may expense 100 percent of all their well expenses regardless of success.[66]

Normally, of course, the additional petroleum production fostered by those tax breaks would mean lower prices. Also, lower prices would alter the decisions of consumers regarding their use of conventional versus alternative fuels. However, in the case of domestic oil production, increased supply did not translate into lower prices because of the activities of the Texas Railroad Commission in restraining output.[67] During the 1935–1973 period, the Texas Railroad Commission, assisted by the federal government, ran a more effective and longer-lived cartel than OPEC. Production in excess of what the commission allowed every year was a Texas, as well as a federal, crime from 1935 until 1973.[68] In 1965, Texas producers were allowed to produce only 29 percent of capacity. The price of oil during the Commission's heyday was basically constant in real terms, but it was above what it otherwise would have been because of the actions of the Texas cartel and the restrictions on imports from 1959 to 1973.[69]

The tax subsidies to oil and gas were greatly reduced after 1975, but the oil shocks increased the price of oil until 1985. In 1990, the Congress enacted excise taxes on gasoline that for the first time went to general revenues rather than transportation-related trust funds.[70] These taxes were estimated to be 10 times the value of the remaining tax subsidies to the oil industry in fiscal year 1992.[71]

Thus, the net effect of tax subsidies on the oil industry over the last 70 years has *not* lowered the price of oil. During the time period when the subsidies were large, the actions of Texas producers did not allow increased supply to lower prices. After 1975, the tax privileges were greatly restricted. In 1990, oil started to pay excise taxes to the general fund. The Energy Information Administration estimates that the new gasoline taxes completely offset the other tax subsidies. The net effect of tax subsidies and taxes places a net *tax* (rather than subsidy) on oil on the order of from $2 to $3 billion a year as of fiscal year 1992.[72]

R&D Subsidies

Research-and-development subsidies for energy sources started with nuclear in the 1940s and 1950s. Coal interests argued that such subsidies unfairly subsidized a competitor. Congress responded not by terminating nuclear subsidies but by funding coal R&D, particularly research that would reduce coal pollution and allow it to compete as a clean fuel.

The practice of accommodating political opposition from other fuels by including them in the pork barrel game continued in the political response to the energy crisis when Congress initiated funding for soft energy. Over the past 20 years, soft energy technologies have received (in inflation-adjusted 1996 dollars) $24.2 billion in federal R&D subsidies. Nuclear energy received $20.1 billion and fossil fuels received only $15.5 billion.[73]

Clearly, there is little to the argument that federal R&D programs have unbalanced the marketplace by shifting research dollars away from soft energy sources.

Military Expenditures in the Persian Gulf

Some policy analysts have argued that the costs of U.S. Persian Gulf military and foreign aid activity are a subsidy for the use of petroleum and should be included in any accounting exercise that determines whether conventional fuels have received policy advantages relative to alternative fuels.[74] If these costs are added to the price of Middle East oil on a per-barrel basis, the cost is about $60 a barrel, making the price of Saudi oil $75 instead of $15. At such a price, numerous other alternatives become financially viable. In this view, sound public policy requires that Middle East military costs be added to the cost of imports and used as a basis for establishing subsidies for domestic alternatives.

From an economic perspective, a key question to ask is whether a reduction in U.S. military and foreign aid expenditures would result in an increase in the price of oil? Those who believe Persian Gulf expenditures are a subsidy believe that the termination of U.S. assistance would create a power vacuum, which would make the stability of contracts and property rights more uncertain. This uncertainty, in turn, would reduce investment and oil production and, thus, reduce supply and increase prices.

To be sure, if the termination of U.S. assistance implied the termination of all military, police, and court services in the region, petroleum extraction investments would become more risky. However, remember that oil companies in the region are largely creatures of government. So the question is really whether Middle East governments would produce less oil if the United States ended its military and foreign aid. Would they provide or pay others to provide their own military services?

Saudi Arabia and Kuwait paid for about 55 percent of the Gulf War.[75] One could argue that the size and scope of the U.S. operation was excessive. The war could have been won at a much cheaper cost. Thus, it is certainly possible for the Middle East oil kingdoms to pay for the defense of their oil production facilities.

Even if oil regimes paid for their own military protection, and the protection of their own shipping lanes, would U.S. Middle East military expenditures really go down? The answer might very well be "No" for two very different reasons. First, the U.S. Middle East military presence stems from our commitment to defend Israel as well as the oil kingdoms and would not end simply if the Arab oil regimes suddenly defended themselves. Second, bureaucratic and congressional inertia might leave military expenditures constant regardless of Israeli or petroleum defense needs because of the pork barrel aspects of defense expenditures. In this admittedly cynical view, the importance of defense is not only its security role, but its role as a provider of jobs and a purchaser of goods and services in congressional districts.

Thus, U.S. Persian Gulf expenditures should not be viewed as a subsidy that lowers oil prices below what they otherwise would be. Instead, the expenditures should be thought of as a transfer or a gift that has wealth (U.S. taxpayers are poorer and oil-regime and Israeli governments are richer) rather than efficiency (oil prices are too low) effects.

Summary

The pattern of final demand by American consumers for various fuels has not been distorted to any significant degree toward the use of oil and gas and away from other soft alternatives. The net effect of public policy has been largely to raise the price of energy from fossil fuels above what it would have been in the absence of government intervention in the market.

The subsidies to nuclear power have distorted the mixture of fuels used to produce electricity away from coal and toward nuclear. In fact, subsidies to nuclear power have likely resulted in higher overall electricity prices, not lower prices.

The Economic and Environmental Truths About "Soft Energy"

Thus far, we have reviewed the case for government intervention in the energy economy and found it wanting. Still, a lingering belief exists that solar power, wind power, and energy efficiency—the main technologies that compose "soft energy"—are nearly competitive with fossil fuels and are far more environmentally benign than oil, coal, or natural gas. "The world today," it is argued, "is already on the verge of a monumental energy transformation . . . [to] a renewable energy economy."[76] If only fossil fuel subsidies and preferences were removed and modest incentives for soft energy put in place, America would undergo a major transition based on the economic and environmental virtues of solar power, wind power, and energy efficiency.[77]

Although renewable energy is often thought of as an "infant industry" facing an uphill and unfair struggle against "Big Oil," the truth is that the largest corporate conglomerates in America have long devoted themselves to making renewable energy a reality. Starting in the mid-1970s, Exxon, Shell, Mobil, ARCO, Amoco, General Electric, General Motors, Texas Instruments, and Grumman all had in place sizable renewable energy R&D and development projects.[78] Although many of those projects went bust given the unfavorable economics of renewable energy, the most aggressive renewable energy development initiatives today continue to be undertaken by Shell (the world's second largest energy company), British Petroleum (one of Europe's largest energy companies), Bechtel (one of the world's largest construction firms), Amoco, and Enron (the world's largest integrated natural gas company).

To soft energy advocates, this is evidence of the inevitability of the triumph of renewables over fossil fuels in the near future. But the alleged gains for soft energy need to be put into perspective. Total private-sector investment in solar, wind, and biomass in 1995, the most recent year in which data are available, was less than 1 percent of total world energy investments.[79] Shell's highly publicized plan to spend $500 million over 5 years on renewable energy, for instance, is only half its budget for developing three deepwater offshore oil rigs in the Gulf of Mexico.[80]

Most renewable energy sources have similar common denominators: extremely high capital costs, spotty power output, environmental complications, serious NIMBY opposition (the not-in-my-back-yard phenomenon), struggling economics, yet they continue to earn the support of activists and some public officials as a hoped-for unlimited source of super-clean energy that promises to transform America's economy.[81,82]

Most important, renewable energy is competing against continually plunging fossil fuel prices and rapidly advancing technologies—primarily natural gas turbines—that result in electricity costs of 2 to 3 cents per kilowatt-hour if the waste heat from the natural gas turbines is also used for heating and cooling.[83] According to projections by the U.S. Department of Energy's Energy Information Administration, almost all the growth in new electricity capacity over the next 15 years will come from natural gas turbines.[84]

The Lost Hope of Solar Power

In 1987, Scott Sklar, executive director of the Solar Industries Association and the nation's leading proponent of solar power, told a congressional subcommittee that the consensus among energy analysts was that solar power would provide between 10 and 20 percent of America's energy needs by the year 2000 "quite easily."[85] As we approach that date, solar provides but .05 percent of America's energy needs, but Sklar and his colleagues continue to sell the same "solar's around the corner" message to congressional appropriators and the public.[86]

The main problem for all solar technologies is cost.[87] Generating electricity from solar power from thermal, photovoltaic, or microapplications costs between 11 and 12 cents per kilowatt-hour,[88] at least quadruple the cost of it's main competitor today—combined-cycle natural gas—and quadruple the cost of surplus gas-fired electricity in the marketplace.[89] Even those figures, however, are understatements. According to Solarex, a subsidiary of a partnership between Amoco and Enron and the largest U.S. manufacturer and marketer of photovoltaic systems, "using typical borrowing costs and equipment life, the life cycle cost of PV generated energy generally ranges from 30 cents to $1 per kilowatt hour."[90] Those high solar costs, according to the California Energy Commission, are related to "problems such as high materials costs, fabrication cost, corrosion, erosion, fatigue, and thermal stress."[91]

Perhaps the greatest economic obstacle to solar power is the problem referred to in the trade as *intermittency*—the fact that the sun doesn't always shine and, thus, solar plants are not reliable sources of electricity. In fact, a typical plant only operates at 13 percent of its theoretical capacity over a given year.[92]

Moreover, the land requirements for solar power are truly monumental: between 5 and 17 acres per megawatt of production (compared with 1/25th of an acre per gas-fired megawatt). Because the solar facilities must be cited in desert areas to achieve maximum efficiency, solar power can only be achieved on a significant scale by "paving the deserts." If preserving the Arctic National Wildlife Refuge, home of potentially major oil fields, from development is important, then surely it would be unacceptable to sacrifice the remaining American deserts, referred to by the Wilderness Society as containing "some of the most wild and beautiful landscapes in America."[93]

Wind Power: The Last, Best Hope for Renewables

Wind power's economic potential has long beguiled policymakers and environmental activists. In 1976, the U.S. Department of Energy estimated that wind power could supply about 20 percent of America's electricity needs by 1995, a projection echoed by the American Wind Energy Association in congressional hearings in 1984.[94] In 1985, an executive of the American Wind Energy Association told a congressional hearing that an "achievable goal" for the industry is for wind power to be "the lowest-cost source of electricity, along with hydro, available to a utility by 1990."[95]

Today, such projections look patently ridiculous: Wind power is only slightly less of an economic white elephant than is solar, costing about 7 cents per kilowatt-hour once subsidies are factored out of the picture[96] and responsible for only 0.2 percent of America's electricity generation.[97] Yet, soft energy advocates and the Department of Energy continue to confidently assert that wind power will soon dominate the U.S. energy market despite all evidence to the contrary; wind-driven electricity generation from the very best locations is *still* twice as expensive as combined-cycle natural gas units and triple the price of existing underutilized fossil fuel generation.[98]

A conservative estimate of the total federal subsidy for wind power totals $1200 per installed kilowatt-hour of generation capacity.[99] That's even greater than the direct capital cost of wind power at around $860 per kilowatt-hour and far more than installed capacity of fossil fuel–generated electricity, such as gas-fired combined-cycle plants that cost only $580 per installed kilowatt-hour to build.[100] If we convert those numbers to subsidy per kilowatt-hour consumed, we arrive at an aggregated, real price of wind-generated power of 10 cents per kilowatt-hour.[101]

Wind energy's problems are akin to those found in solar energy production. The wind does not blow around the clock, much less at peak speeds, which means that wind power facilities only operate at about 23 percent maximum capacity even at prime locations.[102] This intermittency problem is a serious obstacle to wind power ever being a primary source of electricity.

The most serious noneconomic issue that threatens wind power is the fact that wind turbines are responsible for the death of approximately 10,000 predatory birds over the past 20 years.[103] Red-tailed hawks, turkey vultures, American kestrels, and even bald and golden eagles are killed annually because the "wind farms have been documented to act as both bait and executioner—rodents taking shelter at the base of turbines multiply with the protection from raptors, while in turn their greater numbers attract more raptors to the farm."[104] According to Dick Anderson of the California Energy Commission—a supporter of wind power—birds are more than five times as likely to die near wind turbines than they are farther away.[105] Given the nature of the problem (towers attract bird prey, which in turn attract predatory birds), it's hard to envision a solution to the avian mortality matter save for abandonment of land-based wind generation.

It's begun to dawn on environmentalists that wind power might well prove to be an encore to hydroelectric power; a renewable energy that had the unforeseen problem of decimating species. Accordingly, green opposition to wind turbines is mounting. The National Audubon Society has called for a moratorium on new wind facilities.[106] The Sierra Club is wavering on the issue, having termed wind towers "the Cuisinarts of the air."[107] The U.S. Fish and Wildlife Service is considering prosecuting wind farm operators for killing birds protected under the federal Migratory Bird Treaty Act and the Bald Eagle Protection Act.[108]

Another major constraint on wind-powered electricity is the enormous amount of land required for wind farms; from 10 to 80 acres per megawatt, or from 2 to 25 square miles for a typical 50-megawatt facility, a total that is from 30 to 200 times more land than is required for a competing natural gas plant.[109] Because wind farms to be efficient must generally be isolated from urban centers, massive land development in uninhabited areas is a prerequisite for wind-powered electricity. An official at the Guadeloupe Mountains National Park, for example, noted that "I've got a lot of mixed feelings" about a wind farm being constructed in that West Texas area. "I understand that wind power is supposed to be clean, yet I don't have to look just at the visual intrusion. We're tearing up a lot of country putting up those wind towers."[110] A report concerning Altamont Pass referred to the near-wild area as "a visual blight. Acre after acre of 100-foot-tall turbines in long curved rows line the softly rolling hills . . . Altamont is where neighbors complain—loudly and with media coverage—that the noise from the turbines is unbearable."[111] If antidevelopment sentiment doesn't stymie the widespread introduction of wind power, NIMBY sentiment surely would.

Energy Efficiency: The Nonsense of "Negawatts"

In the late 1970s, energy analyst Daniel Yergin popularized the argument that "conservation energy" was "no less an energy alternative than oil, gas, or nuclear,"[112] which has come to be known as *negawatts*. Negawatts is perhaps America's most heavily subsidized "renewable" energy. State governments have spent approximately $17 billion to subsidize the harvest of negawatts, while the federal government has shelled out between $8 and $9 billion to further support the industry.[113]

Although there are a number of federal programs that prohibit the use of energy-intensive appliances, the main vehicle for the public exploitation of negawatts are utility-run programs known as *demand-side management* (DSM). The theory behind DSM is that energy conservation and increased efficiency are cheaper than generating new energy. Public utility commissions thus often require that utilities offer consumers services, such as free energy audits and heavily subsidized technologies designed to reduce demand for electricity. The costs of those subsidies are then passed on to ratepayers, who in theory will be required to pay less for the conservation program than they would have had to pay for new generation capacity.

The supply of negawatts is alleged to be between 22 and 64 percent of current electricity consumption, depending on who's doing the counting.[114] Such calculations are made by comparing the current use of electricity with a hypothetical scenario in which the same consumption occurs but with the most energy-efficient technology on the market or on the drawing boards. If the value of the energy saved in any particular application exceeds the cost of replacement over some set period of time (from 4 years to literally decades, depending on the study), then the energy savings qualifies as a negawatt resource.

Of course, those sorts of calculations are of limited policy value. After all, the existing stock of appliances and machinery tagged as "energy inefficient" is worth hundreds of billions of dollars and, in many cases, has decades of useful service still in front of it. It would be uneconomic (to say the least) to scrap it all overnight in favor of alternative technologies.

DSM in Theory

As with the alleged need for other renewable sources of power, the rationale for DSM has a quasi-economic basis. During the 1970s, the regulation of electric utility prices resulted in consumers receiving incorrect information about the true costs of power. The marginal cost of electricity was greater than the rates charged consumers because rates were not allowed to rise as fast as fuel and capital costs during the period from 1970 through 1984.[115] Under such circumstances, utilities lost money on every marginal increase in electricity supply and, therefore, would undertake conservation investments on their own as long as regulation permitted them to do so. However, notice that the market failure here is the rate controls that prevent utilities from pricing at marginal cost rather than any inherent defect in an unregulated electric utility market. The first-best policy would be to remove rate controls. Demand-side management is what is called a second-best policy necessitated by the political difficulty of eliminating or at least significantly reforming rate regulation.

In any event, the current pricing problem of utilities is the opposite of the 1970s situation that prompted the initiatives for utility-directed energy conservation. In the 1990s, marginal costs are lower than average costs because of an excess supply of electric generation capacity.[116] Under such circumstances, economic efficiency requires that electricity consumption *increase* rather than decrease.

A second market failure rationale offered by DSM program advocates is pollution reduction. As argued earlier, a first-best pollution reduction policy would use charges or tradable emission rights for all emissions and not just those from electric utilities. Demand-side management is not an effective substitute for more explicit pollution policies, because it simply subsidizes the installation of various capital items that use less energy. Because these new "toys" lower the marginal costs of additional electricity use, consumers respond by using more electricity in what is known as the "snapback" or "rebound" effect.[117]

The final and most currently used market failure rationale for DSM mandates is the failure of consumers to save money by purchasing new appliances and lights that use less electricity. It is alleged that even though the initial costs of the new devices are higher than conventional equivalent appliances, the marginal costs are so much lower that consumers would save money in a short period of time. In their reluctance to purchase such devices, consumers appear to be irrational because the implicit rates of return that they appear to require before they purchase energy-saving innovations exceed 100 percent, a return that is far greater than can be obtained on alternative investments.[118] Soft energy advocates argue that such high rates of return are prima facie evidence of market failure. They believe that the appropriate policy response is twofold: Adopt standards so that the devices that consumers buy use less energy, and mandate DSM programs by utilities.[119]

Minimizing the use of energy is not necessarily compatible with maximizing the efficient use of economic resources. Declining energy costs may well indicate that economic efficiency demands that *more*, not *less*, energy be consumed. This is particularly true if energy can be substituted easily for capital, labor, or other resource inputs. If energy costs are lower than the cost of other resources, then it is economically efficient to consume more energy and conserve other more scarce resources. Summarizes economist Ronald Sutherland:

> The economics paradigm emphasizes the efficient use of all resources, while the conservation paradigm emphasizes the cost-effective use of energy resources. A discussion of these paradigms indicates that energy conservation programs, even when estimated to be cost-effective, will almost never enhance economic efficiency. Similarly, policies that promote the overall efficient allocation of resources are unlikely to include current conservation programs.[120]

Although it is certainly true that people in the marketplace ought to be comparing the cost of energy conservation with the cost of electricity generation (and making economic choices accordingly), it is doubtful that electric utility companies or public energy planners are the best candidates for that task. The energy market is far too large and complex to allow any one economic actor or state public utility planner to consider all the options involved in energy generation and use. As economist Larry Ruff explains:

> The cost-effectiveness of any specific DSM device in any specific application by any specific consumer depends on details of the device, the consumer, the application, the timing, the delivery method, etc., in ways that are not directly observable or controllable by the utility. There are now high information and transaction costs involved in implementing a utility DSM program—unless one is willing to accept the assumption . . . that utilities have, at near-zero cost, near-perfect knowledge of and control over the detailed preferences, options, and actions of millions of economic consumers.
>
> There is a name for a utility with the knowledge and control necessary to implement a DSM give-away program efficiently: God. Even to come reasonably close to the truly cost-effective result in any but the simplest cases requires a degree of knowledge and control that is unrealistic for any real-world institution. Mere mortals or even utility regulators cannot hope to handle this job by centralized command-and-control methods.[121]

DSM In Practice

An extensive study of energy consumption in Denmark illustrates the difficulties of implementing DSM programs.[122] The Institute for Local Government Studies found that immediate installation of the most energy-efficient technology presently on the market could reduce electricity consumption by 42 percent. If that pool of potential energy savings, however, were restricted to those technologies that were economically attractive (defined as technologies that could produce savings that would be relevant in the short term, investments that would pay for themselves in less than 4 years, and savings that would prove measurable in an audit process), 74 percent of the negawatt pool disappears and only an 11.2 percent increase in electricity efficiency can be obtained.

Analysts for the Institute offered 37 large companies a rigorous and wide-ranging electricity audit free of charge (audits that they allege "were more comprehensive than what is typically found in Demand Side Management activities").[123] They worked closely with corporate officers to show them where they could save energy costs profitably (using the criteria for economic investments discussed above) and left the investment decision entirely up to the company. A year later, Institute analysts revisited the 37 companies and found that they had realized a 3.1 percent increase in electricity efficiency on average, only 28 percent of the potential they reported to the companies.[124]

> Sometimes it turns out that the recommended savings cannot be realized. The consultant may have overlooked some important aspect or the description in the report may be too optimistic. 29 percent of the managers felt that the savings report was not fully credible. In some cases, the company could clearly say that the projects could not be realized. Occasionally, we have recommended savings whose returns were poorer than what the individual company wants from electricity savings . . . several checkup measurements have revealed errors and deficiencies in the savings reports, leading to an over-evaluation of the potential for saving electricity. Some checkup measurements show that the realized savings are only half of what we had expected.[125]

The study concluded that "the cost of finding electricity conservation projects (i.e., the electricity audit) is higher than the savings due to the realized investment."[126] Moreover, although "the background is experience from Danish industry, we judge the results as general for most industry."[127] The true potential for DSM, according to the authors, is the realized savings of 3.1 percent of total electricity consumption. "The realized savings illustrate what is possible to develop practical policy instruments to harvest profitable electricity savings."[128]

A second example of DSM in practice is the supposed success of public utility subsidies for the purchase of magnetic fluorescent lighting ballasts.[129] Researchers from the Lawrence Berkeley National Laboratory claimed that consumers demonstrated a demand for returns of between 37 and 199 percent annually before they would invest in magnetic fluorescent lighting ballasts; clear evidence, they said, of market (actually consumer) failure. It is exactly this sort of finding that prompts Amory Lovins to confidently pronounce that "modern energy-efficient technologies in all sectors often yield after-tax returns of upward of 100 percent a year, while providing superior service quality."[130] If the authors of the study and Amory Lovins are correct about the incredible potential for profitable energy investments and also correct about the irrational unwillingness of consumers to invest in such technology, then the business world is indeed full of idiots.

Energy economist Paul Ballonoff, however, found that a series of simple but profound analytical errors led to a conclusion, in the magnetic lighting ballast case, that was exactly the opposite of reality:

- The study's authors used the average, rather than incremental, cost of energy in their calculations. However, if consumers switch one light bulb from incandescent to fluorescent, they save only the cost of the incremental reduction in electricity use, less than 3 cents per kilowatt rather than the 7½ to 9 cents cost savings alleged by the authors.

- The authors ignored the fact that electricity prices fell a full 10 percent during the period of their study, a fact that surely was considered by investors facing decisions about energy efficiency investments.

- The authors assumed that the ballasts would be used over the full course of the device's life before being replaced, but consumers frequently abandon devices before they deteriorate. Businesses, in particular, often retire otherwise useful equipment; they may go out of business before they get a chance to recoup long-term investments. They frequently redesign facilities, making previous investments obsolete. Ballasts may even break due to sloppy maintenance. In fact, consumer studies show that equipment and appliances are frequently retired before they are inoperable.

After correcting the errors and recrunching the numbers, Ballonoff found that the true rates of return offered to consumers by "improved" magnetic fluorescent lighting ballasts ranged from negative values to only 14.3 percent! Moreover, a full 70 percent of those consumers would face negative rates of return were they to invest in the technology.[131] Thus, the failure of consumers to purchase the improved ballasts was fully justified.

The Costs and Benefits of DSM

Evaluations of the net costs and benefits of DSM programs have not been kind, although DSM advocates predictably dispute those findings.[132,133] Still, evaluations of DSM consistently find that those programs have proven far more expensive than advertised. The Illinois Commerce Commission, for instance, examined the full costs of state natural gas DSM programs from their inception through 1994 and found not one program in which benefits exceeded costs; in fact, most programs demonstrated benefits only 25 percent of costs. Similar findings were uncovered in electric utility DSM programs.[134]

The cost of DSM programs appears to average 5.55 cents per kilowatt-hour, according to a report from the DOE's Energy Information Administration.[135] Subsidized energy conservation, then, is about twice as expensive as generated energy at the margin and can in no way be thought of as efficient.[136] Moreover, studies indicate that there are diminishing returns to DSM and that the cheapest negawatts have already been harvested. Notes one recent study by analysts at the National Renewable Energy Laboratory:

> Despite variations in exact costs among studies such as the National Academy of Sciences and Office of Technology Assessment reports, the trend of increasing costs for additional energy efficiency is less controversial, especially when reductions of 38 percent or more from today's energy intensity are needed within 18 years (to comply with expected international agreements to constrain greenhouse gas emissions).[137]

Electric Utility Restructuring: A Soft Energy Comeback?

Without additional subsidies or preferences, soft energy will likely all but disappear from the economy (and at only 1.5 percent of total energy market share, it's already pretty close to irrelevance). The introduction of more transparency into electricity rates threatens the invisible subsidies that renewable energy and DSM programs receive in the current franchise-monopoly setting. The challenge for soft-energy advocates is to keep those subsidies invisible to consumers, who are largely unaware of the price they're paying for soft energy and who, would not voluntarily pay for "green" power.

The soft energy response to the challenge is a federal mandate that each power generator either generate from 4 to 20 percent of their electricity from renewable energy sources (defined as solar, wind, biomass, geothermal, or a few other less important exotics but *not* including hydroelectric power) or purchase vouchers from other companies that will generate that load. The exact percentage requirement of renewable energy purchases varies by the bill and the timing of the requirements within the legislation.[138]

Soft energy lobbyists also have been successful in getting purchase mandates [known as *renewable portfolio standards* (RPS)] enacted at the state level where most of the restructuring of the industry today is actually occurring.[139] Maine, Nevada, Massachusetts, Connecticut, and Arizona have already adopted some form of RPS, and nearly a dozen other states have either provided some form of state fund to subsidize renewable energy or are seriously considering expanding subsidies for renewable energy.[140,141]

Despite periodic predictions that the world is running out of petroleum, reserves and production continue to increase while real prices dipped in early 1999 to levels not seen since the 1940s. (*Credit:* Courtesy of Loffland Bros. Co. and American Petroleum Institute Photographic and Film Service.)

Purchase mandates are not free. Back-of-the-envelope calculations indicate that a 4 percent renewables generation mandate would increase electricity prices by 2.3 percent; a 20 percent mandate would increase prices by 11 percent.[142]

Global Climate Change = Global Energy Change?

The global warming issue purportedly adds increased urgency to the advocacy for soft energy. "The roots of the global warming crisis lie in the energy revolution that transformed the world economy a century ago," write analysts from the Worldwatch Institute. "Another energy revolution—one as dramatic as the changes that have swept the computer and telecommunications industries in the past decade—will almost certainly be needed to solve the problems created by the first one. Such fundamental changes in the world's energy system may seem farfetched, but are actually well within reach."[143]

Furthermore, it is argued that while we fundamentally reengineer our energy economy, we will also become wealthier as a result. When President Clinton on October 22, 1997, announced his administration's negotiating position for the upcoming Kyoto Summit, he declared "protecting the climate will yield not costs, but profits; not burden, but benefits; not sacrifice, but a higher standard of living."[144] Then-DOE Secretary Fredrico Pena further claimed that cost-free technology could cut greenhouse gas emissions by 15 percent below current levels if consumers would adopt it.[145]

The statements of Clinton and Pena resemble those made by Amory Lovins, who recently contended in the *Washington Post* that "climate protection is actually a lucrative business opportunity disguised as an environmental problem. The same energy efficiencies that reduce global warming are hugely profitable in strictly business terms, without even ascribing any value to the environmental benefits of squeezing more work out of fossil fuels. Energy efficiency is a competitive advantage, not a burden, because it's cheaper to save fuel than to buy and waste it, even at today's low prices."[146]

As we demonstrated in our discussion of DSM programs, however, such claims are unfounded. Saving electricity is not cheap. Stage 1 (1999–2003) of the administration's global warming plan is intended to put the nation "on a smooth path" to reducing greenhouse gas emissions by increasing research and development into soft energy technologies, establishing tax credits for energy-efficient products, and restructuring the electricity industry to promote the consumption of renewable energy (as discussed previously). Stage 1 is expected to cost the federal government $6.3 billion over 5 years and ratepayers billions more if the administration's proposal for electricity restructuring is put into place.

Although our earlier discussion of DSM should suffice to convince us that EPA's initiative will have little practical environmental effect (but very real economic costs), EPA's boosterism to the contrary should be monitored closely. In reporting on the success of selected voluntary climate change programs managed by the agency, for instance, the General Accounting Office discovered that EPA frequently took credit for improvements in energy efficiency that had nothing to do with their programs. Such improvements can be responsible for 60 percent of the energy savings reported.[147] Let's examine the rest of the near-term free-lunch menu offered by the administration.

The Chimera of Federal R&D

The administration's research-and-development initiative is unlikely to have any positive effect on greenhouse gas emissions because federal R&D has been a spectacular bust in the past and there's little reason to believe that its track record will improve with a few hundred million dollars more per year in federal outlays.[148]

Over the past 4 decades, the federal government has poured $17 billion into general nondefense nuclear science and $63 billion into general energy research and development.[149] The administration proposes to add $331 million in soft energy R&D spending in fiscal year 1999 and an additional $729 million between 2000 and 2003.

Perhaps the most rigorous examination of federal R&D programs—conducted for the Brookings Institution by economists Linda Cohen of the University of California at Irvine and Roger Noll of Stanford University—found that federal R&D has been an abject failure and nothing but a pork barrel for political gain. "The overriding lesson from the case studies is that the goal of economic efficiency—to cure market failures in privately sponsored commercial innovation—is so severely constrained by political forces that an effective, coherent national commercial R&D program has never been put in place."[150] Simply put, if the energy research and development investments made by the DOE were made by a private corporation, that company would have gone bankrupt long ago.

Why don't government investments have a better track record? As former Senator William Proxmire once remarked, "Money will go where the political power is. Anyone who thinks government funds will be allocated to firms according to merit has not lived or served in Washington very long."[151] Eric Reichl, former director of the Synthetic Fuel Corporation and long-time member of the DOE's Energy Research Advisory Board, agrees:

> We have lots of ideas. The problem is how to select the right ones to pursue. If we have many ideas their relative merit will vary from high merit to extremely marginal. It also follows that the more R&D dollars are available the more of them will go to some marginal ones. The high merit ideas will always find support, even from—or particularly from—private industry. In general then government R&D dollars will tend to flow to marginal ideas. Exceptions always exist, but they are just that, exceptions.[152]

Solar Roofs: From Carter to Clinton

The second key aspect of Stage 1 is $3.6 billion in tax credits over 5 years for the purchase of various soft energy technologies. The main element is contained in the President's "Million Solar Roof Initiative," which would offer a 15 percent tax credit for the installation of solar panels, capped at $1000 for solar thermal panels and $2000 for photovoltaic panels.

A 40 percent tax credit for solar panels was adopted in 1979 and half a million homeowners responded by installing those panels on their roofs (half the number President Clinton hopes to buy in to his proposed program).[153] When the tax credits dried up in 1985, so did the market for panels, and when energy prices collapsed, 30 percent of the solar panels were uninstalled.[154]

Even with the proposed tax credits, solar panels are still a more expensive way to heat a home than through traditional means. A full-blown photovoltaic system, even assisted by a $2000 tax break, would only pay for itself after 50 years in a typical California residential setting.[155] A more trimmed-down thermal system, designed just to heat water, would pay for itself over 5 years with the subsidy.[156] Based on a recent DOE report that $5 million was handed over by the federal government to select businesspeople to install 1000 solar systems, the House Appropriations Committee found that "at this rate each roof system will cost an average of $32,000, of which taxpayers will pay $5,000. To install one million roof systems by 2010 would require $32 billion, of which $5 billion would be taxpayer funded."[157]

The "Million Solar Roof Initiative" will not contribute significantly to greenhouse gas reduction. Few will install solar panels even with the tax preferences.

The Costs of Reducing Carbon Emissions

In December 1997, at the third conference of the parties to the United Nations Framework Convention on Climate Change in Kyoto, Japan, the approximately 160 attending countries, including the United States, agreed to reduce greenhouse gas emissions by an average of 5.2 percent from 1990 levels during the years 2008 to 2012. The reduction assigned to the United States was 7 percent below 1990 levels. In the year since the Kyoto protocol was signed, numerous estimates have been issued of the costs of compliance with its provisions.

CEA Estimate

The most optimistic and pessimistic estimates both come from agencies of the U.S. government. In July 1998, the Council of Economic Advisors (CEA) issued its analysis of compliance costs.[158] The Council found that compliance would be relatively cheap because we would not actually cut back emissions very much in the United States. The notion that the United States could reduce carbon emissions cheaply through rapid adoption of alternative technologies, a strategy favored by federal energy laboratories and environmentalists, is not the basis for the low costs in the CEA scenario.[159] Instead, we would purchase the right to emit greenhouse gases from other countries (primarily the former Soviet Union) that would not be emitting as many greenhouse gases as they are entitled to emit under the quotas allocated by the Kyoto protocol.

The availability of surplus emission capacity in the former Soviet Union stems from the use of 1990 as the base year from which each country's emissions reduction obligation is calculated. Soviet industry had not yet collapsed in 1990 and emitted much CO_2 because Soviet industrial boilers and electric generators burned coal rather than oil or natural gas, and coal emits more CO_2 than oil or natural gas.[160]

Under the Kyoto protocol, 40 industrialized countries have been assigned carbon emission quotas relative to their 1990 emission levels.[161] If the European Union allows trading of its countries' quotas only within Europe, then the price of permits supplied by the former Soviet Union would fall, reflecting the lack of European demand for them. The Council of Economic Advisors estimates that under such a scenario, the costs of Kyoto compliance would be very low: around $14 per ton of carbon emissions, an increase in the price of gasoline of about 4 to 6 cents per gallon, and a total cost to the economy of 0.1 percent of GDP.[162] If trading were allowed among all Annex I countries and European countries could bid for unused carbon emission rights from Russia, the price per ton of carbon emissions would be higher: approximately $61 per ton.[163]

EIA Estimate

The most pessimistic estimate of the costs of compliance with the Kyoto accord comes from the Energy Information Administration (EIA), an independent governmental agency that gathers and disseminates data about energy markets. The EIA estimates that the worst-case scenario in which no trading of carbon emission permits across countries is permitted (and the United States had to reduce emissions to 7 percent below 1990 levels rather than buy permits to emit) would result in a price for carbon emissions of $348 per ton, an increase in the price of gasoline of 66 cents per gallon, and a total cost to the economy of 4.2 percent of GDP.[164]

These two particular EIA and CEA estimates differ because they model completely different scenarios. However, even if different economic models are used to predict the cost of nearly identical carbon emission scenarios, the results can differ substantially. For example, if the United States reduces carbon emissions domestically by the full amount required under the Kyoto protocol without any international trading, the EIA model predicts that the cost of a permit to emit 1 ton of carbon will be $348. The model used by the CEA estimates that without international trading the cost of a permit to emit 1 ton of carbon would be $193, a little more than half the EIA estimate.[165]

Why Do Models Produce Different Estimates?

Why do the estimates of different models vary so much even when they model the same scenario? The economic models, although technically quite complex, calculate their results through four conceptually straightforward tasks:

- Generate an estimate of the level of economic activity in the year 2010 in the absence of any policy changes.

- Predict the level of carbon emissions in 2010.

- Calculate the cost of reducing carbon emissions to their level in 1990 minus 7 percent as permitted by the Kyoto protocol.

- Calculate the cost of reducing carbon emissions by lesser amounts and purchasing the right to emit the remainder from countries that emit less than their quota.

Thus, the differences in predictions must arise from differences in the four tasks. The models differ in their predictions about expected GDP and carbon emissions in the absence of any policy changes.[166] However, the models differ even more on how costly it will be to reduce carbon emissions by a given amount. The cost differences stem from:

- Differences in predictions about the ease of transition from coal- to natural-gas-fired electricity

- Differences in the rate at which energy efficiency increases autonomously[167]

- Differences in how energy costs translate into costs in other sectors of the economy

- Differences in how much consumers factor future prices into current decisions

The optimistic model used by the administration assumes that electricity producers respond very rapidly to carbon permit prices. Existing coal-fired plants are carbon emission–intensive. Thus, if they shut down and are easily replaced by natural-gas plants at low cost, complying with Kyoto is not economically costly.[168] Other models assume that the transition from coal to natural-gas electricity will be slower and more costly. If coal-fired electricity persists, then carbon emission reduction must come from sectors of the economy other than electricity, like transportation. Because petroleum combustion is less carbon emission–intensive than burning coal, the consumption cuts, and hence the permit price required to achieve a given level of carbon emissions reduction is greater than if the cuts come from coal-fired electricity.

The effects of the differences in the ease of transition from coal- to natural-gas-fired electricity and the rate at which autonomous energy efficiency increases, have important effects on the estimates of Kyoto compliance costs. For example, Charles River Associates estimates that the cost of reducing carbon emissions in 2010 to 1990 levels would result in a carbon permit price of $148 per ton of carbon emissions. If the assumptions in the Charles River model about the coal natural-gas transition and autonomous energy efficiency increases are modified to be the same as those used in the CEA model, the predicted carbon-permit price is reduced to $109, the same as predicted by the CEA model.[169]

Other important differences exist between the models. The optimistic models only assess the direct costs of Kyoto compliance on the energy sector. Other sectors in the economy are assumed to adjust costlessly and instantaneously.[170] Fiscal and monetary policy are assumed to adjust to maintain full utilization of resources in the rest of the economy.[171] In addition, consumers have perfect foresight in the optimistic models.

The less optimistic models, like the EIA model, assume that the adjustments will not be smooth and costless, and residential consumers will not have perfect foresight.[172] In addition, the EIA model does not calculate the benefits of permit trading directly. Instead, it only estimates the willingness of the United States to pay for reduction (based on our marginal costs). If other countries sell us permits to emit at a lower price than our costs of emissions reduction, the EIA cost estimates are too pessimistic.[173]

Scientific Versus Empirical Validity of the Models

How should we evaluate the various scenarios in the models? First, economic models are simply a series of if-then relationships. As long as the mathematical links between the *ifs* and the *thens* are algebraically true, then the predictions of the model are scientifically accurate.

All the models used in estimation of the costs of Kyoto protocol compliance are scientifically accurate. However, the relevance (rather than the scientific validity) of the predictions depends on the plausibility of the assumptions (the *ifs*). Both the highest- and lowest-cost scenarios rely on assumptions that are unlikely to occur.

The high-cost scenarios require the United States to reduce emissions to 1990 levels minus 7 percent on its own. The cutback of approximately 550 million metric tons of carbon emissions per year (approximately a 31 percent cut from projected emissions in 2010) would require a massive shutdown of coal-fired electricity capacity and a shift to natural gas by 2010.[174] Such a shift is not unprecedented but would exceed our recent experience in natural-gas plant construction.[175]

The importance of the high-cost scenario is not that it is likely to occur; rather, that it demonstrates that carbon emissions reduction without a trading scheme would have a large negative impact on the production of coal-fired electricity and require a massive investment in electricity produced from natural gas. These two changes are likely to generate political disputes involving coal unions and producers, railroads (which would lose from one-quarter to over one-third of their revenue), and the siting of natural-gas plants.[176] The political disputes make the costs of Kyoto compliance higher than a strict economic analysis would suggest.

The lowest-cost scenarios rely on global international trading, flexible markets, and rational consumer behavior all occurring by 2010.[177] The importance of the low-cost scenario is not that it is likely to happen, but rather how smooth and rapid responses to changes in prices and general market flexibility are essential to cost minimization. Consumer and institutional rigidities raise the costs of compliance.

A more likely scenario than either the absence of trading or complete worldwide trading is trading limited to Annex I countries and some rigidities in the responses of firms and consumers to higher prices in the short run. Under a full Annex I country trading regime, the price per ton for carbon emissions is predicted by all the models (except the CEA) to be in the range of $100 to $130. The GDP losses are predicted to range from 0.4 to 1.7 percent.[178]

How much confidence should we have in the economic predictions? If past experience is any guide, the predictions should be discounted. The use of large-scale models to predict the future costs of policy options does not have a very good track record. In 1975, Resources for the Future, an organization respected for its economic analysis, projected that the total costs of nuclear plants from 1985 to 1988 would be cheaper than the total costs of equivalent coal plants. A set of costly nuclear plants came on-line during the early 1980s, however, and electricity rates rose 60 percent from 1978 to 1982. By 1990, nuclear plants had total costs that were about double those for coal plants.[179] In its study of the energy crisis in the 1970s, the Ford Foundation used a doubling of real (inflation-adjusted) oil prices from 1979 to 2000 in its models.[180] The actual price of oil in inflation-adjusted dollars in mid-1998 was less than one-half of its 1979 price.[181]

Conclusion

When you cut through all the technobabble, U.S. compliance with the Kyoto protocol is really a fight over the future of coal-fired generation of electricity.[182] How costly would it be to eliminate coal-fired electricity and switch to natural gas?

If we have to reduce drastically coal use in the United States by 2010, the costs are likely to be high even if we only consider economic factors. Given the likely political resistance of coal interests, the costs are likely to be even higher. For example, during congressional action on the 1990 Clean Air Act, the last time the coal industry was challenged, union miners almost won the right to taxpayer compensation for any job losses that occurred.[183]

The cheapest method of reducing Kyoto compliance costs for the United States is to reduce our coal use very little and pay others to give up their rights to emit. The most realistic trading scheme is likely to involve only Annex I countries rather than the entire world and cost the United States about 1 percent of GDP.

Natural-gas-fired electric plant costs are now competitive with new coal plants, and most new electric plants in the 1990s have been natural gas. If this trend continues, market forces alone, in the long run, will replace carbon-intensive coal-fired electricity plants.

The only reason, therefore, to rush the conversion from coal to natural gas is if the benefits are large. However, the amount of warming prevented by full Kyoto compliance is likely to be so small (0.07°C by 2050) that it will not be easily measurable. The almost totally symbolic benefits of the Kyoto protocol are not worth the real costs it would create.

Market Actors Versus Policy Merchants: Who's Right?

Numerous rationales are used to justify the management of energy markets by government. Many people believe that a series of market failures and existing policy subsidies have the net effect of encouraging too much consumption of fossil fuels and too little consumption of "better" alternatives. In this chapter, we have examined these arguments and found them not supported by theoretical and empirical evidence:

- We are not running out of fossil fuels. If and when we do at current prices, futures markets will signal firms and consumers to switch to alternatives.

- Oil shocks have very real short-run effects on the economy, but government attempts to prevent the wealth transfers that accompany oil shocks have made the effects much worse than they need to be. The 1990 Iraqi oil shock in which the government left oil markets alone had the fewest negative effects on the economy.

- The percentage of oil imported by the United States does not alter the effects of oil shocks. Because the oil market is worldwide, effects on supply anywhere affect oil prices everywhere.

- Fossil fuel combustion is now much cleaner than it was 30 years ago. The benefits from further reductions in emissions are low relative to the costs and certainly do not justify mandates to use fossil fuel substitutes. Even if the benefits from further emissions reduction were large, they would justify the use of tradable emissions permits rather than command-and-control mandates.

- The belief that industrial and residential consumers pass up energy conservation investments that are cost-effective is not supported by economic evidence.

- Fossil fuels have been subsidized, but, historically, they did not lower the price of petroleum to consumers because other government programs raised prices above market levels. At present, the taxes on gasoline are estimated to be much larger than the value of the subsidies to petroleum that remain. In addition, R&D subsidies to alternative fuels now exceed those to nuclear and fossil fuels.

- Persian Gulf military expenditures are a wealth transfer from the United States to Middle East regimes rather than a policy that lowers oil prices below what they otherwise would be.

- Solar and wind power, as well as DSM, do not have a sound economic basis.

Markets have judged soft energy technologies to be inefficient and excessively expensive. To be sure, market judgments are not infallible. However, markets have the virtue of imposing discipline on investors by forcing them to accept the costs of being wrong and minimizing the social damage that might stem from poor investments. Governmental intervention, by definition, overrides the judgment of the best-informed people in the economy and socializes the costs of any misstep. Because governmental agents do not bear the direct costs of bad investments, they are more likely to take poor risks than the private investor, who may face bankruptcy as a consequence of guessing wrong in the marketplace.

Government's record of success when it intervenes in markets is so bad that one suspects that even random chance would have produced a better track record. MIT's Thomas Lee, Ben Ball, Jr., and Richard Tabors argue that "the experience of the 1970s and 1980s taught us that *if a technology is commercially viable, then government support is not needed; and if a technology is not commercially viable, no amount of government support will make it so*" (emphasis in original).[184]

Experience is a good teacher, and experience teaches us that governments are rotten at second-guessing the marketplace. How many times must government mess up the energy marketplace before we learn our lesson?

Chapter 7

RICHER IS MORE RESILIENT
Dealing with Climate Change and More Urgent Environmental Problems

Indur M. Goklany

HIGHLIGHTS

- *Despite any warming that may have occurred over the last century, matters have improved for many climate-sensitive sectors and indicators of well-being, mainly because of human ingenuity (technological change), economic growth, and trade.*

  - *Global agricultural productivity has never been higher. Each acre of cropland sustains about twice as many people today as it did in 1900. Although the population increased 84 percent between 1961 and 1995, food supplies per person increased 19 percent; people have never been fed better or more cheaply; and between 1969–1971 and 1990–1992, people in developing countries suffering from chronic hunger declined from 35 to 21 percent.*

  - *Deaths due to climate-sensitive infectious and parasitic diseases are the exception rather than the rule in the richer countries, and are on the decline in developing countries due to better nutrition and public health measures. These helped overall death rates in developing countries drop from 19.8 to 9.3 per 1000 population between 1950–1955 and 1990–1995, and global life expectancy at birth increased from 46.4 to 64.7 years.*

  - *Although increased population and wealth has put more property at risk, which has helped increase U.S. property losses due to floods and hurricanes during this century, there are no clear trends in losses in terms of wealth. More important, deaths due to hurricanes, tornadoes, floods, and lightning have decreased between 46 and 97 percent, compared with their earlier peaks (based upon 9-year moving averages), whereas death rates declined between 60 and 99 percent.*

- *For other sectors, matters have continued to worsen overall, but not because of warming.*

  - *Forested area is now increasing in developed nations, but declining in developing nations, largely because of land clearance for low-yield agriculture. The resulting habitat loss and fragmentation is also the greatest threat to global biodiversity and to carbon stores and sinks.*

  - *Sea level has risen a relatively modest 8 inches in the past century, but it is not clear what portion, if any, is attributable to global warming. Regardless, its impacts are secondary to other human impacts on coasts and coastal resources.*

- *Poorer societies are the most vulnerable to adversity, no matter what its cause. Comparing the poorest with the richest nations:*

  - *Food supplies per capita are 30 to 40 percent lower, and malnourishment and hunger rates are much higher.*

  - *Only 50 to 60 percent of the people have access to safe water and sanitation compared with 90-plus percent in the richer nations.*

  - *Child mortalities are 20 times higher.*

  - *Life expectancies are 30 years lower.*

- Land use is more inefficient due largely to lower-yield agriculture, which increases deforestation and potential loss of biodiversity.

The root cause of each of these is insufficient technological progress and economic growth. If it were not for trade, poorer nations would be in worse straits, because they import about 15 percent of their grain.

- With respect to the future, assuming the validity of analyses underlying the United Nations' Intergovernmental Panel on Climate Change's (IPCC's) 1995 Impact Assessment, the following are the potential (though not necessarily, probable) impacts due to warming:
  - Agricultural production may decline in now developing—but increase in the already developed—countries, resulting in a net change in global production of +1 or −2 percent in 2060. Without warming, global production would have to increase 83 percent from 1990 to 2060 to meet projected additional food demand. Thus, a future food crisis is more likely if economic growth, technological change, and trade falter. Warming would have minimal impact.
  - If all else remains the same, by 2050, global forest area may increase between 1 and 9 percent due to global warming alone, but if land use change due to greater agricultural and other human demands is also considered, forest cover may decline by 25 percent, putting enormous pressure on the world's biodiversity.
  - Sea levels may rise from 3 to 19 inches, with a "best estimate" of 10 inches by 2060, and about twice that by 2100. The global cost estimate for protecting against a 20-inch rise in 2100 is about $1 billion per year.
  - By 2060, incidences of climate-sensitive infectious and parasitic diseases may increase by about 1/20th to 1/10th of the base rate in the absence of warming. The increase may be double that in 2100.
  - Poorer nations will be most vulnerable to warming, not because their climates are expected to change the most, but because of a deeper disease—poverty. They lack economic resources to easily afford the technologies to adapt to or cope with any adversity, or purchase food surpluses produced elsewhere to make up for projected shortfalls.
- Hence, stabilizing greenhouse gas concentrations immediately, even if feasible would, except for accelerated sea level rise, do little or nothing over the next several decades to solve those problems that are offered as the major reasons for concern about warming:
  - Land and water conversion will continue unabated, with little or no reduction in the threats to forests, biodiversity, and carbon stores and sinks.
  - Chances of feeding, clothing, and sheltering a larger world population will not have been substantially improved, if at all.
  - Incidence rates of infectious and parasitic diseases will be virtually unchanged.
  - Poorer nations will continue to be vulnerable to all kinds of adversity, natural or manmade.

- Thus, although warming may be a serious problem in the long run, it is not now—nor is it likely to be in the next several decades—among the world's list of urgent environmental or health problems.

- The key to addressing the urgent public health and environmental problems of today and tomorrow without ignoring the potentially serious problems of the day after, is to strengthen the institutions underpinning the mutually reinforcing forces of economic growth, technological change, and trade. These institutions include free markets, secure property rights, and honest and predictable bureaucracies and governments. Strengthening them would:
  - Address the root cause for the vulnerability of the poorest nations to climate change as well as other sources of adversity, including hunger, malnutrition, and infectious and parasitic diseases.
  - Increase the productivity and efficiency of land and water use, thereby reducing diversion of land and water to meet human needs for food, clothing, shelter, paper, and other material goods, and reduce the major causes of the loss of forests, habitat, biodiversity, and carbon sinks and stores.
  - Increase the voluntary movement of food and other goods to move from surplus to deficit areas, thereby alleviating shifts in competitive advantage caused by warming or any other factor.
  - Increase the ability of developing nations to obtain mitigation and adaptation technologies.
  - Reduce physical barriers to "allow[ing] ecosystems to adapt naturally to climate change."

- Adaptation can also be boosted by developing and implementing technologies to address those environmental and societal problems that would be further aggravated by climate change. If malaria, for instance, is the concern, it is more cost-effective to invest in malaria-related R&D today than to focus on limiting climate change. An additional 0.2 percent per year reduction in malaria incidence between now and 2100 would more than compensate for any increases due to climate change—and if sufficient emphasis is placed on eradicating malaria, the potential increase in the ranges of malaria-bearing mosquitoes due to climate change could become moot.

- Successful adaptation will raise the thresholds at which greenhouse gas concentrations become "dangerous." This would reduce the cost of controls. Therefore, there can be no optimal strategy for addressing climate change that ignores adaptation.

Our overriding environmental challenge tonight is the worldwide problem of climate change, global warming, the gathering crisis that requires worldwide action.

President Clinton, January 27, 1998
State of the Union Address

Scientists worldwide consider climate change the greatest danger to the environment, followed by population growth, water shortages, and pollution, according to a poll of 1,000 sponsored by the European Commission and the French education and environment ministries

Agence France Presse, January 28, 1998
reported by Greenwire, February 5, 1998

Some laymen and scientists believe that there is no greater environmental threat today than anthropogenic climate change, or as it is sometimes called—global warming. Does the evidence, however, support such a claim? Are the projected effects of global warming going to be dangerous in the foreseeable future (that is, over the next several decades)? Perhaps the best approach is to reduce vulnerability and enhance human and natural adaptability to the environmental and health problems that might be caused—or aggravated—by anthropogenic climate change?

This analysis focuses on the economic sectors and environmental consequences and indicators that are thought to be the most sensitive to climate change—namely, agriculture and food security, forests and biodiversity, human health, hurricanes and other extreme weather events, and sea level rise. For brevity, these will be called the "climate-sensitive" sectors or indicators.

The Importance of Climate Change

Two approaches will test the claim that anthropogenic global warming is the most important environmental problem facing the globe. First, this analysis will ascertain whether over the recent past, damages and threats to human and natural systems due to changes in the "climate-sensitive" sectors increased and, if they have, the extent to which those effects can be attributed to man-made warming, rather than to other environmental problems. Then, the analysis will examine whether—and why—human and natural systems may be more or less vulnerable today than previously. Second, assuming that the United Nations' Intergovernmental Panel on Climate Change's 1995 Impacts Assessment[1] is valid, a comparison will be made between the magnitudes of the effects of global warming projected over the next several decades and those effects due to other environmental changes.

The Present and the Recent Past

Analysis of past trends in the ability of the climate-sensitive sectors to meet human demands can help determine not only whether it is becoming harder to meet those demands, but also to identify factors or attributes of societies that help them cope better with adversity in general. Such information can help reduce the future vulnerability of societies to the negative consequences of climate change.

Agriculture and Food Security

Today, almost twice as many people are fed per acre of cropland as were fed about a century ago (Figure 7-1). Between 1900 and 1995, while global population increased 250% [from 1.6 billion to 5.7 billion), cropland only increased 90 percent (from 0.77 billion hectares (Bha) to 1.48 Bha).[2] Not only are we using less land per human being to grow food (0.26 ha per capita in 1995 versus 0.48 ha in 1900), globally the average person is eating a lot better.

Between 1961 and 1995, for instance, global population increased 84 percent (from 3.1 to 5.7 billion), but cropland increased only 10 percent (from 1.34 to 1.48 Bha), as did total

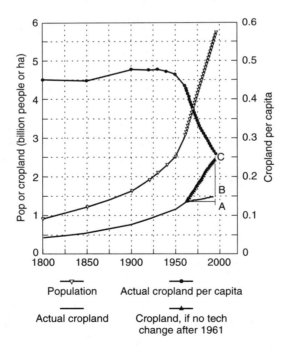

FIGURE 7-1 Global cropland area, 1800 to 1995. (*Note:* AB = increase in cropland from 1961 to 1995 = 0.13 Bha. BC = land not converted to cropland from 1961 to 1995 = 1.00 Bha.)

Sources: Updated from Goklany (1998) using FAO (1998).

agricultural area (from 4.5 to 4.9 Bha) (Figure 7-1). The 74 percent gap between the increases in population and in agricultural area (equivalent to 3.3 Bha of agricultural land, including 1.00 Bha of cropland) is the amount of land saved from conversion to agricultural uses because of technological progress.[3] If it were not for that progress, deforestation and loss of habitat might well have reached apocalyptic levels. Simultaneously, between 1961–1963 and 1994–1996, global food supplies per capita increased 19 percent (from 2269 to 2707 kcal/day), protein supplies increased 15 percent (from 63 to 72 g/capita/day), and between 1961 and 1992, world food prices (in constant dollars) declined 47 percent.[4] Consequently, although global population increased 45 percent between 1969–1971 and 1990–1992, the absolute number of people suffering from chronic undernourishment in developing nations decreased from 917 million (or 35 percent of their population) to 839 million (or 21 percent).[5] Clearly, the global population, despite being larger, is less vulnerable to famine and malnourishment today than it was a few decades ago, which, in turn, is partly responsible for the overall improvements in the world's health status, including lower infant and maternal mortality rates, and higher expected life spans.

However, the IPCC report notes that some global warming has occurred in the last several decades. Some analysts suggest that warming may reduce agricultural productivity through more frequent floods, droughts and loss of soil moisture, and pest and disease outbreaks, which would make it harder for the world's population to be fed. Therefore, how can one explain the historical increases in agricultural productivity and improved food security?

There are three possible explanations for this divergence. First, perhaps the net effects of global warming are not particularly detrimental to agricultural productivity, especially at present CO_2 and temperature levels. In fact, there is no evidence that CO_2-enhanced warming has decreased either global agricultural production or, more important, global food security. Some areas do suffer from food deficits largely as the result of the failure of social, economic, and political institutions.[6] Preliminary evidence suggests that CO_2-enhanced warming may be contributing to increased agricultural productivity. One observer estimated that from 30 to 50 percent of the increase in corn yields in Australia since 1950 may be due to higher minimum temperatures.[7] Second, in the far northern latitudes, the active growing season seems to have lengthened by 12 to 14 days in the 1980s and plant growth apparently accelerated.[8] In addition, numerous controlled field experiments show that increasing atmospheric CO_2 concentrations increases crop yields.[9] One estimate of the increase in global agricultural productivity due to increased CO_2 concentrations puts it at between 8 and 12 percent.[10] However, between 1961 and 1996, global yields for all cereals increased 114 percent (from 1.35 T/ha to 2.90 T/ha), whereas CO_2 concentrations increased only 14 percent (from 317.5 ppm to 362.6 ppm at Mauna Loa), and annual global temperature increased less than 0.3°C.[11,12] Thus, it is unlikely that increased CO_2-enhanced warming can explain more than a small portion of the increase in global agricultural productivity.

A second explanation for the increased agricultural productivity and the resulting decreases in the global vulnerability to food insecurity could be human ingenuity (or technological progress or adaptability).[13] A third and, perhaps, the most plausible explanation is a combination of the first two (i.e., CO_2-enhanced global warming and technological progress have reinforced each other to reduce human vulnerability).

Technological progress is driven by the coevolution of technology, economic growth, and trade, not just in the food and agricultural sector, but in general because technologies invented or perfected in other sectors often were applied to agriculture (e.g., personal computers, microprocessors, plastics, global positioning systems, and bioengineering) and because economic growth in one sector often generates investments for use in another.[14] Economic growth allows more resources to be spent on researching and developing new, or modifying existing, technologies. Economic growth also enables the purchase of new or underused and more efficient food and agricultural technologies as well as the inputs needed to use those technologies. Finally, economic growth boosts the creation and maintenance of the infrastructure required to move agricultural inputs and outputs between farms and markets, making the food and agricultural sector more efficient and reducing waste. Thus, economic growth is critical to implementing and realizing the technological improvements that, in the past, increased the productivity of land. The result is that the richer nations, which encouraged institutions fostering economic growth and technological change, produce large crop and food surpluses.[15] Increased crop production caused food prices to drop relative to other goods and services. In turn, new technologies reinforced economic growth. Continuing this "virtuous cycle," economic growth made it possible for people and countries who did not grow enough food to purchase it and improve their food security. (Currently, 55 percent of the world's population is not engaged in agriculture.)[16] Increased internal and global trade (and, to a lesser degree, aid) were essential to voluntarily redistributing food from surplus to deficit areas and populations. In effect, freer trade globalized sustainability.[17] Moreover, increased economic growth also allowed societies to improve their safety nets for individuals and families who may otherwise have been priced out of the food market. Trade further intensified the cycle by increasing economic growth, as well as the dissemination and implementation of new technologies. As a result of all these factors, economic growth, technology, and trade reinforced each other to increase global productivity and reduce global vulnerability to malnourishment and famine.

Current data on food security, crop yields, food, and aid strongly support the above argument. First, food supplies per capita increase with affluence [as measured by gross domestic product (GDP) per capita] until they level off at about 3500 calories per day (kcal/day) at around $7000 GDP per capita [based on constant purchasing power parity

Low-yield agriculture in Africa and other developing countries poses far greater dangers to the natural environment than does any predicted global warming. (*Credit:* WorldBank.)

(PPP) using 1985 international dollars).[18] For East Asian countries, the plateau may be around 2800 to 2900 kcal/day based on data from Japan, Singapore, and Hong Kong. Thus, food security is not a significant problem in wealthy nations, even if they produce relatively little food (e.g., Japan, Singapore, and Hong Kong); it is a major problem, however, in the least-developed countries, although the majority of their people are engaged in agriculture. The experience of the five most populous developing nations (China, India, Indonesia, Brazil, and Pakistan), which together contain 46.5 percent of humanity, also indicates that economic growth is critical to enhancing food security. In these nations, between 1961–1963 and 1992, GDP per capita (using PPP-adjusted 1985 international dollars) increased,[19] and available food supplies per capita increased between 17 and 64 percent.[20] The converse is also true: Food supplies per capita declined 8 percent between 1988 and 1992 in the "transition" nations of Eastern Europe and the former Soviet Union because of their economic decline.[21] The linkage between poverty and food security is also illustrated by the case of Africa. Unlike other parts of the developing world, production and availability of food have fallen behind population growth in many African nations, mainly because of poverty and civil strife.[22]

Second, a wealthier nation (and wealthier farmers) can afford productivity-enhancing technologies and the inputs needed to wring the most out of those technologies. Because of their poverty, many African nations cannot afford fertilizers or other currently available technologies. From 1991 through 1993, fertilizer use in developing Africa was 16.6 kg/ha, compared with 80.4 kg/ha for all developing nations and 84.7 kg/ha for the world. Therefore Africa's total cereal yield was 1.1 T/ha compared with 2.5 and 2.7 T/ha, respectively.[23] Moreover, many African nations cannot afford the technologies to reduce pre- and postharvest losses to rats, locusts, and other pests, which claim between 30 and 45 percent of production.[24] Therefore, it is hardly surprising that even though chronic malnutrition rates declined between 1969–1971 and 1990–1992 in other developing regions of the world, they climbed in sub-Saharan Africa from 38 to 43 percent of the total population. Without international trade, however, the price of food in these African nations would have increased and, with it, their rates of chronic malnutrition. Nor is it surprising that most of the world's grain surpluses come from 14 of the richer nations, whereas the majority of developing countries are net importers. In 1995/1996, for instance, developing nations' cereal imports amounted to 16 percent of their production.[25] Similarly, virtually all food aid is donated by the richer nations. Thus, patterns of trade and aid also confirm the significance of affluence in increasing the world's food security.

Forest Cover and Biodiversity

Human demand for land for agriculture and—to a much lesser extent settlements and infrastructure—has been, through the ages, the major reason for the loss of forest cover and diversion of habitat away from the rest of nature.[26] Such deforestation and habitat conversion, in turn, are responsible for much of the current threat to global biodiversity. Between 1980 and 1995, global population increased 28 percent. To meet the additional food demand, net agricultural land increased by about 4 percent, or 200 Mha (including 80 Mha of cropland), and net forest cover decreased by about 170 Mha.[27] In the developing countries, net forest cover declined about 190 Mha.[28] By contrast, forest cover increased by about 20 Mha in the developed countries.

There is no evidence that warming has contributed to the loss of forest cover, significantly or otherwise. In fact, for forests, as for agriculture, warming may have increased timber growth and forest mass. The trends in developing and developed countries confirm the importance of economic growth and technological progress in limiting deforestation.[29] Forest cover is declining in developing countries because their increases in agricultural productivity lags behind the demands of their growing populations for food. Meanwhile, developed countries are being reforested because—despite diversion of land for urbanization and infrastructure projects—productivity in the agricultural and forestry sectors is growing faster than the increase in demands for food and timber. Without science-based and market-nurtured increases in food and agricultural productivity, global deforestation would have been much greater—between 1980 and 1995, at least an additional 1230 Mha of agricultural land (including 400 Mha of cropland) would have been needed, much of it at the expense of forests and woodlands.[30]

Trade also enhances adaptability. Nevertheless, some trade skeptics argue that trade allows richer nations to continue their excess consumption of timber products and beef by despoiling tropical forests in developing nations. Moreover, roads built to move products to markets further destroy or degrade forests by enabling easier colonization and exploitation. However, logging, converting natural forests to plantations for agricultural and forest crops, and large-scale cattle ranching, do not seem to be principle causes of changes in the quality and quantity of forest cover. Most deforestation is a result of the need for poor people to increase agricultural production via relatively low productivity techniques (particularly in Africa and Asia), bad government policies (e.g., subsidies, resettlement schemes, creation of water reservoirs), uncertain land tenure and property rights, social disruptions that displace people who then resort to deforestation to free up land for settlements and agriculture, and corrupt political structures and bureaucracies.[31] In 1994, tropical and subtropical nations exported only 1.4 and 8.2 percent of their total and industrial roundwood production, respectively; net exports were even lower (1.2 and 7.0 percent, respectively).[32] Between 1980 and 1990, 4.2 and 0.6 percent of the losses of closed and open tropical forests, respectively, could be attributed to agricultural and forest plantations.[33] Although ranching may be a factor in Latin American deforestation, its effects are magnified by poor policies favoring land clearance as a way to assert property ownership.[34]

Finally, losses in forest cover in the developing countries, due to trade in timber, beef, and plantation products with developed countries, are partially offset by global trade in basic food and agricultural products whose net flow, as noted previously, is from developed to developing nations. Trade also reduces the exploitation of marginal lands for growing crops, provided that neither trade nor production are subsidized. If in 1993 there had been no trade in cereals and if each country increased (or reduced) cereal production by an amount equal to its net imports (or exports), then at least an additional 35 Mha more would need to have been harvested worldwide, an area that exceeds the total area of forests in Viet Nam, Cambodia, and Laos.[35] This rough estimate assumes that each country's average cereal yields would be maintained even as new and, possibly, more marginal lands were brought into production. Most of the increases in cropland would have been in the developing nations, whereas the reductions would have been in developed nations.

Because terrestrial species richness generally seems to increase closer to the tropics,[36] the net effect of trade in cereals on global biological diversity is most likely positive; that is, trade helped save habitat and, therefore, conserved biodiversity.[37]

Mortality and Property Loss Due to Storms, Floods, and Other Extreme Weather Events

Long-term data on U.S. fatalities due to tornadoes, floods, lightning, and North Atlantic hurricanes and cyclones hitting the U.S. mainland show that annual deaths due to such events are in general decline (Table 7-1, Figure 7-2).[38] For the most recent 9-year period for which data are available (1989 through 1997) for tornadoes, floods, and hurricanes; 1988 through 1996 for lightning), average annual deaths for these extreme weather events have declined 86.5, 53.5, 97.3, and 46.5 percent since their 9-year averages peaked in 1917–1925, 1969–1977, 1900–1908, and 1959–1967, respectively.

TABLE 7-1 Annual Deaths and Death Rates in the United States* Due to Tornadoes, Floods, Hurricanes,† and Lightning

	Tornados (T)	Floods (F)	Hurricanes	Lightning (L)	T + F + L
Period of record	1916–1997	1903–1997	1900–1997	1959–1996	1959–1996
Annual deaths					
1989–1997 average	45.1	95.0	24.7	NA	
1988–1996 average	41.1	88.2	24.7	64.2	193.6
Maximum 9-yr average	334.3	204.3	925.3	120.0	403.4
(Period for maximum)	(1917–1925)	(1969–1977)	(1900–1908)	(1959–1967)	(1969–1977)
Reduction (from maximum to latest period)	86.5%	53.5%	97.3%	46.5%	52.0%
Annual death rates					
1989–1997 average	0.175	0.369	0.096	NA	NA
1988–1996 average	0.162	0.345	0.097	0.252	0.759
Maximum 9-yr average	3.059	1.265	12.111	0.642	1.917
(Period for maximum)	(1917–1925)	(1913–1921)	(1900–1908)	(1959–1967)	(1969–1977)
Reduction (from maximum to latest period)	94.3%	70.9%	99.2%	60.7%	60.4%

*Nine-year moving averages.
†Includes only Gulf and Atlantic hurricanes landfalling in the mainland United States.

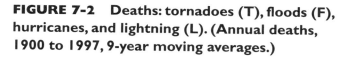

FIGURE 7-2 Deaths: tornadoes (T), floods (F), hurricanes, and lightning (L). (Annual deaths, 1900 to 1997, 9-year moving averages.)

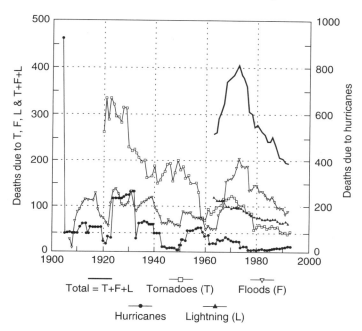

The declines in death rates, perhaps more appropriate indicators because they correct for the increases in risk of fatalities due to the gross increase in population, are even more dramatic. The average annual death rate (measured as deaths per million population) for the latest 9-year periods are 94.3, 70.9, 99.2, and 60.75 percent below the 1917–1925, 1913–1921, 1900–1908, and 1959–1967 peaks for tornadoes, floods, hurricanes, and lightning, respectively (Table 7-1, Figure 7-3).[39]

Perhaps a portion of the declines in deaths and death rates for hurricanes could be attributed to the reduction in the number and wind speeds of violent Atlantic hurricanes that apparently has occurred since the 1940s.[40] On the other hand, the intensity of heavy and extreme precipitation events apparently has modestly increased for the United States since 1910, which, all else being equal, ought to increase the frequency and intensity of floods and, with that, the risk of fatalities due to floods.[41] The bulk of the decreases in fatalities and death rates in Figures 7-2 and 7-3 are likely due to increased wealth and new technologies that enable people to adapt to any bad weather. Such adaptations include more reliable forecasts, early-warning systems, better evacuation plans, stronger houses

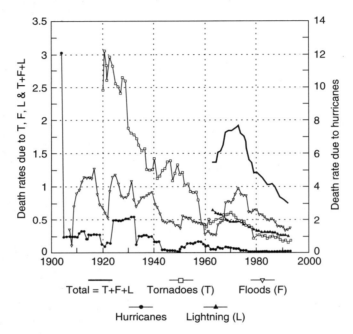

FIGURE 7-3 Death rates: tornados (T), floods (F), hurricanes, and lightning (L). (Annual deaths per million population, 1900 to 1997, 9-year moving averages.)

and infrastructure, a good transportation network, and the constant drumbeat of television and radio weather forecasters once storms show up on their radar screens, all of which have reduced Americans' vulnerability to severe weather.

One might expect that as a society grows wealthier, people may make extra efforts to reduce the loss of life (Figures 7-2 and 7-3), but they might also be relatively less concerned about preventing property losses. Moreover, a wealthier society simply has more property at risk. So, property losses due to extreme weather might increase with increasing wealth even though deaths and death rates may decline. Since the United States has become wealthier over the last century, property losses due to various extreme weather events might be expected to trend upward in time. In addition, one might expect higher property losses because of broader availability (and knowledge) of insurance schemes, and because a richer society is more able to subsidize private losses by compensating victims of extreme events as a token of its increasingly affordable compassion. Finally, as noted, the frequency and intensity of floods in the United States may have increased since 1910.[42]

Between 1903 and 1997, property losses (PL) due to U.S. floods (adjusted to real dollars using the construction cost index) do trend a bit upward, even though there are wide year-to-year fluctuations in PL (Figure 7-4).[43]

However, a better indicator of the amount of property at risk to floods is estimating losses as a percent of the nation's wealth measured as fixed tangible reproducible assets. Using this measure, the overall direction of the trend between 1925 (the first year for which such wealth data are available) and 1997 (Figure 7-4) is flat.[44] Property losses due to hurricanes in terms of real dollars between 1900 and 1997 also trend upward, but—despite the increase in precipitation intensities in the heavy and extreme daily precipitation events—the overall direction of trend is much less clear if losses are measured in terms of percent of wealth (Figure 7-5).[45]

Infectious and Parasitic Diseases

The potential spread of vector-borne diseases in a warmer world has been raised as one of the major reasons for being concerned about anthropogenic climate change. Some fear that vectors such as the anopheles mosquito, the carrier of malaria, could become more widespread with warming.[46] A change in climate could alter the range and abundance of

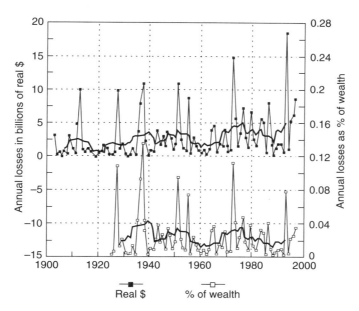

FIGURE 7-4 Property loss from floods, 1903 to 1997. (*Note:* Smoothing based upon 9-year moving average.)

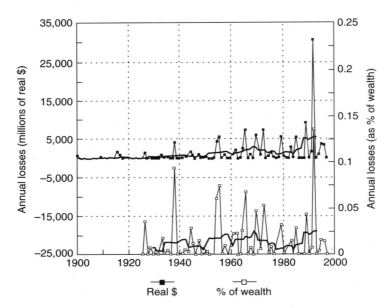

FIGURE 7-5 Property loss: hurricanes, 1900 to 1997. (*Note:* Smoothing based upon 9-year moving average.)

species, but many researchers dispute that global warming would necessarily cause an expansion in the range of all vectors.[47] Today, the prevalence of these diseases has less to do with their potential ranges than with the public health measures taken to deal with the vectors and the diseases they spread. For instance, in the "good old days," malaria, cholera, and other diarrheal and parasitic diseases used to be found around the world, including in the United States and Western Europe (e.g., outbreaks of malaria regularly occurred in New York City and Philadelphia). Today, however, these diseases are found only in countries that cannot afford the necessary public health measures or where those measures have been compromised. In 1900, the cumulative death rate in the United States for typhoid, paratyphoid, various gastrointestinal diseases (gastritis, duodenitis, enteritis, and colitis), and all forms of dysentery was 1860 per million population.[48] (By comparison, the total death rate for the United States in 1996 was 8750 per million.) Today, due to a host of public health measures (such as chlorination of water supplies, sewage treatment, draining of swamps, insect eradication efforts, and mesh screens in windows and doors), deaths due to these diseases barely show up in current statistics.[49] Those statistics show that 7 and 842 deaths in 1996 were due to shigellosis and amebiasis, and "certain other intestinal diseases." In addition, 82 infant deaths were recorded for gastritis, duodenitis, enteritis, and colitis, and 192 for "remainder of diseases of digestive system." Together, these accounted for a death rate of less than 5 per million.

The United States and the developed world are not alone in reducing death rates due to infectious and parasitic diseases, which substantially increased life expectancies. Mainly because of reductions in such diseases, particularly among the young in developing countries, death rates in developing countries dropped from 19.8 per 1000 population in 1950–1955 to 9.3 in 1990–1995 helping to push global life expectancy at birth from 46.4 to 64.7 years.[50] Better nutrition, increased availability of medical and public health technology, and greater investments in public health programs and infrastructure led to the global decline in death rates. Without the wealth generated by economic growth, these improvements would have been impossible. Table 7-2 shows, for a sampling of countries, how various public and environmental health indicators improve with wealth.

Poor sanitation, lack of safe water, and indoor air pollution are among the major causes of higher mortalities and lower life expectancies in developing countries. An estimated 2.9 billion people lack adequate sanitation, and 1.1 billion have no access to safe drinking water in developing countries. These deficiencies are largely responsible for about 2.5 million deaths due to diarrheal diseases (in 1996). According to the World Health Organization, another 3 million premature deaths, mainly in developing countries, were caused by air pollution globally. Nearly 2.8 million deaths were due to indoor air pollution that resulted from cooking and heating with solid fuels (dung, crop residues, wood, and coal) indoors.[51] In addition, malaria, a water-related, vector-borne disease, caused an estimated

TABLE 7-2 Improvement in Public and Environmental Health Status with Wealth

Country	Child Mortality Rate, 1995 (per 1000)	Access to Safe Water, 1994 (% of Population)	Access to Adequate Sanitation, 1994 (% of Population)	Food Supplies per Capita, 1994 (kcal/day)	Life Expectancy at Birth, 1900–1995 (years)	GNP per Capita 1993 (US $)
Sweden	6	100	100	3,239	78.2	24,740
Chile	17	96	71	2,755	73.8	3,170
Philippines	48	84	75	2,393*	66.3	850
Ghana	113	56	42	2,585	56.5	430
Guinea-Bissau	207	57	20	2,443	43.5	240
Afghanistan	251	10	8	1,670*	43.5	<200

*1990–1992 average.

1.5 to 2.7 million deaths in 1996, virtually all of which occurred in the developing countries. There is little evidence that global warming so far is a significant contributor to death and disease around the globe. Some have suggested that warming may be responsible for some of the recent resurgences in diseases such as malaria and dengue in the Americas, and cholera in Peru and Rwanda. However, increases in drug resistance, increased urbanization (which can lead to unsanitary conditions and can facilitate the spread of infectious diseases), and faltering mosquito control and public health measures (e.g., reduction in DDT usage and chlorination) aggravated by poor nutrition are more likely causes.[52]

Accelerated Sea Level Rise

One of the major concerns related to global warming is that it might accelerate the rate at which sea level has been rising for millennia. Preliminary results from the *TOPEX/POSEIDON* satellite observations for 1993 to 1996 are consistent with the historical tide gauge record, which shows mean sea level rising about 18 cm (about 8 inches) over the last 100 years.[53] We do not know what fraction, if any, of that rise might be due to any anthropogenic warming. However, it is important to note that the IPCC's Science Assessment asserts that there is "no detectable acceleration of sea level rise this century . . . nor would any necessarily be expected to from the climate change observed to date."[54] Thus, any sea level rise due to manmade warming has had minimal impacts on human or natural systems compared with other environmental stressors, such as development of coastlines, conversion of lands for aquaculture, drainage for other human land uses, sediment diversion due to dam construction upriver, construction of seawalls, and subsidence owing to water, oil, and gas extraction.[55]

Summary

Nothing so far indicates that current effects of any man-made climate change on the climate-sensitive sectors are close to rivaling the magnitude of effects caused by other environmental changes. Indeed, for some climate-sensitive sectors, matters have markedly improved in spite of whatever climate change that may have occurred. By and large, agricultural productivity and food security are up, relative loss of life due to storms and floods is down in the United States, death rates continue to decline, and life expectancies have increased. Trends with respect to property losses due to floods and hurricanes are much less clear. For those climate-sensitive sectors where matters have continued to worsen (e.g., deforestation, possible loss of biodiversity, and sea level rise), the effect of any climate change so far has, at worst, been very minor. In fact, forests, at least in the northern latitudes, may have become more productive, thereby helping reduce net global loss of forest cover and biodiversity.

Overall, the average person's well-being, continues to improve, and richer countries are better off than poorer ones (Table 7-2), although the world may have warmed a bit. Table 7-2 also suggests that richer countries are less vulnerable to adversity, in general. The richest countries have the highest per capita availability of food, lowest incidences of infectious and parasitic diseases, lowest mortality rates, and the highest life expectancies. Moreover, these countries also use land more efficiently. They have the highest crop yields producing more food per hectare which, in turn, has enabled them to increase forest cover. All this is due mainly to technological progress, driven by science-based economic growth and trade. Such progress has also reduced the vulnerability of the human enterprise to climate change. As a result, technological progress has had a much greater impact on the climate-sensitive sectors (with the exception of sea level rise) than has climate change itself. The experiences of numerous nations in sub-Saharan Africa (where per capita income and per capita food supplies have both declined over the last two decades), and in Eastern Europe and the former Soviet Union (where the aggregate indicators of human well-being worsened along with their economic situation during the last decade), confirm the importance of economic growth and the institutions responsible for nurturing and sustaining such growth. For example, between 1985–1990 and 1990–1995, life expectancies at birth fell from 69.2 to 67.6 years in Russia, and from 71.3 to 69.8 years in Belarus.

In the Next Few Decades

Will man-made climate change likely be the overriding environmental problem facing the globe over the next several decades? For the sake of argument,[56] let's assume that the impact studies reported in the United Nations' Intergovernmental Panel on Climate Change's (IPCC's) 1995 assessment are reasonably accurate, despite numerous reasons for skepticism (see Chapter 2). Despite this willingness to suspend any disbelief regarding the accuracy of models to project the emissions of greenhouse gases a century or more into the future, to transform those emissions into atmospheric concentrations, to translate those concentrations into climatic changes on a fine enough resolution, to convert those changes into biophysical effects, and, finally, to transform those effects into socioeconomic impacts,[57] the IPCC assessments still suffer from systematic biases that tend to overestimate effects.[58] These biases arise partly because these studies do not adequately account for technological progress and adaptation.[59] Numerous postmortems of studies projecting future use of natural resources (including, for instance, the *Limits to Growth* and *Global 2000* reports) have shown that their inability to accurately estimate future environmental impacts a few decades, let alone a few generations, ahead, stems mainly from underestimations of technological change and human responses to social and economic costs associated with the production and use of resources.[60] In fact, the vital importance of technological progress is underscored in the declines of cropland use per capita, deaths, and death rates in Figures 7-1 through 7-3. Yet, another reason for a bias toward overestimation of climate change impacts are that the climate change scenarios used in those studies are often more extreme than the IPCC's "best estimate" scenarios.

Agriculture

One of the major sources of the IPCC's 1995 Impacts Assessment's chapter on agriculture—an EPA- and USAID-sponsored study—estimated that the *baseline* global cereal production (i.e., production in the absence of climate change), would rise 83 percent between 1990 and 2060.[61,62] The baseline assumed a 2060 population of 10.3 billion and a 330 percent economic growth between 1980 and 2060. With climate change, some production would shift from developing to developed nations, increasing the former's food imports and vulnerability to chronic malnutrition and hunger. However, the net change in global production would be relatively modest: The baseline production level would be perturbed from −2.4 to +1.1 percent in 2060 due to an "equivalent doubling of CO_2 concentrations."

The climate change scenarios used by the same EPA/USAID-sponsored study effectively assumed a global warming of 4.0° to 5.2°C in 2060. By comparison, the IPCC estimated a range of 0.7 to 1.7°C (with a best estimate of 1.1 to 1.2°C) in 2060, and 0.8 to 4.5°C in 2100 (with a best estimate of 2.0°C). Nevertheless, despite these huge overestimates, the agricultural and food security impacts due to climate change (−2.4 to +1.1 percent) will be lost in the "noise" due to uncertainties in future levels of population and economic output, either of which could be off by as much as 20 percent by 2060. For instance, the United Nations' 1996 population projections for 2050 is 9.4 billion plus or minus 20 percent.[63] Clearly, at least till the middle of the next century, the effects of climate change on food security will be relatively minor compared with population and economic growth. If we can't feed the world's population in 2060 adequately, it will not be because of climate change, but because of insufficient technological progress and economic growth.[64] Moreover, if the quest for food security leads to massive land conversion, and consequent habitat and biodiversity losses, that, too, will be due to insufficient technological progress, rather than CO_2-enhanced warming.[65]

Forests and Biodiversity

With respect to forest cover, the effects of climate change are likely to be swamped by non-climatic factors already in motion. Poorer countries in the absence of technological improvements would likely convert much of their forests to relatively low-yield agricultural uses to meet increasing food demand, whereas in richer countries agricultural lands will revert to forests as a result of increasing agricultural productivity. One computer model esti-

Both Hurricane Mitch (1998) and Tropical Storm Claudette (1979) released 50 inches of rainfall. Whereas Mitch killed more than 10,000 people in Central America, Claudette killed only 9 people in Texas. The difference in the death tolls is largely due to poverty in Central America. (*Credit:* Christopher Jennings.)

mates that in the absence of any additional human demand for land, climate change alone (but excluding the largely beneficial direct effects of CO_2 on plant growth) could, by 2050, actually increase global forest area by 1 to 9 percent over 1990 levels.[66] A similar model that includes human land use changes *and* direct CO_2 effects estimates global forest cover would decline by 25 percent, including a 47 percent decline in tropical forests and a 10 percent increase in boreal forests.[67] Thus, for the sake of argument, arbitrarily discounting the notion that CO_2-enhanced warming could conceivably be beneficial, even if global warming were to be completely halted, according to the models used in the studies relied on by the IPCC, we might still see massive loss of forests. Changes in land use would far exceed any deforestation due to any warming. Not surprisingly, the IPCC's own assessment states, "Land use change is obviously the greatest threat to species diversity of tropical forests."[68] Once again, we see that over the next few decades, the impacts of climate change will be relatively small compared with the other agents of environmental change.

Climate change could also affect the rate of forest growth. Carbon dioxide–enhanced warming may, in fact, accelerate wood production, though some have suggested that much of the increased growth could fall prey to pests, diseases, and fires.[69] Nevertheless, in more carefully managed forests, it will be possible to harness technology to take advantage of the positive features of CO_2-enhanced warming, while minimizing any negative effects.[70] For instance, one estimate suggests that due to equivalent CO_2 doubling, vegetative carbon could increase 12 to 16 percent owing to climate change alone, and 31 to 37 percent if CO_2 fertilization is also considered.[71] Recent evidence indicates that the Northern latitudes may already have become more productive.[72] Even a 12 percent increase in sustainable yield could reduce the amount of forest land needed to meet human needs for forest products in 2050 by 100 Mha.[73]

Sea Level Rise

According to the IPCC, between 1990 and 2100, sea level may rise between 13 and 94 cm (5 to 37 inches) due to anthropogenic climate change, with a best estimate of 49 cm (19 inches) by 2100, with only about half that occurring by 2060.[74] Notably, the IPCC furnishes a global estimate of about $1 billion per year to protect against a sea level rise of 50 cm by 2100, which translates into less than 0.005 percent of the world's economic product.[75,76]

Public Health

The IPCC suggests that malaria cases may increase 10 to 16 percent by 2100, based on studies that have focused on changes in the potential ranges of anopheles mosquitoes.[77] Public health specialists point out that such prognostications disregard historical fact that disease incidence depends far more on public health measures (or lack thereof), which is determined by a nation's economic status and state of the knowledge regarding the disease, rather than the potential range or by climatic factors.[78] This is exactly why the current geographical distribution of incidences of a number of infectious and parasitic diseases no longer corresponds to their historic potential ranges. The studies underlying the IPCC report also assume essentially no medical progress against these diseases over the next 100 years, which seems quite unlikely, given the experience of the past 100 years and the accelerating rate of the creation of new knowledge in the fields of medicine and the supporting sciences. Nevertheless, let's assume that the 10 to 16 percent estimate is valid, which translates into about 50 to 80 million potential additional cases in 2100, compared with a baseline of 500 million in the absence of climate change. If the additional cases due to climate change increase exponentially with time, that implies a 5 to 8 percent increase by 2060. Further, assuming a similar increase in *all* infectious and parasitic diseases, the public health impact no doubt would be significant because, currently, globally 17 million people, including 1.5 to 2.7 million due to malaria, die prematurely from such diseases each year (over 99 percent of which occur in the developing world).[79] Nevertheless, until at least the middle of the twenty-first century, such an increase would be less than 1/10th of the global base rate in the absence of climate change.

Summary

At least until the middle part of the next century, the contribution of climate change to the cumulative global environmental impacts on the climate-sensitive sectors most affecting human and natural systems will probably be small (Table 7-3). By 2100, only the impact of sea level rise (as estimated by the IPCC's 1995 Assessment) may verge on becoming significant. For the next several decades, other environmental and public health problems plaguing the world will be substantially more urgent than climate change. This conclusion is very robust unless the estimates of the impacts reported in the IPCC are substantially underestimated.

Substantial underestimation of impacts by the IPCC seems unlikely for several reasons. First, the studies underlying the IPCC's Impact Assessment generally do not fully account for human responses to adverse consequences and technological change. Figures 7-1

TABLE 7-3 Impacts of Climate Change Compared with Those Due to Other Global Environmental Problems

Area/Sector	Year	Baseline, Includes Impacts of Other Environmental Problems but Not of Climate Change	Impacts of Climate Change, on Top of the Baseline
Agricultural production	2060 for baseline; >2100 for climate change (see text)	Must increase 83% relative to 1990	Would change net global production by only −2.4 to +1.1%, but could substantially redistribute production from developing to developed countries
Global forest area	2050	Decrease 25 to 30(+)%	Loss of global forest area would be reduced
Malaria incidence	2060	500 million	25 to 40 million additional cases
	2100	500 million	50 to 80 million additional cases
Sea level rise	2060	Varies	less than 25 cm (or 10 in)
	2100	Varies	less than 50 cm (or 20 in)

through 7-3, as well as the current absence of malaria, cholera, and other infectious and parasitic diseases in the developed countries, for instance, show that these responses, although they may be difficult to model in advance of their occurrence, are real and quite substantial, and ignoring them will only inflate estimated negative impacts.[80] In fact, these figures show that adaptations have, so far, more than offset any increases in negative impacts due to any climate change. Second, recent analyses of agricultural and sea level impacts of climate change show that they could be less adverse than reported by the IPCC.[81] Third, for some sectors, the IPCC's underlying impact studies assume, as noted, a greater climatic change than that estimated by the IPCC's Science Assessment (e.g., agriculture). Fourth, empirical data on CO_2 concentrations suggest that carbon fertilization is real and probably already taking place, which, by itself, ought to moderate CO_2 growth rates; increase timber production, at least, in managed forests; and help reduce loss of forest cover.[82-84] Empirical data also indicate that between 1984 and 1996, the growth in atmospheric concentrations of methane, another greenhouse gas, had slowed down by about 75 percent.[85]

Therefore, if climate change is not globally urgent now or in the foreseeable future, is it reasonable to conclude that it is premature to take any actions on climate change now? Probably yes, but let's take a look at some other considerations. First, although the impacts of climate change may be relatively small for a number of decades, this additional stress on top of other environmental stresses may, like the proverbial last straw on the camel's back, prove to be catastrophic for humanity and the rest of nature. Second, this argument focuses only on the net global effects, ignoring the much larger regional impacts that vulnerable poor nations, which have the least ability to adapt to climate change, might experience. Finally, the conclusion may overlook the inertia of the climate system; that is, by the time the adverse effects of climate change become evident, it may be too late to prevent catastrophe.

The Problem of the Last Straw[86]

First, let's take the case of the last straw. Even though CO_2-enhanced warming may not be today, or over the next several decades, the world's overriding environmental problem, perhaps that should not, however, be construed as a prescription for deferring action on climate change. Climate change could be the straw that breaks the camel's back, particularly with respect to forests, ecosystems, and biodiversity.

There are at least two approaches to dealing with the problem of the last straw, neither of which have to be mutually exclusive. The first, more common approach is to concentrate only on reducing the size of, or eliminating altogether, the last straw. In this case, that would be equivalent to minimizing, if not eliminating, climate change. A different approach would be to lighten the entire burden before the last straw descends (i.e., reduce societal and environmental vulnerability by reducing the more urgent environmental and public health problems that might be intensified by climate change before the latter's impacts become significant).[87] This second approach is tantamount to reducing the cumulative environmental impacts by dealing with the whole rather than merely the part—and that, in the case of climate change, a relatively small part. Such an approach effectively enhances the ability of human and natural systems to adapt and cope with climate change *and* other environmental stressors. With respect to malaria, for instance, under the first approach—focusing on the last straw—one would attempt to eliminate the 50 to 80 million new cases in 2100 by totally eliminating climate change. Under the second approach, one could try to reduce the total number of cases, whether it is 500 million this year or 550 to 580 million in 2100 through mosquito control, the development of vaccines, and so forth.

With regard to malaria, there are numerous advantages to the latter approach (i.e., enhancing adaptability, thus reducing vulnerability). First, even a small reduction in the baseline rate could provide greater aggregate benefits, at least in terms of public health, than a large reduction in the additional number of cases due to climate change. In fact, assuming an exponential growth in the relative number of additional malaria cases due to climate change, if the number of baseline malaria cases were reduced an additional 0.2 percent per year between now and 2100, that would more than compensate for any increases due to any hypothesized climate change. Second, resources employed to reduce the base rate would provide substantial benefits to humanity decades before any significant benefits are realized from limiting climate change. Moreover, the benefits of reducing the base rate are much more certain than those related to limiting climate change. Fourth, the lessons learnt, technologies developed, and public health measures implemented to reduce the base rate of malaria cases would themselves serve to limit additional cases due to climate change when, and if, they occur. In addition, reducing the base rate would serve as an insurance policy against adverse impacts of climate change, whether that change is due to anthropogenic or natural causes, or if it comes more rapidly than the IPCC's "best estimates." In effect, by reducing the base rate of malaria today, one would also be solving the cumulative malaria problem of tomorrow, whatever its cause.

Sixth, due to the inertia of the climate system, it is unrealistic to think that future climate change could be completely eliminated even if greenhouse gas (GHG) emissions were to be frozen immediately at today's level—a most unlikely occurrence. Consider, for instance, that a greater-than-50-percent emission reduction (beyond 1990 levels) is required to stabilize atmospheric CO_2 concentrations at 450 ppmv, about 25 percent above current levels.[88] However, as the recent Kyoto conference indicates, such reductions would be phased in over several decades, if at all. Thus, the first approach—lightening the last straw—can, at best, only be partially successful, and that, too, for only a small portion of the malaria problem.

Finally, the stated objective of the Framework Convention on Climate Change is to "prevent dangerous anthropogenic interference with the climate system" (i.e., limit GHG concentrations so that climate change does not become "dangerous"). However that term may be defined, what is "dangerous" depends on societal and environmental adaptability. Analogous to lightening the burden on the camel's back to make room for not just that "last" straw but several more straws, enhancing adaptation would increase the level at which GHG concentrations become dangerous, potentially resulting in substantial savings in the cost of controls. In fact, although adaptation is not cost-free, there can be no optimal strategy for addressing climate change that ignores adaptation.[89]

The same logic applies to the other climate-sensitive sectors where the problems now and in the foreseeable future are caused largely by nonclimate change-related factors. As Table 7-3 indicates, these sectors include agricultural production, food security, forest cover, ecosystems, and biodiversity.

Climate Change Impacts on Developing Nations and Regions

A second criticism of the conclusion that climate change is not the globe's most urgent environmental problem is that its underlying rationale places too much emphasis on *net global impacts*, ignoring the possibility of severe dislocations that may occur in specific areas because of climate change. As noted above, currently most developing nations have food deficits. This imbalance may worsen in the future if economic growth in developing nations falls behind population growth. Assuming the worst, their situation would deteriorate even further if climate changes. Therefore, climate change could impose a disproportionately large burden on developing nations, which have the least ability to adapt to the adverse impacts of climate change.

Indeed, relative to developed nations, developing nations' adaptability is low. However, the fundamental problem is not climate change itself, but a lack of effective institutions (including free markets, secure property rights, and honest and predictable bureaucracies and governments), which hinders economic growth and the development, acquisition, and implementation of technologies to adapt to or cope with any hardship or misfortune. Just as someone suffering from AIDS is less immune to an infectious disease, so is a poorer society less immune to adversity, no matter what its proximate cause (see Table 7-1). Thus, developing better institutions to foster economic growth, particularly in the poorer nations, will increase their resiliency and boost their ability to cope with adversity in general, including those due to climate change.[90]

Today, developing countries import food from developed countries and, clearly, expansion of this trade would help developing countries cope with any additional shortfalls in food (whether or not the shortfalls are due to climate change). In fact, any regional effect, whether caused by climate change or another agent of global change, can be, at least partly, mitigated through international trade. However, such trade is only possible if developing countries' economies produce and sell other goods, which then can generate the revenues to purchase food grown elsewhere.

Developing countries also need to boost their economic growth rates to afford new technologies and the inputs to increase their agricultural production and productivity. Developing countries will need about $166 billion by 2010 for agriculture-related investments for pre- and postproduction operations and rural infrastructure.[91] Some 25 percent of those funds should come, according to the FAO, from the richer nations and international aid sources. By 2050, developing countries may need as much as $250 billion annually.[92] However, developing nations cannot—and should not—count on obtaining more than an insignificant fraction of these sums through overseas development aid. Such aid for agriculture declined almost 50 percent between 1986 and 1994 to $10 billion. Investments of the magnitudes needed in the future can only be generated if developing countries improve their institutions to enable free markets, protect private property rights, ensure honest bureaucracies, and enable freer movement of capital so that they can attract the necessary investment from abroad. In fact, private capital flows from developed to developing nations quintupled from 1990 to 1996 to $244 billion, although official aid (for all sectors) declined over 25 percent to $41 billion.[93]

Third, all else being equal, economic growth increases the likelihood of establishing (or extending) safety nets for the poorest in society who are the least able to afford adequate food and nutrition. Increased food availability and better nutrition would reduce the severity of infectious and parasitic diseases, whether they are climate-sensitive or not. In addition, more vigorous economic growth would help developing nations better afford public health measures (such as immunization and better sanitation) to combat such diseases, which are diseases of poverty.[94] Sixth, economic growth helps create and maintain conditions conducive to reducing developing nations' population growth rate. Seventh, economic growth will enhance their ability to afford technologies to limit climate change, such as more efficient power plants, particularly those which entail a higher initial cost. Finally, noting that economic growth has generally helped reduce a nation's economic dependence on its climate-sensitive natural resource sectors (i.e., agriculture and forestry), such growth could help reduce developing nations' economic vulnerability to climate change. (In 1996, 55 percent of the developing world's population was engaged in agriculture, compared with 22 percent in the transition countries, and 5 percent in the rest of the developed world.[95])

Longer-Term Perspective

Although climate change may not be an urgent problem over the next several decades, some may still argue that because of the inertia of the climate system, it may be too late to do much about it by the time it becomes urgent, unless we act now. Therefore, from a longer-term perspective, climate change is an urgent problem now. First, even the analyses based on IPCC's 1995 Assessment, and coupled with the analyses of greenhouse gas control proponents like Wigley, and Ha-Duong, Grubb, and Hourcade,[97] suggest that even with a 50-year lag between initiation of climate change controls to comply with specified targets and final adherence to those targets, humanity can wait 2 (or more) decades until initiation of control efforts without the impacts of climate change becoming excessive, particularly in comparison with those of other environmental stressors.[96,97] In the meantime, the overall benefit obtained from reducing vulnerability not only to climate change but to other environmental stressors through bolstering economic growth, technological change, and trade will be greater.

Second, one cannot get to the long term without getting through the short and medium terms. Consider the interrelated problems of agriculture, food security, forest cover, and biodiversity. Even if climate change were halted completely, by 2050 more than 25 percent of the world's forest area could be lost (Table 7-2). Not only would this affect biodiversity, it would add to CO_2 emissions by reducing carbon stores and removing sinks. In fact, the world would be undergoing the very same catastrophe that the control of climate change hopes to avoid. The issue, therefore, is how to deal with the urgent problems of today and tomorrow without impairing our ability to deal with the problems of the day after tomorrow—which drastically cutting emissions could compromise.

To address the problems of deforestation and loss of biodiversity, one ought to attack their major cause—the conversion of land and water to satisfy the demands of a larger and wealthier population for food, fiber, and timber.[98] Neo-Malthusian analysts contend that it is, therefore, necessary to decrease demand by reducing populations and/or modifying dietary and consumption habits.[99] This is much easier said than done. In a democratic society, where families are free to choose their own sizes and individuals their diets and consumption patterns (as constrained by the market), it is doubtful whether such recommendations can have a significant impact because they ignore human nature.[100] An alternative approach—and one more likely to succeed because it accepts and tries not to change human nature—would be to increase the productivity of land and water to produce more food, timber, and other products per acre of land or gallon of water diverted to human use.[101] This would limit conversion of these natural resources to human use while meeting human demands adequately.

FIGURE 7-6 Trade-off between productivity growth and habitat loss—net conversion of land to cropland from 1993 to 2050. (Assumptions: (1) 2050 population is 9.6 billion; (2) cereal supplies per capita increase at the 1969/71 to 1989/91 rate.)

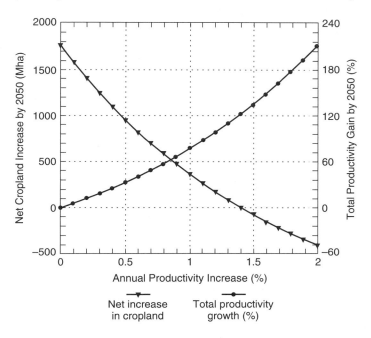

Source: Goklany (1998).

Figure 7-6 indicates how much additional land would have to be converted to cropland between 1993 and 2050 as a function of increases in the productivity of the food and agricultural sector.[102] It assumes that the global population will be 9.6 billion (which may be too high), consistent with the World Bank's 1994 "medium" projection, that food supplies per capita would increase at the historical 1969–1971 to 1989–1991 rate, and that new cropland will, on average, be just as productive as cropland in 1993 (an optimistic assumption). Figure 7-6 shows that if productivity does not increase, cropland would have to increase by 1750 Mha. Much of this would necessarily have to come from forested areas.[103] On the other hand, a 1 percent per year increase in productivity would reduce additional (net) cropland requirements to 370 Mha, whereas a productivity increase of 1.5 percent per year would result in a net reversion of 80 Mha of cropland to forests or other uses. In fact, such increases in productivity are not unprecedented, given that between 1961–1963 and 1995–1997, agricultural productivity has increased at a rate of over 2.3 percent per year.[104] More important, there are numerous existing-but-unused opportunities to enhance productivity in an environmentally sound manner—unused, in large part due, directly or indirectly, to the lack of sufficient economic resources.[105] In addition, current average yields, while increasing, are still substantially behind what is possible, and technological change has yet to run its course.

To boost technological progress to meet global food needs while also limiting habitat conversion, economic growth is essential to generate the investments needed for researching, developing, and purchasing improved and more efficient technologies. Research and development into productivity-enhancement measures for conditions that exist today, but either would persist or become more prevalent due to climate change, would advance global food security regardless of climate change. Accordingly, R&D could emphasize developing and improving seeds and crops for dry and saline conditions, methods to mitigate soil erosion, technologies to reduce pre- and postharvest and end-use wastage and spoilage, and technologies and economic instruments to use or reuse water more efficiently. Investments will also be needed for technology transfer and for additional infrastructure needed for food production and distribution.[106]

The resulting decrease in forest conversion due to enhanced food productivity would also reduce projected atmospheric CO_2 concentrations, as well as reduce habitat loss and fragmentation, which would otherwise create barriers to the "natural" adaptation (via migration and dispersion) of species if climate changes. Notably, Article II of the Framework Convention on Climate Change regarding its stated "ultimate objective" to stabilize atmospheric GHG concentrations "at a level that would prevent dangerous anthropogenic interference with the climate system" refers to, among other things, allowing "ecosystems to adapt *naturally* to climate change" (emphasis mine). Finally, increased agricultural productivity would lower the demand for cropland, which would reduce land prices, thereby decreasing the costs of purchasing or reserving land for conservation, carbon sequestration, or both.

Similarly, sustainably increasing the effective amount of forest products produced per acre of intensively managed forests would reduce the amount of forestlands diverted to intensive human use. In effect, forest plantations would also help conserve habitat and biodiversity, and make land for conservation and carbon sequestration more affordable. Productivity of forests will likely be increased through boosting R&D on faster-growing tree species, decreasing wastage from felled trees, extending the useful life of timber and wood products, combatting pests and diseases, improving extension services to transfer technology, and using inputs like fertilizers more carefully to increase growth rates without undue environmental effects.[107]

Conclusion: Dealing with the Urgent Without Ignoring the Serious

Over the last century or more, according to the IPCC, the globe has warmed between 0.3 and 0.6°C, and some of that warming is perhaps due to humanity's influence. During that period, certain climate-sensitive biophysical indicators—forest cover, biodiversity, and sea level—deteriorated. So far, however, anthropogenic warming has had very little to do with that. On the other hand, for other climate-sensitive sectors and indicators, matters have improved substantially. Land is more productive (Figure 7-1); the average person is better fed; infectious and parasitic diseases are no longer prevalent in many areas where they once were endemic; infant and child mortality are down; life expectancies are up; and even though property losses (relative to wealth) due to various extreme weather-related events may or may not be increasing (Figures 7-4 and 7-5), more significantly, deaths and death rates due to such phenomena have declined (Figures 7-2 and 7-3). Although some of the increased productivity of agriculture could be due to CO_2-enhanced global warming, the lion's share of these improvements is due to technological progress driven by the mutually reinforcing forces of economic growth (or wealth), technology, and trade. Wealth alone can explain much of the variability in the vulnerability of societies to environmental and natural stresses: Just as a person afflicted with AIDS is less immune to infectious diseases, so is a poorer society more susceptible to such stresses (Table 7-2).

With respect to the future, based on the IPCC's 1995 Impact Assessment, over the next several decades, with the possible exception of sea level, which may rise about 10 inches or so by 2060, the environmental and health impacts of climate change are projected to be smaller than the impacts due to other environmental stressors by an order of magnitude or more (Table 7-3). Thus, although warming might be a serious problem in the long run, it is not now or in the foreseeable future, on the world's list of urgent environmental or health problems. Just as lightening the burden on a camel's back creates more room for additional straws to be added, so would reducing the impacts due to the more urgent problems reduce human and natural systems' vulnerability to climate change in the long (and short) run. Reducing vulnerability to the urgent environmental problems will also augment human and natural systems' resilience and ability to adapt to and cope with climate change.

There are yet other reasons for reducing vulnerability (or enhancing adaptability) to climate change. First, like it or not, because of the inertia of the climate system, some climate change is unavoidable. Under the Kyoto agreement, for example, whatever temperature *increase* that is projected for 2100 will be reduced by less than 10 percent.[108] Thus, even if there is agreement to eventually stabilize GHG concentrations, any negative impacts might persist long after emission reductions commence. In the meantime, the world will have to adapt to, and cope with, whatever the consequences of climate change might be. However, although adaptation is inevitable, doing it well is not, and—if proponents of controlling climate change are right—given the stakes in the long term, we must adapt well. Second, adaptation and mitigation of climate change are not mutually exclusive. Many adaptation measures will automatically help limit CO_2 emissions. Moreover, successful adaptation will raise the thresholds at which greenhouse gas concentrations become "dangerous."[109] This would reduce the cost of controls. Therefore, there can be no optimal strategy for addressing climate change that ignores adaptation.

Human and natural vulnerability to climate change would be reduced by strengthening the forces of economic growth, technology, and trade. Each of these mutually reinforcing activities are sustained by many of the same underlying institutions (namely, free markets, secure property rights, honest and predictable bureaucracies and governments). These institutions are also the foundations for a strong civil society. Strengthening these institutions is, therefore, a must. This is particularly true for the poorer countries. They are the ones most vulnerable to climate change, not because their climate is likely to change the most, but because they lack the wealth to buy technologies to cushion them from the adverse effects of any climate change. Their greater vulnerability to any possible warming is merely a symptom of a deeper disease—poverty. Stimulating economic growth would boost their immunity to all types of stressors, including climate change; stimulating technology would help reduce the amount of land, water, and other resources diverted to meet human needs for food (Figure 7-6), clothing, shelter, and other material goods—the key to conserving habitat, biodiversity, and carbon stores and sinks while limiting effluents. Stimulating trade would help the world cope with geographically nonuniform effects and outcomes, whether they are due to climate change or other factors.[110]

Economic growth would also make it easier for societies to better afford not just adaptation, but also limitation, technologies to deal with climate change and the other environmental and public health problems which, over the next several decades, are likely to be more urgent.

A more direct approach to adaptation would be to develop and implement technologies to address those environmental and societal problems which would be further aggravated by climate change. However, the success of the direct approach will ultimately also hinge on that of the indirect approach, partly because economic growth generates the resources needed to develop, obtain, and implement new and more efficient technologies (regardless of sector), and because improvements in technology depend as much, if not more, on developing and nurturing institutions conducive to the creation, development, and dissemination of technology. Harkening back to the AIDS analogy, the direct approach would be tantamount to attempting to protect an HIV-infected individual from future exposure to a particular strain of *E. coli*, whereas the indirect approach is equivalent to ridding one of HIV altogether.

Clearly, augmenting adaptability and thereby reducing vulnerability to climate change through science-based increases in the productivity of the food and forestry sectors and improvements in public health, and the strengthening of the institutions responsible for economic growth, technological change, and international trade would be as close to a perfect "no-regrets" strategy as can be devised. Many of these actions would result in net benefits to society and the environment whether climate changes or not, regardless of the rate and magnitude of change, and whether or not the change is due to man-made or natural causes. Nevertheless, adaptation continues to get shortchanged in the climate change policy debate and in its access to resources for research and programs. For instance, the IPCC report on "Impacts, Adaptations, and Mitigation" devoted only 32 out of its 878 pages to adaptation,[111] and in Fiscal Year 1997, the U.S. Global Change Research Program allocated only $4 million of its $1810 million to the U.S. Department of Health and Human Services for health-related research. Perhaps more revealing of our misplaced global priorities is that, despite its massive global death toll (between 1.5 and 2.7 million deaths per year), as of 1997, only $170 million (or less) was spent annually on malaria research worldwide, of which the U.S. government spent about $25 million.[112] Yet, if the number of malaria cases were reduced an additional 0.2 percent per year between now and 2100, that would more than compensate for any increases due to climate change—and if sufficient emphasis is placed on eradicating malaria, the potential increase in the ranges of malaria-bearing mosquitoes due to climate change could become moot.[113]

Finally, focusing on limiting climate change, but not according the more urgent environmental and health problems their due, is tantamount to intercepting the last straw while allowing the rest of the burden to bend, if not break, the camel's back.[114] If research and policy priorities do not stress the urgent, and if the IPCC's impact assessment is even qualitatively credible, then all the problems that we hope to avoid by limiting climate change may well be visited on us even if further anthropogenic climate change is halted. Eliminating climate change would do little or nothing, for instance, to reduce conversion of land and water to human uses—the major, imminent threat to global forests, ecosystems, biodiversity, and loss of carbon sinks and stores—or the rates of infectious and parasitic diseases. This suggests that, at least for the next several decades, resources devoted to limiting climate change might be better used to address today's urgent environmental and public health problems. However, we do not have to choose one over the other, because decreasing the vulnerability to existing and emerging problems that could be further exacerbated by climate change would increase adaptability and help address both the urgent, and the potentially serious, problems facing humanity and the environment.

Chapter 8

ENDOCRINE DISRUPTORS
New Toxic Menace?

Stephen H. Safe

HIGHLIGHTS

- *Recent claims that some synthetic chemicals are behaving like hormones, disrupting the endocrine systems of both animals and humans and thus leading to reproductive and other health problems, are overstated, though more research is needed.*

- *Synthetic environmental endocrine-disrupting compounds tend to be weakly active, and human dietary exposures to them are several thousandfold less than normal intakes of naturally occurring estrogenic compounds in vegetables, fruits, and other foods. For example, the amount of estrogenic compounds found in a single glass of cabernet wine is 1000 times greater than the estimated daily intake of estrogenic organochlorine pesticide residues.*

- *Disruption of endocrine activity by persistent organochlorines has been found to cause some wildlife developmental problems, particularly in highly contaminated environments. Since the 1970s, the reduction in emissions of persistent organochlorines has resulted in substantially lower environmental levels of these compounds in most locations. These reductions have been accompanied by dramatic improvements in the reproductive success of wildlife.*

- *Recent studies on sperm counts indicate that some researchers jumped to too hasty a conclusion when they suggested that "there has been a genuine decline in semen quality over the past 50 years." Researchers have found no correlation between chemical exposures and measures of decreased male reproductive capacity. Demographic differences are more likely to account for the differences seen in the initial studies.*

- *Farm animals are also exposed to synthetic endocrine disruptors. Recent studies show that in sheep, bulls, and boars, no significant changes in sperm counts have been observed since the 1930s. One researcher concluded that "if the fall in human sperm counts is real, then it must be due to something which is not affecting farm animals."*

- *Recent studies on breast cancer patients in Europe, Northern California, the Nurses Health Study, and Mexico, coupled with results of laboratory animal studies, do not support the contention that organochlorine compounds are causes of human breast cancer.*

The public and policymakers have recently become alarmed by recent studies suggesting that certain man-made chemicals may be causing reproductive and developmental problems in wildlife and human beings. These include infertility, low sperm counts, genital deformities, breast and prostate cancers, and neurological disorders such as hyperactivity and attention deficits. Among the chemicals suspected of disrupting normal hormonal processes are organochlorine pesticides, such as DDT and dieldrin; PCBs, which were used as insulators in electric transformers; and dioxins, which are the by-products of certain industrial processes.

The Endocrine System and Endocrine Disruptors

The endocrine system in wildlife species and humans plays a critical role in reproduction and development and maintaining cellular homeostasis. Endocrinology studies the function of endocrine glands, their secretion products, and their biological and physiological effects on various target organs. The hypothalamus in the brain first receives a neural signal to initiate one or more endocrine responses, resulting in secretion of one or more polypeptide hormones that are transported in the blood to selected tissues. These organs subsequently synthesize various hormones such as corticosteroids (adrenal gland), thyroid hormones (thyroid gland), the male sex hormone testosterone (testis), and the female sex hormone 17β-estradiol [E2 (ovaries)] that are secreted and taken up by various target organs. This illustration serves to remind us that the endocrine system is highly complex, involving different hormones and a large number of organs that both produce or synthesize hormones and receive and transmit hormonal signals. For purposes of this chapter, an endocrine disruptor is an exogenous compound that not only can disrupt one or more endocrine response pathways, but also leads to an adverse or harmful effect. This definition is important because the human diet contains high levels of naturally occurring chemicals in fruits, vegetables, and other food products that exhibit hormonelike activity, and there is an increasing number of endocrine-active pharmaceuticals used to treat hormone-dependent diseases such as breast cancer, osteoporosis, and other problems associated with estrogen deficiencies.[1,2]

Endocrine Disruptors—The Wildlife Connection

The discovery of the organochlorine pesticide DDT and its metabolite DDE as residues in wildlife populations in the 1960s raised concerns about the possible effects that these compounds might have on wildlife reproduction. These concerns led to studies that found diverse organochlorine compounds (OCs) almost everywhere in the global ecosystem.[3] Among this group of organochlorine compounds are numerous pesticides, polychlorinated biphenyls (PCBs), 2,3,7,8-tetrachlorodibenzo-*p*-dioxin (TCDD), and related halogenated aromatics (Figure 8-1). Several reports correlated developmental and reproductive problems in wildlife populations to exposure to some of these compounds. These observations were instrumental in the development of the endocrine disruptor hypothesis, which suggests that many of these same chemical compounds may also be affecting human health.[4,5] Zoologist Theo Colborn and coworkers listed these OCs, other fungicides, insecticides, herbicides, and industrial chemicals as endocrine-disrupting environmental contaminants, based on their reproductive or developmental toxicity to laboratory animals or wildlife.[4] Human and laboratory animal experience with diethylstilbestrol (DES) (Figure 8-1), a drug that was used between 1940 and 1970 to prevent spontaneous abortions during pregnancy, lent additional support to the endocrine disruptor hypothesis. Diethylstilbestrol is a potent estrogenic compound that was administered to women during a period in which the fetus is highly susceptible to small changes in sex hormone concentrations.[6] Children of DES mothers have experienced a higher incidence of reproductive tract problems, including increased malformed genitalia in men and an increased occurrence of a rare form of vaginal adenocarcinoma in women. These observations with DES also suggest that fetal/early postnatal exposures to synthetic estrogenic compounds (xenoestrogens) and other endocrine-active chemicals during "critical" periods of development may lead to permanent damage in the offspring. However, it should also be noted that DES is not only a potent estrogen, but it was administered at relatively high doses ranging from 5 to 150 mg per day during late pregnancy. In contrast, synthetic environmental endocrine-disrupting compounds tend to be weakly active, and dietary exposures to organochlorine xenoestrogens in the diet are approximately 2.5 micrograms per day

FIGURE 8-1 Structures of organochlorine environmental contaminants including 2,3,7,8-TCDD, PCBs, and DDE, and two estrogenic compounds (DES and nonylphenol).

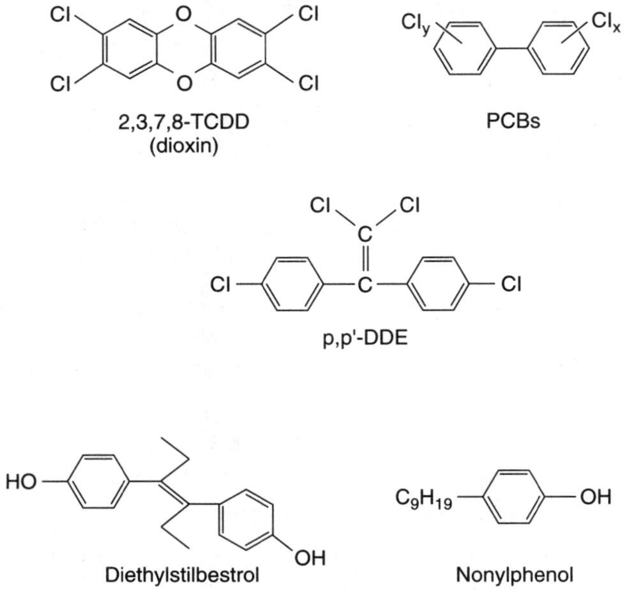

(μg/day). This is several thousandfold lower than DES dosages, as well as several thousandfold less than normal intakes of naturally occurring estrogenic compounds in vegetables, fruits, and other foods.

Numerous wildlife studies, particularly those around the lower Great Lakes where relatively high levels of organochlorine contaminants have been identified in wildlife populations, support the endocrine disruption hypothesis. Because wildlife are exposed to highly complex chemical mixtures, it can be difficult to assign causality to individual chemicals; nevertheless, there is good evidence that reproductive problems in some Great Lakes fish and birds are associated with exposures to TCDD (dioxin) and related OCs that induce their toxic responses through binding the aryl hydrocarbon receptor (AhR or dioxin receptor).[7] Receptors such as the dioxin receptor and estrogen receptor are widely expressed in most tissues, and these receptors can bind the body's own hormones such as estrogens, other naturally endocrine-active chemicals in food and some man-made compounds. It is highly unlikely that trace levels of endocrine disruptors in the human diet would affect the normal action of receptors.

A number of earlier problems with birds correlated with their high exposures to DDT/DDE, which caused eggshell thinning and may not be directly linked to endocrine disruption but to inhibition of calcium-dependent ATPase activity in the eggshell gland.[8] However, recent studies indicate that DDE is also an antiandrogen, and *in utero*/early postnatal exposure to this compound can affect important male sex hormone (testosterone)-dependent responses.[9] Field and laboratory animal studies with alligators suggest that DDE may contribute to male alligator reproductive problems, including decreased penis size in alligators in Lake Apopka, Florida.[10] This lake was contaminated by a spill of sulfuric acid and OC pesticides including DDT and dicofol from the Tower Chemical Company, located in the southwest corner of the lake, and by sewage effluent and runoff from agricultural chemicals.

Thus, disruption of endocrine activity by persistent organochlorines has been found to be the cause of some wildlife developmental problems, particularly in highly contaminated environments. In the 1970s, regulatory agencies in most industrialized countries banned the use of DDT and PCBs, which has resulted in substantially decreased emissions of synthetic and combustion-derived OCs (e.g., dioxin-like compounds). Although pollution hot spots and long-range transport of these chemicals are still a problem, Neil Tremblay and Andrew Gilman from the Canadian Environmental Health Directorate recently reported that "While there is dissention over the adequacy of the rate at which contaminant levels in Great Lakes sediments and biota are declining, it is certain that levels of all 11 critical pollutants have dropped significantly since the 1970s, some by over 90%."[11] Moreover, they also state that as contaminant levels have decreased, there have been

People eat thousands of times more natural estrogenic compounds found in fruits and vegetables than they do synthetic ones. (Credits: Peter Cazamias, CEI.)

"dramatic improvements in reproductive success and significant increases in the populations of cormorants, gulls, terns, herons, and other predatory birds in the Great Lakes basin. Even the bald eagle has returned to nest in the lower Lakes."

Based on the DES model, "critical-period" exposure to estrogenic compounds has been an important component of the endocrine disruptor hypothesis; however, many of the reproductive effects of OCs on wildlife populations may not be related to their estrogenic activity. For example, Sumpter and coworkers in Great Britain identified a dramatic estrogenic response in wildlife.[12] They observed that levels of the estrogen-responsive yolk protein, vitellogenin, were highly elevated in male fish taken from British rivers. Initial studies near sewage outfalls implicated a detergent ingredient, nonylphenol and its breakdown products, as a source of synthetic environmental estrogens found in fish from rivers in the United Kingdom. However, more extensive field and analytical surveys of various rivers in Great Britain have now shown that a major source of estrogenic compounds in these rivers comes primarily from the natural human urinary estrogenic metabolites, estradiol and estrone, and ethinylestradiol, the active component in some birth control pills.

Thus, although it is true that endocrine-disruptive chemicals can affect reproduction and development of various wildlife species, the reduction of synthetic chemical emissions in recent decades has resulted in substantially lower environmental levels of organochlorine compounds in most locations. These have been accompanied by dramatic improvements in the reproductive success of wildlife in the Great Lakes area.[7,11]

Endocrine Disruptors and Decreased Male Reproductive Capacity

In 1992, Elizabeth Carlsen and her coworkers at the University of Copenhagen reported results of their meta-analysis of 61 selected studies of sperm counts from 14,947 men who had no history of infertility.[13] Their analysis found that mean sperm counts had decreased from 113×10^6 in 1940 to 66×10^6/mL in 1990, and seminal volume had also decreased from 3.40 to 2.75 mL. They concluded that "Such remarkable changes in semen quality and the occurrence of genitourinary abnormalities over a relatively short period is more probably due to environmental rather than genetic factors." Subsequently, Sharpe and Skakkebaek suggested that "the incidence of reproductive abnormalities in the human male may be related to increased estrogen exposure *in utero*."[14] They also suggested that "dioxin-like" compounds and DDE (an antiandrogen) may also contribute to decreased male reproductive capacity.[14,15] These reports, when linked to wildlife data (including decreased alligator penis size), provided the impetus for a host of articles in the popular press, a book entitled *Our Stolen Future*, and television programs and congressional testimony in which it was intimated that "we're half the men our fathers were."

Recent reanalyses of the original Carlsen paper has provided both support and criticism of their results and conclusions.[16–20] More important, this paper sparked a number of new studies that focused on temporal changes in sperm counts in patients from clinics in North America, Australia, and Europe.[21–31] Studies from clinics in Paris, Belgium, Athens, Scotland, and Italy reported significant declines in sperm counts during the past 15 to 25 years. For example, analysis of semen quality in Scottish men by year of birth showed that total number of sperm, sperm concentration, and total number of motile sperm were lower in men born after 1970 compared with men born before 1959.[24] Individuals in this study were volunteer sperm donors for a gamete biology research program and, unlike many other studies, these individuals were not semen bank donors, infertility patients, or candidates for vasectomy.

Other studies in Toulouse, the United States, Finland, Sydney, and Denmark have shown that sperm counts have not decreased during the last 15 to 25 years. For example, sperm concentrations were unchanged from 1977 to 1992 in 302 sperm donors in a clinic in Toulouse (Figure 8-2).[27] These results were surprising in light of an earlier report showing sperm counts in 1352 fertile men in Paris "decreased by 2.1% per year from 80×10^6/mL in 1973 to 50×10^6/mL in 1992 ($p < 0.001$)."[22] Results from the French studies were among the first to show that sperm counts within the same country may be highly variable and that demographic differences may be an important variable that was not considered in the original meta-analysis.

Columbia University fertility specialist Harry Fisch and coworkers reported on 1283 men who banked sperm prior to vasectomy in clinics located in New York, California, and Minnesota.[29] Their results (Figure 8-2) showed that sperm quality had not significantly changed from 1970 through 1994 at any of the clinics; however, there were significant differences in mean sperm counts in New York (131.5 ;ci 3.5×10^6/mL), Minnesota (100.8 ;ci 2.9×10^6/mL), and California (72.7 ;ci 3.1×10^6/mL). Three recent studies have confirmed that demography is an important variable in semen quality.[32–35] For example, among Danish infertility clients at centers in Aalborg, Aarhus, Odense, and Sinderborg, there were differences in mean sperm count values between centers; however, semen quality and

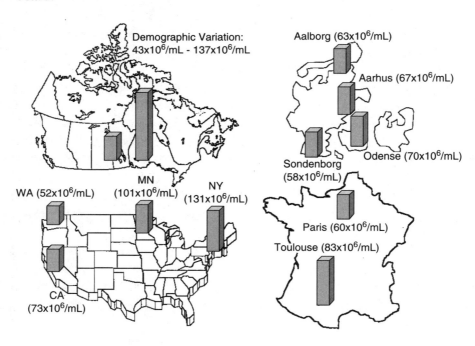

FIGURE 8-2 Demographic variability of sperm counts. The results illustrate sperm count variability in France (Toulouse and Paris), Denmark, the United States, and Canada.[22,27–29,33,35] Only differences in mean values within each country are illustrated to scale.

quantity had not declined during the period from 1922 to 1972 (by birth), whereas from 1950 onward, there was a decline in sperm counts but not in semen volume. A study of infertility clients from 11 centers in Canada showed that sperm count differences between centers in 1984 (51 to 121 × 10^6/mL) and 1996 (43 to 137 × 10^6/mL) were greater than mean value differences in sperm concentrations in the meta-analysis by Carlsen and coworkers.[13,35] Over the 1984 to 1996 period, sperm counts decreased in 6 and increased in 5 of the centers, and analysis of the combined results showed that sperm counts decreased slightly over the 13-year period, whereas no changes were observed if results from 1975 to 1983 were included. Geographic variability was also observed among 4710 fertile semen donors in the following cities in France: Paris, Caen, Grenoble, Toulouse, Bordeaux, Lille, Rennes, and Tours.[32] Sperm concentration varied from 103 (Lille) to 82 × 10^6/mL (Grenoble); sperm motility varied from 69 percent (Bordeaux) to 59 percent (Tours); and seminal volume varied from 4.3 (Caen) to 3.2 mL (Toulouse and Rennes). Handelsman also reported an additional variable that emerged after analysis of sperm counts from 5 different groups of self-selected volunteers at the Andrology Unit, Royal Prince Albert in Sydney, Australia.[31] The variability in sperm counts was greater than 100 percent (142 × 10^6/mL to 63 × 10^6/mL), and he concluded that "This highlights the invalidity of extrapolating similar finding on sperm output of self-selected volunteers to the general male community or in using such study groups to characterize sperm output in supposedly 'normal' men."

Results obtained from recent studies on sperm counts indicate that researchers jumped to too hasty a conclusion when they suggested that "there has been a genuine decline in semen quality over the past 50 years."[13] It seems that the problem of evaluating temporal trends in sperm counts is more complicated than anticipated. The large demographic differences within countries mean that a meta-analysis that does not carefully account for these differences is invalid.[20] Moreover, if demographic differences are observed in "normal" (i.e., randomly sampled) populations, then it is highly unlikely that persistent OC contaminants play an important role in affecting sperm counts, because levels of these compounds in humans and foods are relatively similar in most developed countries. For example, Ekbom and coworkers examined the relationship between DDE levels and the incidence of testicular cancer in Scandinavia.[36] The incidence of testicular cancer has been increasing in Scandinavia and most other countries; moreover, in 20- to 24-year-old men in Denmark, Norway, Sweden, and Finland, the incidence was 14.5, 12.6, 8.1, and 3.6 per 100,000, respectively (1985 to 1989), indicating that the incidence in Denmark was almost four times higher than in Finland. However, it was also reported that since the late 1960s, breast milk DDE levels have been similar in all Scandinavian countries and, over the past 20 to 25 years, levels have decreased by more than 80 percent in all four countries. Thus, differences in testicular cancer rates in Scandinavia are not correlated with differences in breast milk DDE levels. Ekbom and coworkers stated "Furthermore, the alleged increase in cryptorchidism, hypospadias, and other urogenital malformations cannot be linked to p,pN-DDE since the concentrations have decreased during the past 20 years."[36] Similar inverse correlations between DDE levels and prostate cancer incidence in the United States have also been reported.[37] Thus, it is unclear if sperm counts in the general population have, in fact, changed. Also, researchers have found no correlation between chemical exposures and measures of decreased male reproductive capacity. These conclusions have been bolstered by a recent report by the U.S. National Academy of Sciences' National Research Council.[38] Testicular cancer is increasing in most countries; however, the highly variable incidence between similar countries suggests that new hypotheses that include multiple variables (diet, smoking, alcohol, genetics, chemicals, etc.) must be examined to delineate factors responsible for this disease.

Endocrine Disruptors and Semen Quality in Domestic Animals

Semen samples from domestic animals have been collected for artificial insemination for several decades, and two recent studies[39,40] investigated temporal changes in sperm concentration potential markers for decreased male reproductive capacity in humans. Data collected from studies published in many countries showed that in sheep, bulls, and boars, no significant changes in sperm counts were observed since the 1930s. Another study in the Netherlands also reported no decline in sperm concentrations in bulls since 1962. Setchell concluded that "if the fall in human sperm counts is real, then it must be due to something which is not affecting farm animals."[39]

Endocrine Disruptors and Breast Cancer

Over 180,000 women in the United States were diagnosed with breast cancer in 1996, and it is estimated that 1 in 9 women will develop this disease in their lifetime. Genetic predisposition accounts for a relatively low percentage of this disease (approximately 5 percent). A woman's lifetime exposure to endogenous estrogens is an important risk factor, and several studies show an increased incidence of breast cancer is associated with earlier age at menarche, late age at menopause, late age of first pregnancy, obesity (age-dependent), and hormonal therapies. The environment (including diet) must also be an important factor in development of breast cancer because there are dramatic geographical differences in incidence of this disease.[41] For example, the incidence of breast cancer in Japanese and Chinese

Recent studies using data from U.S. sperm banks like this one contradict sensational claims that synthetic estrogenic compounds are causing sperm counts to decline. (Credit: CEI. Special thanks to Fairfax Cryobank.)

women (73 per 100,000) is significantly lower than in Caucasian women from the United States (159 per 100,000); however, when women from Asia move to the United States, their incidence of breast cancer increases. Interestingly, there are also significant differences in mortality from breast cancer among Western countries (e.g., England and Wales, 28.4 deaths/100,000 versus Greece, 14.9 deaths/100,000). Clearly, finding the factors that are responsible for country/region-specific differences in breast cancer incidence and mortality will be important for future prevention of this disease.

The specter of environmental contaminants as important causes of breast cancer and other diseases has been an important consideration for many individuals and groups. The geographical differences in breast cancer incidence noted previously do not necessarily correlate with differences in environmental levels and human exposure to persistent OCs, which are similar in most developed countries. Nevertheless, these differences do not exclude a potential role in causing breast cancer for OCs and other chemical contaminants in some areas. Two studies on breast cancer patients in Connecticut (1992) and New York (1993) greatly heightened concern that background environmental exposures to PCBs and DDE may be causes of breast cancer in women.[42,43] Polychlorinated biphenyl levels were higher in breast cancer patients compared with controls (undergoing reductive mammoplasty) in Connecticut and, in a New York study, serum levels of DDE were higher in breast cancer patients versus controls (Figure 8-3). These observations triggered public and scientific concern regarding the role of pesticides and environmental contaminants on development of breast cancer, particularly in the Northeastern part of the country, and it was hypothesized that xenoestrogens (including PCBs and DDE) are preventable causes of breast cancer in women.[44] Because being exposed to her own naturally produced estrogen is known to increase a woman's risk for breast cancer, it has been suggested by some researchers that some man-made estrogenic chemicals may contribute to this response provided there is sufficient exposure. However, this is highly unlikely because the human diet contains relatively low levels of man-made estrogenic chemicals in the diet, whereas much higher levels of naturally occurring estrogenic compounds are present in fruits, nuts, vegetables, dairy, and meat products.[45] For example, a recent study used several bioassays to compare the estrogenic content in a 200-mL glass of red cabernet wine and the estimated daily intake of estrogenic organochlorine pesticide residues. The "estrogenic equivalents" in one glass of wine were approximately 1 µg/day, whereas "estrogenic equivalents" of the organochlorine compounds were greater than 1000 times lower than wine.[46]

Although the reported correlations between PCBs/DDE and breast cancer were initially a cause for concern, evidence from animal and human studies show that the role of these compounds as estrogens or mammary carcinogens was weak.[45,47] The NAS report on hormonally active agents in the environment concluded that recent "studies do not support an association between DDE and PCBs and cancer in humans."[48] Occupational exposure to high levels of DDE or PCBs has not been linked to increased incidence of breast cancer. Laboratory animal studies with DDE show both increased or decreased mammary tumor formation, and it is unlikely that these effects are related to the carcinogenic or estrogenic activity of this compound. In contrast, long-term feeding with higher chlorinated biphenyl mixtures inhibited spontaneous mammary tumor formation in female Sprague-Dawley rats that spontaneously develop both mammary and uterine tumors as they age.[49] Recent studies on breast cancer patients in Europe (5 countries), Northern California, the Nurses Health Study (11 states), and Mexico City have concluded that it is unlikely that PCBs or DDE cause breast cancer in women.[50-53] The results (Figure 8-3) showed that DDE/PCB levels were not significantly different for the nearly 800 breast cancer patients and a similar number of controls in the four studies. It was concluded by Hunter and coworkers that "Our data do not support the hypothesis that exposure to 2,2-bis(*p*-chlorophenyl)1,1,1,-trichloroethane (DDT) and PCBs increases the risk of breast cancer."[50] These reports, coupled with results of laboratory animal studies,

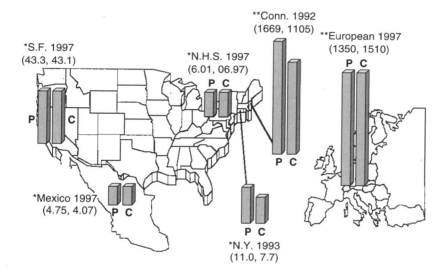

FIGURE 8-3 DDE levels in breast cancer patients and control. Initial studies in New York and Connecticut showed that DDE levels were higher in patients versus controls.[42,43] Subsequent studies in Europe, the United States, and Mexico City showed no significant differences in DDE levels in patients versus controls.[50–53] Only differences in mean values in each study are illustrated to scale. Key: P, patients; C, controls; * serum; ** fat.

do not support the contention that these organochlorine compounds are causes of human breast cancer.

Summary

This chapter has summarized the hypotheses linking synthetic endocrine disruptors with human health problems and the current state of the science in this controversial area. Many scientists (including this author) are skeptical that trace amounts of synthetic chemicals in the environment can adversely impact the human endocrine system because the human diet contains much larger quantities of natural endocrine-active compounds (EACs) that exhibit a broad range of activities. Nevertheless, some scientists remain convinced that serious problems may exist. Resolution of these scientific differences may be difficult because of the inherent problems associated with proving or disproving linkages between exposure to environmental/dietary chemical mixtures with increased/decreased incidence of human health problems. It is reassuring that today's emissions of many contaminants have been significantly reduced, with the result that environmental and human levels of organochlorine compounds have decreased dramatically. Future studies on the role of xenoestrogens and other EACs in human disease will require more information on both levels and timing of exposure, as well as dietary endocrine contributions from foods such as fruits and vegetables that are generally considered to enhance human health.

Chapter 9

BIOLOGICAL DIVERSITY
Divergent Views on Its Status and Diverging Approaches to Its Conservation

Rowan B. Martin

HIGHLIGHTS

- *Estimates of the numbers of species living on Earth range from 3 million to 30 million. Estimates of the number of species recorded so far range from 1.4 million to 1.8 million.*

- *Estimates on the number of species going extinct are very speculative. They range from 1000 species to 100,000 species going extinct annually.*

- *Extinction rates such as 1000 species per year sound dramatic. However, assuming that there are 10 million species, that rate translates to losing 0.01 percent of the species on earth per year or, at linear rates of extrapolation, a loss of 1 percent of the total complement of global species in the next 100 years. That, however, does not sound as alarming. Despite these ominous numbers, there is a paucity of real data to support these assertions.*

- *Nearly 75 percent of known global extinctions in recent times have occurred on islands. Stephen Edwards, Head of World Conservation Union's Sustainable Use Initiative, shows that the frequency of known extinctions from 1900 through 1990 exhibits neither an upward nor a downward trend.*

- *The extent of the loss of species and the consequences for human welfare are difficult to assess. Many biologists have reached the reluctant conclusion that not all species are of equal weight in their impact on ecosystem functions and processes. The evidence so far indicates that much of the utilitarian rhetoric about the potential value of species as yet undescribed and the likely damaging effects of species loss on human prospects for survival are clearly overstatements.*

- *The widely ranging estimates of minimum viable populations of a species that are required to guarantee its survival shows that there are no hard scientific criteria for determining whether any given species is in danger of going extinct.*

- *Defining biological diversity has proven difficult. Some researchers focus on species, others on genetic variability within species and between species, and still others on the relationships between genes, species, and their physical environments.*

- *The species/area curve relationship is derived from the fact that, in most cases, large areas have more species than small areas. This species/area curve relationship is central to the theory of island biogeography, but the parameters used to describe the species/area curve have been shown to be a statistical artifact with no theoretical significance. The balance between immigration and extinction of species on islands is a logical necessity and is a truism rather than a fundamental relationship. Island biogeography wrongly strengthens the common assumption that ecological communities are in equilibrium or in a deterministic progression toward a successional climax.*

- *Theories based on a presumption of "the balance of nature" are no longer accepted by most biologists. Many ecosystems and populations of species undergo rapid change naturally.*

- Western scientists, activists, and agencies favor the creation of reserves in developing nations to preserve biological diversity. However, this strategy is often an unworkable form of "eco-imperialism." Recent studies show that the majority of reserves are failing to conserve biodiversity, are financially unsustainable, and were irrelevant to 95 percent of the people in the countries where they were located.

- An alternative strategy, which has had considerable success, is empowering local people to control the wildlife resources in their area. In many parts of Southern Africa, where full rights of access and control over wildlife have been granted to landholders (of both private and communal land), biodiversity is better conserved in the areas surrounding national parks than in the parks themselves. Additionally, the areas surrounding parks are economically more productive than the state-protected areas.

- In Southern Africa and other parts of the world, conservation of biological diversity would be a profitable activity and not a cost if the correct institutional arrangements were developed, including a stronger reliance on private property and communal tenure systems.

- "Blueprint" measures like the Endangered Species Act (ESA) or the Convention on International Trade in Endangered Species (CITES) have proven to be largely ineffective in protecting and restoring populations of endangered species. Land use restrictions under the ESA and trade bans under CITES, which "force" land owners and national governments to conserve species have the effect of creating conditions in which species become legally valueless. Consequently, many endangered species will likely disappear through a process of attrition and through illegal trade (e.g., the black rhino in Zimbabwe).

The State of Biological Diversity

Considering Species

In most popular accounts, the measure of biological diversity is based on species numbers; therefore, rates of extinction and the listing of endangered species are treated as measures of the trends in biological diversity. The numbers of species presently recorded in the major types of organisms is given in Figure 9-1. The actual number of species that are properly named and recorded is uncertain, and there is no single database that lists them all. The difference between the highest and the lowest estimates is some 400,000 species (29 percent) (see Table 9-1).

The numbers of species in each of the major classes of the vertebrates is shown in Table 9-2. Of the total numbers of species on the globe, the mammals make up about 0.2 percent and the birds about 0.5 percent. However, of all taxonomic groups, the mammals display the greatest diversity, ranging from the pygmy shrew with a body weight of 1.5 grams (g) to the blue whale with a body weight of some 120,000 kilograms (kg). The topic of bio-

FIGURE 9-1 Phylogenetic tree showing the major division of organisms into prokaryotes and eukaryotes.

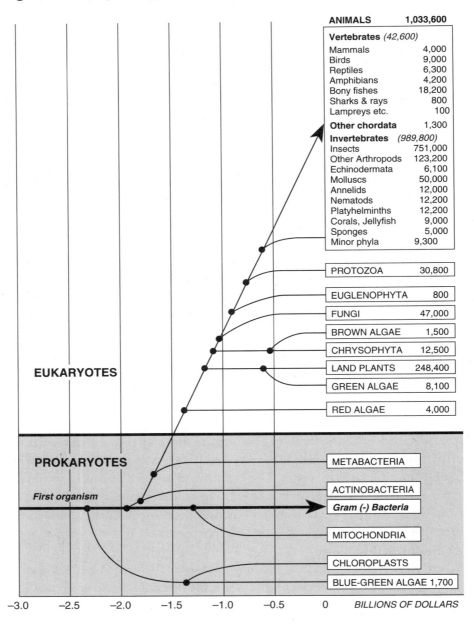

Sources: Phylogenetic tree from Hori[20] and species data from Wilson.[6]

TABLE 9-1 Estimates of the Total Number of Species Recorded

Author	Date	Number (millions)
Grant	1973	1.5
Southwood	1978	1.4
Parker	1982	1.4
Stork	1988	1.8

Sources: Grant,[1] Southwood,[2] Stork,[3,4] Parker,[5] Wilson.[6]

TABLE 9-2 Estimates of Vertebrate Species Numbers

Group	Number	Percent Total
Mammals	4,000	0.22
Birds	9,000	0.50
Reptiles	6,300	0.35
Amphibians	4,200	0.23
Fishes	19,000	1.05

Source: Wilson.[6]

logical diversity is fraught with subjectivity and the fate of "furry or feathery animals"[7] will probably continue to dominate judgments of biodiversity above any formal scientific measures in the future.

How many species are there? Here, we enter the realms of extreme speculation. Insects make up about 75 percent of all known species and recent work in the neotropics (see Table 9-3) suggests that there are very high numbers of species yet to be recorded.[8] The eminent British mycologist Hawksworth also speculates about numbers as dramatic as Erwin's.[9] However, May (the well-known biologist/mathematician of Oxford University) has reviewed a large number of estimates critically (Table 9-3), and he considers that Gaston's estimate is probably closest to the truth, with the final number of species on earth likely to be closer to 5 million than to 10 million.[4]

The cataloging of species is done by taxonomists. May notes that taxonomists (on whose expert opinions the foundations of biodiversity depend) are mismatched with regard to geography and species.[4] Although there are over 3 million invertebrate species,

TABLE 9-3 Estimates of the Total Number of Species

Author	Date	Number (millions)
Simon	1983	6–7
Raven	1985	3–5
Hodkinson	1982	3–5
Erwin	1983	~30
Gaston	1991	5–10

Source: May.[4]

there are approximately 10 vertebrate taxonomists for every plant taxonomist and approximately 100 vertebrate taxonomists for every invertebrate taxonomist. Additionally, only about 6 percent of practicing taxonomists are based in developing countries where the bulk of species are found. May pleads for 'quick-and-dirty' techniques to redress the deficiency and strongly recommends the creation of a central database as a repository for information about species.

Extinctions

The main proponents of high projected rates of species extinctions are Norman Myers, Paul Ehrlich, and Anne Ehrlich, and Edward O. Wilson.[7,10] While conceding that it is very difficult to make estimates because of confounding factors, Wilson nevertheless projects that the current rates of species extinctions are between 1000 and 10,000 times that which existed before human intervention. Tuxill and Bright are apparently using Wilson's estimates when they claim in a recent edition of the Worldwatch Institute's *The State of the World*, that "at least 1,000 species are lost a year." More recently, Hellman et al. have projected that "at least 10,000 species are going extinct per year, or one per hour."[12] Even these rates of loss pale into insignificance when compared with the Chief Scientist of the IUCN Jeffrey McNeely's statement that ". . . if present trends continue, some 25% of the world's species will be lost in the next 25–50 years,"[13] or May's statement that "it is reasonable to suggest that something like half of all terrestrial species are likely to become extinct over the next 50 years, if current trends persist."[14] Assuming some 10 million species on the globe, at linear rates of extrapolation, McNeely's figures translate into 50,000 to 100,000 species per year and May's into 75,000 species per year (assuming terrestrial species amount to 75 percent of all species).

Are these figures believable? The wild variation in the projected rates of extinction found in Table 9-3 suggests that they are not based on sound scientific estimates or are made to sound worse than they are. Extinction rates such as 1000 species per year certainly sound dramatic. Another way of putting it might be that we are losing 0.01 percent of the species on earth per year or, at linear rates of extrapolation, we can expect to have lost 1 percent of the total complement of global species in the next 100 years. That, however, does not sound as alarming. Despite these ominous numbers, there is a paucity of real data to support these various assertions.

Closer to home, these high estimated rates of species loss do not accord with my own experience of the Southern African region. Southern Africa makes up approximately 3 percent of the global land area and, on a crude basis, we should expect 3 percent of all global extinctions to happen in this region. My considerations are limited to a few vertebrate classes for which it is possible that news of an extinction would reach me. In Table 9-4, I

Elephant herds are increasing in Zimbabwe because local communities essentially own them. Villagers no longer see elephants as dangerous pests but as valuable resources to be preserved. (*Credit*: Urs Kreuter.)

make rough estimates of the global number of species of mammals, birds, reptiles, and amphibia that may exist (increasing the number roughly according to the information given by May on rates of discovery of new species in the various classes of vertebrates).[4] On a simple pro rata basis (which is highly challengeable), if 10,000 species (from all classes, using Hellman et al.'s latest estimate) are going extinct annually and the total number of species (of all classes) is 5.9 million (my scaling up), then the expected rates of extinction given in the third column are based on the proportions that each of the listed classes forms of the total number of species on earth.[12] The final column estimates the number of those extinctions expected to take place in Southern Africa (again, on a pro rata and linear basis) over a period of 35 years (3 percent of the global area multiplied by 35 years), which is approximately the time I have been involved in field work in the region.

The fact that I am unaware of *any* extinctions that may have taken place in the region over the period from 1963 to date neither proves nor disproves the estimates. However, it might suggest that some authors are deliberately alarmist in their estimates.

Furthermore, because a large part of Southern Africa is within the tropics, simple pro rata calculations underestimate the numbers of species in the region, and the extinction

TABLE 9-4 Expected Extinctions in the Southern African Region in a Period of 33 Years Based on the Global Extinction Rates of Wilson[6]

Order and Estimated Global Number of Species	Estimated Global Rate of Extinction (spp/year)	Expected Number of Extinctions in Southern Africa in 35 Years (rounded)
Mammals 5,000	0.85	1
Birds 10,000	1.69	2
Reptiles 7,500	1.27	1
Amphibians 5,000	0.85	1

rate should be correspondingly higher than shown in the table if Wilson's calculations are to be believed. The number of mammal species in Southern Africa is actually 338 (the expected number is 120) and the number of bird species is 920 (the expected number is 300). Of the Southern African mammals, the last recorded species to go extinct were the quagga [*Equus quagga* (around 1875)] and the blue antelope, [*Hippotragus leocophaeus* (around 1800)]. No Southern African bird species are known to have become extinct this century.

The majority (approximately 75 percent) of global extinctions in recent times have occurred on islands.[14,15] Stephen Edwards, Head of IUCN's Sustainable Use Initiative, shows that the frequency of known extinctions from 1900 to 1990 exhibits neither an upward nor a downward trend.[16] Although in the past extinction rates of plants have been lower than those of animals, this may change in the future because invasions of alien plants are increasing competitive pressures. Invasions, which displace local species, have been responsible for a large proportion of all the extinctions known to have occurred during the recent historical period.

The extent of the loss of species and the consequences for human welfare are difficult to assess. Many biologists have reached the reluctant conclusion that not all species are of equal weight in their impact on ecosystem functions and processes, and the concept of "functional" and "interstitial species" clearly has relevance.[17] Certain extinctions have had no impact on life as we know it. The sea cow—a huge mammal over 7 meters in length, which lived in the Bering and Medny Island waters—became extinct around 1750

A.D. Sokolov remarks that "... available evidence suggests that no calamitous, or at least, very noticeable, changes occurred..." as a result of the extinction.[18] The population fluctuations of the sea otter in the same period and locality had "... no substantial effect in terms of loss of biological diversity on the functioning of the marine coastal ecosystem." Similarly, the reduced whale populations around the globe have had no marked effects on the biosphere.

The evidence so far indicates that much of the utilitarian rhetoric about the potential value of species as yet undescribed and the likely damaging effects of species loss on human prospects for survival are clearly overstatements.[15] Extinctions are a natural process and it is incorrect to assume that all change is negative.

Endangered Species

Some researchers offer grave figures for the numbers of species in danger of extinction (Table 9-5) based on the recently updated World Conservation Union IUCN Red List of Threatened Animals (1996).[11] The number of species in each IUCN category is entirely dependent on the questionable criteria adopted to define probabilities of extinction over various time spans. The lay reader is given the impression by IUCN Red List that there are generally agreed scientific criteria for deciding what an endangered species is.[11] There are no such absolutes.

For example, the Minimum Viable Population (MVP) needed to ensure the persistence of a population for a certain length of time is a statistical construct based on genetic and demographic properties of the population and environmental factors that may act upon it. Genetic variation and demographic effects can be predicted with some degree of precision,

TABLE 9-5 Conservation Status of the Higher Orders of Animals Based on the 1996 IUCN Red Data List*

Order	Immediate Danger of Extinction	Vulnerable to Extinction	Nearing Threatened Status
Mammals	11	14	14
Birds	4	7	9
Reptiles	8	12	6
Amphibians	10	15	5
Fish	13	21	5

Source: IUCN Red Data List, Data for reptiles, amphibians, and based on partial surveys.
*All values are percentages.

but assumptions about environmental variability are fairly unreliable. The Effective Population Size (Ne) used in MVP calculations is the number of effective breeding animals in any population, which could be *as few as 10 percent* of the actual population, and obviously varies by species. The typical criterion used is that population size should be large enough to ensure a probability of extinction less than a given threshold (e.g., less than a 1 percent likelihood in 100 years).

There has been an historical trend toward increasing MVPs:[19]

1960s   MacArthur and Wilson put forward numbers between 25 and 50 individuals.

1980s   The 50/500 rule was derived from genetic analyses: It was thought that an effective population size of 50 would provide some protection against short-term loss of fitness due to inbreeding, whereas a population of 500 would prevent loss of genetic variation over a longer term.

1990s   We are now in the era of MVP hyperinflation (10,000 to 1 million) based on effects of random fluctuations in the environment. The practical implications of such figures do not bear inspection. If these figures were applied to mountain lions, an area larger than that of the United States would be required for effective conservation.

Definition of Biological Diversity

So what is biological diversity? The Convention on Biological Diversity (CBD) has defined biological diversity as:

> The variability among living organisms from all sources including, inter alia, terrestrial, marine and other aquatic ecosystems and the ecological complexes of which they are part; this includes diversity within species, between species and of ecosystems. (Article 2, CBD)

Biodiversity is not an entity or a resource—rather it is a property, a characteristic of nature. Species, populations, and certain kinds of tissues are resources, but not their diversity as such. Counting species may be a convenient indicator of biological diversity, but it is not an absolute measure of the diversity present at any given site. For example, a grass sward with 20 different grass species is not as diverse a habitat for wildlife as a woodland that has five grass species, five herbaceous species, five shrub species, and five tree species. The first habitat will support a limited community of grazing animals; the second provides habitats for both grazers and browsers and a collection of birds, insects, and other *taxonomic* groups. Unfortunately, all too often, species numbers are the only measure used to describe the status of the world's biota.

The Classification of Biological Diversity

The fact that 4 years after its inception, the CBD has not yet come up with an agreed system for classifying and measuring biological diversity is an indication of the complexity of the construct.

Genes

It is entirely human to see the world's biodiversity as being divided into the simple categories of plants, animals, and microorganisms. However, if we seek to measure the extent to which organisms are differentiated genetically (i.e., how far and how much they have evolved over the history of life on earth), then counting simple numbers of species (or the numbers of individuals in species populations) will not achieve this.

Biologists use DNA and RNA sequences to construct phylogenetic trees (cladograms), which depict the points of separation of the phyla making up today's classification of living organisms (see Figure 9-1). These points of separation may be the most objective measure of diversity: Put into metaphor, there may be less diversity among thousands of species living on one branch of the tree than there is between the major phyla represented by the larger boughs of the tree.

An objective measure for biodiversity might be one that reflects the increasing phylogenetic divergence (cladistics) of the organisms present at any particular site, but the scientists suggesting it concede "it will elicit a wringing of hands and even apoplexy from those who might have to apply it."[21] Simply counting species is an easier, even if less accurate, way of defining the biodiversity of a particular site.

Species

The emphasis on species as the basic building blocks of biological diversity is probably the commonest approach among laypersons and scientists. While recognizing that biodiversity can be quantified in many ways, the noted English biologist May argues for counting species for the simple practical reasons that it is easier to raise money for species and easier to make species the targets for preservation.[4] However, the biological diversity of an area is much more than the number of species it contains.[21] Consider some of the subtleties that using species as the measure of biological diversity misses:

> All species, by their presence or absence, do not contribute equally to biological diversity. Huston from the Oak Ridge National Laboratory has developed the concept of *structural* and *interstitial* species: Structural species are those key species that determine the physical structure of ecosystems and influence the environment for the many other,

generally smaller, interstitial organisms (e.g., if an oak tree is present at a site, then a whole subset of fauna and flora will also be present).[17] The implication is that not all species are of equal weight in their importance to biological diversity.

Species with complex life cycles may contribute "two [or more] doses" of biological diversity during their lifetimes (e.g., a frog in its tadpole stage and adult stage).[1] Thus, the time of sampling of sites can influence the outcomes of biodiversity assessment.

The *grain*, or patch size, of sampling systems will affect outcomes of biodiversity assessments based on species. Surveys that include only higher-level organisms are likely to present a very different picture from those that sample microorganisms and, indeed, if every bacterium species were to be accorded equal weight with the elephant in biodiversity compilations, then the importance of the pachyderm would be minimal.

Comparisons between sites of the species present in like groups (e.g., vascular plants) may show valid differences in biological diversity, but such comparisons are less useful when a number of phyla are lumped together (e.g., reptiles and amphibia along

Under the Endangered Species Act administered by the U.S. Dept. of the Interior, only 11 of the 1761 species listed as endangered or threatened have been recovered. (*Credit:* CEI.)

with vascular plants). It is essential not to "mix apples and pears" in biodiversity assessments.

Even at the species level, complete counts of organisms are impractical. Cheap, quick solutions are needed to quantify biological diversity over the global landscape. The continued focus on species for measuring biodiversity suggests a certain inner comfort with familiar terrain. Repeated assessments of the species present at a single site may provide information of changes taking place at that site but do not explain the changes or provide meaningful comparisons with other sites. The larger danger inherent in a preoccupation with species numbers is a "failure to see the woods for the trees" (i.e., the relationships between species and the contributions that species make to the functioning of the ecosystem).

Ecosystems

The Convention on Biological Diversity (CBD) is moving toward adopting an ecosystem approach for the conservation and sustainable use of biodiversity. The CBD has developed 12 principles that characterize the ecosystem approach to measuring biodiversity.[22] Perhaps Principle 5 is the most relevant:

> Principle 5: A key feature of the ecosystem approach includes conservation of ecosystem structure and functioning.
>
> Rationale: Ecosystem functioning and resilience depends on a dynamic relationship within species, among species, and between species and their abiotic environment. The conservation of these interactions and processes is of greater significance for the long-term maintenance of biological diversity than simple protection of species.

Since the late 1970s, the major nongovernmental organizations [World Wildlife Fund (WWF), International Union for the Conservation of Nature (IUCN)] have advocated a shift in focus from species conservation to ecosystem conservation. They recognize the dangers of frittering away scarce conservation funds on missions to save species where the causes of their decline lie at the ecosystem level. Whereas fluctuations in species' presence and numbers within ecosystems are normal and part of the dynamics of the larger system, it is the constant functioning and resilience of whole ecosystems that human managers should logically strive to maintain.

Notwithstanding all of the assertions that biodiversity is a characteristic of relationships between and within genes, species, and ecosystems, the tendency to lapse back into regarding species as the fundamental building blocks of biological diversity remains dominant. This tendency is shared even by the most eminent of scientists and suggests that the fundamental concept of biological diversity is problematic.

Explaining Biological Diversity

If the underlying determinants of the biodiversity of any area are known then, presumably, the task of conserving it should be made simpler. If we know the significance of different aspects of biodiversity for key ecosystem attributes (such as life-support systems), we ought to be able to focus on these. Achieving this level of knowledge, however, is a very difficult task. A large number of correlations exist between species diversity and various environmental parameters. However, it seems that no sooner has one group of scientists established one relationship, then another group will produce the data to indicate an opposite trend. Let's examine some of the parameters that determine how biological diversity is distributed across the earth.

> *Underlying geological effects.* Many of the current patterns of biodiversity can be understood as resulting from the geological and environmental events. Four times in the last million years, glaciers have swept across Europe destroying its magnificent tertiary forests; however, the same types of forest did not disappear in parts of North America and Eastern Asia because more southerly ice-free refuges existed (e.g., the Southern Appalachian Mountains and the mountains of Szechwan and Kwangsi in China. The migration of species during the ice ages was also affected by the nature of barriers—both north–south and east–west mountain ranges. The big-tree (Sequoiadendron) avoided extinction by migrating westward over the Sierra Nevada mountains before they evolved to their present height.
>
> *Latitudinal and Altitudinal Gradients.* Species diversity generally increases toward the equator simply because the majority of plant species (which provide the habitats for animal species) have little or no tolerance for cold climates. Brazil, for example, has over 40,000 species of vascular plants compared with less than 400 species in the larger area of the Canadian Arctic Archipelago. Species diversity also generally declines with altitude. However, there are exceptions to these rules (e.g., species of coastal sea birds increase away from the Equator, and regions linking plains and high mountain tops may possess a greater diversity than lower altitude plains).
>
> *Productivity.* On a global scale, the primary productivity of terrestrial vegetation is positively correlated with plant species diversity and this, in turn, accounts for increased

diversity of animals. However, the addition of nutrients to aquatic ecosystems or fertilizers to herbaceous plant communities can result in decreased diversity by allowing those species that are best adapted to take advantage of the increased nutrition to outcompete other species. Certain infestations of water "weeds" (e.g., Pistia) in African waterbodies are examples of this process in operation.

Temporal variation. Biodiversity also varies continuously at many different time scales linked to the generation times of the species under consideration, the seasonal aspects of life cycles, longer-term successional processes and, finally, at evolutionary rates of change.

Type of Diversity

It is also necessary to distinguish amongst several types of diversity, which are themselves changing constantly.[17]

"Within-habitat" diversity (alpha diversity). Characterizes the coexistence among organisms that are interacting with one another by competing for the same resources or otherwise using the same environment.

"Between-habitat" diversity (beta diversity). Reflects the way in which organisms respond to environmental heterogeneity and depends not only on the numbers of species in the habitat, but also on the identity of those species and where they occur in different geographical areas. It is here that the use of simple presence/absence measures of species do not provide meaningful quantitative comparisons of the biological diversity between two sites. The presence of a species in a place is ample evidence that the environment is suitable and that the species has been able to get there. The absence of a species from a place tells us nothing in itself. It may be absent for one or more of several reasons, such as the fact that the area may be outside its tolerance range, or barriers may have prevented its arrival, or it may once have been there but was eliminated either by a paleological event or some more recent disturbance. Few species actually occupy their potential geographic range and many of the factors discussed earlier in this section are responsible (e.g., geological history).

Large-scale regional diversity (gamma diversity). Tends to reflect evolutionary, rather than ecological, determinants of diversity. The tolerance range of a species is made up of the tolerance ranges of all the individuals in the population. Species that are young in terms of evolutionary time have usually not persisted long enough to develop considerable genetic variation and are less diverse than species that have survived for hundreds of thousands of years. Species that reproduce vegetatively (as opposed to sexually) also tend to have less genetic diversity.

All of these various types of diversity are dynamic; that is, they are changing all the time.

Global Unifying Theories of Biodiversity

Biologists have long sought to explain the biological diversity that exists in different areas—a diversity that far exceeds that expected according to simple ecological theories. A feature of the various explanations that have been put forward is their short shelf-life or limited applicability. A number of authors note the "changing fashions" of conservation ecology, and Soulé and Mills remark that the current drive toward ecosystem analysis has left species specialists and, by association, conservation geneticists as the "species chauvinists."[17,19] Some of the theories that have achieved prominence this century are discussed briefly below.

Species/Area Curves

With few exceptions, large areas have more species than small areas, and relationships from limited samples in small areas have been used to predict the total number of species in larger areas. This species/area curve relationship is central in MacArthur and Wilson's theory of island biogeography, but the parameters used to describe the species/area curve have been shown to be a statistical artifact with no theoretical significance.[23] The number of species in an area is strongly correlated with the heterogeneity of the area, which affects the diversity of both plant and animal communities.[17] Such a situation can easily give rise to spurious correlations (e.g., where the inclusion of a greater area leads to inclusion of more heterogeneity in the environment, it is intuitively obvious that this will also result in the presence of more species). However, the obverse is not true: If the consideration of a greater area does not include any new heterogeneity, then there is no reason to expect that the number of species will be greater than in the original sample (i.e., species numbers are *not* correlated with area per se—they are correlated with variation in the environment).

Many scientists have criticized attempts to extrapolate species numbers over large areas. May observed that "if long-distance movement is an important cog in the machinery maintaining overall diversity, then you cannot extrapolate a 'local' rate of adding species with area beyond the characteristic distance scale on which the dispersal/diversity mechanism operates."[4] In other words, it is reasonable to expect that as the size of samples is increased, more and more species will be encountered up to the point where adding further samples at certain distances away from the starting point results in some of the original species dropping out of samples and their replacement with a completely new suite of species. To ignore this phenomenon is to attempt to apply the species/area relationship beyond the limited physical range over which it may be valid.

Urban et al., in examining the number of habitat niches in forests that can be occupied by birds, found that the age of forest stands determined the number of niches, but the same number could be reached by sampling over larger areas of forest.[24] The relationship was affected by disturbance, landscape patterns, and varied geographically. In determining the biodiversity of animal communities, the type and geometry of habitats play an important role.

The implications of this for the species/area effect of MacArthur and Wilson are significant and raise concerns at any attempt to use species/area curves to extrapolate the number of species going extinct on a continental scale. Thus, recent claims that the species/area curve is the best descriptor of hundreds of sets of data "from the scale of laboratory experiments to continental studies" would seem to be trying to attribute some magical properties to this commonsensical issue and fly in the face of more objective reasoning.[12]

Competitive Exclusion

The principle of competitive exclusion dates back to the 1920s and predicts that if two species are competing for the same limited resources, one of them will become extinct. This led to the concept of *competitive equilibrium*, which has now been largely discredited because a far larger number of species actually coexist in natural communities than the theory predicts. Huston notes that the theory ". . . seems to persist largely because of its elegance, simplicity and heuristic value rather than because of its mechanistic validity."[17]

Equilibrium Theories

Theories based on a presumption of equilibrium in nature are no longer accepted by most biologists. Holling and Meffe discuss the differences between "equilibrium resilience" and "ecosystem resilience"—the former being the manner in which a system returns to an equilibrium state after minor perturbations, and the latter reflecting conditions far from any equilibrium where systems may even change state.

There is no real dichotomy in the two concepts of resilience. If resilience per se is conceived of as an inherent characteristic of an ecosystem conferred on it by the amount of biological diversity it possesses, then equilibrium resilience is the behavior of that ecosystem in response to small disturbances. Ecosystem resilience is the full suite of responses that that ecosystem may display, not only in response to external perturbations, but also through its own internal dynamics.

The apparent dichotomy is the result of the approaches taken by people attempting to manage ecosystems, not an inherent feature of ecosystems themselves. Earlier conservationists conceived of and would have liked to maintain nature in a stable state: Each minor change in an ecosystem was to be "corrected" by remedial management. However, such an approach denies reality and, far from conserving resilience, it may actually destroy it. From time to time environmental and ecological conditions may act in concert to cause an ecosystem to undergo massive changes—changes that are not gradual or continuous, but episodic. Ecosystems that have been subjected to a long history of management by those seeking to maintain stability are often the least able to accommodate such disturbances, and the perturbation may result in far-reaching changes and havoc. For example, the history of attempts to constrain the Mississippi River through locks, levees, and channelization has reduced the resilience of the ecosystem with the result that when the right combination of perturbations occurs (as happened in the storms of 1993), massive flooding takes place.

The resilience in ecosystems lies in the variability they possess—the ability to respond to changes without the collapse of their essential functioning. However, those who would embrace ecosystem management need to put aside preconceived notions of any absolute desirable state for an ecosystem and be willing to accept gross superficial changes where they are clearly the results of normal ecological processes. It is difficult for managers to conceive of their ecosystems as moving targets and doubly difficult because virtually every ecosystem requiring management has been already tampered with to some extent by "control freaks." Where there is no convenient benchmark at which to aim, the Golden Rule—natural resource management should strive to retain critical types and ranges of natural variation in ecosystems—becomes a more and more important maxim.[25]

Nonequilibrium Processes

One of the major ecological insights of the 1970s was the importance of nonequilibrium processes in the maintenance of species diversity.[17] Two explanations for the persistence of biological diversity at levels higher than predicted by the competitive exclusion theory are currently in favor.

In the first, it is thought that systems are prevented from reaching the equilibrium at which a number of species would go extinct by virtue of time lags, disturbances, and effects of predation or herbivory. The second explanation is that patchiness in the environment permits a stochastic equilibrium of high species diversity to be maintained through processes of local extinctions and reimmigrations. Both of these theories acknowledge the possible validity of competitive exclusion, but in neither case does the ecosystem ever reach the equilibrium at which it would take effect. The high species diversity of East Africa's Serengeti might be explained by either effect: The ecosystem provides a number of niche habitats and simultaneously depends on local migrations for its persistence.

Island Biogeography

MacArthur and Wilson's very influential theory of island biogeography falls in the category of "intermediate-scale equilibria."[17,23] It hypothesizes that the species diversity on islands ("true" islands or "habitat" islands) will reflect a balance between immigration and extinction. The model has been a major stimulus to investigations by ecologists in general and conservation biologists in particular over the past 2 decades. However, the theory has also come under considerable criticism because of the large number of cases for which its predictions fail or cannot be demonstrated. Berry's experimental work with rodents on islands surrounding the United Kingdom has allowed many aspects of the theory to be tested over a significant time period.[15]

The balance between immigration and extinction of species on islands is a logical necessity and is a truism rather than a fundamental relationship. In Berry's opinion, island biogeography wrongly strengthens the common assumption that ecological communities are in equilibrium or in a deterministic progression toward a successional climax. In fact, the major lesson from island studies is the importance that opportunism and random chance play in determining which species inhabit an island ecosystem.

Berry makes four points about island populations (which have a significant bearing on the philosophy of biological diversity in general):

1. The genetic composition of island species is largely determined by founding colonizers, not subsequent evolution.
2. Species survival is largely the result of lessened competition, not adaptation to island environments. All species must be seen as contemporary survivors potentially susceptible to a change of conditions on a micro- or macroscale.
3. Island ecology should teach us that equilibrium and determinism assumptions are unjustified. The romantic concept of a "balance of nature" is a fruit of medieval theology not confirmed by modern science.
4. If a species is found in a particular environment, it is difficult to tell whether it arrived 100,000 years ago or yesterday. Conservation is too full of attempts to rescue species or ecosystems that are transients in the dynamic progression of life—the enormous efforts

that go into preserving island endemics *are a case in point*. Conservation biologists are prone to preservationism, whereas their science demands acceptance that extinction is a natural process.

Genetics

Ultimately, it is at the genetic level that all biological diversity originates. When we assess biological diversity in terms of species, we ignore the possibility that there may be a greater difference between two individuals of the same species when their genetic makeup is considered than there may be between two individuals of different species (e.g., the entire Cisticola genus of Southern African birds contains species that are visually so similar that it is quite possible that there is greater variation within species than between species among some members of the genus). Species are constructs of taxonomists and the differences between species are subject to the whims of taxonomists: The evidence of genetic differences revealed by electrophoresis is not.

Biological diversity could be seen as one large soup of genes grouped together at any instant of time into a number of gene associations—all individual organisms. One of the dangers of studying biological diversity solely at the species level is that a vast bank of information of intraspecies diversity is ignored. The process is akin to placing a large amount of information in files, writing names on the covers of the files, destroying the information in each file and working thereafter only with the names of the files. Ironically, there is less difficulty in accommodating the concept of genetic diversity into the biological diversity of ecosystems than there is in using species as the units of biodiversity. At the ecosystem level, our concern is with conserving biological variation and, hence, ecosystem resilience.

Conservation of Biological Diversity

The motivations for conserving biological diversity include at the highest level a philosophy and ethic, not limited to the Northern Hemisphere, which sees it as our responsibility to keep evolutionary options open, so far as we can, for the sake of future humans. Thereafter, perceptions diverge as to how this huge task should be approached.

There is little that will be of help to a field manager in the global theories of biological diversity presented previously, or that will even facilitate the conservation of biodiversity in local situations. The nice differences between island biogeography and competitive exclusion are largely irrelevant when compared with the gross effects of externalities that result in land use changes. Land use is at the core of conserving terrestrial biodiversity. Decisions on land use and development are inextricably linked to the issues of tenure and resource valuation. The prevalent global approaches to the conservation of biodiversity being offered to the developing world by international donor agencies and nongovernmental organizations are often very different from the approaches being attempted at local and national levels. Local and global conservationists are talking past each other and could easily be conducting two different debates in adjacent rooms.

Thinking Globally

There appears to be a strong degree of eco-imperialism inherent in the global approach to conservation—even if this is the innocent product of differing backgrounds between first-world and third-world scientists. A noted Asian scientist, Agarwal argues that the statement that "biodiversity is a global resource" is a colonialist intervention.[26] Any programs to protect biodiversity that do not simultaneously address the problem of poverty will be viewed with suspicion by developing countries. Global rules are being set and global discipline is being demanded, but global sharing of costs and burdens is not on the global agenda.

Perhaps the three most important features which characterize the global approach to conservation are:

1. A belief in central planning as opposed to decentralized institutions. Hand in hand with this goes an emphasis on a "blueprint approach" versus a process-based or adaptive-management approach.
2. A focus on protected areas rather than the more general problem of land use systems.
3. A faith in international treaties as a means to coerce recalcitrant states into conserving their biological resources.

Each of these topics is dealt with briefly and, in the concluding remarks, I surmise that, to a large extent, politics and funding explain the syndrome.

Central Planning

A large number of western scientists see biodiversity as a matter for global assessment and global planning and, simultaneously, define a central role for themselves in this process.[7,27-30] Some feel that this global centralized planning "... will require a holistic approach focused on ecosystems at national, regional and global levels."[31] My interpretation of what is meant by "holistic" here is that it implies a massive data collection exercise, which will enable scientists to design the correct blueprint.

The chief environmental scientist to the British Government, May says, "Efforts to conserve biological diversity, both in local areas and more globally, must be based on facts."[4] This may be true, if you see the process as one vast centrally planned exercise by governments based on priorities established by Western scientists. The implications of this incredible assertion are that, without a knowledge of the "facts," attempts to conserve biological diversity are a waste of time. I am not a post-Modernist, but I do believe that efforts could be based on adaptive management in which the facts emerge under trial-and-error systems.

Brian Walker, the head of the Wildlife Division of the CSIRO in Australia, observes that "The most complex and desirable ecosystems that we wish to conserve are markedly unstable (nonconstant), and achieving our conservation goals depends on their remaining that way. It is the continued instability of these systems which allows for the coexistence of their many species, whether or not the systems have strong internal regulation.... Unfortunately, conservation management is often intuitively opposed to this."[32] Inflexible blueprints emanating from global planners may entail a stasis that is unfavorable for ecosystems, reduces their resilience, and ends up in the command-and-control pathology defined by Holling and Meffe.[25]

The CBD has recognized that change is inevitable in ecosystems (Principle 9) and has postulated that adaptive management is the appropriate tool for dealing with changes that will occur on time scales varying from instantaneous episodic events to long-term evolutionary change.[22]

Protected Areas

Theory

Frankel, regarded by many as a founding father of modern genetics, sees the prime parameters for continuing biological evolution as:[33]

1. Level and distribution of variation
2. Size of minimum viable populations (see earlier discussion of MVPs)
3. Optimal and minimal sizes of reserves

Focusing on the last of these, it is apparently inconceivable to Frankel that there is life outside of reserves. Second, he has no qualms about recommending that land should be sequestered solely for biodiversity conservation. Third, he believes that the larger the reserves the better.

Unfortunately, many share his innocent eco-imperialism. Van der Hammen, from the University of Amsterdam, recommends that, in order that species may recolonize areas that may be depleted in the future, reserves should take the form of corridors along temperature and rainfall gradients and, in the tropics, there should be "very large nature reservations."[34] This view of the world as a biologist's tabula rasa is remarkable—and unreal. The majority of third-world governments would send even the most eminent scientist packing if he arrived in their countries with the bright announcement that he had found the right combination of protected areas for persistence of long-term genetic variability.

A cadre of global biodiversity planners work on the supposition that large areas of the globe must be set aside to preserve biological diversity and that each (hypothetical) natural reserve should be created with the object of maximizing global biodiversity.[29] Thus, the addition of each new protected area must bring to the table additional aspects of biodiversity in order to be valuable or to justify investment.

In a bottom-up system, the views of the people who live in any given ecosystem might be sought. They will not be impressed to be told that they are not a global conservation priority, because the biodiversity contained in their area will not contribute additionally to global biodiversity. The same applies to those prevalent modeling efforts, which presuppose that the landscape is tractable and can be rearranged as a result of research findings—a situation that is unlikely to be true for most real life situations.[35]

McNeely, head of the Biodiversity Policy Coordination Division of IUCN, is sensitive to the eco-imperialism inherent in creating reserves. "When a central government establishes a national park because of its outstanding value to the nation and humanity, it simultaneously denies access to any marketable value of the area to the local people who once benefited from the goods and services that the area formerly provided."[13] However, he does not consider alternative solutions and sees the answer in compensation of the affected parties.

Practice

The Southern Africa Sustainable Use Specialist Group of IUCN recently reviewed the sustainability of state protected areas in southern Africa.[36] It concluded that the majority of reserves were failing to conserve biodiversity, were financially unsustainable, and were irrelevant to 95 percent of the people in the countries where they were located. The creation of national parks could be seen as "a crude attempt by governments to capture land and resources for the public good when neither the public nor the good had been defined." Whether the objectives are to conserve biological diversity or to promote economic growth, there are better ways of doing it than through the mechanism of state conservation areas.

The situation that now exists in many parts of Southern Africa is that, where full rights of access and control over wildlife have been granted to landholders (of both private and communal land), biodiversity is better conserved in the areas surrounding national parks than in the parks themselves. Additionally, the areas surrounding parks are economically more productive than the state-protected areas.

The existing array of protected areas and international conventions is not going to plug the species drain. The key in the future will be to find a way to allow these protected areas to be used by local people while maintaining as high a level of biodiversity as possible.[30] The International Board for Plant Genetic Resources concluded in 1983 that the existing system of protected areas was inadequate for survival of numerous valuable species and their intraspecific diversity and similar conclusions have been reached by others on conservation of genetic resources of tropical woody species. There should be concern for the increasing concentration of much of the world's biota in small, quasi-insular protected areas because of the vulnerability to invasions by introduced species, which, together with other effects, is likely to result in a net loss in biodiversity.[37] Trying to preserve biological diversity largely within reserves is a recipe for failure.

Far from being regarded as the pinnacle of conservation, protected areas could as well be seen as a failure highlighting humanity's inability to live with nature. I have no difficulty with protected areas being established as viable forms of land use based on the recreational needs of national citizenry and international tourists. The problem is that governments are probably the least suitable agencies to manage such areas effectively and efficiently. As soon as there is a dual agenda for national parks, when they are required both to conserve biological diversity and be viable tourism ventures, the outcome is usually a failure to satisfy either objective. Far more promising for conserving biological diversity in Southern Africa is the move toward land use based on natural resource management (on wildlife in particular). The primary motive for this shift is greater financial viability than alternative land uses: The conservation of biological diversity is a secondary benefit.

It therefore has to be viewed with some concern that IUCN—The World Conservation Union—is making recommendations to the Convention on Biological Diversity (CBD) for an increased emphasis on state-protected areas. The statement that "Protected areas are essential for biodiversity conservation" is demonstrably untrue. Indeed, the alternative hypothesis is easier to establish.

International Treaties

The State of the World 1998 asserts that "... international agreements have probably made their biggest contribution in reducing the overexploitation of species, particularly those that are traded globally."[11] This is a highly questionable claim.

The Convention on the International Trade in Endangered Species (CITES)

CITES deals only with internationally traded species and only with those that are in danger of extinction (as a result of trade) or those that may become endangered as a result of trade. It does not address any local consumption of species, which, in most of the countries of the world, is likely to be the largest use. In 1994, the CITES Parties decided to commission a review of the performance of the treaty, and consultants examined a sample of 12 species and found that CITES may have been effective for only 2 of these.[39] The consultants stated that "The impact of CITES on the conservation status of individual species is very complex and cannot be measured easily or precisely." This is a remarkable finding. If the impact of CITES is so easily obscured, perhaps there is no impact. My own involvement with CITES extends over a period of 15 years, and I cannot think of a single species for which CITES has been instrumental in reversing its decline or (more important) increasing its population size.

The problem with CITES is that it is a "blueprint" treaty. It relies on listing species on Appendices and, having listed them, its prescriptions are inflexible. It was apparent by 1992 that the criteria for listing species on the Appendices were inadequate and had resulted in many species being incorrectly listed (i.e., they were not on the brink of extinction, and/or international trade had nothing to do with their status). Several Southern African nations submitted proposals for more rigorous criteria based on the Minimum Viable Population approach of Mace and Lande.[40] With some modifications, these criteria were adopted by CITES in 1994. They have made little difference to the CITES Appendices—these remain as subjective as ever. However, the exercise served to demonstrate the problem of attempting to "hard-link" management prescriptions to criteria of this sort. The status of species is irrelevant to the management measures by which their populations may be increased. Even very small populations (less than 100 animals) can sustain offtakes and, if such an offtake is likely to benefit the conservation of the species through reinvestment of funds, there is no basis for prohibiting the particular transaction that would result in this improvement. As long as CITES continues to operate under its present articles, it will act against the conservation of species more frequently than it will improve their status.

In this respect, CITES is identical to the United States Endangered Species Act, which contains the same inflexible linkages between the perceived degree of endangerment and the management prescription. The sooner the Act moves away from a blueprint approach and adopts a process-based approach, the sooner it is likely to have a beneficial impact on conservation.

Far from CITES trade bans forcing national governments to conserve species, they have rather the effect of creating conditions whereby species become legally valueless and will simply disappear through a process of attrition and through illegal trade (e.g., the black rhino in Zimbabwe). Sustainable use requires a very different suite of measures and, where

Western powers are frustrated with the apparent inability of any particular developing nation to conserve a charismatic species, there is only one option—to assist that country in developing its management skills, not to prohibit its trade.

The Convention on Biological Diversity (CBD)

Unlike those of CITES, the Articles of the CBD are not inflexible or prescriptive and lend themselves ideally to the development of a process-based approach to conservation and sustainable use. The greatest threat to the CBD is the drive of many of the participants who seek to transform it into a blueprint-type treaty.

The CBD has carried out a preliminary identification of the proximate threats to and ultimate causes of the loss of biological diversity and lists them in Table 9-6.

Much of what is being attempted in global scientific diagnosis of the needs for biodiversity conservation goes no further than identifying symptoms (proximate threats) and fails to highlight the underlying problems (ultimate causes). It is significant that international trade in wildlife products—the raison d'être for CITES—is not identified by the CBD as one of the ultimate causes of loss of biological diversity.

A worrying feature of many of the methods of assessing biodiversity being advocated by certain Western scientists is that they are aimed not so much at ongoing monitoring of biological diversity (which is the process-based approach needed by field managers) as they are aimed at being a one-off "snapshot" of global diversity with the information to be used for global planning—and judgment.[17] These two approaches are mutually incompatible.

The Politics and Funding of Biodiversity Conservation

Conservation of biological diversity has become a politically important issue. A measure of this importance is the fact that the Earth Summit in Rio de Janeiro in 1992 was

TABLE 9-6   Threats to and Causes of Loss of Biological Diversity

Proximate Threats	Ultimate Causes
1. Overharvest or overkill of wild species	1. Land tenure
2. Introduced species	2. Population change
3. Habitat destruction or deterioration	3. Cost-benefit imbalances
4. Pollution	4. Cultural factors
5. Climate change factors	5. Misdirected economics
	6. National policy failure

attended by over 120 heads of state. No other global meeting on any other issue has achieved this prominence. The results are several:

1. A greater proportion of global funding than ever before has been allocated to conservation of biological diversity.
2. National budgets and international donor funding for biodiversity conservation have increased.
3. A large proportion of this funding is being allocated to first-world research institutions.
4. Donor funding for developing countries has shifted significantly toward biodiversity conservation and sustainable development.

The pressures on Western research institutions to align their research agendas with this large potential source of funding are considerable. It is inevitable that researchers who receive government funding will be asked to give advice to national and international agencies. Unfortunately, it is very often the case that the more alarmist the advice, the greater is the opportunity for increased research funding. Equally, there are pressures on developing countries to accept certain Western philosophies of conservation and certain Western technical assistance, because it is to these conservation approaches that funds are tied.

Thinking Locally

Land Use

Of all the factors affecting biological diversity, land use is the most important. Our concerns have to lie with the 90 percent of land in each country that is not designated as state-protected areas. The decisions affecting this land use have two key components:

1. Land and resource tenure (the complete system of property rights affecting landholders)
2. Resource values (financial, economic, and intrinsic)

These two factors are tightly linked and inseparable. Neither factor on its own will address all of the problems of land use decisions and, hence, biodiversity conservation. Equally, the two taken together are the necessary and sufficient variables that provide the entire domain in which land use issues will be decided. This automatically implies that the scale at which problems are addressed is that of the ecosystem or landscape.

The typical proportions of land in various categories in Southern African countries are shown in Figure 9-2. Most countries have at least 10 percent of their land set aside as state

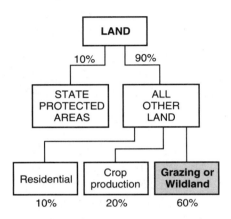

FIGURE 9-2 Typical distribution of land categories in a Southern African savanna country.

conservation areas. Good arable land suitable for crop production is only about 20 percent of the total national land area (in Botswana and Namibia, it is considerably less than this). The remainder is suitable only for extensive cattle grazing or wildlife habitat and management. It is largely the future of this land that will affect the amount of biodiversity retained in Southern Africa.

The first of the land use problems relates to arable land. In most Southern African countries, sufficient crops could be grown on this land to meet the food requirements of the entire population but, for various reasons, marginal land is being cultivated and is degrading land that should never be placed under the plough. The second land use issue is what the remaining nonarable land will be used for. The options are domestic livestock or wildlife management or a combination of both (however, the presence of any significant number of domestic livestock on savanna range land reduces the carrying capacity for wildlife). It is in respect of these two land use issues that many scientists (and laypeople) from the first world make incorrect assumptions because of the very different circumstances obtaining in the temperate zones.

As land that is not required for agricultural production in Europe becomes available for "return to nature," rich countries are effectively gardening their landscapes and providing for their aesthetic and recreational needs (which is not to ignore the improved ecosystem services such as watershed protection arising from the process).[41] This land is not expected to be agriculturally productive: A wealthy society can afford to put it to uses that are popular and that the taxpayer is prepared to subsidize. No such situation pertains in Africa.

Poverty is so intense that all land with agricultural potential will be exploited and even that with very little potential will be put to use—even if that use is unsustainable.

This is but the first of the two problems mentioned above. The attempts to scratch a living from marginal soils affects only a fraction of the land in a country like Zimbabwe. Typically, the arable proportion of the country is about 20 percent of the land area, and the encroachment of cultivation onto marginal soils is only likely to result in the clearance of an additional 10 percent of the country's land. The remaining soils are too poor even for a destitute peasant to invest his labor in attempting to cultivate them. The next big question is what will the future be for that largest proportion of the land, which is nonarable and whose productivity can only be realized through grazing and browsing animal production?

In Europe or North America, it might be possible to view such wild lands as unable to pay for themselves but, nevertheless, desirable adjuncts to human living that should be subsidized and set aside either as state-protected areas or recreational land under private ownership. Intense poverty makes the choices in Africa almost wholly economic ones. The only question is: Which of the options (wildlife or cattle) will provide the higher or more secure return from the land?

A large number of studies has demonstrated that wildlife management is the highest-valued use for nonarable land in Southern Africa.[42-52] The returns from such land may be derived from a variety of activities including ecotourism, sport hunting, sale of live animals to other landholders who are attempting to build up their wildlife populations, the sale of meat and wildlife products—and combinations of all of these activities. The returns can outcompete cattle farming by a large margin depending on skills in marketing. In these cases, there is no financial sacrifice to be expected from society at large in pursuing that land use, which is most favorable for biodiversity conservation and sustainable development. Managing land for wildlife is a highly viable form of land use in Africa. Logically, every farmer ought to be pursuing it. Yet, the uses to which the land is put are often lower-yielding financially than the original wilderness. The explanations for why farmers choose lower-yielding cattle ranching rather than wildlife production lie in the critically interlinked role of tenure and resource values.

Tenure

The tragedy of the commons must be one of the most discussed issues in biodiversity conservation.[53] The commons by definition is unowned, and the incentive for the individual is to gain benefits from the commons before another individual does so. The romantic notion is that somehow open access situations are seen as more moral, more natural and superior to fenced private property. This is a commonly held belief among environmentalists in the United States, but it finds its parallel in a very different culture in Southern Africa.[54] Many Africans share an inherent discomfort with the notion of enclosing the commons. Wildlife is perceived as a resource belonging to all the people and attempts to privatize it are seen as antisocial (see box). This perception may have been appropriate during earlier times when subsistence forms of economic life were possible because wildlife resources were so abundant relative to population. Smith notes that "The tragedy of the commons is more likely to persist to its end in poorer societies—societies discouraging technological innovation, reluctant to allow private property ownership, and societies in which government subsidies are common."[55]

Defining "ownership" for wild animals is a vexatious problem in legislation. By definition, something that is wild cannot be owned. The Roman-Dutch legal systems in South Africa and Zimbabwe assign wildlife the status of res nullius (i.e., owned by nobody). Zimbabwean law assigns powerful rights of access and use to landholders (both on private land and on land that is held under customary communal tenure), which effectively empower them to manage wildlife for their own benefit without government interference. This empowerment has resulted in a major resurgence of wildlife in the rural areas since the 1960s and, correspondingly, the retention of wildlife habitats.

> *The law doth punish man or woman*
> *That steals the goose from off the common,*
> *But lets the greater felon loose,*
> *That steals the common from the goose.*
> "On enclosures,"
> 18th century—Anonymous

However, in many countries in Africa, as great a problem as the tragedy of the commons is the tragedy of state ownership. The "natural justice" of such ownership is highly questionable, as it is based on the assumption that wildlife is a "free good" without overhead costs in management—a situation far from the truth. Successful wildlife husbandry entails costs as much as cattle ranching does. Where the state lacks the capacity to enforce its ownership, the situation is identical to the open-access commons. Political management, which stems from this option, has not had a good track record in developing countries. "Politicizing the situation does not resolve the tragedy of the commons; rather it institutionalizes it".[55]

Agarwal remarks that when British colonists nationalized grazing lands and forests in India, they converted these managed common property resources into free-access common property resources—which led to their degradation.[26] He notes that the independent government has unfortunately continued the system. This is true also for many postindependence African governments: They have unthinkingly adopted the practices of their former colonial masters.

Of course, individual ownership doesn't guarantee that the owner will necessarily protect biological diversity on his land. Numerous factors affect the economics of private individuals, and it is possible for a private landholder to exercise his rights to eliminate the biodiversity on his land if it appears to be in his interest. Group ownership of natural resources may be more likely to protect biodiversity, provided the group (or community) is not too large. Communal checks and balances tend to preclude sweeping overnight decisions that could negatively affect wild resources.

However, no property rights system can be effective if the underlying legal system fails to protect and defend it. Partially empowering individuals or groups to manage their resources is seldom adequate for encouraging the protection of biological diversity. Among McNeely's solutions for conserving biodiversity is the recommendation that indigenous conservation efforts by local people should be supported.[13] It requires far more than support. The incentives for local people to conserve their biological diversity will not be sufficient if they do not include full empowerment over the use of their resources. In Southern African situations, one must consider how land use rules and regulations encourage cattle ranching. People will choose to raise cattle if the legal and bureaucratic constraints relating to wildlife husbandry render it an unattractive option.

In Southern Africa and, I suspect that in a large part of the world, conservation of biological diversity would not be a cost if the correct institutional arrangements were developed, including a stronger reliance on private property and communal tenure systems. A potential win-win situation would exist if the insistence on establishing protected areas were abandoned or, alternatively, if such areas were not conceived of as national parks and became rather the local conservation areas at a district level. To this end, much of the global thinking advocated by international agencies and nongovernmental organizations is largely missing the target and is underpinned by a set of assumptions about the way the world works that are demonstrably false.

The economic future of the developing countries will depend on them finding a competitive niche in world markets. In Southern Africa, that niche lies in the valuable large wild mammal resource that few other countries have. Today, more than 75 percent of the land on every continent, except Europe, is available for wildlife. The set of incentives that control land use decisions is critical to the success or failure of protecting biological diversity.

If Southern Africa opts to focus on its charismatic wildlife as a land use, it will very likely be competitive because it is an exclusive resource denied to other countries. For this land use option to be adopted by the citizenry, it will require the devolution of rights to the smallest accountable community units; full market value for wildlife resources; the removal of artificial barriers to trade and the perverse economic incentives that drive land use to lower valued options like cattle ranching. There are no simple solutions to this last problem and it is very relevant to Southern Africa. It does not need the unwitting negative contributions from major donors that promote alternative land uses (e.g., clearance of tsetse flies to promote cattle production). It also requires African governments to reevaluate their slavish adherence to the development paradigms and institutional systems of the first world.

Sustainable Development

In the developing countries, sustainability has to be achieved at two levels simultaneously—the sustainability of natural resources and the sustainability of livelihoods. Biodiversity conservation has, therefore, to be linked to conservation of livelihoods derived from using biodiversity. Biodiversity cannot be conserved until its conservation helps local people make a living.[56]

The growing numbers of poor people in the developing world are seen as the greatest threat to conservation of biological diversity and, indeed, they may well be. However, give communities (or private landholders) secure property rights to their resources and simultaneously make them bear all costs and receive all income related to those resources, and they will have the proper set of incentives to husband those resources sustainably to ensure their own future.

Conclusions

Briefly, the most significant points from each of the main sections in this paper are:

1. Biodiversity is a property or characteristic of living organisms that captures the essence of their variability derived from evolutionary history. It is difficult to define unequivocally.
2. There is no agreed system for the classification or quantification of biological diversity at the genetic, species, or ecosystem levels.
3. No theories adequately explain biodiversity. Generally, species diversity is higher than would be expected from competitive exclusion theories, and this is thought to be a result of nonequilibrium processes maintained either by disturbances or by patchiness in the environment. The predictions obtained from island biogeographical theory and species/area curves do not correspond with the realities of species abundance in the field. Most of the scientific research is directed at explaining species diversity rather than biological diversity per se.
4. There is considerable divergence among scientists about the status of the biodiversity of the world's species and ecosystems:
   a. Uncertainty reigns over the number of species that have actually been taxonomically described, and even greater uncertainty over the number of species that remain to be identified.
   b. There is a paucity of data on the numbers of species that have become extinct this century. The majority of extinctions have occurred on islands, and there are weaknesses in attempts to extrapolate from small areas to global scales. Theoretically

derived rates of extinction remain to be verified with real data, and the manner in which figures have been presented appears designed to be alarmist.

   c. Those losses of species that have been clearly documented do not appear to have dire implications either for ecosystem functioning or for human survival.

   d. The most recent figures on numbers of endangered species are more an artifact of new criteria used than they are indicative of any sudden change in the rate of loss of biodiversity. The criteria on minimum viable populations for species are controversial.

   e. The loss of forest cover and the decrease in species population sizes of marine organisms is a cause for concern. The implications of these losses for biological diversity are, however, difficult to predict, despite alarmist predictions to the contrary.

   f. Directly linked to the loss of forest cover and perhaps the greatest threat to terrestrial biodiversity are the land use changes that are taking place all over the world. This problem is particularly serious in the savanna regions of Africa and provides a logical focus for conservation efforts.

5. There are major differences between what are perceived as conservation priorities by scientists addressing problems at a global level of understanding and those seen by practitioners at a local level. Even within the global scientific community, there is disagreement as to whether the global focus should be on genetic, species, or ecosystem aspects of biological diversity.

6. Global solutions, such as increasing the number of protected areas and bringing pressure to bear on sovereign nations through international conservation treaties, do not appear to offer any significant prospect for improving the status of biological diversity. Indeed, in many instances their net contributions are not merely not positive: They may actually have negative effects on conservation.

7. The lack of emphasis in the bulk of the scientific literature on adaptive management, both as the primary research method needed to understand biological diversity at the ecosystem level and as the necessary management tool, is disappointing. In the imperialist drive toward global planning, the emphasis is on blueprint designs instead of process-based approaches.

8. The conservation of biodiversity requires local solutions in the majority of cases. Both in the oceans and in terrestrial ecosystems, the key problem is that of the unmanaged open-access commons, including those areas that are effectively open-access systems by virtue of ineffectual state ownership. The necessary and sufficient factors that have to be addressed to solve this problem are tenure (property rights systems) and resource economics. These two factors are critically linked and consideration of one without the other will not solve any conservation problems or produce any useful scientific results.

   a. Secure tenure is essential for landholders to invest in biodiversity conservation.

Effective ownership needs to be devolved to the smallest accountable institutional level in order to be effective. Partial or comanaged systems seldom provide the suite of incentives necessary to prevent landholders from adopting alternative land uses. In the case of marine systems, stakeholders require secure property rights.

    b. Given secure tenure, the higher the value of biological resources the greater is the likelihood that viable forms of land use will be adopted and that these will outcompete the alternatives that remove biodiversity. Any artificial constraints, such as barriers to trade or prohibitions on wildlife use, are simply likely to drive land use in the direction that eliminates biodiversity.

9. These two requirements imply a reduced direct involvement of governments in conservation issues in the future. The major requirement of governments will lie in adopting facilitatory policies, promulgating enabling legislation, providing demand-driven services to landholders and stakeholders, and defending their citizens' interests in international agreements.

Given these conditions, there is every possibility that downward trends in biological diversity in many areas of the world can be reversed.

BENCHMARKS
The Global Trends That Are Shaping Our World

Compiled by Paul Georgia, Indur Goklany, and
the Competitive Enterprise Institute Staff

1

WORLD DOMESTIC PRODUCT

Global economic output has increased dramatically since World War II. World gross domestic product (GDP) has more than doubled from 1970 to 1996, rising from just under $9.5 trillion to just over $20.3 trillion. During the 1970s, 1980s, and 1990s, global gross national product per capita has also increased significantly. Individual productivity rose considerably in the latter half of the 1980s, spurred by advances in technology and a wave of market liberalization around the globe. The world GDP chart on the facing page reflects the level of global prosperity by measuring the cumulative domestic product values for all national economies. Growth in GDP per capita slowed between 1979 and 1982 due to a worldwide global recession and the debt crisis that affected many developing countries, but it has since rebounded.

While North America and Western Europe have enjoyed steady and significant economic growth for the past two centuries, many of the world's less developed regions are catching up at an accelerated rate, taking advantage of modern methods of production and the wider acceptance of free markets.

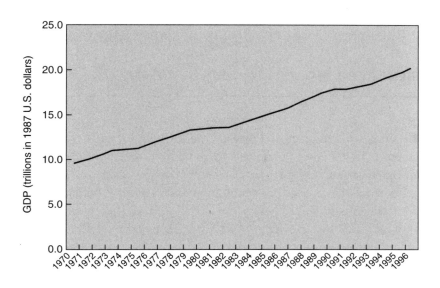

Year	World Gross Domestic Product	Year	World Gross Domestic Product
1970	9,450,166,076,034	1984	14,674,484,342,781
1971	9,816,371,377,560	1985	15,158,234,906,451
1972	10,340,064,984,779	1986	15,624,911,230,455
1973	10,990,194,678,911	1987	16,175,354,872,414
1974	11,141,790,374,487	1988	16,884,927,157,508
1975	11,273,552,089,835	1989	17,481,077,283,547
1976	11,833,788,308,760	1990	17,870,020,909,942
1977	12,292,473,709,311	1991	18,028,672,967,877
1978	12,803,273,274,312	1992	18,329,438,118,253
1979	13,278,366,711,110	1993	18,634,043,334,043
1980	13,447,958,987,563	1994	19,190,956,808,051
1981	13,629,730,465,989	1995	19,715,785,040,303
1982	13,674,043,097,086	1996	20,314,198,529,127
1983	14,056,314,083,121		

Source: World Bank, *World Development Indicators, 1998* (Washington, D.C.: IBRD/World Bank, 1998).

2

SATELLITE-BASED MONTHLY GLOBAL TEMPERATURES 1979–1998

Ground-based temperature measurements have shown a warming of the planet of about 0.1 to 0.15°C per decade in the last century, giving rise to concern that man-made greenhouse gases may be dangerously warming the planet. The ground-based temperature record, however, suffers from many problems, such as the urban heat island effect, which make it difficult to tell whether the observed warming is real or an artifact of instrument or measurement error.

Highly accurate temperature measurements, however, have been taken from space using microwave sounding units (MSUs) aboard satellites since 1979. At the end of 1997, the satellite data showed a slight cooling trend of 0.01°C per decade. Most of 1998, however, was very warm creating a small warming trend in the satellite data of +0.04° over the last 20 years. The satellite data are highly correlated with balloon temperature data taken from radiosonde instruments, strengthening the confidence in the accuracy of the satellite data.

MSUs measure the temperature of the lower troposphere, the atmospheric layer from the surface to 20,000 feet. This layer of the atmosphere is important for climatic research because global circulation models predict that global warming will be much more pronounced in the lower troposphere than at the surface. The failure of the satellite data to verify global climate model predictions seriously challenges the idea that greenhouse gas emissions are likely to cause significant global warming in the next century.

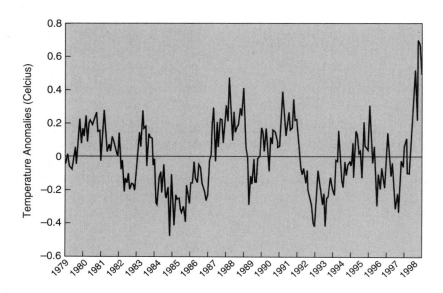

Satellite-Based Monthly Global Temperature

Year	Monthly Global Temperature	Year	Monthly Global Temperature	Year	Monthly Global Temperature	Year	Monthly Global Temperature	Year	Monthly Global Temperature
1979	−0.047	1982	−0.014	1986	−0.023	1990	0.211	1994	0.087
1979	0.013	1983	0.148	1986	0.005	1990	0.393	1994	−0.117
1979	−0.021	1983	0.056	1987	0.225	1990	0.286	1994	0.16
1979	−0.068	1983	0.278	1987	0.295	1991	0.133	1994	0.136
1979	−0.083	1983	0.17	1987	−0.026	1991	0.181	1995	0.022
1979	−0.042	1983	0.183	1987	0.213	1991	0.268	1995	0.041
1979	0.05	1983	−0.055	1987	0.055	1991	0.165	1995	−0.12
1979	−0.052	1983	0.139	1987	0.233	1991	0.183	1995	0.211
1979	0.103	1983	0.121	1987	0.23	1991	0.349	1995	0.065
1979	0.225	1983	0.113	1987	0.086	1991	0.227	1995	0.061
1979	0.072	1983	−0.056	1987	0.175	1991	0.233	1995	0.047
1979	0.167	1983	−0.012	1987	0.315	1991	0.11	1995	0.316
1980	0.116	1983	−0.277	1987	0.221	1991	0.013	1995	0.134
1980	0.246	1984	−0.288	1987	0.482	1991	−0.082	1995	−0.036
1980	0.089	1984	−0.127	1988	0.327	1991	−0.103	1995	0.064
1980	0.206	1984	−0.093	1988	0.102	1992	−0.065	1995	−0.187
1980	0.218	1984	−0.22	1988	0.272	1992	−0.149	1996	−0.289
1980	0.196	1984	−0.052	1988	0.163	1992	−0.076	1996	−0.1
1980	0.193	1984	−0.235	1988	0.19	1992	−0.204	1996	−0.187
1980	0.23	1984	−0.25	1988	0.191	1992	−0.237	1996	−0.062
1980	0.265	1984	−0.183	1988	0.292	1992	−0.277	1996	−0.103
1980	0.151	1984	−0.474	1988	0.243	1992	−0.394	1996	−0.183
1980	0.158	1984	−0.107	1988	0.421	1992	−0.413	1996	−0.035
1980	−0.033	1984	−0.315	1988	0.191	1992	−0.318	1996	0.146
1981	0.19	1984	−0.412	1988	0.06	1992	−0.077	1996	0.006
1981	0.278	1985	−0.227	1988	0.006	1992	−0.133	1996	−0.112
1981	0.187	1985	−0.255	1989	−0.281	1992	−0.204	1996	−0.033
1981	0.027	1985	−0.244	1989	−0.113	1993	−0.282	1996	−0.113
1981	0.072	1985	−0.319	1989	−0.159	1993	−0.211	1997	−0.307
1981	0.026	1985	−0.333	1989	−0.017	1993	−0.406	1997	−0.21
1981	0.121	1985	−0.297	1989	−0.153	1993	−0.244	1997	−0.324
1981	0.101	1985	−0.386	1989	−0.149	1993	−0.237	1997	−0.259
1981	0.059	1985	−0.173	1989	−0.011	1993	−0.161	1997	−0.021
1981	0.02	1985	−0.24	1989	0.006	1993	−0.12	1997	−0.055
1981	−0.002	1985	−0.286	1989	0.175	1993	−0.191	1997	0.073
1981	0.126	1985	−0.156	1989	0.15	1993	−0.224	1997	0.113
1982	−0.08	1985	−0.156	1989	0.032	1993	−0.017	1997	−0.096
1982	−0.025	1986	−0.034	1989	0.17	1993	−0.029	1997	−0.097
1982	−0.217	1986	−0.128	1990	0.03	1993	0.157	1997	0
1982	−0.131	1986	−0.155	1990	−0.087	1994	0	1997	0.158
1982	−0.158	1986	−0.048	1990	0.124	1994	−0.131	1998	0.323
1982	−0.104	1986	−0.063	1990	0.08	1994	−0.182	1998	0.525
1982	−0.197	1986	−0.157	1990	0.164	1994	−0.028	1998	0.227
1982	−0.161	1986	−0.177	1990	0.154	1994	−0.107	1998	0.705
1982	−0.166	1986	−0.206	1990	0.126	1994	−0.039	1998	0.681
1982	−0.204	1986	−0.26	1990	0.06	1994	−0.023	1998	0.509
1982	−0.122	1986	−0.228	1990	0.065	1994	−0.053		

3

POPULATION PROJECTIONS, WORLD

World population has more than doubled since 1950 almost entirely because of the large reduction in worldwide death rates, not a major increase in global birthrates. The decline in death rates should continue as economic growth and scientific advances improve human health.

The United Nations issues a series of population projections for the twenty-first century, but population projections vary widely depending on the assumptions used. Without further understanding of how the projections were calculated, one might assume that the "medium projection" is the most likely. In fact, the medium U.N. projection assumes that acceleration or deceleration of death and fertility rates will continue as they have in recent years. However, much evidence suggests that this assumption is wrong. Historically, in a given society, after a lag period, a rapid reduction in fertility rates follows a drop in mortality rates due to economic progress. When economic development modernizes an economy by improving women's education, per capita incomes, and the infant mortality rate, fertility rates quickly decline to the point at which the population's fertility rate is at or below zero. This process has already been completed in all Western nations, and even in Asia and Latin America, and some parts of Africa, fertility rates are dropping rapidly. Several Asian countries, including Bangladesh, India, Pakistan and others, have experienced much faster decreases in fertility rates than previously expected. Bangladesh's fertility rate, for example, dropped 45 percent from its 1980–1985 average of 6.2 births per woman to an average of 3.4 births per woman. Future reductions in the world fertility rate are likely to produce populations more in line with the U.N.'s low projection, at which point world population would reach 8 billion around 2040 and then begin to decline. In any event, population will slow at some point; even the highest projected U.N. trend has the world's population stop growing in 2075.

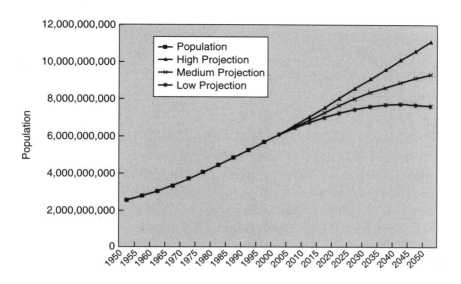

Population Projections, World

Year	Population	High Projection	Medium Projection	Low Projection
1950	2,524,000,000			
1955	2,759,000,000			
1960	3,027,000,000			
1965	3,343,000,000			
1970	3,702,000,000			
1975	4,081,000,000			
1980	4,447,000,000			
1985	4,847,000,000			
1990	5,282,000,000			
1995	5,687,000,000			
2000		6,123,000,000	6,091,000,000	6,062,000,000
2005		6,581,000,000	6,491,000,000	6,409,000,000
2010		7,060,000,000	6,891,000,000	6,726,000,000
2015		7,554,000,000	7,286,000,000	7,010,000,000
2020		8,062,000,000	7,672,000,000	7,264,000,000
2025		8,581,000,000	8,039,000,000	7,474,000,000
2030		9,099,000,000	8,372,000,000	7,625,000,000
2035		9,614,000,000	8,669,000,000	7,715,000,000
2040		10,123,000,000	8,930,000,000	7,746,000,000
2045		10,633,000,000	9,159,000,000	7,725,000,000
2050		11,156,000,000	9,367,000,000	7,662,000,000

Source: UN Population Division (1997): World Population Prospects: The 1996 Revision (draft).

4
ESTIMATED AND PROJECTED TOTAL FERTILITY RATES, WORLD

Fertility rates worldwide have been declining over the past several decades. One of the clearest indicators of fertility, the total fertility rate (TFR), corresponds to the average number of births per woman over the course of childbearing ages. The world's TFR has dropped by two-fifths since 1960/1965, from roughly 5 children per woman to 3 children per woman today, and appears to be heading toward further decline. The TFR for the world's developed regions dropped by nearly a third, from 2.7 children per woman in 1960/1965 to 1.7 children per woman in 1990/1995. This is below the replacement level of 2.1 children per woman. The less developed regions of the world have witnessed a steep 45 percent reduction in their TFRs while the least developed regions have experienced a nearly a 17 percent reduction in their TFRs.

These fertility declines are due, in part, to significant advancements in contraceptive technology since World War II. However, changes in desired fertility that have accompanied economic development appear to have been the dominant force behind lower fertility rates.

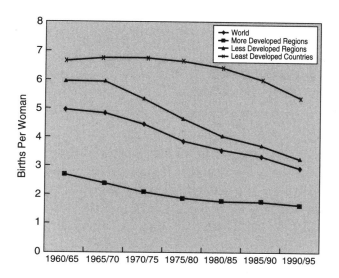

Estimated and Projected Total Fertility Rates, World

Period	World	More Developed Regions	Less Developed Regions	Least Developed Countries
1960/1965	5	2.7	6	6.6
1965/1970	4.9	2.4	6	6.7
1970/1975	4.5	2.1	5.4	6.7
1975/1980	3.9	1.9	4.7	6.6
1980/1985	3.6	1.8	4.1	6.4
1985/1990	3.4	1.8	3.8	6
1990/1995	3	1.7	3.3	5.5

Source: U.N. Population Division (1997): World Population Prospects: The 1996 Revision (draft).

5

ESTIMATED AND PROJECTED LIFE EXPECTANCY AT BIRTH, WORLD

The twentieth century has witnessed an explosion in global health, as evidenced by the dramatic increase in human longevity. Life expectancy since 1950 has increased by just over 38 percent, from 46.5 years to 64.3 years. Life spans for populations in the less-developed regions have increased over 50 percent, from 40.9 years in 1950/1955 to 62.1 years currently. Life spans in even the least developed regions rose dramatically from 35.5 years in 1950 to nearly 50 years today. Populations from the world's more developed regions have extended their average life span by nearly eight full years in the same period, from 66.5 years to 74.2 years.

Technological progress has been a driving force behind the extension of the human life span. Medical breakthroughs, infrastructure improvement, and innovations in communications and transport have improved the quality and capacity of medical relief to be administered to the world's populations. Improved medical care has factored into the nearly 60 percent decline of infant mortality rates, which in turn strongly affects life expectancy at birth. Agriculture innovations also have yielded an increase in the supply and availability of the world's food. Increased food availability has averted millions of deaths from starvation that would have otherwise occurred.

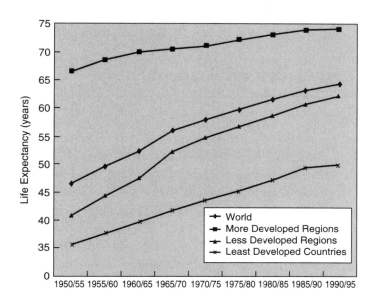

Estimated Life Expectancy at Birth, World

Period	World	More Developed Regions	Less Developed Regions	Least Developed Countries
1950/1955	46.5	66.5	40.9	35.5
1955/1960	49.6	68.5	44.4	37.7
1960/1965	52.3	69.8	47.7	39.6
1965/1970	56	70.5	52.2	41.8
1970/1975	57.9	71.2	54.7	43.6
1975/1980	59.7	72.2	56.7	45.2
1980/1985	61.3	73	58.6	47.1
1985/1990	63.1	74	60.6	49.3
1990/1995	64.3	74.2	62.1	49.7

Source: U.N. Population Division (1997): World Population Prospects: The 1996 Revision (draft).

6

WETLANDS LOSSES AND GAINS, UNITED STATES

One of the main concerns about economic development is the effect it has on land use. In particular, some fear that species habitat and environmentally sensitive areas will be converted to other uses. In the United States, much of this concern has focused on wetlands because they serve to filter water and can play an important role in coastal buffer zones. Many animal species, including whooping cranes, alligators, and two-thirds of North American species of ducks and geese, either live or breed on wetlands.

In the postwar period, wetlands have been converted to other uses at a dramatic rate in the United States: 300,000 to 450,000 acres per year. Most wetlands were lost by being drained and converted into farmland. As farm productivity has increased, however, the rate of wetland conversion has slowed dramatically, from an average of 458,000 between 1954 and 1974, to an average of 135,000 acres per year between 1982 and 1992. At the same time, wetland restoration has emerged as a significant trend in the United States. Beginning in 1987, various incentive and restoration programs have been responsible for the restoration and creation of several hundred thousand acres of wetlands per year. The significant drop in wetlands restoration in 1993 was the resulted from the loss of funding for the Wetlands Reserve Program that year. In 1994 restoration resumed its previous pace and in 1995 wetland restoration occurred on 210,000 acres. The result is that there was no net loss of wetlands that year.

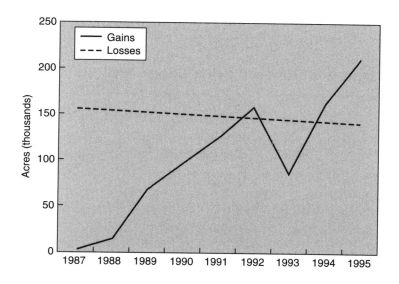

Wetlands Losses and Gains, United States

Year	Adjusted Restoration	Wetland Loss
1954–1975 (avg.)		
1974–1983 (avg.)		
1982–1992 (avg.)		
1987	2	156
1988	14	154
1989	68	152
1990	96	150
1991	125	148
1992	158	147
1993	85	145
1994	160	143
1995	210	141

Source: Wetlands Reserve Program, 1998.

7

ARABLE AND PERMANENT CROPLAND, WORLD

The amount of arable and permanent cropland worldwide has been increasing at a slow but relatively steady rate over the last 15 years. Global cropland area expanded by just over 1.5 percent between 1980 and 1995. While the overall trend was toward more cropland, many regions saw a decrease. The amount of European land under crops declined by about 4 percent between 1980 and 1995. Though North America has registered a slight cropland increase since 1980, cropland area has remained basically flat for the last 5 years. The former Soviet Union's area under crops declined by just under 1 percent between 1980 and 1993. The greatest increases in cropland from 1980 to 1993 occurred in Africa (7.2 percent), Oceania (5.7 percent), and Asia (2.9 percent). The large declines that occurred in 1991 and 1993 were the result of steep drops in food commodity prices.

Before the twentieth century, the world increased its food supply chiefly by expanding the amount of land cleared and planted in crops. By dramatically increasing the amount of food grown on land already under cultivation, humanity has already managed to save up to 10 million square miles—the total area of North America—of rain forests, wetlands, and mountain terrain from being plowed down. Higher agricultural yields were achieved by substituting more productive crop varieties, pesticides, and fertilizers for extra acreage.

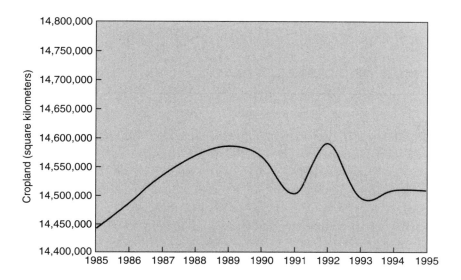

Arable and Permanent Cropland

Year	Cropland (square kilometers)
1970	13,772,210
1975	13,941,490
1980	14,273,070
1985	14,440,290
1986	14,485,500
1987	14,534,720
1988	14,568,330
1989	14,584,650
1990	14,566,890
1991	14,501,530
1992	14,590,050
1993	14,495,480
1994	14,508,380
1995	14,508,380

Source: Organization for Economic Cooperation and Development, *OECD Environmental Data, Compendium 1997* (Paris: OECD, 1997 & 1993).

8

PRODUCTION OF CEREALS, WORLD

World cereal output increased from close to 877 billion metric tons in 1961 to over 1.95 trillion metric tons in 1995. Japan and China are the globe's greatest net importers of cereal, while the United States, Canada, and France remain the world's leading net exporters of cereals. The world's developed countries accounted for most of this period's cereal production.

Cereal production expanded rapidly from 1974 to 1989 as Green Revolutoin technologies were adopted by farmers throughout developing regions, particularly in Asia. Since 1989, a slowdown in the growth rate of aggregate cereal production is discernible. This slowdown is primarily the result of grain surpluses that have driven down commodity prices and diminished the incentive to invest in cereal production, irrigation development projects, and agriculture infrastructure.

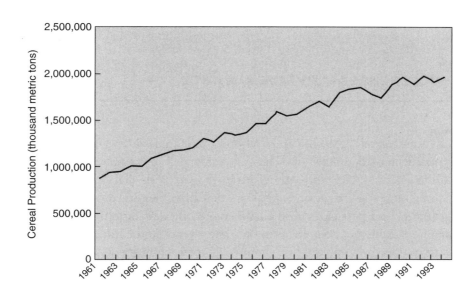

Production of Cereals, World

Year	Cereal Production (thousand metric tons)	Year	Cereal Production (thousand metric tons)
1961	876,892	1978	1,582,254
1962	933,474	1979	1,538,482
1963	949,459	1980	1,548,813
1964	1,001,434	1981	1,632,723
1965	998,321	1982	1,693,999
1966	1,078,437	1983	1,625,989
1967	1,123,716	1984	1,786,572
1968	1,160,578	1985	1,822,721
1969	1,170,656	1986	1,835,803
1970	1,192,086	1987	1,768,183
1971	1,299,007	1988	1,725,544
1972	1,258,139	1989	1,868,766
1973	1,357,972	1990	1,946,554
1974	1,326,081	1991	1,876,297
1975	1,361,274	1992	1,960,172
1976	1,462,286	1993	1,891,578
1977	1,455,421	1994	1,950,600

Source: World Resources Institute, World Resources 1996–1997 data on diskette (Washington, D.C.: World Resources Institute, 1996).

9

AREA OF CEREALS HARVESTED, WORLD

The acreage devoted to cereal production increased from 1961 to 1981 and has since decreased somewhat. The dispersion of Green Revolution farming technologies into Asia and other developing regions boosted cereal production through massive irrigation expansion, new high-yielding crop varieties, enhanced fertilizers and pesticides, and newer, more efficient farming methods. India was able to double its wheat yields in only a few years, and China now supports 22 percent of the world's population on just 7 percent of its arable land. Since the 1970s, global rice yields have risen 49 percent, wheat yields have risen 50 percent, and corn and sorghum have risen 28 percent.

The coming years promise even more productive cereal varieties. For example, the Veery wheats, particularly suited to Africa's subtropical climate, could boost the region's yields by up to 15 percent. Similarly, new Chinese hybrid rice and acid and salt-tolerant plant varieties that can thrive in hot, arid, and previously uncultivable areas are under development. Plant breeders at the International Rice Research Institute in the Philippines estimate that they can boost the productivity of rice by 15 to 20 percent in the next decade.

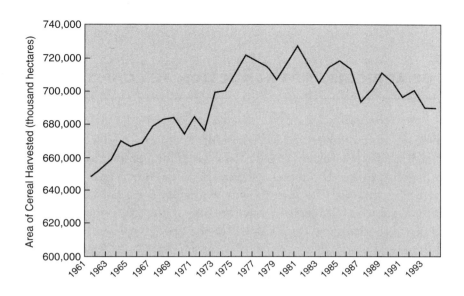

Year	Area of Cereals Harvested, World	Year	Area of Cereals Harvested, World
1961	647,738	1978	714,981
1962	653,361	1979	707,214
1963	658,781	1980	717,013
1964	670,185	1981	727,184
1965	666,335	1982	714,811
1966	668,768	1983	704,359
1967	678,790	1984	714,141
1968	682,732	1985	718,507
1969	683,858	1986	713,205
1970	673,793	1987	693,299
1971	684,705	1988	700,145
1972	675,848	1989	710,840
1973	699,024	1990	705,458
1974	699,814	1991	696,205
1975	711,261	1992	700,409
1976	721,851	1993	689,412
1977	718,875	1994	689,146

Source: World Resources Institute, World Resources 1996–1997 data on diskette (Washington, D.C.: World Resources Institute, 1996).

10

INDEX OF AGRICULTURE PRODUCTION PER CAPITA, WORLD

Agriculture production has consistently outpaced population growth over the past 30 years. The pattern of per capita agricultural production has also been fairly consistent: a period of impressive growth, followed by a brief period of stagnation or decline, followed by more growth. Although there has been a recent measurable slowdown of per capita agriculture output due to economic factors, it appears to be on the upswing again. Causes of the brief slowdown included tremendous surpluses in world food supplies that prompted North America and Europe to restrain their production. Moreover, the chaos that followed the demise of communism in Eastern Europe and the former Soviet Union dramatically reduced the region's contribution to global agriculture production. Meanwhile, the third world has managed to increase agricultural productivity (recently) at an annual rate of 5 percent. It is noteworthy that each of the low points or dips in the cycle (1965, 1972, 1980, 1983, 1987, and 1992) is higher than the previous dip.

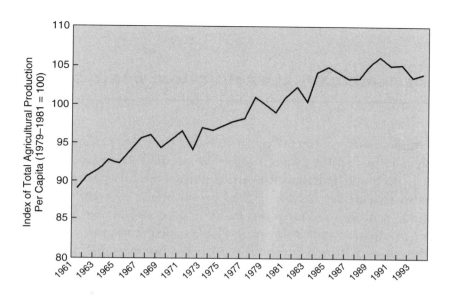

Year	Index of Agriculture Production Per Capita, World	Year	Index of Agriculture Production Per Capita, World
1961	88.98	1978	100.86
1962	90.61	1979	100.06
1963	91.41	1980	98.98
1964	92.85	1981	100.96
1965	92.29	1982	102.3
1966	93.9	1983	100.23
1967	95.53	1984	104.09
1968	96.06	1985	104.81
1969	94.3	1986	104.05
1970	95.37	1987	103.13
1971	96.55	1988	103.22
1972	94	1989	105.03
1973	97.05	1990	105.95
1974	96.68	1991	104.88
1975	97.24	1992	104.97
1976	97.82	1993	103.36
1977	98.18	1994	103.81

Source: World Resources Institute, World Resources 1996–1997 data on diskette (Washington, D.C.: World Resources Institute, 1996).

11

INDEX OF AGRICULTURAL PRODUCTION, WORLD TOTAL

Almost without exception, agricultural productivity worldwide has risen year after year since 1961. Some of this increase can be attributed to cropland expansion, but most is the result of technological advances in farming, which have boosted yields per hectare of land exponentially over the past 25 years. The world's agriculture research system has proven international collaboration to be one of the most critical boons to global agricultural productivity. The International Rice Research Institute, the Centro Internacional de Mejoramiento de Maiz y Trigo, and the Consultative Group on International Agricultural Research work collectively to bring new scientific ideas to bear on the world's agricultural sectors.

The outlook for the future of yield performance is bright. The fact that the overall yield performance of most crops shows little sign of slowing down indicates that higher yields are still attainable. Developing countries showed considerable progress with certain crops in the 1980s and into the 1990s. For example, worldwide yields of maize grew at about 47 kilograms per hectare for each year in the 1980s, and 55 kilograms per hectare for each year in the 1990s. Many developing countries have enjoyed yield gains that were even higher than the world average. Chile experienced an astronomical gain of just over 400 kilograms per hectare per year in the 1980s, and has continued to outpace worldwide average yields at nearly 180 kilograms per hectare per year during the 1990s.

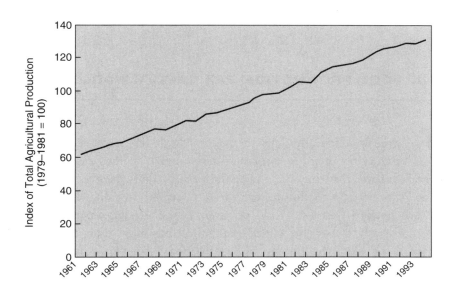

Year	Index of Agriculture Production, World Total	Year	Index of Agriculture Production, World Total
1961	61.68	1978	97.48
1962	64.06	1979	98.36
1963	65.92	1980	98.97
1964	68.33	1981	102.68
1965	69.31	1982	105.85
1966	71.97	1983	105.51
1967	74.74	1984	111.48
1968	76.72	1985	114.23
1969	76.88	1986	115.41
1970	79.34	1987	116.41
1971	81.97	1988	118.57
1972	81.42	1989	122.72
1973	85.73	1990	125.89
1974	87.05	1991	126.7
1975	89.2	1992	128.8
1976	91.35	1993	128.82
1977	93.29	1994	131.14

Source: World Resources Institute, World Resources 1996–1997 data on diskette (Washington, D.C.: World Resources Institute, 1996).

12

INDEX OF FOOD PRODUCTION PER CAPITA, WORLD

The world's continuing growth in population has sparked some concern that food production might not increase fast enough to feed everyone. However, if trends continue as they have over the past 30 years, people will be better nourished than ever in the future regardless of population gains. There a is fairly consistent upward trend in world per capita food production from 1961 to 1994, despite the fact that the world's population has more than doubled since 1950. Over this period, the amount of food produced per person increased about 19.5 percent, mostly due to advances in farming technology.

The same kind of research that has brought about life-extending discoveries in vaccines, sanitation, and nutrition has also fostered advances in genetic engineering, irrigation, and pesticides that have kept food productivity well ahead of global increases in population. It is important to note that population growth is closely related to food abundance. More abundant food has helped reduce starvation and malnutrition and thus cut global death rates. This results in higher population growth rates. Economic growth and technological change have kept the food supply several steps ahead of the growing population.

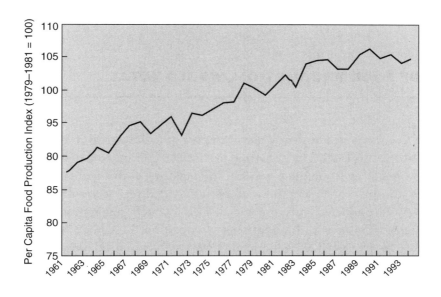

Year	Index of Food Production Per Capita, World	Year	Index of Food Production Per Capita, World
1961	87.59	1978	100.95
1962	89.12	1979	100.12
1963	89.86	1980	99.17
1964	91.41	1981	100.71
1965	90.48	1982	102.24
1966	92.74	1983	100.31
1967	94.56	1984	103.85
1968	95.21	1985	104.45
1969	93.37	1986	104.46
1970	94.7	1987	103.02
1971	95.89	1988	102.98
1972	93.06	1989	105.21
1973	96.49	1990	106.18
1974	96.07	1991	104.75
1975	97.07	1992	105.29
1976	98.05	1993	103.93
1977	97.97	1994	104.67

Source: World Resources Institute, World Resources 1996–1997 data on diskette (Washington, D.C.: World Resources Institute, 1996).

13
INDEX OF FOOD PRODUCTION, WORLD TOTAL

There was a steady, nearly uninterrupted growth in total world food production from 1961 to 1994. The growth in production continued despite ever lower world food prices over the same period. The majority of this increase in production is due to the implementation of better agriculture technology resulting from research conducted since the 1950s. This research, much of it done by the Consultative Group on International Agriculture Research, has fostered major advances in pesticides, genetic engineering, fertilization, prevention of soil erosion, crop rotation, irrigation techniques, and livestock production techniques.

In general, the rate of improvement seems to be increasing. After yields exceed 2000 kilograms per hectare per year, it requires less time to achieve each next 1000 kilograms per hectare per year in productivity. The reason is that the shift from subsistence agriculture to technological agriculture is an initially expensive procedure. After the shift is made, it is much easier to incorporate new scientific findings into farming practice. Most countries in the developing world have recently gone through this shift toward technology or will soon. The potential for increased implementation of the latest agriculture knowledge suggests that the growth in world food production will not slow in the near future.

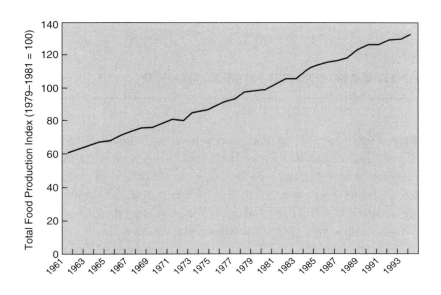

Year	Index of Food Production, World Total	Year	Index of Food Production, World Total
1961	60.71	1978	97.56
1962	63	1979	98.42
1963	64.81	1980	99.16
1964	67.27	1981	102.43
1965	67.95	1982	105.79
1966	71.08	1983	105.6
1967	73.98	1984	111.23
1968	76.05	1985	113.84
1969	76.12	1986	115.86
1970	78.78	1987	116.29
1971	81.41	1988	118.3
1972	80.61	1989	122.94
1973	85.24	1990	126.16
1974	86.5	1991	126.55
1975	89.04	1992	129.19
1976	91.56	1993	129.53
1977	93.09	1994	132.23

Source: World Resources Institute, World Resources 1996–1997 data on diskette (Washington, D.C.: World Resources Institute, 1996).

14

TOTAL FOOD COMMODITY INDEX, WORLD

Global food prices have been dropping steeply for more than 2 decades. This index of food commodity prices shows that throughout the 1960s, prices remained somewhat steady. A large peak in price came in the mid-1970s, followed by dramatic gains in food production that greatly outpaced population increases. The price surges in the 1973/1974 and 1977 were related directly and indirectly to the oil crisis of those years, which increased the costs of some aspects of food production and gave the Soviet Union (a major oil exporter) the wealth to purchase grain on the world market for livestock production, radically increasing demand. These productivity improvements have led to a relatively steady increase in food abundance since the late 1970s, when food prices were much higher. This abundance has brought about a near end to mass famine. Those that have occurred in the past few decades have been caused by political strife, not lack of resources.

Several factors contribute to the reduction in world food prices. One of the most significant has been the myriad of recent advances in agricultural technology. Another important factor in the drop in food prices was increased liberalization of global trade, which reduced the tariffs and price subsidies that previously had inflated food prices. Competition and increased crop specialization brought about a more efficient market in agricultural commodities.

There was a sharp price spike for corn and wheat in 1996 due to a temporary grain shortage that created when the United States and Western European governments abruptly began cutting their farm price support programs. As a result of these programs, the United States and the European Union had essentially been holding the world's grain stocks at their taxpayers expense for decades. While the United States and the European Union were cutting their stocks, they were also idling farmland. So when 1995 feed grain harvest was down 75 million tons from the year before, prices rose. Predictably, higher prices led to more production. The grain harvest in the OECD countries was up 15 percent the following year and world production rose 7 percent. Consequently, grain prices resumed their historic declines.

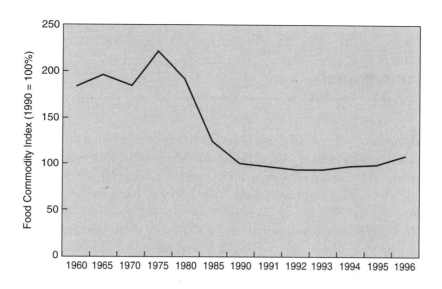

Year	Total Food Commodity Index, World (1990 = 100%)
1960	184
1965	196
1970	184
1975	221
1980	191
1985	124
1990	100
1991	97
1992	94
1993	93
1994	97
1995	98
1996	108

Source: World Resources Institute (WRI) in collaboration with the UN Environment Programme (UNEP), the UN Development Program (UNDP) and the World Bank, *World Resources 1998–1999: A Guide to the Global Environment* (New York: Oxford University Press, 1998), table 6.3.

15

FISH CATCH, WORLD

The growing demand for fish products has fueled the increase of the world's commercial fishing industry. Worldwide, the fishery harvest is over 100 million metric tons per year, an increase of over 55 percent above the harvest of just 2 decades ago. Advanced technologies have enabled ocean harvesting on an unprecedented scale.

It appears that the current rate of harvest is depleting many marine populations. In 1994, the U.S. government shut down portions of George's Bank, historically one of the world's most fertile fishing grounds, due to fishery depletion. Many species of marine mammals, in particular, are facing serious population declines as well. Worldwide, the fish catch had declined somewhat after 1989 but has resumed its steady climb.

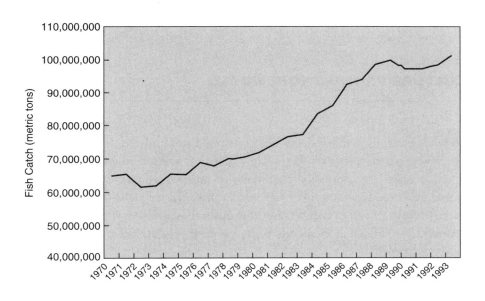

Year	Fish Catch, World	Year	Fish Catch, World
1970	65046654	1982	76449528
1971	65478919	1983	77027200
1972	61468284	1984	83584542
1973	61979968	1985	86019356
1974	65444914	1986	92386580
1975	65356812	1987	93916012
1976	68844401	1988	98589311
1977	67706662	1989	99782016
1978	69820914	1990	97130494
1979	70617192	1991	97006210
1980	71889590	1992	98155916
1981	74349198	1993	100946938

Source: World Resources Institute, World Resources 1996–1997 data on diskette (Washington, D.C.: World Resources Institute, 1996).

16

AQUACULTURE PRODUCTION, WORLD

As demand for fish products has continued to climb, some people have developed methods to raise fish on the equivalent of farms. Known as aquaculture, this practice holds the potential to reduce pressures on marine fisheries; more fish would be raised for human consumption rather than caught on the open seas. Per capita consumption of fish has not diminished even though marine catches have leveled off somewhat in recent years because production from aquaculture has made up the difference.

Aquaculture production increased by over 125 percent between 1984 and 1993, with the greatest increase occurring in Asia. Successful aquaculture techniques have been developed to farm salmon, tilapia, catfish, trout, abalone, oysters, crawfish, and shrimp, among others. Already in the United States, most trout and catfish served in restaurants are farm-raised, as are significant portions of crawfish and oysters. Worldwide, shrimp farms produce approximately one-fifth of the shrimp sold on the market.

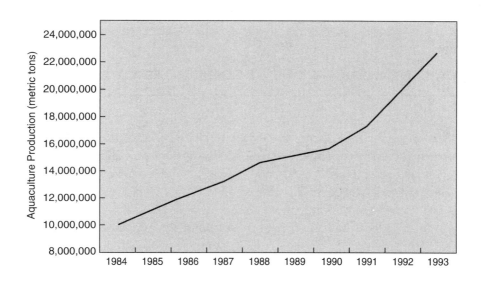

Aquaculture Production, World

Year	Africa	South America	North America	Central America	Europe	Asia	Oceania	USSR	World
1984	24511	57473	334173	66834	917435	8319422	25437	270754	10016039
1985	40220	58769	332171	69182	1006288	9375084	27840	293292	11202846
1986	40851	57457	382896	70465	1044097	10304842	36277	323501	12260386
1987	43283	108937	396131	88117	1080114	11120041	38487	348824	13223934
1988	51456	135171	381291	95863	1138697	12382939	41358	364783	14591558
1989	72117	154882	401346	99441	1158660	12868773	51047	354165	15160431
1990	63057	186327	348248	101159	1228683	13344221	52135	404278	15728108
1991	75761	256970	409761	88105	1221594	14690044	74566	437610	17254411
1992	77776	295267	461452	85546	1355389	17450848	79743	0	19806021
1993	75088	295275	485000	77413	1351224	20233529	84133	0	22601662

Source: World Resources Institute, World Resources 1996–1997 data on diskette (Washington, D.C.: World Resources Institute, 1996).

17

PER CAPITA EMISSIONS OF CARBON DIOXIDE, WORLD

Global emissions of carbon dioxide (CO_2) have increased since the 1950s, primarily driven by the rise in fossil fuel consumption throughout the world. The dramatic increase in the 1960s and 1970s has since slowed, however, with CO_2 emissions actually declining from 1979 to 1983. In 1991, CO_2 emissions increased only 1.5 percent over the previous year, and much of that was due to the Kuwaiti oil fires. Indeed, had the fires not resulted in the emission of 130 million metric tons of CO_2, global CO_2 emissions would have declined in 1991.

The global emission of CO_2 has slowed, in large part due to the leveling off of per capita CO_2 emissions, which peaked at 1.23 metric tons of carbon per capita in 1979. Since then per capita CO_2 emissions have fluctuated mildly, with no significant increase or decrease.

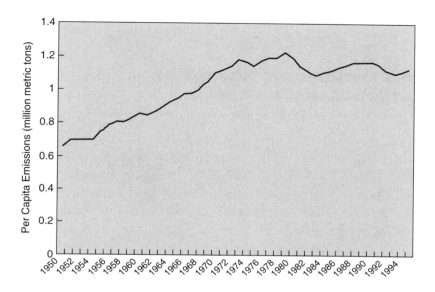

Per Capita Emissions of Carbon Dioxide, World

Year	Per Capita Emissions (million metric tons)	Year	Per Capita Emissions (million metric tons)
1950	0.65	1973	1.18
1951	0.69	1974	1.16
1952	0.69	1975	1.13
1953	0.69	1976	1.17
1954	0.69	1977	1.19
1955	0.74	1978	1.18
1956	0.78	1979	1.22
1957	0.8	1980	1.19
1958	0.8	1981	1.13
1959	0.83	1982	1.1
1960	0.85	1983	1.08
1961	0.84	1984	1.1
1962	0.86	1985	1.11
1963	0.89	1986	1.13
1964	0.92	1987	1.14
1965	0.94	1988	1.16
1966	0.97	1989	1.16
1967	0.98	1990	1.16
1968	1.01	1991	1.15
1969	1.05	1992	1.11
1970	1.1	1993	1.09
1971	1.12	1994	1.1
1972	1.14	1995	1.12

Source: G. Marland, R. J. Andres, T. A. Boden, C. Johnson, and A. Brenkert, "Revised Global CO2 Emissions from Fossil-Fuel Burning, Cement Manufacture, and Gas Flaring: 1751–1995," in *Trends Online: A Compendium of Data on Global Change,* (Oak Ridge, TN: Carbon Dioxide Information Analysis Center, Oak Ridge National Laboratory, January 1998), http://cdiac.esd.ornl.gov/trends/trends.htm.

18

ESTIMATED ATMOSPHERIC RELEASES OF CHLOROFLUOROCARBONS, WORLD

Chlorofluorocarbons (CFCs) were first used in the 1930s as refrigerants. After World War II, CFC-11 and CFC-12, the two most prominent CFCs, were also used as blowing agents for closed-cell foams (used for insulation) and as propellants for aerosol sprays. CFCs were popular because they are nonflammable and nontoxic, unlike the substances they replaced.

In the 1970s, concerns were raised about the potential impact of CFCs on the stratospheric ozone layer. Releases of CFCs into the atmosphere, it is believed, initiate a chain reaction that thins the ozone layer and potentially exposes the earth's surface to an increase in damaging ultraviolet solar radiation. These concerns led to the ban of CFCs for use in aerosols in the United States and an overall decline in the release of CFC-11 and CFC-12 into the atmosphere. However, this downward trend was quickly overtaken by a rapid increase in the use of CFCs in the developing world. This trend was reversed with the ratification of the Montreal Protocol in 1987 (subsequently amended in 1990 and 1992), which calls for phasing out all CFC production. Due to the widespread use of CFCs, particularly in refrigeration units and air conditioners, the phaseout will come at considerable costs: an estimated $100 billion in the United States alone.

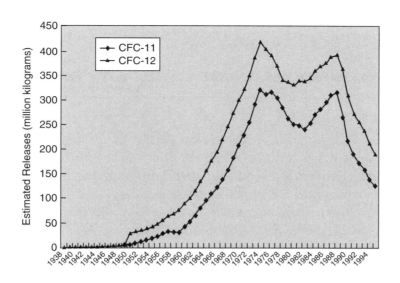

Estimated Atmospheric Releases of Chlorofluorocarbons, World

Year	Atmospheric Release (million kilograms)		Year	Atmospheric Release (million kilograms)	
	CFC-11	CFC-12		CFC-11	CFC-12
1938	0.1	0.1	1967	137.6	219.9
1939	0.1	0.1	1968	156.8	246.5
1940	0.1	0.1	1969	181.9	274.3
1941	0.1	0.2	1970	206.6	299.9
1942	0.1	0.4	1971	226.9	321.8
1943	0.2	0.5	1972	255.8	349.9
1944	0.2	0.8	1973	292.4	387.3
1945	0.3	1.2	1974	321.4	418.6
1946	0.6	1.7	1975	310.9	404.1
1947	1.3	2.3	1976	316.7	390.4
1948	2.3	3	1977	303.9	371.2
1949	3.8	3.7	1978	283.6	341.3
1950	5.5	29.5	1979	263.7	337.5
1951	7.6	32.4	1980	250.8	332.5
1952	11	33.7	1981	248.2	340.7
1953	15	37.9	1982	239.5	337.4
1954	18.6	42.9	1983	252.8	343.3
1955	23	48.2	1984	271.1	359.4
1956	28.7	56.1	1985	280.8	368.4
1957	32.2	63.8	1986	295.1	376.5
1958	30.2	66.9	1987	310.6	386.5
1959	30.9	74.8	1988	314.5	392.8
1960	40.5	89.1	1989	265.2	364.7
1961	52.1	99.7	1990	216.1	310.5
1962	65.4	114.5	1991	188.3	271.6
1963	80	133.9	1992	171.1	255.3
1964	95	155.5	1993	157.9	237.8
1965	108.3	175.4	1994	137.4	211.5
1966	121.3	195	1995	123.8	188.6

Source: Alternative Fluorocarbons Environmental Acceptability Study, January 1997, *Production, Sales and Atmospheric Release of Fluorocarbons Through 1995*.

19

METALS AND MINERALS, WORLD COMMODITY INDEX

There was a sustained, though erratic, decline in the world prices of metals and minerals from 1960 to 1996. Although metals and minerals exist in fixed quantities, prices have tended to decrease over time rather than increase. The chief reason for lower prices is that the supply of metals and minerals is increasing. New supplies of these resources have been discovered with improvements in technology and scientific knowledge that allow miners to locate sources for metals and minerals more precisely. Also, new technologies have made mining of less-concentrated minerals, or minerals located in previously inaccessible areas, economically feasible. Improvements in mining technology were spurred by the volatility of the market, as depicted in the graph. Despite the long-term downward trend in prices, occasional increases in price caused by sudden scarcity made advanced technologies profitable. This encourages further research, and once demand is met, market forces fostered increases in efficiency, which in turn lower the price of new technology. This spiral of ever more productive technology increases supply faster than demand can grow.

On the demand side, the occasional price spikes encourage conservation efforts. More abundant substitutes for the commodity were found, technologies that use less of scarce resources were developed, and more efficient methods of waste recovery were discovered. Markets ceaselessly encourage the development of more efficient resource uses, making the limited supply of any physical commodity ultimately irrelevant.

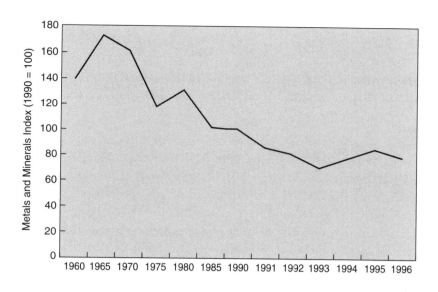

Year	Metals and Minerals, World Commodity Index
1960	139
1965	173
1970	162
1975	118
1980	132
1985	102
1990	100
1991	87
1992	81
1993	70
1994	77
1995	85
1996	78

Source: WRI, UNEP, UNDP, The World Bank, *World Resources 1998–1999: A Guide to the Global Environment*, table 3.

20

CRUDE OIL DOMESTIC FIRST PURCHASE PRICES

The price of crude oil declined steadily from 1959 to the early 1970s. Prices increased sharply in 1974 due to the Arab oil embargo and jumped again in 1979 in response to the Iranian revolution. After regional political crises and domestic energy regulations relaxed, the price of oil dropped steeply. In 1994, crude oil prices adjusted for inflation were lower than they had been in 20 years. The years 1995 and 1996 saw a rise in prices once again. Although not shown here, 1999 global petroleum prices in real terms reached levels that were lower than they had been at any time since the 1940s. Prices spiked up again at the end of 1999.

When crude oil prices exceeded $40 per barrel in 1981, new techniques for locating and drilling for oil were developed. This increased the supply, thus loosening the OPEC nations' ability to affect oil prices. New geological research boosted the exploration of oil in many countries that had previously produced little or none. Brazil, for example, eventually produced as much as a half a million barrels per day. Similar new production capabilities in countries around the globe greatly increased non-OPEC sources of oil.

Higher oil prices also encouraged switching to alternative sources of energy, chiefly coal and natural gas. New research in these competing energy sources yielded similar gains in production capacity, greatly increasing overall energy supplies. This diversification of energy sources and technologies has both cut oil prices to precrisis levels and made the oil market more resilient to other potential global crises.

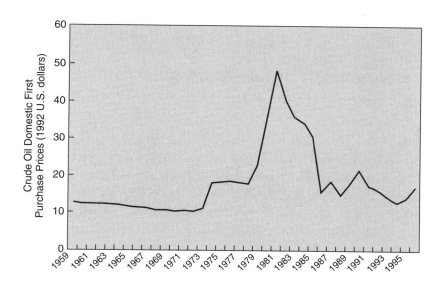

Crude Oil Domestic First Purchase Prices

Year	Real (1992 dollars)	Year	Real (1992 dollars)
1959	12.66	1978	17.65
1960	12.36	1979	22.86
1961	12.25	1980	35.75
1962	12.13	1981	48.21
1963	11.94	1982	40.68
1964	11.76	1983	35.83
1965	11.44	1984	34.1
1966	11.21	1985	30.73
1967	11.02	1986	15.52
1968	10.61	1987	18.53
1969	10.66	1988	14.61
1970	10.39	1989	17.68
1971	10.53	1990	21.4
1972	10.12	1991	17
1973	10.99	1992	15.99
1974	17.84	1993	13.89
1975	18.18	1994	12.57
1976	18.36	1995	13.59
1977	18.08	1996	16.59

Source: Energy Information Administration, *Annual Energy Review 1997* (Washington, D.C.: U.S. Department of Energy, July 1998), http://www.eia.doe.gov/bookshelf.html, table 5.16.

21

TOTAL CONSUMPTION OF ENERGY, WORLD

As the world's economy has grown, so has its demand for energy. Demand has increased consistently, with only occasional lulls, such as the recession of the early 1980s that temporarily suppressed energy demand. Total final consumption of energy worldwide increased by nearly 65 percent from 1970 to 1995. This figure reflects the use of energy in all economic sectors—industrial, agricultural, residential, and commercial—as well as the nonenergy uses of fossil fuels. Over the same time period, the amount of electricity generated more than doubled, with the greatest increase occurring from the upswing in use of nuclear power to generate electricity.

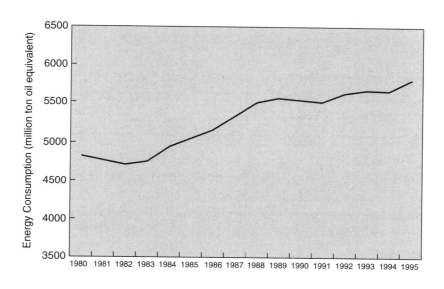

Year	Total Consumption of Energy, World (million ton oil equivalent)
1980	4821.4
1981	4768.3
1982	4709.6
1983	4753
1984	4940.4
1985	5042.1
1986	5155.8
1987	5324.8
1988	5505.3
1989	5565.9
1990	5544.5
1991	5518.1
1992	5623.5
1993	5662.5
1994	5646.3
1995	5801.5

Source: OECD Environmental Data Compendium, 1997.

22

CONSUMPTION OF ENERGY PER UNIT OF GROSS DOMESTIC PRODUCT, ORGANIZATION FOR ECONOMIC COOPERATION AND DEVELOPMENT NATIONS

Energy use has increased substantially over the past 2 decades. However, as nations become more economically advanced, pursuing economic development through a market economy, energy efficiency increases significantly. Consider the trend in energy consumption per unit of gross domestic product (GDP) in developed countries. In Organization for Economic Cooperation and Development nations (Western Europe, the United States, Canada, Japan, Australia, and New Zealand), energy consumption per unit of GDP declined by nearly 16 percent between 1980 and 1990, though there has been a recent decrease in energy efficiency.

The same trend toward greater energy efficiency did not occur in the former communist nations. Centralized economies lack the market pressures that constantly encourage increased efficiency and innovation. As a result, the technological breakthroughs that allow industries to produce more using a constant resource or energy base fail to materialize, and potential efficiency gains are sacrificed.

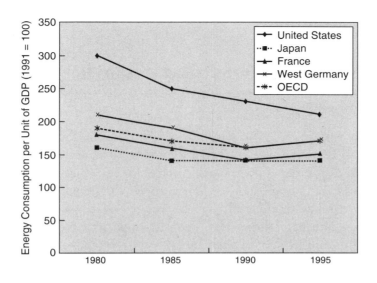

Consumption of Energy Per Unit of Gross Domestic Product

Year	United States	Japan	France	West Germany	OECD
1980	300	160	180	210	190
1985	250	140	160	190	170
1990	230	140	140	160	160
1995	210	140	150		170

Source: OECD Environmental Data Compendium, 1997.

23

WATER QUALITY VIOLATIONS, UNITED STATES

The percentage of U.S. rivers and streams violating Environmental Protection Agency (EPA) standards for fecal coliform bacteria, dissolved oxygen, and phosphorus is declining. High concentrations of fecal coliform bacteria can cause a variety of infectious diseases, including cholera and typhoid. Common sources of this bacteria are insufficiently treated sewage and runoff from pastures, feedlots, and cities. The graph shows a fairly consistent decline in the rate of fecal coliform bacteria until 1988. Since then violations have fluctuated rather significantly. Analysts at the U.S. Department of Interior suspect that the fluctuations are the result of unaccounted for measurement changes rather than a actual trend.

A violation of the dissolved oxygen standard means the tested water lacks oxygen concentrations high enough to support aquatic life fully. Low levels of dissolved oxygen can reduce the solubility of trace elements and affect the taste and odor of the water. The violation rate for this standard has dropped slightly even though larger population densities have increased oxygen demanding loads. Large technology investments in point source controls have helped keep this indicator of environmental health low.

Phosphorus in streams could add to oxygen depletion and increase the growth of aquatic vegetation, which can then clog water intake pipes. This figure dropped rapidly following limits put on the phosphate content of detergents in the late 1960s and early 1970s. Improvements in the 1980s can be attributed to a reduction in phosphorus fertilizer use and point source controls at sewage treatment, food processing, and other industrial plants.

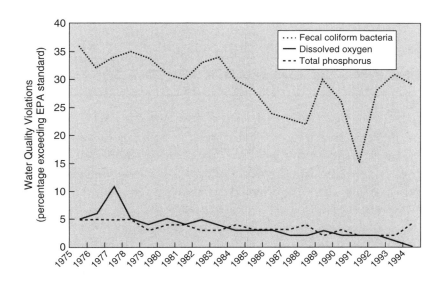

Water Quality Violations

Year	Fecal coliform bacteria	Dissolved oxygen	Total phosphorus
1975	36	5	5
1976	32	6	5
1977	34	11	5
1978	35	5	5
1979	34	4	3
1980	31	5	4
1981	30	4	4
1982	33	5	3
1983	34	4	3
1984	30	3	4
1985	28	3	3
1986	24	3	3
1987	23	2	3
1988	22	2	4
1989	30	3	2
1990	26	2	3
1991	15	2	2
1992	28	2	2
1993	31	1	2
1994	29	<1	4

Source: Council on Environmental Quality, Environmental Quality 1994–1995 (Washington, D.C.: Council on Environmental Quality, 1994–95), table 40.

24

ESTIMATED PHOSPHORUS LOADING TO THE GREAT LAKES

The Great Lakes region is often viewed as a microcosm of the interaction between economic and environmental concerns. The Great Lakes Basin is the site of significant agricultural production, particularly in Canada, as well as a large portion of U.S. manufacturing. At the same time, there has been considerable concern over the ecological health of the Great Lakes in the past two decades.

Important environmental progress in this region has been made since the 1970s. Factory emissions—so-called point sources—now account for only 1/10th of the water pollution in the Great Lakes. Pollution of the Great Lakes, as measured by estimated phosphorus loadings, declined significantly in all five of the Great Lakes from 1976 to 1989 though the graph shows a slight increase from 1989 to 1991. The reduction was greatest in Lake Erie, where phosphorus loadings declined by over 50 percent. Phosphorus loading in 1991 was still over 40 percent below the high level reached in 1978. Phosphorus is discharged from municipal sewage treatment plants and factories and can be found in agricultural runoff. Phosphorus is of concern because it stimulates excess blue-green algae growth, which can result in eutrophication, harming species and making water unfit for drinking and recreation.

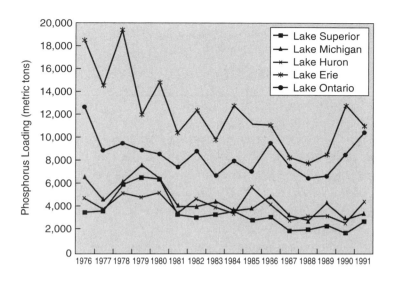

Phosphorus Loading to the Great Lakes

Year	Lake Superior	Lake Michigan	Lake Huron	Lake Erie	Lake Ontario
1976	3,550	6,656	4,802	18,480	12,695
1977	3,661	4,666	3,763	14,576	8,935
1978	5,990	6,245	5,255	19,431	9,547
1979	6,619	7,659	4,881	11,941	8,988
1980	6,412	6,574	5,307	14,855	8,579
1981	3,412	4,091	3,481	10,452	7,437
1982	3,160	4,084	4,689	12,349	8,891
1983	3,407	4,515	3,978	9,880	6,779
1984	3,642	3,611	3,452	12,874	7,948
1985	2,864	3,956	5,758	11,216	7,083
1986	3,059	4,981	4,210	11,118	9,561
1987	1,949	3,298	2,909	8,381	7,640
1988	2,067	2,907	3,165	7,841	6,521
1989	2,323	4,360	3,227	8,568	6,728
1990	1,750	3,006	2,639	12,899	8,542
1991	2,709	3,478	4,460	11,113	10,475

Source: Council on Environmental Quality, Environmental Quality 1994–1995 (Washington, D.C.: Council on Environmental Quality, 1994–1995), table 40.

25

U.S. CANCER DEATH RATES

Cancer was estimated to cause nearly 24 percent of the person-years of premature loss of life and about 520,600 deaths in the United States in 1996. Cancer death rates for all sites combined increased by 0.4 percent per year from 1973 to 1990, but from 1990 to 1995 the annual death rate for cancer decreased 0.5 percent per year. This decline was mostly confined to persons under the age of 65 at the time of death.

Lung, female breast, prostate, or colon/rectum cancers cause over 50 percent of all cancer deaths. Much of the decrease can be attributed to a steep decline in the death rates of lung cancer due to a decline in smoking rates. In 1965, 42 percent of adults smoked compared with less than 25 percent in 1995.

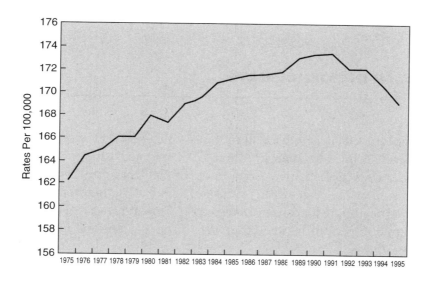

U.S. Cancer Death Rate

Year	Rate
1975	162.3
1976	164.5
1977	165.1
1978	166.1
1979	166.1
1980	168
1981	167.4
1982	169
1983	169.6
1984	170.9
1985	171.3
1986	171.5
1987	171.6
1988	171.9
1989	173
1990	173.3
1991	173.4
1992	172.1
1993	172
1994	170.7
1995	169.1

Source: L. A. G. Ries, C. L. Kosary, B. F. Hankey, B. A. Miller, B. K. Edwards (eds). "SEER Cancer Statistics Review, 1973–1995," National Cancer Institute, Bethesda, MD, 1998.

26

U.S. CANCER INCIDENCE RATE

Cancer incidence rates for all cancers combined and for most of the top 10 cancer sites declined between 1990 and 1995, reversing a 20-year trend of increasing cancer cases in the United States. Cancer incidence rates for all sites combined increased by 1.2 percent per year from 1973 to 1990, but from 1990 to 1995 the annual death rate for cancer decreased 0.7 percent per year. The largest decreases occurred in persons between the ages 35 and 44 years and in persons who were above 75 years.

The four leading cancer sites for 1990–1995 were lung and bronchus, prostate, female breast, and colon/rectum, which account for approximately 54 percent of all newly diagnosed cancers. The largest declines in incidence rates occurred in colon/rectum cancer (−2.3), lung cancer (−1.1), and prostate (−1.0). There was no change in female breast cancer incidence rates. It should be noted that less than 2 percent of cancers are caused by exposures to synthetic chemicals in the environment.

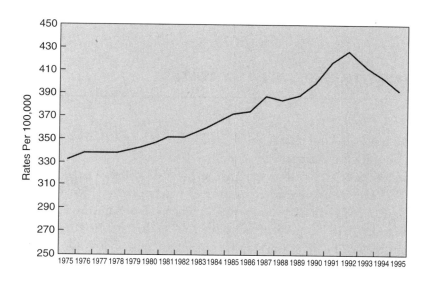

U.S. Cancer Incidence Rate

1975	332.7
1976	338
1977	337.6
1978	337.7
1979	341.3
1980	345.7
1981	351.9
1982	351.6
1983	357.4
1984	364.5
1985	372.4
1986	374.4
1987	387.5
1988	384.9
1989	387.8
1990	399.5
1991	417.5
1992	426.2
1993	412.5
1994	403.4
1995	392

Source: L. A. G. Ries, C. L. Kosary, B. F. Hankey, B. A. Miller, B. K. Edwards (eds). "SEER Cancer Statistics Review, 1973–1995," National Cancer Institute, Bethesda, MD, 1998.

27

AIR QUALITY TRENDS, UNITED STATES

As the following charts show, air pollution trends in the United States have been improving dramatically since the 1960s and 1970s. Ambient levels of both sulfur dioxide and carbon monoxide have dropped over 75 percent since the 1960s. Lead levels have fallen by over 95 percent since 1975. Total suspended particulates (TSP), such as soot, ash, and dust from fuel burning and industrial operations, declined 50 percent between the 1950s and 1990. Since then, PM-10, which replaced TSP as the standard for particulate matter air quality because it is a more sophisticated indicator of the potential public health impact, has declined about 20 percent. Ambient ozone, a prime constituent of smog, and ambient nitrogen dioxide, which contributes to the formation of smog, are both down by 30 percent or more from the levels seen in the 1970s. Cleaner air is a direct consequence of better technologies and the enormous and sustained investments that only a rich nation could have sunk into developing, installing and operating these technologies. [Reference: Indur M. Goklany, *Clearing the Air: The True Story of the War on Air Pollution* (Washington, DC: Cato Institute, 1999).]

AIRBORNE PARTICULATES

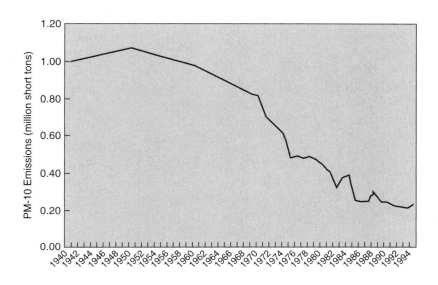

Year	PM-10 (million short tons) Normalized to 1940	Year	PM-10 (million short tons) Normalized to 1940
1940	1.00	1968	0.84
1941	1.01	1969	0.82
1942	1.01	1970	0.82
1943	1.02	1971	0.71
1944	1.03	1972	0.67
1945	1.04	1973	0.64
1946	1.04	1974	0.60
1947	1.05	1975	0.48
1948	1.06	1976	0.49
1949	1.07	1977	0.48
1950	1.07	1978	0.49
1951	1.06	1979	0.47
1952	1.05	1980	0.44
1953	1.04	1981	0.41
1954	1.03	1982	0.33
1955	1.02	1983	0.37
1956	1.01	1984	0.39
1957	1.00	1985	0.26
1958	0.99	1986	0.24
1959	0.98	1987	0.25
1960	0.98	1988	0.30
1961	0.96	1989	0.25
1962	0.94	1990	0.24
1963	0.92	1991	0.23
1964	0.91	1992	0.22
1965	0.89	1993	0.21
1966	0.87	1994	0.23
1967	0.86		

Source: Goklany, 1999.

TOTAL SUSPENDED PARTICULATES

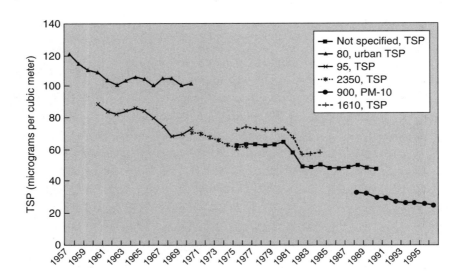

National Ambient Air Pollutant Concentrations
Total suspended particulates: 1957 To 1996
Composite annual averages (in micrograms/cubic meter)

No. Monitors	Not Specified, TSP	80, Urban TSP	95, TSP	2350, TSP	900, PM-10	1610, TSP
1957		120.5				
1958		114.4				
1959		110.7				
1960		109.1	88			
1961		103.8	84			
1962		101	82			
1963		103.6	84			
1964		105.6	86			
1965		104.7	84			
1966		100.7	80			
1967		105.2	74			
1968		104.9	69			
1969		100.6	69			
1970		101.7	72	70.4		
1971			68	69.6		
1972				67.1		
1973				65.4		
1974				62.5		
1975	61.9			60.8		72.3
1976	62.8			61.8		73.7
1977	62.9					73.1
1978	62.4					71.8
1979	63.1					71.8
1980	64.2					72.5
1981	57.4					66.7
1982	48.7					56.4
1983	48.4					56.7
1984	49.9					57.3
1985	47.7					
1986	47.6					
1987	48.6					
1988	49.7				32.2	
1989	48				32	
1990	47.3				29.4	
1991					29.1	
1992					26.8	
1993					26	
1994					26.2	
1995					25.1	
1996					24.2	

Sources: EQ, 1991; EQ, 1971; EQ, 1981; EQ, 1979; EPA, 1998; AQT, EPA/OAQPS, 1995; EPA, 1990; Goklany, 1999.
Is may be too high because of the measurement procedure.

SULFUR OXIDES

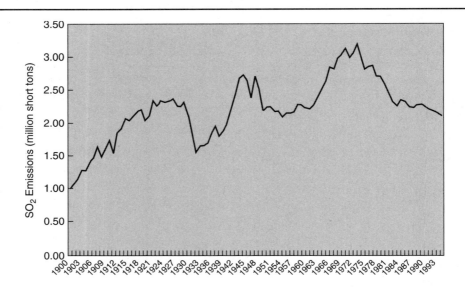

Year	SO2 Emissions (million short tons) Normalized to 1900	Year	SO2 Emissions (million short tons) Normalized to 1900	Year	SO2 Emissions (million short tons) Normalized to 1900	Year	SO2 Emissions (million short tons) Normalized to 1900
1900	1.00	1924	2.31	1948	2.53	1972	3.04
1901	1.07	1925	2.33	1949	2.18	1973	3.18
1902	1.15	1926	2.37	1950	2.24	1974	3.01
1903	1.28	1927	2.25	1951	2.26	1975	2.80
1904	1.27	1928	2.24	1952	2.18	1976	2.85
1905	1.40	1929	2.32	1953	2.18	1977	2.86
1906	1.47	1930	2.11	1954	2.09	1978	2.69
1907	1.64	1931	1.79	1955	2.15	1979	2.70
1908	1.47	1932	1.55	1956	2.15	1980	2.59
1909	1.61	1933	1.66	1957	2.16	1981	2.46
1910	1.73	1934	1.66	1958	2.29	1982	2.32
1911	1.53	1935	1.70	1959	2.28	1983	2.26
1912	1.85	1936	1.84	1960	2.23	1984	2.35
1913	1.92	1937	1.96	1961	2.21	1985	2.33
1914	2.08	1938	1.80	1962	2.28	1986	2.25
1915	2.03	1939	1.88	1963	2.40	1987	2.22
1916	2.10	1940	2.00	1964	2.50	1988	2.27
1917	2.18	1941	2.24	1965	2.64	1989	2.28
1918	2.21	1942	2.43	1966	2.84	1990	2.25
1919	2.03	1943	2.68	1967	2.80	1991	2.21
1920	2.12	1944	2.73	1968	2.96	1992	2.19
1921	2.34	1945	2.64	1969	3.03	1993	2.15
1922	2.26	1946	2.38	1970	3.12	1994	2.11
1923	2.34	1947	2.71	1971	2.97		

Source: Goklany, 1999.

ATMOSPHERIC CONCENTRATIONS OF SULFUR DIOXIDE

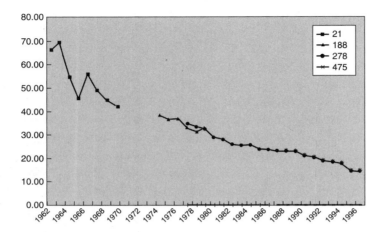

National Ambient Air Pollutant Concentrations
Sulfur Dioxide, 1962 to 1996
(Composite of annual averages based on 24-hour averages micrograms per cubic meter)

No. Monitors	21	188	278	475
1962	66.40			
1963	69.40			
1964	55.10			
1965	45.40			
1966	55.80			
1967	49.20			
1968	45.10			
1969	42.50			
1970				
1971				
1972				
1973				
1974		38.40		
1975		36.70		
1976		37.10		
1977		33.20	34.58	
1978		31.50	33.28	
1979		32.60	32.50	
1980			29.12	
1981			28.08	
1982			26.00	
1983			25.48	
1984			25.74	
1985			23.92	
1986			23.66	
1987			23.14	23.14
1988			23.14	23.14
1989			22.62	22.62
1990			21.06	21.06
1991			20.28	20.28
1992			18.98	18.98
1993			18.46	18.46
1994			17.68	17.68
1995			14.56	14.56
1996			14.56	14.56

Source: Q, 198; A, 198; 1994 AQT Data (EPA, 1995) Appendix; 1996AQT (EPA, 1998); Goklany, 1999.

CARBON MONOXIDE (CO)

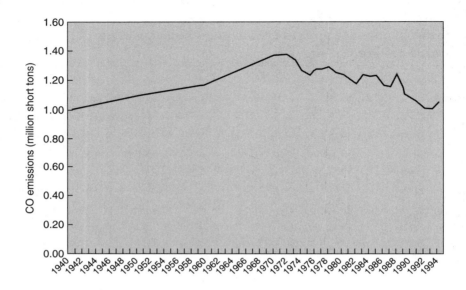

Year	Carbon Monoxide Emissions (million short tons) Normalized to 1940	Year	Carbon Monoxide Emissions (million short tons) Normalized to 1940
1940	1.00	1968	1.33
1941	1.01	1969	1.35
1942	1.02	1970	1.37
1943	1.03	1971	1.37
1944	1.04	1972	1.36
1945	1.05	1973	1.33
1946	1.06	1974	1.27
1947	1.07	1975	1.23
1948	1.08	1976	1.27
1949	1.09	1977	1.27
1950	1.10	1978	1.29
1951	1.10	1979	1.25
1952	1.11	1980	1.24
1953	1.12	1981	1.20
1954	1.13	1982	1.17
1955	1.13	1983	1.23
1956	1.14	1984	1.22
1957	1.15	1985	1.23
1958	1.16	1986	1.17
1959	1.16	1987	1.15
1960	1.17	1988	1.24
1961	1.19	1989	1.10
1962	1.21	1990	1.08
1963	1.23	1991	1.04
1964	1.25	1992	1.00
1965	1.27	1993	1.01
1966	1.29	1994	1.05
1967	1.31		

Source: Goklany (1999).

ATMOSPHERIC CONCENTRATIONS (CO)

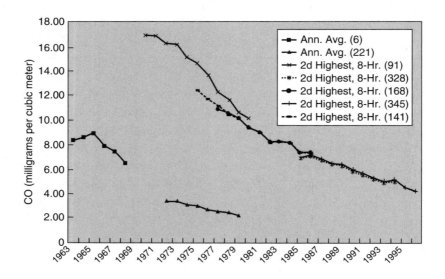

National Ambient Air Pollutant Concentration
Carbon Monoxide, 1963–1992
(milligrams per cubic meter)

Avg. Time No. monitors	Ann. Avg. Ann. Avg. (6)	Ann. Avg. Ann. Avg. (221)	2nd. Max 8-Hr. (91)*	328 2nd. Max 8-Hr. (328)	168 2nd. Max 8-Hr. (168)	345 2nd. Max 8-Hr. (345)	141 2nd. Max 8-Hr. (141)
1963	8.36						
1964	8.59						
1965	8.93						
1966	7.90						
1967	7.45						
1968	6.53						
1969							
1970			17.0				
1971			16.9				
1972		3.4	16.3				
1973		3.4	16.2				
1974		3.1	15.1				
1975		3.0	14.7				12.4
1976		2.7	13.8				11.7
1977		2.5	12.2		10.9		11.1
1978		2.4	11.7		10.5		10.4
1979		2.2	10.6		10.1		10.1
1980			10.1		9.3		9.3
1981					8.90		9.00
1982					8.20		8.10
1983					8.20		8.20
1984					8.10		8.10
1985				6.90	7.30		
1986				7.10	7.30		
1987				6.70		6.7	
1988				6.40		6.4	
1989				6.30		6.4	
1990				5.80		5.9	
1991				5.50		5.6	
1992				5.20		5.2	
1993				4.90		4.9	
1994				5.00		5.1	
1995						4.5	
1996						4.2	

Sources: EQ, 1971; SA, 1981; EQ, 1981; AQT, 1994; AQT, 1996; AQT, 199; AQT, 1994; EPA, 1995; EPA, 1998; EPA, 1998; EPA, 1995; Goklany, 1999.
*Data represent composite averages of pollutant based on the second-highest, nonoverlapping, 8-hour average.

NITROGEN OXIDES (NO$_x$)

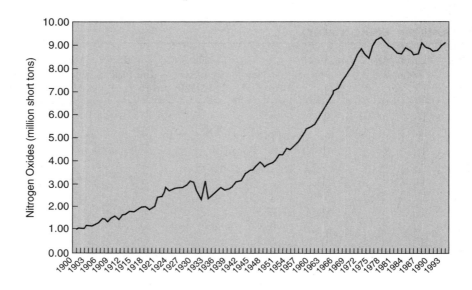

Year	NOx Emissions (million short tons) Normalized to 1900	Year	NOx Emissions (million short tons) Normalized to 1900	Year	NOx Emissions (million short tons) Normalized to 1900
1900	1.00	1932	2.31	1964	6.37
1901	1.06	1933	3.13	1965	6.67
1902	1.06	1934	2.37	1966	7.02
1903	1.20	1935	2.54	1967	7.13
1904	1.18	1936	2.66	1968	7.45
1905	1.27	1937	2.81	1969	7.66
1906	1.32	1938	2.72	1970	7.90
1907	1.47	1939	2.73	1971	8.13
1908	1.35	1940	2.82	1972	8.57
1909	1.47	1941	3.09	1973	8.86
1910	1.57	1942	3.14	1974	8.55
1911	1.45	1943	3.36	1975	8.38
1912	1.65	1944	3.54	1976	8.91
1913	1.71	1945	3.57	1977	9.19
1914	1.81	1946	3.74	1978	9.29
1915	1.79	1947	3.92	1979	9.12
1916	1.88	1948	3.74	1980	8.92
1917	1.98	1949	3.84	1981	8.84
1918	2.01	1950	3.87	1982	8.62
1919	1.88	1951	3.98	1983	8.57
1920	1.98	1952	4.20	1984	8.88
1921	2.44	1953	4.24	1985	8.76
1922	2.42	1954	4.48	1986	8.56
1923	2.85	1955	4.47	1987	8.58
1924	2.68	1956	4.61	1988	9.05
1925	2.80	1957	4.79	1989	8.90
1926	2.83	1958	5.12	1990	8.83
1927	2.83	1959	5.34	1991	8.68
1928	2.92	1960	5.42	1992	8.75
1929	3.13	1961	5.51	1993	8.92
1930	3.07	1962	5.76	1994	9.05
1931	2.61	1963	6.05		

Source: Goklany, 1999.

ATMOSPHERIC CONCENTRATIONS OF NITROGEN DIOXIDE (NO₂)

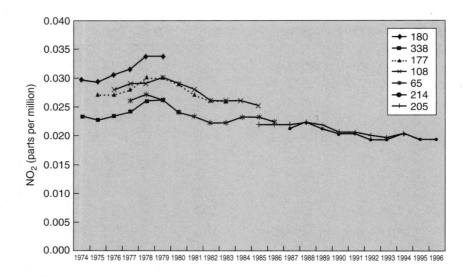

National Ambient Air Pollutant Concentrations
Nitrogen Dioxide: 1972 to 1996*

No. Monitors/Year	180	338	177	108	65	214	205
1974	0.030	0.023					
1975	0.029	0.023	0.027				
1976	0.031	0.023	0.027	0.028			
1977	0.032	0.024	0.028	0.029	0.026		
1978	0.034	0.026	0.030	0.029	0.027		
1979	0.034	0.026	0.030	0.030	0.026		
1980		0.024	0.029	0.029	0.024		
1981			0.027	0.028	0.023		
1982			0.026	0.026	0.022		
1983			0.026	0.026	0.022		
1984				0.026	0.023		
1985				0.025	0.023		0.0217
1986					0.022		0.0218
1987						0.021	0.0217
1988						0.022	0.022
1989						0.021	0.0216
1990						0.02	0.0204
1991						0.02	0.0203
1992						0.019	0.0197
1993						0.019	0.0192
1994						0.02	0.02
1995						0.019	
1996						0.019	

Sources: AQT, 1996; AQT, 1996; EPA, 1998; EPA, 1998; Environmental Quality 1981, 1984; Statistical Abstract of the United States, 1981, 1988; Goklany, 1999.
*Data represent composite of annual averages (in PPM).

VOLATILE ORGANIC COMPOUNDS

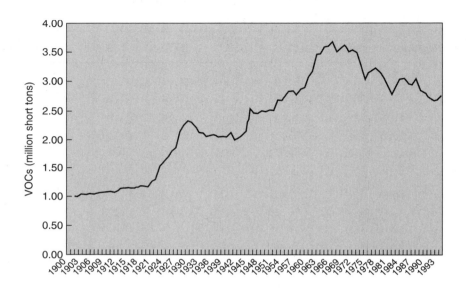

Year	VOCs (million short tons) Normalized to 1900	Year	VOCs (million short tons) Normalized to 1900	Year	VOCs (million short tons) Normalized to 1900
1900	1.00	1932	2.20	1964	3.45
1901	1.00	1933	2.12	1965	3.56
1902	1.00	1934	2.09	1966	3.60
1903	1.04	1935	2.02	1967	3.67
1904	1.04	1936	2.06	1968	3.48
1905	1.04	1937	2.07	1969	3.53
1906	1.04	1938	2.03	1970	3.60
1907	1.04	1939	2.04	1971	3.49
1908	1.07	1940	2.02	1972	3.52
1909	1.07	1941	2.11	1973	3.47
1910	1.07	1942	1.98	1974	3.25
1911	1.07	1943	2.00	1975	3.02
1912	1.08	1944	2.04	1976	3.13
1913	1.15	1945	2.13	1977	3.18
1914	1.14	1946	2.51	1978	3.21
1915	1.15	1947	2.42	1979	3.15
1916	1.14	1948	2.43	1980	3.05
1917	1.14	1949	2.48	1981	2.88
1918	1.17	1950	2.46	1982	2.75
1919	1.17	1951	2.49	1983	2.89
1920	1.18	1952	2.49	1984	3.01
1921	1.25	1953	2.65	1985	3.03
1922	1.29	1954	2.65	1986	2.94
1923	1.54	1955	2.73	1987	2.91
1924	1.61	1956	2.83	1988	3.02
1925	1.68	1957	2.83	1989	2.81
1926	1.77	1958	2.73	1990	2.78
1927	1.85	1959	2.84	1991	2.69
1928	2.11	1960	2.88	1992	2.64
1929	2.22	1961	3.06	1993	2.66
1930	2.29	1962	3.15	1994	2.73
1931	2.27	1963	3.44		

Source: Goklany, 1999.

ATMOSPHERIC CONCENTRATIONS OF OZONE

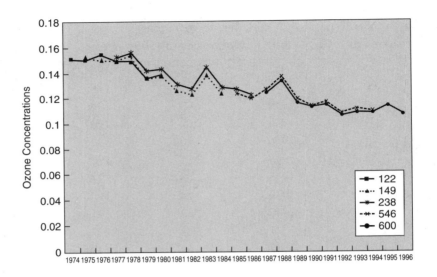

National Ambient Air Pollutant Concentrations
Ozone: 1974 to 1996
(Average of the Second-highest Daily Maximum One Hour Values)

No. Monitors	122	149	549	238	600
1974	0.151				
1975	0.151	0.152			
1976	0.154	0.151			
1977	0.149	0.15		0.152	
1978	0.149	0.154		0.156	
1979	0.136	0.135		0.141	
1980	0.138	0.138		0.143	
1981		0.126		0.131	
1982		0.124		0.127	
1983		0.138		0.144	
1984		0.124		0.128	
1985			0.124	0.127	
1986			0.12	0.122	
1987			0.126		0.124
1988			0.136		0.133
1989			0.117		0.116
1990			0.114		0.113
1991			0.116		0.114
1992			0.107		0.106
1993			0.11		0.108
1994			0.109		0.108
1995					0.113
1996					0.106

Sources: EQ, 1981; EPA/OAQPS, 1995; EPA/OAQPS, 1995; AQT, 1996; EPA, 1998; AQT, 1996; EPA, 1998; Goklany, 1999.

LEAD

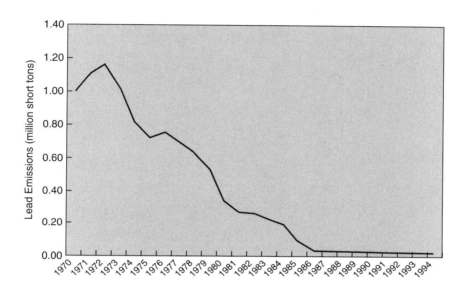

Year	Lead Emissions (million short tons) Normalized to 1970	Year	Lead Emissions (million short tons) Normalized to 1970
1970	1.00	1983	0.22
1971	1.11	1984	0.19
1972	1.16	1985	0.09
1973	1.02	1986	0.03
1974	0.81	1987	0.03
1975	0.72	1988	0.03
1976	0.75	1989	0.03
1977	0.69	1990	0.03
1978	0.63	1991	0.02
1979	0.53	1992	0.02
1980	0.34	1993	0.02
1981	0.27	1994	0.02
1982	0.26		

Source: Goklany, 1999.

ATMOSPHERIC LEAD CONCENTRATIONS

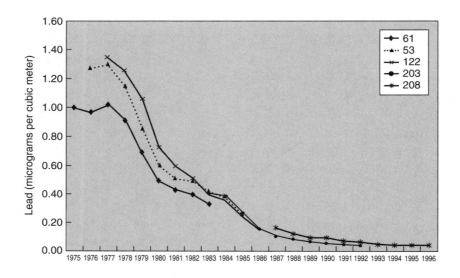

Ambient Lead Concentrations
(Micrograms Per Cubic Meter)

No. Monitors	61	53	122	208	203
1975	1.00				
1976	0.97	1.27			
1977	1.02	1.30	1.35		
1978	0.91	1.15	1.26		
1979	0.69	0.86	1.06		
1980	0.49	0.60	0.73		
1981	0.43	0.51	0.59		
1982	0.40	0.49	0.50		
1983	0.33	0.42	0.40		0.41
1984		0.38	0.36		0.39
1985		0.26	0.25		0.27
1986			0.16		0.15
1987				0.16	0.11
1988				0.12	0.09
1989				0.09	0.07
1990				0.09	0.06
1991				0.07	0.05
1992				0.06	0.04
1993				0.05	
1994				0.04	
1995				0.04	
1996				0.04	

Sources: EPA, 1983; EPA, 1985; EPA/OAQPS, 1998; WF, 1994; SA, 1986; SA, 1988; Goklany, 1999.

NOTES

Chapter 1

1. T. R. Malthus, *An Essay on the Principle of Population*, Geoffrey Gilbert, ed. (Oxford/New York: Oxford University Press. 1993), p. 12.
2. Ibid., p. 13.
3. Ibid., p. 21.
4. Ibid., p. 17.
5. Ibid., p. 21.
6. Ibid., p. 61.
7. Quoted in R. V. Short, "Malthus, a prophet without honour," *The Lancet*, 351, no. 9117 (June 6, 1998): p. 1676 (1).
8. Paul Ehrlich and Anne Ehrlich, *The Population Explosion* (New York: Simon & Schuster, 1990) 71.
9. Paul Ehrlich, *The Population Bomb* (New York: Sierra Club Ballantine, 1968): p. i.
10. Paul Ehrlich, "Looking backward from 2000 A.D.," *The Progressive* (April 1970): 23–25.
11. Paul Ehrlich and Anne Ehrlich, *The Population Explosion* (New York: Simon & Schuster, 1990), p. 193.
12. William and Paul Paddock, *Famine 1975! America's Decision: Who Will Survive?* (Boston: Little Brown, 1967).
13. Lester Brown, *State of the World Report 1994*, p. 178.
14. Lester Brown, *State of the World Report 1997*. p. 1.
15. Donnella Meadows, et al., *The Limits to Growth: A Report for the Club of Rome's Project on the Predicament of Mankind* (New York: New American Library, 1972), p. 29.
16. Paul Ehrlich and Anne Ehrlich, *The End of Affluence* (New York: Ballantine Books, 1976).
17. J. E. De Steiguer, "Three theories from economics about the environment," *BioScience*, 45, no. 8 (September 1995): 552 (6).
18. Donald Winch, *Malthus*, (Oxford/New York: Oxford University Press, 1987), p. 3.
19. Paul Wallace, "The rebirth of Malthusian gloom," *New Statesman*, 127, no. 4367 (January 9, 1998): 21 (2).
20. Donald Winch, *Malthus*, (Oxford/New York: Oxford University Press, 1987), p. 61.

21. Garret Hardin, "Limits to growth are nature's own," *Insight on the News*, 9, no. 51 (December 20, 1993).
22. Jay Forrester, *World Dynamics*, 2nd ed. (Cambridge, MA: Wright-Allen Press, 1973; original ed., 1971), p. 27.
23. Ibid., p. 46.
24. Maurice King, "Health is a sustainable state," *Lancet*, 336, no. 8716 (1990), 664 (4).
25. Matthew Scanlon, "The new population bomb: An interview with Michael Tobias," *Mother Earth News*, no. 163 (August–September 1997): 48 (6).
26. Robert W. Kates, "Population, technology, and the human environment: A thread through time." *Daedalus*, 125, no. 3 (Summer 1996): 43 (29).
27. Ibid.
28. Ibid.
29. Ibid.
30. Gene M. Grossman and Elhanan Helpman, "Endogenous Innovation in the Theory of Growth," *Journal of Economic Perspectives*, Winter, 1994, 8, no. 1 (Winter 1994): 25.
31. Paul Romer, "Beyond classical and Keynesian macroeconomic policy," *Policy Options*, (July–August 1994). P. 3 of 8, accessed online November 10, 1998.
32. Paul Romer, "Why, indeed, in America? Theory, history, and the origins of modern economic growth," *Journal of the American Economics Association*, 86, no. 2 (May 1996): 204.
33. Paul Romer, "Economic growth," in *The Fortune Encyclopedia of Economics*, edited by David R. Henderson (Warner Books, accessed online November 11, 1998).
34. Robert W. Kates, "Population, technology, and the human environment: A thread through time." *Daedalus*, 125, no. 3 (Summer 1996): 43 (29).
35. D. Gale Johnson, *Population, Food and Wellbeing*, Paper No. 90:13, University of Chicago Office of Agricultural Economics (July 9, 1990), p. 11.
36. Dwight Lee, "The perpetual assault on progress," *The St. Croix Review* (October 1991): 13.
37. Paul Romer, "Economic growth," in *The Fortune Encyclopedia of Economics*, edited by David R. Henderson (Warner Books, accessed online November 11, 1998).
38. Ibid.
39. Paul Romer, "Beyond the knowledge worker," *Worldlink* (January/February 1995, accessed online November 11, 1998).
40. Ibid.
41. Paul Romer, quoted by Kevin Kelly in "The economics of ideas," *Wired*, (June 1996).
42. Garrett Hardin, *Living within Limits: Ecology, Economics and Population Taboos*. (New York/Oxford: Oxford University Press, 1993), pp. 130–131.
43. Ismail Serageldin, Consultative Group on International Agricultural Research, Press Release (August 4, 1996), p. 2.
44. Vernon M. Briggs, Jr., "Malthus: The economist," *The Social Contract* (Spring 1998): 213.
45. Paul Waggoner, "How much land can ten billion people spare for nature?", *Daedalus* (Summer 1996): 87.
46. Donnella Meadows, et al., *The Limits to Growth*, 81.
47. Indur Goklany, "Richer is cleaner," *The True State of the Planet*, (New York: The Free Press, 1995), p. 342.

48. Ehrlich and Ehrlich, *The Population Explosion*, p. 175. 175.
49. Maurice King, "Health is a sustainable state," *Lancet*, 336, no. 8716 (1990): 664 (4).
50. Paul Romer, "Endogenous technological change," *Journal of Political Economy*, 98, no. 5 (1990): S71.
51. Ibid., p. S99.
52. Ibid., p. S73.
53. Amartya Sen, "Public Action to Remedy Hunger," Arturo Tanco Memorial Lecture given in London on August 2, 1990, arranged by The Hunger Project and CAB International, in association with The Commonwealth Trust and The Royal Institute of International Affairs.
54. Ibid.
55. Ibid.
56. Paul Romer, "In the beginning was the transitor," *Forbes* (1996), page 6 of 6, accessed on-line.

Chapter 2

1. C. D. Keeling, T. P. Whorf, M. Wahlen, and J. van der Plicht, "Interannual extremes in the rate of rise of atmospheric carbon dioxide since 1980," *Nature*, 375 (1995): 666–670.
2. J. T. Houghton, L. G. Meira Filho, B. A. Callander, N. Harris, A. Kattenberg, and K. Maskell, eds., *Climate Change 1995: The Science of Climate Change* (Cambridge: Cambridge University Press, 1996).
3. J. E. Hansen, M. Sato, A. Lacis, R. Ruedy, I. Tegen, and E. Matthews, "Climate forcings in the industrial era," *Proc. Natl. Acad. Sci. USA*, 95 (1998): 12,753–12,758.
4. J. Hansen, M. Sato, J. Glascoe, and R. Ruedy, "A common-sense climate index: Is climate changing noticeably?" *Proc. Natl. Acad. Sci. USA*, 95 (1998): 4113–4120.
5. V. Ramanathan, B. R. Barkstrom, and E. F. Harrison, "Climate and the earth's radiation budget," *Physics Today* (May 1989): 22–32.
6. G. L. Stephens and P. J. Webster, "Clouds and climate: Sensitivity of simple systems," *J. Atmos. Sci.*, 38 (1981): 235–247.
7. V. Ramanathan, R. D. Cess, E. F. Harrison, P. Minnis, B. R. Barkstrom, E. Ahmad, and D. Hartmann, "Cloud radiative forcing and climate: Results from the earth radiation budget experiment," *Science*, 243 (1989): 57–63.
8. R. S. Lindzen, "Can increasing carbon dioxide cause climate change?" *Proc. Natl. Acad. Sci. USA*, 94 (1997): 8335–8342.
9. S. Manabe and R. F. Strickler, "Thermal equilibrium of the atmosphere with a convective adjustment," *J. Atmos. Sci.*, 21 (1964): 361–385.
10. W. L. Gates, U. Cubasch, G. Meehl, J. Mitchell, and R. Stouffer, "An intercomparison of selected features of the control climates simulated by coupled ocean-atmosphere general circulation models," World Meteorological Organization publ. TD-No. 574 (1993).
11. R. D. Cess et al., "Cloud feedback in atmospheric general circulation models: An update," *J. Geophys. Res.*, 101 (1996): 12,791–12,794.
12. R. W. Spencer and W. D. Braswell, "How dry is the tropical free troposphere? Implications for global warming theory," *Bull. Amer. Meteor. Soc.*, 78 (1997): 1097–1106.

13. K. A. Emanuel, "A cumulus representation based on the episodic mixing model: The importance of mixing and microphysics in predicting humidity," *Meteorological Monographs*, 24 (1994): 185–192.
14. D.-Z. Sun and R. S. Lindzen, "Distribution of tropical tropospheric water vapor," *J. Atmos. Sci.*, 50 (1993): 1643–1660.
15. N. O. Renno, K. A. Emanuel, and P. H. Stone, "Radiative-convective model with an explicit hydrologic cycle 1. Formulation and sensitivity to model parameters," *J. Geophys. Res.*, 99 (1994): 14,429–14,441.
16. F. B. Wood, "Comment: On the need for validation of the Jones et al. temperature trends with respect to urban warming," *Climatic Change*, 12 (1988): 297–312.
17. T. M. L. Wigley and P. D. Jones, "Do large-area-average temperature series have an urban warming bias?", *Climatic Change*, 12 (1988): 313–319.
18. K. P. Gallo, T. W. Owen, D. R. Easterling, and P. F. Jamason, "Temperature trends of the U.S. Historical Climatology Network based on satellite designated land use/land cover," *Preprints, 10th Symposium on Global Change Studies* (Boston: American Meteorological Society, 1999), pp. 91–93.
19. C. K. Folland and D. E. Parker, "Correction of instrumental biases in historical sea surface temperature data," *Quart. J. R. Met. Soc.*, 121 (1995): 319–367.
20. T. R. Karl, P. D. Jones, R. W. Knight, G. Kukla, N. Plummer, V. Razuvayev, K. P. Gallo, J. Lindseay, R. J. Charlson, and T. C. Peterson, "A new perspective on recent global warming: Asymmetric trends of daily maximum and minimum temperatures," *Bull. Amer. Meteor. Soc.*, 74 (1993): 1007–1023.
21. P. D. Jones, "Hemispheric surface air temperature variations: A reanalysis and an update to 1993," *J. Climate* 7 (1994): 1794–1802.
22. J. Lean and D. Rind, "Climate forcing by changing solar radiation," *J. Climate*, 11 (1998): 3069–3094.
23. R. W. Spencer and J. R. Christy, "Precise monitoring of global temperature trends from satellites," *Science*, 247 (1990): 1558–1562.
24. J. Hansen et al., "Forcings and chaos in interannual to decadal climate change," *J. Geophys. Res.*, 102 (1997): 25,679–25,720.
25. F. W. Wentz and M. Schabel, "On the discrepency between observed in situ surface warming and the cooling trend in MSU tropospheric temperatures," *Nature*, 394 (1998): 361–364.
26. J. R. Christy, R. W. Spencer, and W. D. Braswell, "Global tropospheric temperature variations since 1979," *Preprints, 10th Symposium on Global Change Studies* (Boston: American Meteorological Society, 1999), pp. 101–104.
27. E. M. Rasmussen and T. H. Carpenter, "Variations in tropical sea surface temperature and surface winds fields associated with the Southern Oscillation/El Niño," *Mon. Wea. Rev.*, 110 (1981): 354–384.
28. K. E. Trenberth, "El Nino and global warming," *Preprints, 10th Symposium on Global Change Studies* (Boston: American Meteorological Society, 1999), pp. 258–260.
29. W. M. Gray, "On the causes of multi-decadal climate change and prospects for increased Atlantic Basin hurricane activity in the coming decades," *Preprints, 10th Symposium on Global Change Studies* (Boston: American Meteorological Society, 1999), pp. 183–186.
30. F. P. Roberts and M. A. Saunders, "Upward trend in global intense and super-intense tropical cyclone numbers 1969–1997," *Preprints, 10th Symposium on Global Change Studies* (Boston: American Meteorological Society, 1999), pp. 197–198.

31. K. A. Emanuel, "The dependence of hurricane intensity on climate," *Nature*, 326, (1987): 483–485.
32. T. R. Knutson, R. E. Tuleya, and Y. Kurihara, "Simulated increase in hurricane intensities in a CO_2-warmed climate," *Science*, 279 (1998): 1018–1022.
33. L. Bengtsson, M. Botzet, and M. Esch, "Will greenhouse gas-induced warming over the next 50 years lead to higher frequency and greater intensity of hurricanes?" *Tellus*, 48A (1996): 57–73.
34. J. Yoshimura, M. Sugi, and A. Noda, "Influence of greenhouse warming on tropical cyclone frequency simulated by a high resolution AGCM," Preprints, *23rd Conference on Hurricanes and Tropical Meteorology* (Boston: American Meteorological Society, 1999), pp. 1081–1084.
35. R. A. Pielke, Jr., and C. W. Landsea, "Normalized hurricane damages in the United States: 1925–1995," *Weather Forecasting*, 13 (1999, in press).
36. T. R. Karl, R. W. Knight, and N. Plummer, "Trends in high-frequency climate variability in the twentieth century," *Nature*, 377 (1995): 217–220.
37. H. F. Lins and J. R. Slack, "Streamflow trends in the United States," *Geophys. Res. Lett.*, 26 (1999): 227.
38. D. A. Randall et al., "Intercomparison and interpretation of surface energy fluxes in atmospheric general circulation models," *J. Geophys. Res.*, 97 (1992): 3711–3724.

Chapter 3

1. D. H. Meadows, D. L. Meadows, J. Randers, and W. W. Behrens, *The Limits to Growth* (New York: Universe Books, 1972).
2. The phrase "weigh heavily" is borrowed from Jesse Ausubel, in his article, "The Liberation of the Environment," in *Daedalus*, June 22, 1996.
3. Franklin Associates, *Characterization of Municipal Solid Waste in the United States: 1997 Update* (Washington, D.C.: U.S. Environmental Protection Agency, 1997).
4. We forget, for example, that the now-maligned chlorinated fluorocarbons were introduced to replace explosive ammonia as a refrigerant. Solved problems give rise to new problems.
5. Robert Stavins, "Comments on 'Lethal Model 2: The Limits to Growth Revisited," by William Nordhaus," in *Brookings Papers on Economic Activity*, 1993.
6. Robert W. Kates, "A Thread through Time," in *Technological Trajectories and the Human Environment* (Washington, D.C.: National Academy Press, 1997), p. 37.
7. See, for example, Hardin Tibbs, "Ecology: an Environmental Agenda for Industry," *Whole Earth Review*, Dec. 22, 1992. Tibbs writes: "While the industrial system was small, we regarded the natural global ecosystem as limitlessly vast. As a result we treated the functioning of the natural system as irrelevant to our industrial operations. But continuing expansion of the worldwide industrial system will oblige us to reconsider this view."
8. Jesse Ausubel, "The liberation of the environment," *Daedalus*, Summer, 1996.
9. Jesse Ausubel, "Can technology spare the earth?" *American Scientist*, 84, March/April 1996.
10. Ibid., pp. 172–173.
11. Martin Melosi, *Garbage in the Cities* (Chicago: Dorsey Press, 1981), p. 24.
12. Ibid.

13. Ibid., p. 23. In 1987, MSW generation per capita was around 1429 pounds per year contrasted to the 1488 pounds indicated by the Melosi figures for the turn of the century. Since 1987, per capita waste discarded has actually declined slightly as a result of more extensive household recycling.
14. Ausubel, "The liberation of the environment," *Daedalus*, Summer, 1996.
15. Jesse Ausubel, et al. define *dematerialization* as "the decline over time in the weight of materials used in industrial end products or in the 'embedded energy' of the products. More broadly, dematerialization refers to the absolute or relative reduction in the quantity of materials required to serve economic functions." See Iddo Wernick, Robert Herman, Shekhar Govind, and Jesse H. Ausubel. "Materialization and dematerialization: Measures and trends," in *Technological Trajectories and the Human Environment* (Washington, D.C.: National Academy Press, 1997), p. 135.
16. Al Gore, speech to the American Association for the Advancement of Science, Jan. 24, 1999, Anaheim, CA.
17. Iddo Wernick et al., "Materialization and dematerialization: Measures and trends," in *Technological Trajectories and the Human Environment* (Washington, D.C.: National Academy Press, 1997), p. 149.
18. Lynn Scarlett et al., *Packaging, Recycling, and Solid Waste* (Los Angeles: Reason Foundation, 1997), p. 29, note 16.
19. Iddo Wernick et al., "Materialization and dematerialization: Measures and trends," in *Technological Trajectories and the Human Environment* (Washington, D.C.: National Academy Press, 1997), p. 136.
20. Jesse Ausubel, "Can technology spare the earth?" *American Scientist*, 84, March/April 1996: 173.
21. Of the average 31,000 stock-keeping units carried by food stores, the top 520 move a case or more per week; the bottom 7000 move less than one unit per week. Personnel correspondence, H. E. Swift, Procter & Gamble, February 28, 1996.
22. Iddo Wernick et al., "Materialization and dematerialization: Measures and trends," in *Technological Trajectories and the Human Environment* (Washington, D.C.: National Academy Press, 1997), p. 139.
23. Ibid., p. 140.
24. Ibid., p. 141. For example, per capita consumption of commercial timber in the United States was around 500 board feet per capita in 1900; since 1930 per capita consumption has held at about 200 board feet per capita.
25. Iddo Wernick, Paul Waggoner, and Jesse Ausubel, "Searching for leverage to conserve forests: The industrial ecology of wood products in the United States," *Journal of Industrial Ecology*, 1 (Summer 1997): 130, 134.
26. Ibid., p. 133.
27. Ibid., p. 136.
28. Ibid.
29. Ibid., p. 137.
30. W. Mandelbum, World Demand for Raw Materials in 1985 and 2000 (New York: McGraw-Hill, 1978), cited in Oliviero Bernardini and Riccardi Galli, "Dematerialization: Long-term trends in the intensity of use of materials and energy," *Futures* (May 1993).
31. Ibid., p. 433.
32. Ibid.
33. Ibid., p. 138.

34. American Iron & Steel Institute, website at www.steel.org/facts/safercjc.htm.
35. Ibid.
36. Automotive Applications Committee, January 18, 1996.
37. Oliviero Bernardini and Riccardo Galli, "Dematerialization: Long-term trends in the intensity of use of materials and energy," *Futures* (May 1993), p. 440.
38. Franklin Associates, *Analysis of Trends in Municipal Solid Waste Generation: 1972–1987* (Prairie Village, KS: Franklin Associates, 1992), pp. 2–4.
39. Lynn Scarlett, Richard McCann, Robert Anex, and Alexander Volokh, *Packaging, Recycling, and Solid Waste* (Los Angeles: Reason Foundation, 1997), p. iv.
40. Franklin Associates, *Report on Grocery Packaging and Solid Waste Management* (Prairie Village, KS: Franklin Associates, 1995).
41. Franklin Associates, *Analysis of Trends in Municipal Solid Waste Generation: 1972–1987* (Prairie Village, KS: Franklin Associates, 1992).
42. Unless otherwise indicated, general data are from Scarlett et al., *Packaging, Recycling, and Solid Waste* (1997), pp. 85–86. Specific company information is from Grocery Manufacturers of America, *Progress and Performance* (1996).
43. The Anheuser-Busch information is reported in Grocery Manufacturers of America, *Progress and Performance* (Washington, D.C.: GMA, 1996).
44. Personal communication, Flexible Packaging Association. January 1998.
45. Lynn Scarlett, "*Packaging, solid waste, and environmental trade-offs*," in *Illahee: Journal of the Northwest Environment* (Spring 1994).
46. Franklin Associates, *Characterization of Municipal Solid Waste in the United States: 1997 Update*, prepared for U.S. Environmental Protection Agency, Report No. EPA530-R-98-007.
47. Robert A. Frosch, "Industrial ecology: Adapting technology for a sustainable world," *Environment* (December 1995).
48. Iddo Wernick et al., "Materialization and dematerialization: Measures and trends," *Daedalus* (June 22, 1996), p. 183.
49. Ibid.
50. Ibid. Wernick et al. use the term "dissipative" to describe the release of materials into the environment in ways that make recovery virtually impossible. They note that car and truck brake pads and tires, for example, "leave finely distributed powder on highways."
51. Lynn Scarlett et al., *Packaging, Recycling, and Solid Waste* (Los Angeles: Reason Public Policy Institute, 1997), p. ii.
52. Chauncey Starr, "Sustaining the human environment: The next two hundred years," *Daedalus* (Summer 1996).
53. Michael Edesses, "Entropy, economics, and the environment," unpublished essay, January 15, 1993 (on file with the author).
54. Robert A. Frosch, "Toward the end of waste: Reflections on a new ecology of industry," in Jesse Ausubel and Langford, *Technological Trajectories and the Human Environment*, p. 157.
55. Hardin Tibbs, "Industrial ecology: An environmental agenda for industry," *Whole Earth Review* (December 22, 1992).

56. David Wallace, *Environmental Policy and Industrial Innovation: Strategies in Europe, the U.S., and Japan* (London: Royal Institute of International Affairs, Earthscan Publications, 1995).
57. Richard Florida, "Lean and green: The move to environmentally conscious manufacturing," *California Management Review* (September 1996).
58. Ibid.
59. Jesse Ausubel, "The liberation of the environment," in *Technological Trajectories and the Human Environment*, p. 2 (reprint).
60. Oliviero Bernardini and Riccardo Gallo, "Dematerialization: Long-term trends in the intensity of use of materials and energy," *Futures* (May 1993), pp. 440–441.

Chapter 4

1. American Enterprise Institute and Harvard Center for Population and Development Studies. The author would like to thank colleagues at the U.S. Census Bureau's International Programs Center and the United Nations Population Division for their kind advance provision of unpublished research, and Ms. Kelly O'Neal for her able research assistance. The usual disclaimers obtain.
2. Perhaps the two most authoritative sources for estimates and projections of world population are the Population Division of the United Nations' Statistical Office and the United States Bureau of the Census.

    The U.N. Population Division projects population change by five-year increments. The latest update of its work is *World Population Prospects: The 1998 Revision* (New York: United Nations Department of Economic and Social Affairs, forthcoming), upon which this chapter draws.

    The U.S. Census Bureau offers estimates and projections of annual global population change. The most recent revision of the Census Bureau series took place in the spring of 1998. For these annual estimates and projections, see the U.S. Bureau of the Census, "Total Midyear Population for the World: 1950–2050." Available electronically from <http://www.census/gov/ipc/www/worldpop.html>. Accessed October 26, 1998.

    U.S. Census and U.N. Population Division projection of world population for midyear 2000 are extremely close: 6.08 billion versus 6.06 billion.
3. For a range of historical estimates, see U.S. Bureau of the Census, "Historical Estimates Of World Population." Available electronically at <http://www.census.gov/ipc/www/worldhis.html>. Accessed October 26, 1998. The 11 estimates presented on this website average out to 1650 million for world population in 1990. The United Nations Population Division, for its part, offers but a single estimate for world population that year: also 1650 million. United Nations Population Division, "Historical World Population Growth," 6/7/94; available electronically at <http://www.undo.org/popin/wdtrends/historical.html>. Accessed October 26, 1998.
4. Samuel H. Preston, *Mortality Patterns in National Populations*, (New York: Academic Press, 1976), p. 3; United Nations Population Division, *World Population Prospects: The 1998 Revision*, op. cit; U.S. Bureau of the Census International Data Base (IDB), available electronically at <http://www.census.gov/cgi-bin/ipc/agggen>, accessed October 30, 1998.

Note that this has not been an entirely smooth ascent. In particular regions and sometimes even for the world as a whole, progress toward higher life expectancy has been reversed—sometimes brutally—by war, political disasters, and epidemics.

At this writing, indeed, two large areas of the world appear to be in the grip of peacetime deterioration of life expectancy. One area, centering on the Russian Federation, includes a number of former Soviet Bloc countries that have suffered an upsurge in mortality during the course of their "transition" to a post-Leninist political and economic order. The other, which includes many countries in sub-Saharan Africa, has been ravaged by the as-yet-uncontrolled spread of a deadly AIDS epidemic.

One may argue that these pervasive health setbacks fully qualify as "population problems"—even though they have received strangely little attention to date from observers who profess concern with such matters. These recent and troubling regional trends, however, do not alter the broad picture of the twentieth century's remarkable health advances.

5. Calculations based on interpolations from Ansley J. Coale and Paul Demeny with Barbara Vaughan, *Regional Model Life Tables and Stable Populations* (New York: Academic Press, 1983).
6. For further details and background, consult Ansley J. Coale and Susan C. Watkins, eds., *The Decline of Fertility in Europe* (Princeton, NJ: Princeton University Press, 1986), and Jean-Claude Chesnais, *The Demographic Transition: Stages, Patterns and Economic Implications* (New York: Oxford University Press, 1992).
7. See Michael S. Teitelbaum and Jay M. Winter, *The Fear of Population Decline* (New York: Academic Press, 1985), Appendix A. The places in question were England and Wales (1927–39), France (1933–37), Norway (1931–39), West Germany (1926–37), Czechoslovakia (1933–38), Sweden (1927–39), Switzerland (1932–39), and apparently Austria (1933–37).
8. United Nations, *World Population Prospects: The 1998 Revision,* op. cit.
9. The former is the U.N. Population Division "medium variant" projection for 1995–2000; the latter is the U.S. Census Bureau's projection for the year 2000. For sources, see footnote 6.
10. Cf. U.S. Census Bureau, "Historical World Population Growth", op. cit.
11. Western audiences are familiar with the "Black Death's" toll in Europe, but are not always aware that the absolute magnitude of human losses from the "Black Death" may have been at least as great in Asia. See, for example, George C. Kohn, ed., *Encyclopedia of Plague and Pestilence* (New York: Facts On File, Inc., 1995), pp. 25–27.
12. The total fertility rate (TFR) is a demographic measure for the average number of births per lifetime per woman of childbearing ages. Note that Table 4-1 pertains to "period" TFRs (a synthetic "snapshot" for women of all ages in a given year) rather than "cohort" TFRs (the actual number of children ultimately born to women completing childbearing in some given year).
13. Because net replacement requires that every mother, on average, should bear a daughter who reaches the childbearing years, the exact number of births per woman per lifetime needed to achieve a "net reproduction ratio" of 1.0 will, in practice, vary somewhat, according to mortality schedules and the sex ratio at birth (i.e., the number of boys born per 100 baby girls) of the population in question. These technicalities notwithstanding, a TFR of 2.1 can serve as a reasonable general benchmark for judging replacement prospects in today's historically low-mortality settings.

14. In reality, Japan's fertility level may be even somewhat lower. Recently, Japanese authorities reported that the country's TFR had fallen to 1.39 in 1997. Kyodo News Service (Tokyo), June 18, 1998; republished in *United States Foreign Broadcast Information Service* (hereafter, *FBIS*) as "Japan: Hashimoto eyes experts' forum on declining birthrate," *FBIS*, EAS-98-169, June 18, 1998 (electronic version).
15. The U.N. Population Division medium variant projections likewise place China's TFR for the period 1995 to 2000 at 1.8.
16. For more details, see Nicholas Eberstadt, "China's population prospects: Problems ahead," *Edge*, forthcoming.
17. U.N. Population Division, *World Population Prospects: The 1998 Revisions*, op. cit.
18. Calculations derived from United Nations Development Programme, *Human Development Report 1998* (New York: Oxford University Press, 1998), p. 128, and United States Census Bureau, *Statistical Abstract of the United States 1997* (Washington, D.C.: Government Printing Office, 1997), p. 462. Estimations of Vietnam's "PPP adjusted" per capita GDP are problematic for all the obvious reasons; nevertheless, this comparison may give a rough impression of the difference in scale between per capita GDP in Vietnam today and the United States' in the late 1960s.
19. United Nations Development Programme, *Human Development Report 1998*, loc. cit., p. 144.
20. World Bank, *World Development Report 1997* (New York: Oxford University Press, 1997).
21. World Bank, *World Development Report 1997*, loc. cit.
22. For an interesting analysis of the Brazilian experience, see George Martine, "Brazil's fertility decline, 1965–95: A fresh look at key factors," *Population and Development Review*, 24, no. 1 (1996), pp. 47–76.
23. World Bank, *World Development Report 1997*, op. cit.; United Nations Development Programme, *Human Development Report 1998*, op. cit.
24. Those groupings, however, slightly overstate the world's sub-Saharan and Arab country populations. The Census Bureau's "Near East" happens to include Turkey—a non-Arab country of roughly 65 million, where, as we saw in Table 1, fertility levels are thought to have fallen by more than one-half over the past 30 years. Excluding Turkey would leave these three regions with a total midyear 1998 projected population of about 860 million—just over one-seventh of the planetary total.
25. Expert Group Meeting on Below Replacement Fertility, "Future expectations for below replacement fertility," p 1. Paper prepared for U.N. Population Division, 4–6 November 1997. Available electronically at <http://www.undp.org/popin/wdtrends/belowrep/estimate.htm>; accessed October 30, 1998.
26. Cf. Charles F. Westoff, "The return to replacement fertility: A magnetic force?", in Wolfgang Lutz, ed., *Future Demographic Trends in Europe and North America: What Can We Assume Today?* (London: Academic Press, 1991), pp. 227–234.
27. Antonio Golini, "How low can fertility be? An empirical exploration," *Population and Development Review*, 24, no. 1 (1998), pp. 59–74.
28. Nicholas Eberstadt, "Demographic shocks after Communism: Eastern Germany, 1989–93," *Population and Development Review*, 20, no. 1 (1994), pp. 137–152.
29. Dudley Kirk, "The demographic transition," *Population Studies*, 50, no. 3 (1996), pp. 361–387; citation at p. 379.

30. Cf. UNESCO, *UNESCO Statistical Yearbook 1997* (Paris: UNESCO, 1997), Table 1.3. According to Tunisia's 1984 census, 52 percent of the country's women of childbearing age (15 to 44 years) had never been to school.

    Since 1984 is roughly the midpoint of the 1970/1975 to 1995/2000 period, it may roughly approximate the level of schooling for women of childbearing ages for the period as a whole.
31. United Nations Development Programme, *Human Development Report 1998*, p. 147. "Extreme poverty" here refers to the World Bank's stipulated threshold of $1 per day (PPP adjusted); the estimates pertain to the period 1989–1994.
32. Interestingly enough, even quite dramatic shifts in European and North American fertility trends are likely to make relatively little difference to prospective global trends in the next 3 decades. The total difference between the U.N. Population Division's high-variant and low-variant projections for the year 2025 for all of Europe and North America, for example, amounts to just over 120 million. A large number perhaps—but not in comparison with the 1.1 billion discrepancy between high-variant and low-variant projections for total world population.
33. In contemplating that question, one might consider what odds an informed reader in the early 1960s would have placed against the proposition that Asia's fertility levels 30 years hence would be lower than those of the United States at the time of the bet.
34. For an authoritative assessment, see Nathan Keyfitz, "The limits Of population forecasting," *Population and Development Review*, 7, no. 4 (1981), pp. 579–594.
35. Nicholas Eberstadt, "World population implosion?", *Public Interest*, no. 129 (1997), pp. 3–22.
36. Cf. OECD, *Maintaining Prosperity In An Ageing Society* (Paris: OECD, 1998).

Chapter 5

1. Associated Press, press release June 7, 1996.
2. Greenpeace, "Fishing in Troubled Waters", press release found at *http://www.greenpeace.org/~comms/fish/part1.html*, 1993.
3. *http://www.fao.org/waicent/faoinfo/fishery/sidp/htmls/species/ga_mo_ht.htm*, taken from D. M. Cohen, T. Inada, T. Iwamoto, and N. Scialabba, 1990, "Gadiform fishes of the world (Oreder Gadiformes)," *FAO Species Catalogues, FAO Fisheries Synopsis*, 10, no. 125.
4. Commercial extinction occurs when it is no longer economically viable to catch the remaining fish.
5. R. A. Myers, N. J. Barrowman, J. A. Hutchings, and A. A. Rosenberg, "Population dynamics of exploited fish stocks at low population levels," *Science*, 269 (1995), 1106–1108.
6. Julian Simon, *The Ultimate Resource 2* (Princeton, NJ: Princeton University Press, 1996), p. 104.
7. Louis De Alessi, "The economics of property rights: A review of the evidence," *Research in Law and Economics*, 2 (1980), 1–47.
8. This scenario has come to be known as the "Tragedy of the Commons," following the famous essay by Garret Hardin (1968) (who drew on the earlier work of economists like Gordon, 1954, and Scott, 1955).
9. Orna Izakson, "Gulf of Maine cod may be in jeopardy. Scientists: Existing measures not enough," *Bangor Daily News*, July 29, 1998.

10. William DiBenedetto, "Alaska hosts final 'rush to the sea' for halibut derby," *Journal of Commerce* (September 13, 1994), 613.
11. William K. Brooks, *The Oyster* (Baltimore, MD: Johns Hopkins University Press, reprinted 1996), p. 71.
12. See John Wennersten, *The Oyster Wars of Chesapeake Bay* (Centreville, MD: Tidewater Publishers, 1981).
13. Louis De Alessi, 1980.
14. Terry Anderson and Don Leal, *Free Market Environmentalism* (San Francisco: Pacific Research Institute for Public Policy, 1991).
15. See, for example, Elmer Keen, "Common property in fisheries: Is sole ownership an option?", *Marine Policy*, 7 (1983), 197–211; Anthony Scott, "Development of property in the fishery," *Marine Resource Economics*, 5 (1988), 289–311; Steven Edwards, "Ownership of renewable ocean resources," *Marine Resource Economics*, 9 (1994), 253–273; and Kent Jeffreys, "Rescuing the oceans," in Ron Bailey (ed.), *The True State of the Planet* (New York: The Free Press, 1996), pp. 295–338.
16. S. Ciriacy-Wnatrup and R. Bishop, "Common property as a concept in natural resources policy," *Natural Resources Journal*, 15 (1980), 713–727.
17. Margaret McKean and Elinor Ostrom, "Common property regimes in the forest: Just a relic from the past?", *Unasylva*, 46, no. 180 (1995), 6.
18. Donald McCloskey, "The enclosure of open fields: Preface to a study of its impact on the efficiency of English agriculture in the eighteenth century," *Journal of Economic History*, 32 (1972), 15–35.
19. Michael De Alessi, "Oysters and Willapa Bay," Private Conservation Case Study (Washington, D.C.: Center for Private Conservation, 1996).
20. Richard R. Agnello and Lawrence P. Donnelley "Property rights and efficiency in the oyster industry," *Journal of Law and Economics*, 18 (1975), 521–533.
21. Robert Neild, *The English, The French and the Oyster* (London: Quuiller Press, 1995).
22. I. Clark, P. Major, and N. Mollet, "Development and implementation of New Zealand's ITQ management system," *Marine Resource Economics*, 5 (1988), 325–349.
23. Ragnar Arnason, "Property rights as an organizational framework in fisheries: The case of six fishing nations," in Brian Crowley (ed.) *Taking Ownership: Property Rights and Fishery Management on the Atlantic Coast* (Halifax, Nova Scotia: Atlantic Institute for Market Studies, 1997), pp. 99–144.
24. See Tom McClurg, "Bureaucratic management versus private property: ITQs in New Zealand after ten years," in Laura Jones and Michael Walker (eds.), *Fish or Cut Bait!* (Vancouver, BC: The Fraser Institute, 1997), pp. 91–105; and Basil Sharp, "From regulated access to transferable harvesting rights: Policy insights from New Zealand," *Marine Policy*, 21, no. 6 (1997), 501–517.
25. Quoted in *The Economist* (March 19, 1994), p. 24, describing a 1993 decision by the hoki fleet to not fish an extra 50,000 tons of fish allocated to them by the government.
26. Tom McClurg, "Bureaucratic management versus private property: ITQs in New Zealand after ten years," in Laura Jones and Michael Walker (eds.), *Fish or Cut Bait!* (Vancouver, BC: The Fraser Institute, 1997), pp. 91–105.
27. Orange roughy has received a lot of attention in recent years due to new findings about their age and stock sizes, and the industry now fishes them much more conservatively. See Peter Stevens, "ORH 3B—A role model," *Seafood New Zealand* (August 1993), 3.

28. Mike Arbuckle, chief executive of the Challenger Scallop Enhancement Company Ltd., in an e-mail to the *Fishfolk* e-mail discussion group, September 16, 1998.
29. Mike Arbuckle, 1998.
30. "Cyanide Sauce," *The Economist* (May 11, 1996).
31. Michael De Alessi, "Holding out for some local heroes," *New Scientist* (March 8, 1997).
32. Robert Johannes and Mark Ripen, "Environmental, economic and social of the fishery for live coral reef food fish in Asia and the Western Pacific," *SPC Live Reef Fish Information Bulletin* (March 1996).
33. Robert Johannes, *Words of the Lagoon* (Berkeley, CA: University of California Press, 1981).
34. See Yamamoto, 1995.
35. Kent Jeffreys, 1996.
36. Kenneth Ruddle and Tomoya Akimichi, "Sea tenure in Japan and the Southwestern Ryukus," in John Cordell (ed.), *A Sea of Small Boats* (Cambridge, MA: Cultural Survival Press, 1989), p. 364.
37. Margaret McKean and Elinor Ostrom, "Common property regimes in the forest: Just a relic from the past?", *Unasylva*, 46, no. 180 (1995), 3.
38. Elinor Ostrom, 1997.
39. Robert Higgs, "Legally induced technical regress in the Washington State salmon fishery," *Research in Economic History*, 7, (1982), 55–86.
40. Ibid., p. 59.
41. Duncan, 1996. p. 104
42. Tom McClurg, "Bureaucratic management versus private property: ITQs in New Zealand after ten years," in Laura Jones and Michael Walker (eds.), *Fish or Cut Bait!* (Vancouver, BC: The Fraser Institute, 1997), pp. 91–105.
43. I. Clark, P. Major, and N. Mollet, "Development and implementation of New Zealand's ITQ management system," *Marine Resource Economics*, 5 (1988), 331.
44. See Hide and Ackroyd, 1990.
45. Francis Christy, "The death rattle of open access and the advent of property rights regimes in fisheries," *Marine Resource Economics*, 11 (1996), 287–304.
46. Ibid., p. 293.
47. Mark Lundsten, *Halibut Fisherman*, personal communication, April 21, 1998.
48. IPHC annual report, 1996.
49. David Whitmore, letter to the North Pacific Management Council published in the *Alaska Fisherman's Journal* (February 1998).
50. Stanley Wang, "The surf clam ITQ management: An evaluation," *Marine Resource Economics*, 10 (1995), 93–98.
51. Quoted in David Wallace, "An overview of the surf clam and ocean quahog individual transferable quota system," testimony for the Ocean Studies Board of the National Research Council of the National Academy of Sciences, Washington D.C., March 19, 1998.
52. Lawrence Latane, "Watermen's new deal: On Feb. 1, policy lets them exchange harvest shares," *The Richmond Times Dispatch* (January 18, 1998).
53. Francis Christy, "The death rattle of open access and the advent of property rights regimes in fisheries," *Marine Resource Economics*, 11 (1996), 287–304.

54. Walter Griffin, "Monhegan lobster zone draws favor from lawmakers," *Bangor Daily News* (February 4, 1998).
55. James Acheson, "The lobster fiefs revisited," in *The Question of the Commons*, Bonnie McCay and James Acheson, eds. (Tucson, AZ: University of Arizona Press, 1987), pp. 37–65.
56. Ron Johnson, "Implications of taxing quota value in an individual transferable fishery," *Marine Resource Economics*, 10 (1995), 327–340.
57. Hannes Gisurarson, *North Atlantic Fisheries: Lessons from Iceland* (London: The Insitutte of Economic Affairs, forthcoming).
58. Terry Anderson and P. J. Hill, "The evolution of property rights: A study of the American West," *Journal of Law and Economics*, 12 (1975), 163–179.
59. Arthur C. Clarke, *The Deep Range* (New York: Signet, 1958), p. 15.
60. Sound will pen fish inside a sea ranch," *Fish Farming International*, 23, no. 4 (April 1996).
61. T. O'Shea, "Manatees," *Scientific American* (July 1994).
62. James Crittendon, untitled article, *The Boston Herald* (October 30, 1994).
63. quoted in Crittenden, 1994.
64. John Cordell, *A Sea of Small Boats* (Cambridge, MA: Cultural Survival, 1989), p. 1.
65. Fleming Meeks, "Would you like some salmon with your Big Mac?", *Forbes* (December 24, 1990).
66. FAO, *Aquaculture Production 1985–1991* (Rome: Food and Agriculture Organization of the United Nations, 1993).
67. FAO, *The State of World Fisheries and Aquaculture* (Rome: Food and Agriculture Organization of the United Nations, 1997).
68. M. Bittman, "Today's fish: Straight from the farm," *New York Times* (September 18, 1996).
69. S. Mydans, "Thai shrimp farmers facing ecologists' fury," *New York Times* (April 28, 1996).
70. Ibid.
71. Ibid.
72. Conner Bailey, "The social consequences of tropical shrimp mariculture development," *Ocean and Shoreline Management* (1988), 31–34.
73. H. Murray, "Just compensation," *Far Eastern Economic Review* (March 9, 1995).
74. D. Southgate, *Shrimp Mariculture Development in Ecuador: Some Resource Policy Issues*," Working Paper No. 5 of the Environment and Natural Resources Policy and Training Project, University of Wisconsin, November 1992.
75. Ibid.
76. Michael Weber, "The fish harvesters: Farm raising salmon and shrimp makes millionaires, and also creates dead seas," *E Magazine* (November/December 1996).
77. See *Open Ocean Aquaculture '97: Charting the Future of Ocean Farming*, Proceedings of an International Conference, Charles Helsley (ed.), University of Hawaii Sea Grant, April 23–25, 1997.
78. H. B. Herring, "900,000 striped bass, and not a fishing pole in sight," *New York Times* (November 6, 1994).
79. "Greenpeace fisheries campaign: Challenging the global grab for declining fish stocks," *http://greenpeace.org/~comms/fish/index.html* (January 1998).
80. Troubled waters: A call for action, Marine Conservation Biology Institute," *http://www.mcbi.org/release.html* (March 1998).

81. A. Maitland, "Unilever in fight to save global fisheries," *Financial Times* (February 22, 1996), and Rod Fujita and Doug Hopkins, "Market theory can help solve overfishing," *The Oregonian* (September 20, 1995).
82. Rebecca Golburg and Tracy Triplett, *Murky Waters: The Environmental Effects of Aquaculture in the United States* (Environmental Defense Fund publication, October 1997).
83. Elmer Keen, *Ownership and Productivity of Marine Fishery Resources: An Essay on the Resolution of Conflict in the Use of the Ocean Pastures* (Blacksburg, VA: McDonald and Woodward Publishing, 1988).
84. Steve Nadis, "Fertilizing the sea," *Scientific American* (April 1998).

Chapter 6

1. Robert L. Bradley, Jr., "Renewable Energy: Not Cheap, Not 'Green,' " Policy Analysis no. 280, Cato Institute, August 27, 1997, p. 5.
2. List compiled by Bradley, 1997, pp. 4–5.
3. Energy Information Administration, U.S. Department of Energy, *International Energy Outlook 1998* (Washington, D.C.: U.S. Department of Energy, 1998), p. 135.
4. Steven Kelman, *What Price Incentives?* (Boston: Auburn House, 1981), chapter 3.
5. If the factory, however, was isolated and only affected a few neighbors, then any pollution remedy would not have spillover benefits and would not have beneficiaries who would benefit without payment. In such small-number-of-persons situations, parties could resolve the "externality" themselves through contract or the common law. Under those circumstances, air quality would not be considered a "public good" and a market failure would not exist. See Ronald Coase, "The Problem of Social Cost," *The Journal of Law and Economics*, 3 (October 1960): 1–44.
6. In a recent example of such an accounting exercise, the authors conclude that diesel fuel, wood, and coal are undertaxed relative to their external costs; natural gas is substantially overtaxed; and gasoline is taxed correctly. See W. Kip Viscusi, Wesley A. Magat, Alan Carlin, and Mark K. Dreyfus, "Environmentally Responsible Energy Pricing," *The Energy Journal*, 15, no. 2 (1994): 23–42.
7. See Robert W. Crandall, *Controlling Industrial Pollution* (Washington, D.C.: The Brookings Institution, 1983), chapter 3.
8. Peter VanDoren, "The deregulation of the electricity industry: A primer," *Cato Institute Policy Analysis #320*, October 6, 1998.
9. Three issues not discussed are the problem of "capture" in petroleum reservoirs, vertical integration in the oil industry, and natural monopoly issues in oil and gas pipelines. The problem of capture is of historical rather than current significance and the other two result in higher rather than lower than efficient oil prices, the opposite of current policy concern.
10. The arguments come mainly from geologists. See Colin J. Campbell and Jean H. Laherrere, "The End of Cheap Oil," *Scientific American* (March 1998): 78–83.
11. Energy Information Administration, U.S. Department of Energy, *International Energy Annual 1996* (Washington, DC: U.S. Department of Energy, 1997) pp. 3, 109, and 111; Energy Information Administration, 1998, pp. 35, 50; Enron Corporation, *1997 Energy Outlook* (Houston: Enron Corp., 1997), p. 11; World Energy Council, *1995 Survey of Energy Resources* (London: World Energy Council, 1995), p.

32–35, all cited in Robert L. Bradley, Jr., "The Increasing Sustainability of Conventional Energy," in *Advances in the Economics of Energy & Resources*, John Moroney, ed. (Greenwich, CT: Jai Press, 1999).

12. Energy Information Administration, 1997, p. 111.
13. For a good discussion of the real economic meaning of "proven reserves," see Paul Ballonoff, *Energy: Ending the Never-Ending Crisis* (Washington, D.C.: Cato Institute, 1997), pp. 7–8, 17–22.
14. Bradley, 1999, pp. 15–16.
15. William Nordhous, "Resources as Constraint on Growth?" *American Economic Review* (May 1974): 22–26, and "Energy and the Environment: A Power for Good, A Power for Ill," *The Economist* (August 31, 1991): survey, p. 4.
16. Michael Lynch, *Facing the Elephant: Oil Market Evolution and Future Oil Crises* (Boulder, CO: IRCEED, 1998), p. 2, cited in Bradley, 1999, p. 13.
17. Figures calculated from Energy Information Administration 1997, table 1.1, p. 3.
18. For a thorough discussion of the impact of technological advance on petroleum supplies, see Peter Coy, Gary McWilliams, and John Rossant, "The New Economics of Oil," *Business Week* (November 3, 1997): 140–144; Gary McWilliams, " 'Technology is What's Driving This Business,' " *Business Week* (November 3, 1997): 146–148; Allanna Sullivan, "Prudhoe Bay Field Isn't Dying After All, Thanks to Technology," *Wall Street Journal* (October 25, 1995): B1; Daniel Southerland, "Getting a Leg Up: In Gulf of Mexico's Depths, Shell Finds Lots of Oil—And a Way to Restructure," *Washington Post* (March 31, 1996): H1; Ballonoff, pp. 7–22; and Roger Anderson, "Oil Production in the 21st Century," *Scientific American* (March 1998): 86–91.
19. In 1949, gasoline prices were 26.8 cents per gallon, on average ($1.664 in 1998 dollars). In 1972, gasoline prices were 33.42 cents per gallon, on average ($1.21.3 in 1998 dollars). In March 1998, the average price of unleaded gasoline was $104.1. See U.S. Department of Energy, Energy Information Administration, *Annual Energy Review 1997*, Table 5.22, and *Monthly Energy Review* (August 1998): Table 9.4.
20. M. A. Adelman, *The Genie out of the Bottle World Oil since 1970* (Cambridge, MA: M.I.T. Press, 1995), pp. 15–17.
21. See United States Department of Energy, Energy Information Administration, *Annual Energy Review 1996*, Tables 5.16, 6.8, and 7.8.
22. Richard Stroup, "Political Control vs. Sustainable Development," paper submitted for the Cato Institute conference *Global Environmental Crises: Science or Politics?*, June 5–6, 1991; Fred Smith, "The Market and Nature," *The Freeman*, (September 1993).
23. Andrew Chisholm, Peter Hartley, and Michael Porter, "Slogans or Policies: A Critique of 'Ecologically Sustainable Development'," Occasional Paper No. B3, Tasman Institute, October 1990, p. 17.
24. The ideas in this paragraph draw heavily on Steven E. Landsburg, "Tax the Knickers Off Your Grandchildren," *Slate* (March 6, 1997).
25. In the short run, a 1 percent decrease in petroleum supplies results in a price increase of 10 percent. In the long run, a 1 percent decrease in petroleum supplies results in a price increase of only 1 percent. See Adelman, pp. 190–191.
26. United States Department of Energy, Energy Information Administration, *Annual Energy Review 1996*, Table 5.16 ("Crude Oil Domestic First Purchase Prices").
27. Richard Pindyck, "Inter-fuel Substitution and the Industrial Demand for Energy: An International Comparison," *Review of Economics and Statistics* (May 1979): 169–179.

28. Peter VanDoren, *Politics, Markets, and Congressional Policy Choices* (Ann Arbor, MI: University of Michigan Press, 1991), p. 37.
29. Ibid., pp. 38–39.
30. Ibid., pp. 39–44.
31. Peter Passell, "The Oil Reserve: Big Is Beautiful," *The New York Times* (August 29, 1990): D2; Matthew L. Wald, "Sanctions Starting To Pinch Iraq Economy, U.S. Aides Say; UN's Diplomacy Welcomed," *The New York Times* (August 27, 1990): A1. Oil price and supply data come from U.S. Department of Energy, *Historical Monthly Energy Review 1973–1992*, Tables 9.1 ("Crude Oil Price Summary Composite Refiner Acquisition Cost") and 10.1b ("World Crude Oil Production") as well as Adelman, pp. 292–297.
32. Jerry Taylor, "Restructuring the Department of Energy," testimony before the Subcommittee on Government Reform and Oversight Committee on Government Reform and Oversight United States House of Representatives, May 16, 1995.
33. Philip Verleger has argued that the management of market expectations is crucial during an oil shock. The holders of inventory need to be convinced that their largest profit opportunities lie in selling inventory sooner rather than later so that they supply oil that dampens the shock rather than withholding oil to see if they make more money later. In an ideal world, governments would precommit to a stiff and predictably declining tax on oil imports during actual supply reductions to give the holders of domestic inventory incentive to put oil on the market sooner rather than later. See Philip Verleger, Jr., *Oil Markets In Turmoil: An Economic Analysis* (Cambridge, MA: Ballinger, 1982).
34. Douglas Bohi, "Thinking Through Energy Security Issues," *American Enterprise* (September–October 1991): 33.
35. Thomas Lee, Ben Ball, Jr., and Richard Tabors, *Energy Aftermath* (Boston: Harvard Business School, 1990), p. 17.
36. Ibid., p. 30.
37. Murray Rothbard argues that air pollution should be governed by the common law strict liability rule. Murray Rothbard, "Law, Property Rights, and Air Pollution," *The Cato Journal*, 2 (Spring 1982): 55–99.
38. Daniel Klein and Pia Maria Koskenoja, "The Smog-Reduction Road: Remote Sensing vs. The Clean Air Act," Policy Analysis no. 248, Cato Institute, February 7, 1996, p. 6
39. Adam Smith, *The Wealth of Nations* (1776), ed. Edwin Cannan (New York: Modern Library, 1937), p. 423.
40. Over the 1970–1990 period, Clean Air Act direct compliance expenditures are estimated to have been $500 billion. In 1978, Clean Air Act direct compliance expenditures are estimated to have been $35 billion annually. See J. Clarence Davies and Jan Mazurek, *Pollution Control in the United States Evaluating the System* (Washington, D.C.: Resources for the Future, 1998), pp. 128–130.
41. Crandall, 1983, chap. 3.
42. For an excellent discussion of this problem as it relates to electricity consumption, see Ballonoff, pp. 52–56.
43. Albert Nichols, *How Well Do Market Failures Support the Need for Demand Side Management?* (Cambridge, MA: National Economic Research Associates, 1992), p. 9.
44. Viscusi et al., 1994, p. 26 consider only the relationship between optimal pollution taxes and current explicit general taxes not dedicated to a trust fund. They do not consider the cost of existing pollution regulations already embedded in fuel prices.

45. The 1990 Clean Air Act Amendments probably will result in additional costs that are double the additional benefits. See Paul R. Portney, "Economics and the Clean Air Act," *The Journal of Economic Perspectives* 4 (Fall 1990): 173–181.
46. U.S. General Accounting Office, *Electricity Supply: Consideration of Environmental Costs in Selecting Fuel Resources* (May 19, 1995): p. 2, cited in Ballonoff, p. 55.
47. Amory Lovins, "Invited Comments on Kenneth W. Costello's Article 'Should Utilities Promote Energy Conservation?' " *Electricity Journal* (March–April 1986): 4.
48. For overview of the debate, see an issue of *Energy Policy* entirely devoted to the controversy [22, no. 10 (October 1994)]; and "Markets for Energy Efficiency," a report of the Stanford Energy Modeling Forum [report 13, volume 1 (September 1996)].
49. Nichols, 1992, pp. 22–24.
50. Kevin Hassett and Gilbert Metcalf, "Energy Conservation Investment Do Consumers Discount the Future Correctly?", *Energy Policy*, 21 (June 1993): 710–716. Gilbert Metcalf, "Economics and Rational Conservation Policy," *Energy Policy*, 22 (October 1994): 819–825.
51. Nichols, 1992, p. 17.
52. Nichols, 1992, pp. 24–25; and Ruth Johnson and David Kaserman, "Housing Market Capitalization of Energy-Saving Durable Good Investments," *Economic Inquiry*, 21 (1983): 374–386.
53. This holds true even for rental markets that are, according to conservationists, less likely to reflect energy efficiency in rents, which in turn leads to underinvestment in energy efficiency. Nichols, 1992, pp. 26–29.
54. Matthew Wald, "Saving Energy: Still a Tough Sell," *New York Times* (March 30, 1991): 25.
55. Nichols, 1992, p. 30.
56. Jerry Hausman, Conference presentation at the American Enterprise Institute, Washington D.C., October 17, 1997.
57. The details about subsidies come from United States Department of Energy, Energy Information Administration, "Federal Energy Subsidies: Direct and Indirect Interventions in Energy Markets," November 1992. Some analysts describe the Overseas Private Investment Corporation (OPIC) and the foreign tax credit as subsidizing oil production; see Citizen Action, "Subsidizing Big Oil's Foreign Investments: Importing Oil, Exporting Jobs, and Making War" (Washington, D.C.: Citizen Action, September 1996). We will not discuss these policies because they are available to all corporations. However, the government provision of risk insurance for overseas investment does violate market principles.
58. Douglas Koplow, "Federal Energy Subsidies: Energy, Environmental, and Fiscal Impacts," The Alliance to Save Energy, April 1993, p. 35.
59. See for example Robert L. Bradley, *Oil, Gas & Government: The U.S. Experience*, Vols. 1 and 2 (Lanham, MD: Rowman & Littlefield, 1996); and Peter VanDoren, *Politics, Markets, and Congressional Policy Choices* (Ann Arbor, MI: University of Michigan Press, 1991).
60. A truly neutral tax code would not tax capital investments at all, because capital returns are invariably taxed a second time at the point of consumption whereas noncapital consumption is taxed only once. Thus, the subsidies castigated by ASE simply help offset the unfair treatment of capital via the corporate income tax and the capital gains tax.
61. "Federal Government Subsidies and Incentives for U.S. Energy Industries," Management Information Services, Inc., Washington, D.C., May 1993, p. 35.

62. Energy Information Administration, 1992, p. x.
63. Koplow, p. ii.
64. Energy Information Administration, 1992, p. x.
65. Ibid., pp. 117–118. Coal producers receive a 10 percent depletion allowance regardless of output or company size.
66. Coal producers may expense 70 percent of their surface mine stripping expenses.
67. VanDoren, 1991, pp. 37–39, Stephen McDonald, *Petroleum Conservation in the U.S.* (Baltimore, MD: The Johns Hopkins University Press, 1971), p. 189.
68. Actually, the law is still on the books (United States Code Title 15 Sec 715), but during the first oil shock in 1973, the President issued an executive order suspending its operation.
69. VanDoren, 1991, pp. 38–39.
70. The revenues in fiscal year 1992 amounted to $3.1 billion. See Energy Information Administration, 1992, pp. 7 and 40.
71. Ibid., p. 7.
72. Gas and coal receive net subsidies of $1 billion and $300 million, respectively. See Energy Information Administration, 1992, p. 7.
73. Data from the Department of Energy, reported by Bradley, 1997, p. 63.
74. Alan Tonelson and Andrew K. Hurd, "The Real Cost of Middle-East Oil," *The New York Times* (September 4, 1990): A17.
75. Saudi Arabia and Kuwait paid approximately $33 billion (55 percent) toward the total cost of Desert Storm and Desert Shield, which was $60 billion. The U.S. share was only $6 billion (10 percent). Defense Department Press release 125-M, May 5, 1992.
76. John Berger, *Charging Ahead: The Business of Renewable Energy and What It Means for America* (New York: Holt & Co., 1997), pp. 4–5.
77. Typical of this school of thought is Christopher Flavin and Nicholas Lenssen, *Power Surge: Guide to the Coming Energy Revolution* (New York: W. W. Norton, 1994). See particularly pp. 23–28.
78. Bradley, 1999, p. 6.
79. Martin Daniel, "Finance for Energy," *FT Energy News* (Summer 1997); Energy Information Administration, 1998, p. 20.
80. Shell International Limited, "Shell Invests US$0.5 Billion in Renewables," News Release, October 16, 1997; Sam Fletcher, "Shell to Spend $1 Billion on 3 Deep Gulf Fields," *The Oil Daily* (March 20, 1998): 1, cited in Bradley, 1999, pp. 6–7.
81. California Energy Commission, *1996 Energy Technology Status Report*, P500-96-006, December 1997, p. 27.
82. Ibid.
83. Agis Salpukas, "70's dreams, 90's Realities Soft Energy: A Luxury Now. A Necessity Later?" *The New York Times* (April 11, 1995): C1; Michael T. Maloney, Robert E. McCormick, and Raymond D. Sauer, "Customer Choice, Consumer Value: An Analysis of Retail Competition In America's Electric Industry" (Washington, D.C.: Citizens for a Sound Economy Foundation, 1996), p. 38; and Block and Lenard, p. 1-1. Block and Lenard (p. 3-1) report that if the waste heat from the turbines is used for heating, the cost per kilowatt-hour is reduced to 2 to 3 cents per kilowatt-hour.

84. Energy Information Administration, *Annual Energy Outlook 1996*, cited in "Energy Security Analysis Inc., Electricity & Climate Change: Estimating The Effects of Compliance With The Kyoto Treaty," ESAI Power Market Analysis, Winter 1997–1998, pp. 2, 13 (Table 6).
85. Scott Sklar, statement before the Subcommittee on Energy and Power of the House Committee on Energy and Commerce, 100th Congress, 1st Session (Washington, D.C.: Government Printing Office, 1988), p. 26, cited in Bradley, 1997, p. 29.
86. Bradley, 1997, p. 28.
87. There are three subcategories of solar power: thermal solar—systems that collect sunlight on a parabolic dish trough or in a tower, which is then converted to electricity; photovoltaic solar—systems that convert sunlight to electricity via massive panels; and microsolar—small-scale technologies that use microphotovoltaic systems to power specific applications such as communications, lighting, and switching (a good example is the batteryless standard pocket calculator).
88. California Energy Commission, 1997, p. 57.
89. Bradley, 1997, p. 29.
90. "Everything You Always Wanted to Know About Solar Power," Solarex brochure 6121-6, March 1997, p. 3.
91. California Energy Commission, 1997, p. 27.
92. Solarex, p. 11.
93. Karin Sheldon, president, Wilderness Society, prepared statement before the Subcommittee on Public Lands, National Parks, and Forests, Senate Committee on Energy and Natural Resources, 103rd Congress, 1st Session (Washington, D.C.: Government Printing Office, 1993), p. 208, cited in Bradley, 1997, p. 32. For a brief summary of the ecological problems associated with full development of the deserts, see Bradley, 1997, p. 32.
94. Hearings before the Subcommittee on Energy Conservation and Power and the Subcommittee on Fossil and Synthetic Fuels of the House Committee on Energy and Commerce, 98th Congress, 2nd Session (Washington, D.C.: Government Printing Office, 1984), p. 810, cited in Bradley, 1997, p. 24.
95. Angus Duncan, American Wind Energy Association, statement before the Subcommittee on Energy Conservation and Power of the House Committee on Energy and Commerce, 99th Congress, 2nd Session (Washington, D.C.: Government Printing Office, 1985), pp. 189–190, cited in Bradley, p. 14.
96. California Energy Commission, 1997, p. 57. For a review of the various subsidies and preferences affecting the prices consumers pay for wind power, see Bradley, 1997, pp. 8–10.
97. Bradley, 1997, p. 24.
98. Ibid., pp. 7–8 and Bradley, 1999, p. 9.
99. California Energy Commission, *1994 Electricity Report*, November 1995, p. 104, cited in Bradley, 1997, p. 14.
100. Ibid., and ICF Kaiser Study, prepared for Enron Corp., September 1995, cited in Bradley, 1997, p. 14.
101. Bradley, 1997, p. 15.
102. California Energy Commission, *Wind Project Performance: 1994 Summary*, August 1995, p. 1, cited in Bradley, 1997, p. 7.
103. California Energy Markets, May 8, 1992, pp. 16–17, cited in Bradley, 1997, p. 17. Given 10,000 bird deaths from today's 1731 megawatts of installed capacity, we can project that, if all American electricity generation were powered by wind turbines, 4.4 million birds would die for our electricity. If wind power

were able to supply 20 percent of America's electricity (a figure the American Wind Energy Association forwarded some years ago in Congressional hearings), then 880,000 birds would die. Calculations from Bradley, 1997, p. 17.

104. Resource Data International, *Energy Choices in a Competitive Era* (Alexandria, VA: Center for Energy and Economic Development, 1995), p. 2–15.
105. Ros Davidson, "New Rules for the Altamont Pass," *Windpower Monthly* (July 1998): 37.
106. Amy Linn, "Whirly Birds," *SF Weekly* (March 29–April 4, 1995): 11–12, 14, cited in Bradley, 1997, p. 16.
107. Paul Gipe, *Wind Energy Comes of Age* (New York: John Wiley & Sons, 1995), p. 450.
108. Linn, cited in Bradley, 1997, p. 16.
109. Gipe, p. 396, Resource Data International, pp. 2–12.
110. Diane Jennings, "Wind Power Gets a Turn," *Dallas Morning News* (September 24, 1995): 49A; cited in Bradley, 1997, p. 77.
111. Carlotta Collette, "Wind's Eastern Front," *Northwest Energy News* (July–August 1992): 14; cited in Bradley, 1997, p. 76.
112. Daniel Yergin, "Conservation: The Key Energy Resource," in *Energy Future: Report of the Energy Project at the Harvard Business School*, Robert Stobaugh and Daniel Yergin, eds. (New York: Random House, 1979), p. 136; cited in Bradley, 1997, pp. 36–37.
113. Bradley, 1997, p. 37.
114. David Kline et al., "The Role of Renewable Energy in U.S. Climate Strategies," conference proceedings from the 18th Annual North American Conference of the International Association For Energy Economics, published in *International Energy Markets, Competition and Policy* (Cleveland: United States Association for Energy Economics, 1997), p. 499.
115. Nichols, 1992, pp. 7–9.
116. Nichols reports (1992, pp. 12–13) that a survey of 78 utilities by National Economic Research Associates concluded that prices exceeded marginal cost on a capacity-weighted basis by 22 percent.
117. See J. D. Khazzoom, "Economic Implications of Mandated Efficiency Standards," *The Energy Journal*, no. 11 (1980): 21–40; "Energy Savings Resulting from the Adoption of More Efficient Appliances," *The Energy Journal*, no. 8 (1987): 85–89; and "Energy Savings Resulting from the Adoption of More Efficient Appliances: A Rejoinder," *The Energy Journal*, no. 10 (1989): 157–166; H. D. Saunders, "The Khazzoom-Brooks Postulate and Neoclassical Growth," *The Energy Journal*, no. 17 (1992): 131–148; F. P. Sioshansi, "Do Diminishing Returns Apply to DSM?" *The Electricity Journal*, 7, no. 4, (1994): 70–79; Nichols, 1992, p. 17; and Paul Joskow, "Utility-Subsidized Energy-Efficiency Programs," *Annual Review of Energy and the Environment*, no. 20 (1995): 526–534; cited in David Kline et al., p. 499. Robert W. Crandall, "Corporate Average Fuel Economy Standards," *Journal Of Economic Perspectives*, 6 (Spring 1992): 171–180, examines the same phenomenon in the context of regulations that mandate that cars use less gasoline per mile.
118. Nichols, 1992, p. 21.
119. Mark D. Levine, Jonathan G. Koomey, James E. McMahon, Alan H. Sanstad, and Eric Hirst, "Energy Efficiency Policy and Market Failures," *Annual Review of Energy and the Environment*, 20 (1995): 535–555.
120. Ronald Sutherland, "The Debate About Energy Conservation Policy," conference proceedings from the 18th International Association For Energy Economics International Conference, published in *Into the*

21st Century: Harmonizing Energy Policy, Environment, and Sustainable Economic Growth, (Cleveland, OH: International Association For Energy Economics, 1995), p. 82.
121. Larry Ruff, "Equity v. Efficiency: Getting DSM Pricing Right," *Electricity Journal* (November 1992): 27, 29.
122. Mikael Togeby and Anders Larsen, "The Potential for Electricity Conservation in Industry: From Theory to Practice," conference proceedings from the 18th International Association For Energy Economics International Conference, published in *Into the 21st Century: Harmonizing Energy Policy, Environment, and Sustainable Economic Growth*, (Cleveland, OH: International Association For Energy Economics, 1995), pp. 48–55.
123. Ibid., p. 51.
124. They estimate that 15 percent of those savings would have been realized with or without their audit, so the actual benefit of their audits should be reduced accordingly.
125. Togeby and Larsen, p. 53.
126. Ibid., p. 54.
127. Ibid., p. 48.
128. Ibid., p. 54.
129. J. G. Koomey, A. H. Sanstad, and L. J. Shown, "Magnetic Fluorescent Ballasts: Market Data, Market Imperfections, and Policy Success," occasional paper LBL-37702, Lawrence Berkeley Laboratory, 1996.
130. Amory Lovins, "Save Energy, Make Piles of Money," *The Washington Post* (January 5, 1998): A11.
131. Paul Ballonoff, comment on the paper "Market Data, Market Imperfections, and Policy Success," unpublished manuscript (available from the authors), July 1998.
132. Paul L. Joskow and Donald B. Marron, "What Does a Negawatt Really Cost?", *The Energy Journal*, 13, no. 4 (1992): 1–34; Albert L. Nichols, "Demand-side Management: Overcoming Market Barriers or Obscuring Real Costs?", *Energy Policy*, 22 (October 1994): 840–847; and Franz Wirl, *The Economics of Conservation Programs* (Boston: Kluwer Academic Publishers, 1997).
133. Mark D. Levine and Richard Sonnenblick, "On the Assessment of Utility Demand-Side Management Programs," *Energy Policy*, 22 (October 1994): 848–856. Interlaboratory Working Group, "Scenarios of U.S. Carbon Reductions: Potential Impact of Energy Technologies by 2010 and Beyond," U.S. Department of Energy, Office of Energy Efficiency and Soft Technologies, September 1997.
134. Personal communication between Illinois Commerce Commissioner Ruth Kretschmer and Jerry Taylor, 1998.
135. Energy Information Administration, *Electric Power Annual, 1995*, Vol. 2, Table 43, p. 77.
136. Ibid., Table 13, p. 35.
137. David Kline et al., p. 500.
138. As part of a wide-ranging bill to restructure the electricity industry, four separate proposals dominate the political debate regarding restructuring and renewable energy. Rep. Dan Schaefer, chairman of the House Commerce and Energy Power Subcommittee, introduced legislation (H.R. 665) that would mandate that at least 4 percent of the nation's electricity come from renewable energy by the year 2010. The Clinton administration is peddling its own restructuring plan that would require 5.5 percent of the nation's electricity to come from renewable energy by the year 2010. Sen. Dale Bumpers and Sen. Slade Gorton introduced legislation (S. 1401) that would require 14 percent of all electricity come from renewables.

Rep. Edward Markey and Sen. Jim Jeffords introduced legislation (H.R. 1359 & S. 687) requiring that at least 10 percent of the nation's electricity come from renewable energy by the year 2010 and 20 percent by the year 2020.

139. Nancy A. Rader and William P. Short, III, "Restructuring: Hard Ground For Softs," *The Electricity Journal* (April 1998): 74.
140. Lisa Prevost, "Renewable Energy: Toward a Portfolio Standard?", *Public Utilities Fortnightly* (August 1998): 31.
141. "Sampling of State Renewable Energy Activity: Measures Pending and Approved," Public Utilities Fortnightly, August 1998, p. 35.
142. Author's calculation assumes that the current costs for the cheapest renewable energy (wind power at 7 cents per kilowatt-hour) and the current costs for its most common competitor—combined-cycle natural-gas turbines (3 cents per kilowatt-hour) continue. The calculation also assumes an elasticity of consumer demand of −1.0. The results are partial equilibrium estimates that do not reflect the changes that occur in all other areas of the economy because electricity is higher-priced, nor does it attempt to measure the value of services people fail to consume because of higher electricity prices.
143. Christopher Flavin and Seth Dunn, "Rising Sun, Gathering Winds: Policies to Stabilize the Climate and Strengthen Economies," Worldwatch Paper 138, November 1997, p. 18.
144. Ibid.
145. Energy Security Analysis Inc., p. 9.
146. Lovins, 1998.
147. U.S. General Accounting Office, "Global Warming: Information on the Results of Four of EPA's Voluntary Climate Change Programs," GAO/RCED-97-163, June 30, 1997, and Victor Rezendes, testimony before the Senate Committee on Energy and Natural Resources, "Global Warming: Administration's Proposal in Support of the Kyoto Protocol," GAO/T-RCED-28-219, June 4, 1998, pp. 9–10.
148. For a thorough review of the record of government research and development programs, see Jerry Taylor, testimony before the House Subcommittee on Energy and Environment of the House Committee on Science, April 9, 1997.
149. "Historical Tables," *Budget of the Unites States Government, FY 1996* (Washington, D.C.: U.S. Government Printing Office, 1995), pp. 135–140; and "DOE's *Success Stories* Report," United States General Accounting Office, GAO/RCED-96-120R, April 15, 1996, p. 2.
150. Linda Cohen and Roger Noll, *The Technology Pork Barrel* (Washington: The Brookings Institution, 1991), p. 378.
151. Murray Weidenbaum, "A New Technology Policy for the United States?" *Regulation*, 16, no. 4 (Fall 1993): 19.
152. Eric Reichl, "Alternate Opinion on Energy R&D in the U.S.," unpublished manuscript, p. 2.
153. Kelly Barron, "I'm Greener Than You," *Forbes* (March 9, 1998): 45.
154. The DonVito family in California, for example, complain that rooftop solar panels "saved them little if anything and was a plumbing concern. 'It took a lot of work to get that thing out of our lives,' says Michelle DonVito. 'To be here in suburbia with that monster on the roof is stupid.' " Ibid.
155. Ibid.

156. Ibid.
157. Reported in *The Electricity Daily* (July 16, 1998), cited in "Congress Scrutinizes DOE Funding," *Cooler Heads*, Competitive Enterprise Institute, July 22, 1998, p. 2.
158. *The Kyoto Protocol and the President's Policies to Address Climate Change* (cited as CEA report hereafter) available at http://www.whitehouse.gov/WH/New/html/kyoto.pdf.
159. Interlaboratory Working Group on Energy-Efficient and Low-Carbon Technologies, *Scenarios of U.S. Carbon Reductions: Potential Impacts of Energy-Efficient and Low Carbon Technologies by 2010 and Beyond* (Oak Ridge National Laboratory, Lawrence Berkeley National Laboratory, Pacific Northwest National Laboratory, National Renewable Energy Laboratory, and Argonne National Laboratory, September 1997)
160. The CO_2 emissions of fossil fuels per unit energy released vary by over a factor of two. Coal releases the most CO_2. For example, an existing coal-fired electricity plant releases 571 pounds of carbon emissions per megawatt-hour of electricity produced. An advanced combined-cycle natural-gas-fired electricity plant produces only 201 pounds of carbon emissions per megawatt-hour of electricity (65 percent less). See United States Energy Information Administration *Impacts of the Kyoto Protocol on U.S. Energy Markets and Economic Activity* (October 1998), p. 75, Table 17 (cited as EIA report, hereafter).
161. These 40 countries are referred to as "Annex I" countries for the section of the agreement in which their names appear signed in Rio de Janeiro in June 1992 at the first meeting of the parties to the United Nations Framework Convention on Climate Change. See CEA report, p. 93. The full text of the Kyoto protocol including the carbon emissions quota for each Annex I country is available at http://www.cnn.com/SPECIALS/1997/global.warming/stories/treaty/.
162. CEA report, pp. iv, 53–54.
163. Statement of W. David Montgomery in United States House of Representatives, *The Road from Kyoto—Part 4: The Kyoto Protocol's Impacts on U.S. Energy Markets and Economic Activity*, October 9, 1998, a hearing before the Committee on Science, p. 13, Table 2 (cited as Science hearing, hereafter) available at http://www.house.gov/science/montgomery_10-09.htm.
164. See EIA report, p. xv, Table ES1.
165. Ibid., p. 219, Table C8 and Science hearing, p. 13, Table 2.
166. EIA report, Appendix C.
167. Autonomous energy efficiency is a reduction in the use of energy per dollar of economic output that occurs even in the absence of energy price increases to encourage such efficiency.
168. See Science hearing, pp. 16–18.
169. Ibid.
170. Ibid., p. 16.
171. EIA report, p. 139.
172. Ibid., p. 143.
173. Ibid., p. xiv.
174. Ibid., pp. xv, Table ES1, 73–74, 93–94. In 1996, coal-fired power plants produced 92 percent of U.S. carbon emissions in the electricity sector and accounted for over one-third of total U.S. carbon emission.
175. Ibid., p. 105. Since 1983, an annual average of 10 giga(billion)watts of natural-gas-fired electric generation capacity has been added. In the scenario in which the United States has to reduce emissions to 3

percent below 1990 levels, 24 gigawatts of natural-gas-fired electric generation capacity would have to be added annually.

176. Science hearing, p. 17. Coal shipments provided 23 percent of all rail revenue and 39 percent of revenues for major coal-hauling railroads in 1996. See EIA report, p. 143.
177. Ibid., pp. 138–139.
178. EIA report, Appendix C. The CEA model predicts about $61 per ton for carbon emissions (Science report, p. 13). Wigley recently estimated that the amount of global warming prevented by full compliance with the Kyoto protocol by every country would be 0.07°C by the year 2050, an amount so small that it cannot be reliably measured by ground-based thermometers. See T. M. L. Wigley, "The Kyoto Protocol: CO2, CH4, and Climate Implications," *Geophysical Research Letters*, 25 (July 1, 1998): 2285–2288.
179. See William Spangar Peirce, *Economics of the Energy Industries* (Westport, CN: Praeger, 1996), pp. 216–218.
180. Hans H. Landsberg, *Energy: The Next Twenty Years* (Cambridge, MA: Ballinger, 1979), p. 19.
181. United States Energy Information Administration, *Annual Energy Review* 1997, p. 149, Table 5.16, and *Monthly Energy Review October 1998* p. 111, Table 9.1. The average 1979 price of domestic crude oil was $22.90 per barrel in 1992 dollars. The June 1998 price in 1992 dollars was less than $8.90.
182. Reduced use of coal accounts for 68 to 75 percent of carbon emission reduction in the various scenarios modeled by the Energy Information Administration. See EIA report p. ES4.
183. The so-called Byrd Amendment to provide compensation to miners failed in the Senate by only one vote. See Paul L. Joskow and Richard Schmalensee, "The Political Economy of Market-Based Environmental Policy: The U.S. Acid Rain Program," *The Journal of Law and Economics*, 41 (April 1998): 50.
184. Lee, Balls, Tabors, p. 167.

Chapter 7

1. R. Watson et al., *Climate Change 1995: Impacts, Adaptations and Mitigation of Climate Change* (Cambridge, UK: Cambridge University Press, 1996).
2. C. McEvedy and R. Jones, *Atlas of World Population History* (New York: Facts on File, 1978); I. M. Goklany, "Strategies to enhance adaptability: Technological change, sustainable growth and free trade," *Climatic Change*, 30 (1995): 427–449; Food and Agricultural Organization (FAO), *FAOSTAT database* <http://apps.fao.org/> (15 April 1998).
3. See, for example, Goklany, "Strategies to enhance adaptability." *Climate Change*, 30 (1995): 427–449.
4. I. M. Goklany, "Saving habitat and conserving biodiversity on a crowded planet," *BioScience* (forthcoming); *FAOSTAT database* (15 April 1998).
5. FAO, *The State of Food and Agriculture 1996* (Rome: FAO, 1996).
6. I. M. Goklany, "Conserving habitat, feeding humanity," *Forum for Applied Research and Public Policy*, 13 (Summer 1998): 51–56; Goklany, "Strategies to enhance adaptability"; Goklany, "Saving habitat and conserving biodiversity on a crowded planet."
7. N. Nicholls, "Increased Australian wheat yield due to recent climate trends," *Nature*, 387 (1997): 484–485.

8. R. B. Myneni et al., "Increased plant growth in the Northern high latitudes," *Nature*, 386 (1997): 698–702.
9. J. Reilly et al., "Agriculture in a changing climate: Impacts and adaptations," in R. Watson et al., eds., *Climate Change 1995: Impacts, Adaptations and Mitigation of Climate Change* (Cambridge University Press, 1996), pp. 451–454.
10. S. Wittwer, Address to the Western Fuels Association's 1998 Energy Conference.
11. C. D. Keeling and T. P. Whorf, "Atmospheric CO2 concentrations (ppmv) derived from in situ air samples collected at Mauna Loa Observatory, Hawaii," <http://cdiac.esd.ornl.gov/ftp/ndp001r7/ndp001r7.dat> (22 April 1998).
12. P. D. Jones, D. E. Parker, T. J. Osborn, and K. R. Briffa, "Global and hemispheric temperature anomalies—Land and marine instrumental records," in *Trends: A Compendium of Data on Global Change* (Oak Ridge, TN: Carbon Dioxide Information Analysis Center, Oak Ridge National Laboratory, 1998).
13. Goklany, "Strategies to enhance adaptability."
14. I. M. Goklany and M. W. Sprague, *An Alternative Approach to Sustainable Development: Conserving Forests, Habitat and Biological Diversity by Increasing the Efficiency and Productivity of Land Utilization* (Washington, D.C.: Office of Program Analysis, Department of the Interior, 1991); Goklany, "Saving habitat and conserving biodiversity on a crowded planet."
15. I. M. Goklany, "Meeting global food needs: The environmental trade-offs between increasing land conversion and land productivity," *Technology: Journal of the Franklin Institute*, forthcoming.
16. Goklany, "Saving habitat and conserving biodiversity on a crowded planet."
17. Goklany, "Strategies to enhance adaptability."
18. T. T. Poleman and L. T. Thomas, "Report: Income and dietary change," *Food Policy*, 20 (1995): 149–159.
19. World Resources Institute, *World Resources 1996–97* (New York: Oxford Univ. Press, 1996), pp. 244–245.
20. FAO, *Country Tables 1995* (Rome: FAO, 1995); FAO, *Country Food Supply Indicators, 1961–1990*. <http://www.fao.org/WAICENT/FAOINFO/NUTRITIO/Foodindi/findintr.htm> (1 June 1997).
21. FAO, *Country Tables 1995*.
22. FAO, *World Food Summit Fact Sheets* (Rome: FAO, 1996). <http://www.fao.org/wfs/fs/e/FSHm-e.htm> (7 October 1997).
23. FAO, *FAOSTAT database* <http://apps.fao.org/cgi-bin/nph-db.pl> (11 August 1998).
24. FAO, *World Food Summit Fact Sheets*.
25. FAO, *Food Outlook: Global Information and Early Warning System* (June 1998).
26. Goklany and Sprague, *An Alternative Approach to Sustainable Development*; Goklany, "Strategies to enhance adaptability"; Goklany, "Saving habitat and conserving biodiversity on a crowded planet."
27. FAO, *The State of the World's Forests 1997* (Rome: FAO, 1997); FAO, *FAOSTAT database* (11 August 1998).
28. FAO, *The State of the World's Forests*; Goklany, "Saving habitat and conserving biodiversity on a crowded planet."
29. T. Panayotou and J. R. Vincent, ". . . Or Distraction," *Science*, 276 (1997): 55–57.
30. These estimates, based upon *FAOSTAT* data, assume that, although population would continue to grow, technologies would be frozen in place in 1980 (i.e., there would be no new—or wider use of existing—technologies after 1980). For a more detailed explanation of the methodology, see Goklany and Sprague,

An Alternative Approach to Sustainable Development; Goklany, "Strategies to enhance adaptability"; Goklany, "Meeting global food needs: The environmental trade-offs."

31. G. Chichilnisky, "North-South trade and the global environment," *American Economic Review,* 84 (1994): 851–874; Environmental Defense Fund (EDF), *Global Deforestation, Timber, and the Struggle for Sustainability: Making the Label Stick* (Washington, D.C.: EDF, 1997); D. M. Kummer and B. L. Turner II, "The human causes of deforestation in Southeast Asia," *BioScience,* 44 (1994): 323–328; FAO, *The State of the World's Forests 1997.*

32. Goklany, "Saving habitat and conserving biodiversity on a crowded planet."

33. FAO, *The State of the World's Forests 1997.*

34. S. B. Hecht, "The logic of livestock and deforestation in Amazonia," *BioScience,* 43 (1993): 687–695; M. Edelman, "Rethinking the hamburger thesis: Deforestation and the crisis of Central American beef exports," in M. Painter and W. H. Durham, eds., *The Social Causes of Environmental Destruction in Latin America* (Ann Arbor, MI: University of Michigan, 1995), pp. 25–62; M. Painter, "Introduction," in M. Painter and W. H. Durham, eds., *The Social Causes of Environmental Destruction in Latin America,* pp. 1–21; EDF, *Global Deforestation, Timber, and the Struggle for Sustainability;* FAO, *The State of the World's Forests 1997.*

35. Goklany, "Saving habitat and conserving biodiversity on a crowded planet"; FAO, *The State of the World's Forests 1997.*

36. D. L. Hawksworth et al., "Magnitude and distribution of biodiversity," in V. H. Heywood, ed., *Global Biodiversity Assessment* (New York: Cambridge University Press, 1995), pp. 107–191.

37. Goklany, "Saving habitat and conserving biodiversity on a crowded planet."

38. The data for tornadoes and lightning were obtained from National Oceanic and Atmospheric Administration (NOAA), *1996 Annual Summaries* (Asheville, NC: NOAA/National Climatic Data Center, 1997), and Storm Prediction Center, *1997 Tornado Deaths by State* <http://www.spc.noaa.gov/archive/tornadoes/dead97.gif> (31 July 1998). For hurricanes, the data are from P. J. Hebert, J. D. Jarrell, and M. Mayfield, *The Deadliest, Costliest, and Most Intense United States Hurricanes of This Century (and Other Frequently Requested Hurricane Facts),* NOAA Technical Memorandum NWS TPC-1, (Miami, FL: NOAA/National Weather Service, 1997) and National Hurricane Center (NHC), *The 1997 Atlantic Hurricane Season, Preliminary Reports* <http://www.nhc.noaa.gov/1997text.html> (27 July 1998). Flood data were obtained mainly from Hydrologic Information Center (HIC), *Flood Losses: Compilation of Flood Loss Statistics* <http://www.nws.noaa.gov/oh/hic/flood_stats/Flood_loss_time_series.htm> (27 July 1998). It's worth noting that there are discrepancies between the flood data from NOAA's HIC and its NCDC's *Annual Summaries,* and both have some differences with the data published in the *Statistical Abstract* and the *Historical Statistics.* The decision to use the HIC's data set was made after substantial consultation with the keepers of each of these data sets. Also, the keeper of the HIC's data set expresses greater confidence in the data after the mid-1960s on fatalities and mid-1950s on property losses (J. Dionne, personal communication, 1998). However, in the earlier years, even the HIC data set may be prone to error, possibly undercounting fatalities. In 1911, that data set indicates 0 fatalities, however, *The New York Times* indicates that there were at least 55 fatalities that flood year. Similarly, the latter indicates at least 244 in 1928 and 42 in 1931 compared with 15 and 0, respectively, in the HIC data set. See *The New York Times,* October 7, 1911, p. 1; March 18, 1928, p. 22; November 20, 1930; March 15, 1931,

p. 8; April 2, 1931, p. 12; April 6, 1931, p. 3; September 4, 1931, p. 1. However, the corrected values may themselves be lower bounds.

39. The declines in deaths (D) [and death rates (DR)] can be fitted using models that vary linearly with time (t) for D or log D (or DR or log DR). The following table provides results for some curve fitting exercises:

Type of Event	Years, No. of Observations (obs), Period	Equations Fitting the Data	R^2	p for the Slope
Tornados	1916–1997	DR = 2.484 − 0.0341t	0.367	<0.001
	82 annual	Log DR = 0.395 − 0.0154t	0.563	<0.001
	obs.	D = 289.3 − 3.401t	0.269	<0.001
	t = 1 to 82	Log D = 2.395 − 0.0100t	0.354	<0.001
Floods	1903–1997	DR = 0.852 − 0.0219 t	0.094	>0.1
	19 non-overlapping	Log DR = −0.176 − 0.0089t	0.037	>0.1
	5-yr periods,	D = 148.7 − 3.541t	0.630	<0.001
	t = 1 to 19	Log D = 2.180 − 0.0136t	0.613	<0.001
Hurricanes	1900–1997	DR = 5.514 − 0.5141t	0.281	<0.05
	14 non-overlapping	Log DR = 0.640 − 0.1357t	0.702	<0.001
	7-yr periods,	D = 456.2 − 40.07t	0.299	<0.05
	t = 1 to 14	Log D = 2.519 − 0.0960t	0.549	<0.005
Lightning	1959–1996	DR = 0.686 − 0.0137t	0.639	<0.001
	38 annual	Log DR = −0.143 − 0.0140t	0.749	<0.001
	obs.	D = 127.6 − 1.981t	0.507	<0.001
	t = 1 to 38	Log D = 2.110 − 0.0094t	0.576	<0.001

40. C. W. Landsea et al., "Downward trends in the frequency of intense Atlantic hurricanes during the past five decades," *Geophysical Research Letters*, 23 (1996): 1697–1700.
41. T. R. Karl and R. W. Knight, "Secular trends of precipitation amount, frequency, and intensity in the United States," *Bulletin of the American Meteorological Society*, 79 (1998): 231–241.
42. Karl and Knight, "Secular trends of precipitation amount, frequency, and intensity in the United States."
43. Using models linear in t, R^2 for property loss (PL) due to floods and log PL for the period 1903 to 1997 are 0.083 and 0.153, respectively. The R^2 can be improved to 0.283 ($p < 0.02$) and 0.240 ($p < 0.05$), respectively, by dividing the data series into 19 nonoverlapping 5-year periods and using a model linear in t (with t = 1 to 19). See following note.
44. As can be seen from the following table, R^2 for linear curve-fitting models using property losses measured in terms of percent of wealth are poorer than those using real dollars. Wealth was estimated using tangible wealth data for 1925–1996 from the Bureau of Economic Affairs, *15 Tangible Wealth Tables From the*

September 1997 "Survey of Current Business" <http://www.fedstats.gov/index20.html> July 12, 1998, and does not include land values. The value for 1997 was based on a straight-line extrapolation over the previous three years.

Property Loss (in terms of)	Period (no. of observations)	Curve-Fitting Equations	R^2	p for the Slope
Billions of real (1997) $	1903–1997, nineteen 5-yr periods	LR = 1.183 + 0.1732t Log LR = 0.1207 + 0.0257t	0.283 0.240	<0.02 <0.05
Billions of real (1997) $	1926–1997, eight 9-yr periods	LR = 17.11 + 2.900t Log LR = 0.3055 + 0.0423t	0.373 0.358	>0.1 >0.1
Percent of wealth	1926–1997, eight 9-yr periods	LR = 0.2829 − 0.0135t Log LR = −1.525 − 0.0252t	0.136 0.140	>0.3 >0.3

45. Results of the curve-fitting analyses for property losses due to hurricanes are given in the following table:

Property Loss (in terms of)	Period (no. of observations)	Curve-Fitting Equations	R^2	p for the Slope
Billions of real (1997) $	1903–1997, fourteen 7-yr periods	LR = −825.0 + 283.37t Log LR = 1.916 + 0.1223t	0.604 0.826	<0.001 <0.001
Billions of real (1997) $	1926–1997, eight 9-yr periods	LR = −623.9 + 518.39t Log LR = 2.428 + 0.1415t	0.553 0.715	<0.05 <0.01
Percent of wealth	1926–1997, eight 9-yr periods	LR = 0.0087 − 0.0011t Log LR = −2.0389 + 0.0277t	0.152 0.082	>0.3 >0.3

46. A. J. McMichael et al., "Human population health," in Watson, et al., eds., *Climate Change 1995: Impacts, Adaptations and Mitigation of Climate Change*, pp. 561–584; A. J. McMichael, et al., eds., *Climate Change and Human Health* (Geneva: WHO, 1996).
47. P. Reiter, "Global warming and mosquito-borne disease in USA," *Lancet*, 348 (1996): 622; G. Taubes, "Global warming: Apocalypse not," *Science*, 278 (1997): 1004–1006; J. H. Bryan, D. H. Foley, and R. W. Sutherst, "Malaria transmission and climate change in Australia," *Medical Journal of Australia*, 164 (1996): 345–347.
48. I. M. Goklany, "Factors affecting environmental impacts: The effects of technology on long term trends in cropland, air pollution and water related diseases," *Ambio*, 25 (1996): 497–503.
49. H. M. Rosenberg et al., "Births and deaths: United States, 1995," *Monthly vital statistics report*, 45 (no. 3, supp. 2) (Hyattsville, MD: National Center for Health Statistics, 1996), p. 31.
50. WRI, *World Resources 1996–97*.
51. World Health Organization (WHO), *World Health Report 1997* (Geneva: WHO, 1997).

52. R. E. Besser, et al., "Prevention of cholera transmission: Rapid evaluation of the quality of municipal water in Trujillo, Peru," *Bol Oficina Sanit Panam*, 119, no. 3 (1995): 189–194; G. Taubes, "Global warming: Apocalypse not," *Science*, 278 (1997): 1004–1006; F. P. Pinheiro and R. Chuit, "Emergence of dengue hemorrhagic fever in the Americas," *Infections in Medicine*, 15, no. 4 (1998): 244–251; D. R. Roberts et al., "DDT, global strategies, and a malaria control crisis in South America," *Emerging Infectious Diseases*, 3 (1997): 295–301.

53. R. S. Nerem, "Global mean sea level change: Correction," *Science*, 275 (No. 5303, 21 February 1997): 1049–1053; R. A. Warrick et al., "Changes in sea level," in J. T. Houghton et al., eds., *Climate Change 1995: The Science of Climate Change* (Cambridge University Press, 1996), pp. 359–405.

54. R. A. Warrick et al., "Changes in sea level," pp. 365–366.

55. J. A. McNeely et al., "Human influences in biodiversity," in V. H. Heywood, ed., *Global Biodiversity Assessment*, 755–757.

56. See, Goklany, "Eliminate the last straw or reduce the heavier load," in preparation.

57. The substantial uncertainties in every link of the chain connecting economic activities to the impacts of climate change are outlined in the body of the IPCC's 1990 and 1995 Impact Assessments. The uncertainties are hinted at in: "Policymakers' summary," in IPCC, *Climate Change: The IPCC Impacts Assessment* (Canberra: Australian Government Publishing Services, 1991), p. 1; "Policymakers' summary," in Watson et al., eds., *The IPCC's 1995 Impact Assessment*, p. 4.

58. K. M. Frederick, I. M. Goklany, and N. J. Rosenberg, "Conclusions, remaining issues, and next steps," *Climatic Change*, 28 (1994): 209–219; I. M. Goklany, *Adaptation and Climate Change*, AAAS Annual Meeting, Chicago, February 6–12 (1992).

59. Frederick, Goklany, and Rosenberg, "Conclusions, remaining issues, and next steps"; Goklany, *Adaptation and Climate Change*; Goklany, "Factors affecting environmental impacts," P. Rogers, "Assessing the socioeconomic consequences of climate change on water resources," *Climatic Change*, 28 (1994): 179–208; R. Cantor and G. Yohe, "Economic analysis," in S. Rayner and E. L. Malone, eds., *Human Choices & Climate Change, vol. 3: Tools for Policy Analysis* (Columbus, OH: Battelle Press, 1998), pp. 1–103.

60. Frederick, Goklany, and Rosenberg, "Conclusions, remaining issues, and next steps"; Goklany, *Adaptation and Climate Change*; Goklany, "Factors affecting environmental impacts," Rogers, "Assessing the socioeconomic consequences of climate change on water resources."

61. J. Reilly et al., "Agriculture in a changing climate: Impacts and adaptations," in Watson et al., eds., *Climate Change 1995: Impacts, Adaptations and Mitigation of Climate Change*, pp. 451–454.

62. C. Rosenzweig and M. L. Parry, "Potential impacts of climate change on world food supply," *Nature*, 367 (1994), 133–138.

63. United Nations (UN), "World population prospects: The 1996 revision," *POPULATION Newsletter*, no. 62 (December 1996). <http://www.undp.org/popin//popdiv/news62/content.htm> (22 April 1998).

64. Goklany, *Adaptation and Climate Change*; Goklany, "Saving habitat and conserving biodiversity on a crowded planet."

65. Ibid.

66. A. F. Solomon et al., "Wood production under changing climate and land use," in Watson et al., eds., *Climate Change 1995: Impacts, Adaptations and Mitigation of Climate Change*, pp. 492–496.

67. M. U. F. Kirschbaum et al., "Climate change impacts on forests," in Watson et al., eds., *Climate Change 1995: Impacts, Adaptations and Mitigation of Climate Change*, pp. 95–129; A. F. Solomon et al., "Wood production under changing climate and land use."
68. Kirschbaum et al., "Climate change impacts on forests," p. 115.
69. Kirschbaum et al., "Climate change impacts on forests," pp. 99–122; Solomon et al., "Wood production under changing climate and land use," pp. 492–496.
70. Goklany, "Saving habitat and conserving biodiversity on a crowded planet."
71. A. W. King, W. M. Post and S. D. Wullschleger, "The potential response of terrestrial carbon storage to changes in climate and atmospheric CO_2," *Climatic Change*, 35 (1997): 199–227.
72. Myneni et al., "Increased plant growth in the Northern high latitudes."
73. Goklany, "Saving habitat and conserving biodiversity on a crowded planet."
74. Warrick et al., "Changes in sea level," pp. 384–385.
75. D. W. Pearce et al., "The social costs of climate change: Greenhouse damage and the benefits of control," in J. P. Bruce et al., eds., *Climate Change 1995: Economic and Social Dimensions of Climate Change* (New York: Cambridge University Press, 1996), p. 191.
76. WRI, *World Resources 1996–97*, p. 223.
77. A. J. McMichael et al., "Human population health," in Watson et al., eds., *Climate Change 1995: Impacts, Adaptations and Mitigation of Climate Change* (New York: Cambridge University Press, 1996), pp. 561–584.
78. Reiter, "Global warming and mosquito-borne disease in USA"; Taubes, "Global warming: Apocalypse not."
79. WHO, *World Health Report 1997*.
80. Reiter, "Global warming and mosquito-borne disease in USA"; G. Taubes, "Global warming: Apocalypse not."
81. J. G. Titus and V. Narayanan, "The risk of sea level rise," *Climatic Change*, 31 (1996): 151–212; D. Schimmelpfennig et al., *Agricultural Adaptation to Climate Change: Issues of Longrun Sustainability* (Washington, D.C.: Economic Research Service, U.S. Department of Agriculture, 1996); C. Loehle and D. LeBlanc, "Model based assessments of climate change effects on forests: A critical review," *Ecological Modelling*, 90 (1996): 1–31; Cantor and Yohe, "Economic analysis in human choices & climate change."
82. Myneni et al., "Increased plant growth in the Northern high latitudes."
83. M. Cao and F. I. Woodward, "Dynamic responses of terrestrial ecosystem carbon cycling to global climate change," *Nature*, 393 (1998): 249–252; King, Post, and Wullschleger, "The potential response of terrestrial carbon storage to changes in climate and atmospheric CO_2."
84. Goklany, "Saving habitat and conserving biodiversity on a crowded planet."
85. E. J. Dlugokencky et al., "Continuing decline in the growth rate of the atmospheric methane burden," *Nature*, 393 (1998): 447–450.
86. Goklany, "Eliminate the last straw or reduce the heavier load."
87. IPCC, "Chapter 6: Resource use and management," in *Climate Change: The IPCC Response Strategies* (Washington, D.C.: Island Press, 1991); Goklany, *Adaptation and Climate Change*; Goklany, "Strategies to enhance adaptability."
88. D. Schimel et al., "Radiative forcing of climate change," in J. T. Houghton et al., eds., *Climate Change 1995: The Science of Climate Change*, pp. 83–85.

89. Curiously, in a paper titled, "Influence of socioeconomic inertia and uncertainty on optimal (sic) CO2-emission abatement," Ha-Doung et al. are totally silent on adaptation and on the avoided costs (or benefits) associated with alternative paths to stabilize atmospheric CO_2 concentrations at the same eventual level. In it the only optimization is with respect to the costs of alternative paths for emissions and concentrations. See M. Ha-Duong, M. J. Grubb and J.-C. Hourcade, "Influence of socioeconomic inertia and uncertainty on optimal (sic) CO2-emission abatement," *Nature*, 390 (1997): 270–273.
90. Goklany, *Adaptation and Climate Change*; Goklany, "Strategies to enhance adaptability."
91. FAO, *World Food Summit Fact Sheets*.
92. Goklany, "Saving habitat and conserving biodiversity on a crowded planet."
93. World Bank, *Global Development Finance 1997*. <http://www.worldbank.org/images/extpb/gdf97eng/table4.gif> (3 September 1997).
94. WHO, *International Community to Step Up Coordination of Malaria Control*, Press Release WHO/82 (17 November 1997).
95. FAO, *FAOSTAT database* (11 August 1998).
96. T. M. L. Wigley, "Implications of recent CO2 emission-limitation proposals for stabilization of atmospheric concentrations," *Nature*, 390 (1997): 267–270.
97. Ha-Duong, Grubb, and Hourcade, "Influence of socioeconomic inertia and uncertainty on optimal (sic) CO2-emission abatement."
98. Goklany and Sprague, *An Alternative Approach to Sustainable Development*; Goklany, *Adaptation and Climate Change*; Goklany, "Strategies to enhance adaptability."
99. N. Myers, "Consumption: Challenge to sustainable development . . . ," *Science*, 276 (1997): 53–55.
100. Goklany, "Saving habitat and conserving biodiversity on a crowded planet."
101. Ibid.; Goklany and Sprague, *An Alternative Approach to Sustainable Development*; Goklany, *Adaptation and Climate Change*; Goklany, "Strategies to enhance adaptability"; Goklany, "Meeting global food needs: The environmental trade-offs."
102. Goklany, "Meeting global food needs: The environmental trade-offs."
103. Goklany, "Saving habitat and conserving biodiversity on a crowded planet."
104. FAO, *FAOSTAT database* (11 August 1998).
105. Goklany, "Meeting global food needs: The environmental trade-offs"; Goklany, "Saving habitat and conserving biodiversity on a crowded planet."
106. Ibid.
107. Goklany, *Adaptation and Climate Change*; Goklany, "Saving habitat and conserving biodiversity on a crowded planet."
108. E. Masood, "Kyoto agreement creates new agenda for climate research," *Nature*, 390 (1997): 649–650.
109. Goklany, "Eliminate the last straw or reduce the heavier load."
110. Ibid.
111. R. W. Kates, "Climate change 1995: Impacts, adaptations, and mitigation," *Environment*, 39 (1997): 29–33.
112. "Malaria: Avoidable catastrophe?" *Nature*, 386 (10 April 1997), briefing, available at <*http://www.nature.com*>.
113. Goklany, "Eliminate the last straw or reduce the heavier load."
114. Ibid.

Chapter 8

1. K. Verdeal and D. S. Ryan, "Naturally-occurring estrogens in plant foodstuffs—A review," *J. Food Prot.*, 42 (1979): 577–583.
2. R. F. Kauffman, and H. U. Bryant, "Selective estrogen receptor modulators," *Drug News Perspect.*, 8 (1995): 531–539.
3. Great Lakes Water Quality Board, Great Lakes Water Quality Board Report to the International Joint Commission, 1987 Report on Great Lakes Water Quality, (Windsor, ON: International Joint Commission, 1987).
4. T. Colborn, F. S. Vom Saal, and A. M. Soto, "Developmental effects of endocrine-disrupting chemicals in wildlife and humans," *Environ. Health Perspect.*, 101 (1993): 378–384.
5. K. B. Thomas, and T. Colborn, "Organochlorine endocrine disruptors in human tissue," in *Chemically Induced Alterations in Sexual Development: The Wildlife/Human Connection*, T. Colborn and C. Clement, eds. (Princeton, NJ: Princeton Scientific Publishing, 1992), pp. 365–394.
6. R. Newbold, "Cellular and molecular effects of developmental exposure to diethylstilbestrol: implications for other environmental estrogens," *Environ. Health Perspect.*, 103 (1995): 83–87.
7. J. P. Giesy, J. P. Ludwig, and D. E. Tillitt, "Deformities of birds in the Great Lakes region: Assigning causality," *Environ. Sci. Technol.*, 28 (1994): 128A–135A
8. C. E. Lundholm, "Comparison of p,p'-DDE and o,p'-DDE on eggshell thickness and Ca binding activity of shell gland in ducks," *Acta Pharmacol. Toxicol.*, 47 (1980): 377–384.
9. W. R. Kelce, C. R. Stone, S. C. Laws, and L. E. Gray, "Persistent DDT metabolite p,p'-DDE is a potent androgen receptor antagonist," *Nature*, 375 (1995): 581–586.
10. L. J. Guillette, Jr., T. S. Gross, G. R. Masson, J. M. Matter, H. F. Percival, and A. R. Woodward, "Developmental abnormalities of the gonad and abnormal sex hormone concentrations in juvenile alligators from contaminated and control lakes in Florida," *Environ. Health Perspect.*, 102 (1994): 680–688.
11. N. W. Tremblay, and A. P. Gilman, "Human health, the Great Lakes, and environmental pollution: A 1994 perspective," *Environ. Health Perspect.*, 103 (1995): 3–5.
12. J. K. Sumpter, *Xenoendocrine Disrupters—Environmental Impacts* (Paris: International Congress of Toxicology, 1998).
13. E. Carlsen, A. Giwercman, N. Keiding, and N. E. Skakkebaek, "Evidence for the decreasing quality of semen during the past 50 years," *Br. Med. J.*, 305 (1992): 609–612.
14. R. M. Sharpe, and N. F. Skakkebaek, "Are oestrogens involved in falling sperm counts and disorders of the male reproductive tract," *Lancet*, 341 (1993): 1392–1395.
15. R. M. Sharpe, "Reproductive biology. Another DDT connection," *Nature*, 375 (1995): 538–539.
16. G. W. Olsen, K. M. Bodner, J. M. Ramlow, C. E. Ross, and L. I. Lipshultz, "Have sperm counts been reduced 50 percent in 50 years? A statistical model revisited," *Fertil. Steril.*, 63 (1995): 887–893.
17. A. Lerchl, and E. Nieschlag, "Decreasing sperm counts? A critical (re)view," *Exp. Clin. Endocrinol. Diabetes*, 104 (1996): 301–307.
18. S. H. Swan, E. P. Elkin, and L. Fenster, "Have sperm densities declined? A reanalysis of global trend data," *Environ. Health Perspect.*, 105 (1998): 1228–1232.

19. P. Bromwich, J. Cohen, I. Stewart, and A. Walker, "Decline in sperm counts: An artefact of changed reference range of normal," *Br. Med. J.*, 309 (1994): 19–22.
20. S. Becker, and K. Berhane, "A meta-analysis of 61 sperm count studies revisited," *Fertil. Steril.*, 67 (1997): 1103–1108.
21. J. Ginsburg, S. Okolo, G. Prelevic, and P. Hardiman, "Residence in the London area and sperm density," *Lancet*, 343 (1994): 230–230.
22. J. Auger, J. M. Kuntsmann, F. Czyglik, and P. Jouannet, "Decline in semen quality among fertile men in Paris during the past 20 years," *N. Engl. J. Med.*, 332 (1985): 281–285.
23. D. A. Adamopoulos, A. Pappa, S. Nicopoulou, E. Andreou, M. Karamertzanis, J. Michopoulos, V. Deligianni, and M. Simou, "Seminal volume and total sperm number trends in men attending subfertility clinics in the greater Athens area during the period 1977–1993," *Hum. Reprod.*, 11 (1996): 1936–1941.
24. S. Irvine, E. Cawood, D. Richardson, E. MacDonald, and J. Aitken, "Evidence of deteriorating semen quality in the United Kingdom: Birth cohort study in 577 men in Scotland over 11 years," *Br. Med. J.*, 312 (1996): 467–471.
25. F. Menchini-Fabris, P. Rossi, P. Palego, S. Simi, and P. Turchi, "Declining sperm counts in Italy during the past 20 years," *Andrologia*, 28 (1996): 304–304.
26. K. Van Waeleghem, N. De Clercq, L. Vermeulen, F. Schoonjans, and F. Comhaire, "Deterioration of sperm quality in young healthy Belgian men." *Hum. Reprod.*, 11 (1996): 325–329.
27. L. Bujan, A. Mansat, F. Pontonnier, and R. Mieusset, "Time series analysis of sperm concentration in fertile men in Toulouse, France between 1977 and 1992," *Br. Med. J.*, 312 (1996): 471–472.
28. C. A. Paulsen, N. G. Berman, and C. Wang, "Data from men in greater Seattle area reveals no downward trend in semen quality: Further evidence that deterioration of semen quality is not geographically uniform," *Fertil. Steril.*, 65 (1996): 1015–1020.
29. H. Fisch, E. T. Goluboff, J. H. Olson, J. Feldshuh, S. J. Broder, and D. H. Barad, "Semen analyses in 1,283 men from the United States over a 25-year period: No decline in quality," *Fertil. Steril.*, 65 (1996): 1009–1014.
30. P. E. Rasmussen, K. Erb, and L. G. Westergaard, "No evidence for decreasing semen quality in four birth cohorts of 1,055 Danish men born between 1950 and 1970," *Fertil. Steril.*, 68 (1997): 1059–1069.
31. D. J. Handelsman, "Sperm output of healthy men in Australia: Magnitude of bias due to self-selected volunteers," *Human Reprod.*, 12 (1997): 101–105.
32. J. Auger, and P. Jouannet, "Evidence for regional differences of semen quality among fertile French men," *Hum. Reprod.*, 12 (1997): 740–745.
33. Y. Zheng, J. P. E. Bonde, E. Ernst, J. T. Mortensen, and J. Egense, "Is semen quality related to the year of birth among Danish infertility clients," *Int. J. Epidemiol.*, 26 (1997): 1289–1297.
34. H. Fisch, and E. T. Goluboff, "Geographic variations in sperm counts: A potential cause of bias in studies of semen quality," *Fertil. Steril.*, 65 (1996): 1044–1046.
35. E. V. Younglai, J. A. Collins, and W. G. Foster, "Canadian semen quality: An analysis of sperm density among eleven academic fertility centers," *Fertil. Steril.*, 70 (1998): 76–80.
36. A. Ekbom, A. Wicklund-Glynn, and H. O. Adami, "DDT and testicular cancer," *Nature*, 347 (1996): 553–554.

37. P. Cocco, and J. Benichou, "Mortality from cancer of the male reproductive tract and environmental exposure to the anti-androgen p,p'-dichlorodiphenyldichloroethylene in the United States," *Oncology*, 55 (1998): 334–339.
38. Ernest Knobil et al., *Hormonally Active Agents in the Environment*, National Research Council, National Academy Press, prepublication copy, August 1999, pp. 131–137, 251–256.
39. B. P. Setchell, "Sperm counts in semen of farm animals 1932–1995," *Int. J. Androl.*, 20 (1997): 209–214.
40. J. L. van Os, M. J. de Vries, N. H. den Daas, and L. M. Kaal Lansbergen, "Long-term trends in sperm counts of dairy bulls," *J. Androl.*, 18 (1997): 725–731.
41. B. S. Hulka, E. T. Liu, and R. A. Lininger, "Steroid hormones and risk of breast cancer," *Cancer*, 74 (1994): 1111–1124.
42. M. S. Wolff, P. G. Toniolo, E. W. Leel, M. Rivera, and N. Dubin, "Blood levels of organochlorine residues and risk of breast cancer," *J. Natl. Cancer Inst.*, 85 (1993): 648–652.
43. F. Falck, A. Ricci, M. S. Wolff, J. Godbold, and P. Deckers, "Pesticides and polychlorinated biphenyl residues in human breast lipids and their relation to breast cancer," *Arch. Environ. Health*, 47 (1992): 143–146.
44. D. L. Davis, H. L. Bradlow, M. Wolff, T. Woodruff, D. G. Hoel, and H. Anton-Culver, "Medical hypothesis: Xenoestrogens as preventable causes of breast cancer," *Environ. Health Perspect.*, 101 (1993): 372–377.
45. S. Safe, "Environmental and dietary estrogens and human health—Is there a problem?" *Environ. Health Perspect.*, 103 (1995): 346–351.
46. K. Gaido, L. Dohme, F. Wang, I. Chen, B. Blankvoort, K. Ramamoorthy, and S. Safe, "Comparative estrogenic activity of organochlorine pesticide resides in food and wine extracts," *Environ. Health Persp.* [1998 (in press)].
47. S. Safe, "Interactions between hormone and chemicals in breast cancer," *Annu. Rev. Pharmacol. Toxicol.*, 38 (1998): 121–158.
48. Ernest Knobil, *Hormonally Active Agents in the Environment*, National Research Council, National Academy Press, prepublication copy, August 1999, pp. 231–251, 257.
49. B. A. Mayes, E. E. McConnell, B. H. Neal, M. J. Brunner, S. B. Hamilton, T. M. Sullivan, A. C. Peters, M. J. Ryan, J. D. Toft, A. W. Singer, J. F. Brown, Jr., R. G. Menton, and J. A. Moore, "Comparative carcinogenicity in Sprague-Dawley rats of the polychlorinated biphenyl mixtures Aroclors 1016, 1242, 1254, and 1260," *Toxicol. Sci.*, 41 (1998): 62–76.
50. D. J. Hunter, S. E. Hankinson, F. Laden, G. Colditz, J. E. Munson, W. C. Willett, F. E. Speizer, and M. S. Wolff, "Plasma organochlorine levels and the risk of breast cancer," *New Engl. J. Med.*, 337 (1997): 1253–1258.
51. N. Krieger, M. S. Wolff, R. A. Hiatt, M. Rivera, J. Vogelman, and N. Orentreich, "Breast cancer and serum organochlorines: A prospective study among white, black, and Asian women," *J. Natl. Cancer Inst.*, 86 (1994): 589–599.
52. P. Van't Veer, I. R. Lobbezoo, J. M. Martin-Moreno, F. Guallar, J. Gomez-Aracena, A. F. M. Kardinaal, L. Kohlmeier, B. C. Martin, J. J. Strain, M. Thumm, P. Van Zoonen, B. A. Baumann, J. K. Huttunen, and F. J. Kok, "DDT (dicophane) and postmenopausal breast cancer in Europe: Case control study," *Br. J. Med.*, 315 (1997): 81–85.

53. L. López-Carrillo, A. Blair, M. López-Cervantes, M. Cebrián, C. Rueda, R. Reyes, A. Mohar, and J. Bravo, "Dichlorodiphenyltrichloroethane serum levels and breast cancer risk: A case-control study from Mexico," *Cancer Res.*, 57 (1997): 3728–3732.

Chapter 9

1. V. Grant, *The Origin of Adaptations* (New York: Columbia University Press, 1973).
2. T. R. E. Southwood, "The components of diversity," in *Diversity of Insect Faunas*, pp. 19–40, L. A. Mound and N. Waloff, eds. (Oxford: Blackwell, 1978).
3. N. E. Stork, "Insect diversity: Facts, fiction and speculation," *Biol. J. Linn. Soc.*, 35 (1988): 321–337.
4. Robert M. May, "Past efforts and future prospects towards understanding how many species there are," in *Biodiversity and Global Change*, Monograph No. 8 (Paris: International Union of Biological Sciences, 1992), pp. 71–81.
5. S. P. Parker (Ed.), *Synopsis and Classification of Living Organisms*, (New York: McGraw-Hill, 1982).
6. E. O. Wilson, "The current state of biological diversity," in *Biodiversity*, E. O. Wilson, ed. (Washington D.C.: National Academy Press, 1988), p. 521.
7. Robert M. May, "Conceptual aspects of the quantification of the extent of biological diversity," in *Biodiversity Measurement and Estimation*, The Royal Society. (London: Chapman & Hall, 1995), pp. 13–20.
8. T. L. Erwin, "Beetles and other insects of tropical canopies at Manaus, Brazil sampled by insecticidal fogging," in *Tropical Rain Forest: Ecology and Management*, S. L. Sutton, ed. (Oxford: Blackwell, 1983), pp. 59–75.
9. D. L. Hawksworth, "Biodiversity in microorganisms and its role in ecosystem function," in *Biodiversity and Global Change*, Monograph No. 8 (Paris: International Union of Biological Sciences, 1992), pp. 83–93.
10. P. R. Ehrlich and A. Ehrlich, *Extinction: The Causes and Consequences of the Disappearance of Species*. (New York: Random House, 1981).
11. John Tuxill and Chris Bright, "Losing Strands in the Web of Life." in *The State of the World 1998* (A Worldwatch Institute Report), Lester R. Brown, Christopher Flavin, and Hilary French, eds. (New York: W. W. Norton & Co., 1998).
12. Jessica Hellman et al. *Ecofables/Ecoscience* (Stanford, CA: Stanford University, Center for Conservation Biology, 1998).
13. Jeffrey A. McNeely, "The biodiversity crisis: challenges for research and management," in *Conservation of Biodiversity and Sustainable Development*. (Oslo: Scandinavian University Press, 1992), pp. 15–26.
14. M. H. Williamson, *Island Populations* (Oxford: Oxford University Press, 1981).
15. Robert J. Berry, "The role of ecological genetics in biological conservation," in *Conservation of Biodiversity and Sustainable Development* (Oslo: Scandinavian University Press, 1992), pp. 88–104.
16. Stephen R. Edwards, "Conserving biodiversity: Resources for our future," in *The True State of the Planet* (New York: The Free Press, 1995), pp. 211–265.
17. Michael A. Huston, *Biological Diversity: The Coexistence of Species on Changing landscapes* (Cambridge: Cambridge University Press, 1994).
18. Vladimir Sokolov, "The role of mammal biodiversity in the function of ecosystems," in *Biodiversity and Global Change*, Monograph No. 8 (Paris: International Union of Biological Sciences, 1992), pp. 131–138.

19. Michael E. Soulé and L. Scott Mills, "Conservation genetics and conservation biology: A troubled marriage," in *Conservation of Biodiversity and Sustainable Development* (Oslo: Scandinavian University Press, 1992), pp. 55–69.
20. Hiroshi Hori, "Evolutionary outline of living organisms as deduced from 5S ribosomal RNA sequences," in *Biodiversity and Global Change*, Monograph No. 8 (Paris: International Union of Biological Sciences, 1992), pp. 94–104.
21. D. L. Hawksworth (Ed.), *Biodiversity Measurement and Estimation*, The Royal Society (London: Chapman & Hall, 1995).
22. CBD, *Report of the Workshop on the Ecosystem Approach*, Document UNEP/CBD/COP/4/Inf.9 (March 1998).
23. R. H. MacArthur and E. O. Wilson, *The Theory of Island Biogeography* (Princeton: Princeton University Press, 1967).
24. Dean L. Urban, Andrew J. Hansen, David O. Wallin, and Patrick N. Nalpin, "Life-history attributes and biodiversity: Scaling implications for global change," in *Biodiversity and Global Change*, Monograph No. 8 (Paris: International Union of Biological Sciences, 1992), pp. 172–195.
25. C. S. Holling and Gary K. Meffe, "Command and control and the pathology of natural resource management," *Conservation Biology*, 10, no. 2 (1996): 328–337.
26. Anil Agarwal, "Sociological and political constraints to biodiversity conservation: A case study from India," in *Conservation of Biodiversity and Sustainable Development* (Oslo: Scandinavian University Press, 1992), pp. 293–302.
27. P. M. Hammond, "Practical approaches to the estimation of the extent of biodiversity in speciose groups," in *Biodiversity Measurement and Estimation*, The Royal Society (London: Chapman & Hall, 1995), pp. 119–136.
28. David L. Pearson, "Selecting indicator taxa for the quantitative assessment of biodiversity," in *Biodiversity Measurement and Estimation*, The Royal Society (London: Chapman & Hall, 1995), pp. 75–79.
29. Daniel P. Faith, "Phylogenetic pattern and the quantification of organismal biological diversity," in *Biodiversity Measurement and Estimation*, The Royal Society (London: Chapman & Hall, 1995), pp. 45–58.
30. Hans Alders, "Towards biodiversity in politics," in *Biodiversity and Global Change*, Monograph No. 8 (Paris: International Union of Biological Sciences, 1992), pp. 9–12.
31. Odd Terje Sandlund, Kjetil Hindar, and Anthony H. D. Brown (Eds.), "Introduction," in *Conservation of Biodiversity and Sustainable Development* (Oslo: Scandinavian University Press, 1992).
32. Brian H. Walker, "Biological diversity and ecological redundancy." *Conservation Biology*, 6 (1992): 18–23.
33. O. H. Frankel, "Genetic conservation: 'Our evolutionary responsibility.' " *Genetics*, 78 (1974): 53–65.
34. Thomas van der Hammen, "Global change, shifting ranges and biodiversity in plant ecosystems." in *Biodiversity and Global Change*, Monograph No. 8 (Paris: International Union of Biological Sciences, 1992), pp. 159–166.
35. Nils Chr. Stenseth, "Models for predicting ecological change," in *Conservation of Biodiversity and Sustainable Development* (Oslo: Scandinavian University Press, 1992), pp. 137–154.
36. SASUSG, "Sustainability of state conservation areas," in: *Report of the Fourth Meeting of the SASUSG Steering Committee*, Kruger National Park, January 1998. (Harare, Zimbabwe: Southern Africa Sustainable Use Specialist Group, 1998).

37. Ian A. W. Macdonald, "Global change and alien invasions: implications for biodiversity and protected area management," in *Biodiversity and Global Change*, Monograph No. 8 (Paris: International Union of Biological Sciences, 1992), pp. 197–207.
38. IUCN, "Protected areas and the convention on biological diversity, Information Paper prepared by the World Commission on Protected Areas, in *IUCN Background Briefs and Recommendations to the 4th Meeting of the Conference of the Parties to the CBD*, May 1998.
39. Environmental Resources Management, "Study on how to improve the effectiveness of CITES," Final Consultants' Report to the Standing Committee of CITES, September 1996.
40. Georgina M. Mace and Russell Lande, "Assessing extinction threats: Towards a reevaluation of IUCN threatened species categories," *Conservation Biology*, 5 (1991): 148–155.
41. Ricardo Simoncini, "Current changes in agricultural use of natural resources in European countries: A regional overview," Workshop: *Influence of Tenure and Access Rights on Sustainability of Natural Resource Use*, 10th Session of the Global Biodiversity Forum, Bratislava, May 1998.
42. Rowan B. Martin, *Should Wildlife Pay Its Way?* (Keith Roby Memorial Address, Murdoch University, Perth, Western Australia, 8 December 1993. Reprinted by Department of National Parks and Wild Life Management, Zimbabwe).
43. Ivan Bond, *The Economics of Wildlife and Land-Use in Zimbabwe: An Examination of Current Knowledge and Issues* (Project paper no. 35, 1993, WWF Multispecies Production Systems Project, Harare, Zimbabwe).
44. Graham F. T. Child, *Wildlife and People: The Zimbabwean Success.* (Harare, Zimbabwe, and New York: WISDOM Foundation, 1995).
45. V. J. Clarke, D. H. M. Cumming, R. B. Martin, and D. A. Peddie, *The Comparative Economics of African Wildlife and Extensive Cattle Production* (Paper presented at the 8th Session of the Working Party on Wildlife Management and National Parks of the FAO African Forestry Commission, Mali, January 1986).
46. D. H. M. Cumming, *Research and Development for Africa's Wildlife Resources* (Address to the 1984–1985 Annual General Meeting of the Zimbabwe National Conservation Trust of Zimbabwe. *The Conservationist*—Bulletin of the Trust (39/40) July–September 1985, Harare, Zimbabwe).
47. D. H. M. Cumming, *Multispecies Systems: Progress, Prospects and Challenges in Sustaining Rangeland Animal Production and Biodiversity in East and Southern Africa* (Proc. VII World Conference on Animal Production, Edmonton, Alberta, Canada, 28 June–2 July, 1993).
48. R. F. Dassman and A. S. Mossman, "Commercial use of game animals on a Rhodesian ranch." *Wild Life (Nairobi)* 3 (1961): 7–14.
49. R. F. Dassman and A. S. Mossman, "The economic value of Rhodesian game," *Rhodesian Farmer*, 30 (1960): 17–20.
50. D. J. Jansen, I. Bond, and B. A. Child, *Cattle, Wildlife, Both or Neither—Results of a Financial and Economic Survey of Commercial Ranches in Southern Zimbabwe* (Project paper no. 27, 1992, WWF Multispecies Project, Harare, Zimbabwe).
51. Rowan B. Martin, "Indigenous multi-species systems on Southern African rangeland," in *Proc. Regional Workshop Rangeland Potential in the SADCC Region*, Bulawayo, June 1987. (Ministry of Lands, Agriculture and Rural Resettlement, Harare, Zimbabwe, 1989).

52. Rowan B. Martin, *Elephant Outside Protected Areas and Rural Community Involvement* (Paper presented at a Conference, *Elephant Utilisation in the Southern African Region*, Lilongwe, Malawi, 25–27 November 1991).
53. Garrett Hardin, "The Tragedy of the Commons," *Science* (December 13, 1968): 1243–1248.
54. Rowan B. Martin, *The Influence of Governance on Conservation and Wildlife Utilisation*, plenary address at a conference entitled *Conservation Through Sustainable Use of Wildlife*, held at the University of Queensland, Brisbane, Australia, 8–11 February 1994.
55. Fred Smith, "Epilogue: Reappraising humanity's challenges, humanity's opportunities," in *The True State of the Planet* (New York: The Free Press, 1995), pp. 380–392.
56. Vandana Shiva, "The seed and the spinning wheel: Technology development and biodiversity conservation," in *Conservation of Biodiversity and Sustainable Development* (Oslo: Scandinavian University Press, 1992), pp. 280–289.

INDEX

Above-replacement fertility levels, 73–76
Affluence:
    environmental impact of, 18
    as materializer, 46–47
Africa:
    extinctions in, 208–210
    fertility profiles of, 71, 76–78, 79–80, 82
    food security of, 163–164
    land use issues in, 225–226, 229–234
Agarwal, Anil, 223, 232
Agence France Presse, on environmental dangers, 159
Aging population, implications of, 83–84
Agriculture:
    in developing nations, 180–181
    and food security, 160–164
    future productivity of, 182–184
    impact of climate changes on, 174
    impact on deforestation, 16–17
    land use issues and, 229–234
    production tables, 250–265
Air quality trends, 290–310
Akimichi, Tomoya, 100
Alaska, fishing rights in, 101, 103, 105
Alaska Fisherman's Journal, 103
Alexander the Great, 45
Alliance to Save Energy (ASE), 130, 132
Alpha diversity, defined, 217
Altamont Pass, blighted by wind farms, 139
Altitude, effect on biodiversity, 216
Aluminum can, dematerialization and, 54
American Iron and Steel Institute, 50

American Wind Energy Association, 137
Amoco, 136, 137
Anderson, Dick, 138
Anderson, Terry, 107
Anheuser-Busch, 54
Animals, effect of chemicals on, 191–195, 198. *See also* Biodiversity
Anthropogenic climate change. *See* Climate changes; Global warming
Appliances, dematerialization and, 51–52
Aquaculture, 109–112. *See also* Fishing industry
Aquafuture, 112
ARCO, 136
Arctic National Wildlife Refuge, 137
Asia:
    fertility profiles of, 73, 79–80
    and food security, 163
Asnaes electric plant, 61
Australian Wildlife Division of the CSIRO, 224
Ausubel, Jesse, 45–46, 62
Auto manufacturing, environmentally sound trends in, 50
Avian mortality, wind farms and, 138

Bald Eagle Protection Act, 138
Ball, Ben Jr., 125, 154
Ballonoff, Paul, 143
Bangor Daily News, 90
Bechtel, 136
Berry, Robert J., 221
Best Foods, 55
Beta diversity, defined, 217

352 Index

Biodiversity:
  conservation of, 222–234
  defining, 212–216
  deforestation and, 164–166
  ecosystem approach to, 215–216
  endangered species and, 211–212
  extinctions and, 208–211
  genetics and, 213, 222
  global planning and, 223–229
  land use issues and, 229–234
  overview, 204–205, 234–236
  parameters of, 216–217
  species as measure of, 205–208, 213–215
  theories of, 218–222
  types of, 217–218
Biodiversity Policy Coordination Division of IUCN, 225
Biological diversity. See Biodiversity
Biology era, 44–45, 60–61
Biosphere, carbon dioxide in, 26
Birds, effect of chemicals on, 193–195. See also Biodiversity
Birth control. See Family planning
Birth control pills, as endocrine disruptor, 194
Birth rates, linked to economic growth, 9–10
Blue antelope, extinction of, 210
Boundary layer of atmosphere, defined, 30
Bradley, Robert L. Jr., 121
Brazil, as example of deforestation, 16
Breast cancer, effect of chemicals on, 198–201
Bridge fuels, explained, 16
Bright, Chris, 208
British Petroleum, 136
Brookings Institution, 147
Brooks, William, 91–92
Brown, Lester, 6
Bubonic plague, effect on world population, 67
Bureau of the Census. See U.S. Bureau of the Census

California Energy Commission, 137, 138
Canadian Environmental Health Directorate, 193
Cancer:
  breast, 198–201
  statistics, 286–289
Capital-labor ratio, explained, 11
Carbon dioxide:
  agricultural productivity and, 161–162, 184
Carbon dioxide (*Cont.*):
  costs of reducing, 148–153
  global warming and, 25–27, 175–176, 182
  worldwide emissions, 270
Carbon monoxide emissions, 298–301
Caribbean nations, fertility profiles of, 70, 73, 76
Carlsen, Elizabeth, 195, 197
Car manufacturing. See Auto manufacturing
Carrying capacity:
  defined, 5
  of savanna range land, 230
  Stavins on, 44
Catholic societies, and falling fertility levels, 74
CFCs, 272–273
Challenger Scallop Enhancement Company Ltd., 99
Charles River Associates, 150
Chemicals, toxic. See Endocrine disruptors
Chemistry era, 44
China:
  economic growth in, 19–20
  fertility profiles of, 73–74
Chlorofluorocarbons. See CFCs
Christy, Francis, 103
CITES, 227–228
Cladograms, defined, 213
Clam fishing, as example of ITQ program, 104
Clarke, Arthur C., 108
Clean Air Act, 126, 152
Clearing the Air (Goklany), 290
Climate changes:
  future impact of, 177–178, 182–184
  health-related effects of, 169–172, 176–177
  impact on agriculture and food security, 160–164, 174
  impact on developing nations, 180–181
  impact on forests and biodiversity, 164–166, 174–176
  impact on sea level, 172, 176, 177
  "last straw" theory and, 178–180
  man-made versus environmentally caused, 172–174
  overview, 156–160, 185–187
  weather-related effects of, 166–169
  See also Carbon dioxide; Global warming
Climate-sensitive sectors. See Climate changes
Clinton, President, 145–146, 147, 158
Closed-loop manufacturing, 45
Clouds, global warming theory and, 28–29

Club of Rome *Limits to Growth* report, 6
Coal. *See* Fossil fuels
Cod depletion. *See* Fishing industry
Cohen, Linda, 147
Colborn, Theo, 191
Communal property:
   and biodiversity, 231–233
   and fishing rights, 93–94, 99–100
Communications. *See* Telecommunications
Competitive exclusion principle of biodiversity, 219
Computer modeling:
   and carbon emissions, 149–152
   economics-related, 6, 9, 11, 17
   global warming and, 27–29
Computers, effect on generation of paper, 47
Connecticut Agricultural Experiment Station, 17
Conservation:
   of biodiversity, 222–236
   energy-related, 127–129, 139–144
   fishing industry and, 88–89, 106, 112–114
   recycling as, 56–59
   technology and, 44–46
   See also Dematerialization
Construction, environmentally sound trends in, 49–50
Consultative Group on International Agricultural Research, 16
Consumption control:
   explained, 18
   Malthusian theory and, 43
Consumption trends, resource, 46–48
Convention on Biological Diversity (CBD):
   defining biological diversity, 212–213
   ecosystem approach to biodiversity, 215, 224
   on protected areas, 226
   on threats to biodiversity, 228
Convention on the International Trade in Endangered Species. *See* CITES
Cooling processes, global. *See* Global warming
Copper:
   recycling of, 57
   versus silica, 51, 52
Cordell, John, 109
Council of Economic Advisors (CEA), 148, 149

Darwin, Charles, 5
DDE:
   impact on breast cancer, 199–201

DDE (*Cont.*):
   impact on male reproductive capacity, 195
   impact on wildlife, 193
DDT, impact on wildlife, 191–193
Death rates, impact on world population, 66. *See also* Mortality
Deep-layer versus surface temperature controversy, 33–35
Deep Range, The (Clarke), 107–108
Deforestation:
   developing countries and, 16–17
   effect on climate, 164–166
   impact of R&D on, 184
   minimizing effects of, 174–176, 182
Demand-side management (DSM), energy-related, 139–144
Dematerialization:
   and consumption conundrum, 43
   and consumption trends, 46–47
   defined, 42, 46, 60
   examples of trends toward, 48–56
   future of, 62
   industrial ecology and, 60–61
   institution-driven, 59–60
   overview, 42–43
   recycling role in, 56–59
   technology's impact on, 44–46
Democratic governments:
   impact on economic growth of, 18–21
   subreplacement fertility levels and, 68–72
   See also Government control
Demographics. *See* World population
Denmark:
   energy consumption study in, 142
   recycling examples in, 61
Depopulation:
   impact of, 67, 83–84
   predictions regarding, 81–83
   See also Population; World population
DES, impact on offspring, 191–195
Developing nations:
   and biodiversity conservation, 225–234
   impact of climate changes on, 180–181
Diminishing marginal returns. *See* Law of diminishing returns
Dioxins. *See* Endocrine disruptors
Diseases, impact of global warming on, 169–172, 176–177

Diversity, biological. *See* Biodiversity
Domestic animals, effect of chemicals on, 198
DSM. *See* Demand-side management

Earth Day, 5
Earth Summit, 228–229
Eco-imperialism, 223–229
Ecology, industrial. *See* Industrial ecology
Economics:
   environmental, 159, 180–187
   of land use, 229–234
   Malthusian, 1–10, 182
   neoclassical, 10–11
   New Growth, 12–21
Ecosystem approach to biodiversity, 215–216
Ecuador, shrimp depletion in, 111
Edesses, Michael, 60
Education:
   impact on economic growth, 18–21
   linked to fertility rates, 74–76
Edwards, Stephen, 210
Effective Population Size (Ne), defined, 212
Efficiency, defined, 119
Ehrlich, Anne, 5–6, 208
Ehrlich, Paul:
   erroneous prediction of grain shortfall in India, 19
   as neo-Malthusian, 18
   on overpopulation, 5–6
   on species' extinction, 208
EIA. *See* Energy Information Administration
Ekbom, E., 197–198
Electricity. *See* Energy, renewable; Fossil fuels
Electric Power Research Institute, 59
Elemental Research, 108
El Niño, impact on global weather, 35
Endangered species, 211–212
Endocrine disruptors:
   and breast cancer, 198–201
   defined, 191
   and domestic animals, 198
   endocrine system and, 191
   and male reproduction issues, 195–198
   overview, 190, 201–202
   and wildlife, 191–195
End of Affluence, The (Ehrlich), 6
Energy:
   balance of earth's, 26–27
   consumption tables, 278–281

Energy (*Cont.*):
   technological innovation and, 15–16
   See also Energy, renewable; Fossil fuels
Energy, nonrenewable. *See* Fossil fuels
Energy, renewable:
   costs versus benefits of, 135–145
   efficiency of, 119–120
   environmental protection issues of, 145–153
   and fossil fuel myths debunked, 153–154
   versus fossil fuels, 117–131
   government interventionists and, 118–119, 125–127
   government subsidies of, 131–135
   overview, 116–117
   See also Energy; Fossil fuels
Energy Information Administration (EIA), 132, 133, 136, 144, 149, 151
Enron (natural gas company), 136, 137
Entropy, and New Growth Theory of economics, 15
Environmental Defense Fund (EDF), 112
Environmental problems:
   of aquaculture, 110–112
   energy-related, 125–127, 135–153
   and I = PAT equation, 18
   reasons for, 16–17
   See also Climate changes; Global warming; Pollution
Environmental Protection Agency, 55
Environmental transition, defined, 17
Environmental triumphs. *See* Dematerialization
Equilibrium theories of biodiversity, 219–221
Erwin, T. L., 207
Essay on the Principle of Population (Malthus), 3, 4, 8–9
Estrogens. *See* Endocrine disruptors
Europe:
   demographics of, 68–72
   food security and, 163
European Commission, 159
European Union, 149
Evaporation, role in climate system, 29–30
Evolution, biological, 5, 224
Exploratory Fishing Company (ORH 3B) Ltd., 99
Extinctions of species, 208–211
Exxon, 136

Family planning:
    developing countries and, 76
    linked to economic growth, 10
    secular fertility decline and, 66–67
Family structure, impact of subreplacement fertility on, 84
Famine:
    Ehrlich on, 5–6
    land use issues and, 229–234
    Malthus on, 4
    Sen on, 19–20
Famine 1975! (Paddock), 6
Farming. *See* Agriculture
Farming fish. *See* Aquaculture
Feedbacks, climatic, 27–29
Fertility decline, secular, 66–67
Fertility rates:
    above-replacement, 73–76
    declining, 66–67
    high and resistant, 76–78
    linked to economic growth, 10
    linked to education, 74
    linked to income, 74
    for low-income countries, 75, 80
    predicted, 78–81, 244–245
    subreplacement, 68–73
Fiber-optic cable, 51
Fisch, Harry, 196
Fishery cooperative associations (FCAs), 100
Fish Farming International magazine, 108
Fishing industry:
    aquaculture and, 109–112
    Atlantic cod depletion and, 87, 88, 90
    communal rights and, 99–100
    cooperative associations and, 100
    depletion and government control, 89–93
    doomsayers versus cornucopians, 87–88
    environmental pollution from, 110–112
    future of, 106–109
    individual transferable quotas (ITQs) and, 96–99
    overview, 86–87
    oyster depletion and, 91–93, 94–96
    political problems facing, 100–106
    privatization of, 93–106
    property rights and conservation, 88–89, 112–114
    quota management system example, 96–99
    technological advances in, 107–108
    world production, 266–269

Floods:
    and biodiversity, 220
    and global warming, 35–37
    See also Weather
Florida, Richard, 61
Food. *See* Agriculture
Forbes magazine, 109
Forcing, climate-related, 27–30
Forests. *See* Deforestation
Ford Foundation, 152
Forrester, Jay, 6, 9
Fossil fuels:
    domestic crude oil prices, 276–277
    effect of subsidies on production of, 131–134
    environmental issues and, 125–129
    future of, 153–154
    military policy and, 134–135
    overview, 116–117
    reducing carbon emissions from, 148–153
    versus renewable energy sources, 117–131
    reserves of, 121–122
    supply and demand of, 123–125
Framework Convention on Climate Change, 180, 184
Frankel, O. H., 224
Franklin Associates, 55
Franklin, Benjamin, 15, 45
Free markets. *See* Democratic governments
Free troposphere, defined, 30
Frosch, Robert, 61
Fudge factor, computer modeling and, 28–29

Gamma diversity, defined, 217–218
GAO. *See* U.S. General Accounting Office
Garbage. *See* Waste generation; Waste reduction
Gas, natural. *See* Fossil fuels
Gaston's estimate of species' numbers, 207
GDP. *See* Gross domestic product
General Electric, 136
General Motors, 136
Genetics, biodiversity and, 213, 222
Genital abnormalities. *See* Endocrine disruptors
Geography, effect on biodiversity, 221–222
Geology, effect on biodiversity, 217
Geothermal power. *See* Energy, renewable
Gillette, 55
Gilman, Andrew, 193
Global population. *See* World population

Global 2000 report, 173
Global warming:
  conclusions about, 38–39
  deep-layer versus surface temperatures as predictors of, 33–35
  effect of carbon dioxide on, 25–27
  effect of climatic feedbacks on, 27–30
  effect of sun on, 33
  El Niño and, 35
  energy-related, 145–146
  and greenhouse effect, 25–27, 148
  natural variability of weather versus, 35–37
  overview, 24–25
  surface temperatures and, 30–35
  See also Carbon dioxide; Climate changes
Goklany, Indur, 17, 290
Gore, Al, 46
Government control:
  biodiversity conservation and, 223–234
  energy-related, 117–118, 120, 124–135, 145–154
  in fishing industry, 89–93, 100–103
Grand Forks (North Dakota) flood of 1997, 37
"Great Die-Off" (Ehrlich), 5–6
Great Lakes:
  phosphorous loading to, 284–285
  wildlife studies, 193–195
Great Leap Forward, as contributor to Chinese famine, 20
Greenhouse effect:
  and global warming, 25–27, 148
  See also Carbon dioxide; Global warming
Greenhouse gas emissions, 148–153, 178, 179–180, 184, 185–186
Greenpeace, 87, 112
Green Revolution of the 1960s, 19
Grocery stores:
  packaging dematerialization trends in, 52–55
  proliferation of choices in, 47
Gross domestic product:
  and trends toward dematerialization, 48–49
  world, 238–239
Grumman, 136
Guadeloupe Mountains National Park, wind farms in, 139
Gulf War, impact on oil prices, 124, 134–135
Gyproc, 61

Handelsman, D. J., 197
Hardin, Garret, 9, 93
Hausman, Jerry, 130
Hawksworth, D. L., 207
Health issues:
  impact on world population, 65–66, 83
  relationship to global warming, 169–172, 176–177
  See also Cancer; Endocrine disruptors
Hellman, Jessica, 208, 209
Higgs, Robert, 101
High and resistant fertility levels, 76–78
Hill, P. J., 107
Holdren, John, 18
Holling, C. S., 219, 224
Homeostatic hypothesis of fertility patterns, 79
"Homesteading" the oceans, 107
Hormones:
  endocrine system and, 191
  See also Endocrine disruptors
Horses, pollution by, 46
House Appropriations Committee, 148
Human capital, as factor in economic growth, 19
Hurricane Andrew, 36
Hurricanes:
  as cause of mortality and property loss, 166–169, 170
  unpredictability of, 36–37
Hydroelectric power. *See* Energy, renewable
Hunter, D. J., 200
Huston, Michael A., 213–214, 219

I = PAT equation:
  debunked, 20
  as economic theory, 18
Iceland, conservation of marine resources in, 105
Ideas:
  infinite supply of, 21
  as resources, 12–14
Illinois Commerce Commission, 144
Income:
  aging population and, 83
  linked to fertility rates, 74–75
Increasing returns, New Growth Theory and, 13–14
India, economic growth of, 19

Individual fishing quotas (IFQs), 103
Individual transferable quotas (ITQs), 96–99, 101–106
Individuation, effect of wealth on, 46–47
Industrial ecology, 60–61
Industrial waste. *See* Waste generation; Waste reduction
Infectious diseases. *See* Diseases
Infertility. *See* Endocrine disruptors
Infrared radiation, role in earth's temperature, 26–27
Infrastructure construction, environmentally sound trends in, 49–50
Innovation. *See* Knowledge; Technology
Intensity of use, defined, 49
Interface Flooring Systems, 45
Intergovernmental Panel on Climate Change (IPCC):
   biases of, 173–174
   contribution to policy debate, 185–187
   estimate of global warming by year 2100, 30
   malaria predictions, 176, 179
   overestimation of global warming impact, 177–178
   as point of comparison, 159
   on recent global warming, 161
   on sea level changes, 176, 177, 185
Intermittency problem:
   and solar power, 137
   and wind power, 138
International approach to biodiversity conservation, 226–229
International Board for Plant Genetic Resources, 226
International Pacific Halibut Commission, 103
International Union for the Conservation of Nature. *See* IUCN
Internet:
   as example of exponential growth, 12
   shopping, 47
   telephony and, 51
Interstitial species, defined, 213–214
IPCC. *See* Intergovernmental Panel on Climate Change
Island biogeography theory of biodiversity, 221–222
ITQs. *See* Individual transferable quotas

IUCN:
   and ecosystem conservation, 208, 225
   Red List of Threatened Animals, 211
   Sustainable Use Initiative, 210

Japan:
   fishery cooperative associations in, 100
   subreplacement fertility levels and, 73
Johannes, Robert, 100
Johnson, Gale, 14
Johnson, Ron, 106

Kaibab Plateau deer, 51
Kates, Robert, 10, 14
Keen, Elmer, 114
Kelman, Steven, 119
Kern River field oil reserves, 121–122
King, Maurice, 9, 18
Klein, Daniel, 125–126
Knowledge, exponential growth of, 12–13, 21
Koskenoja, Pia Maria, 125–126
Kraft, 55
Kyoto protocol:
   climate treaty meeting of 1997, 25
   greenhouse gas quotas, 148–153, 179
   projected impact on global warming, 185

Labor, capital, and productivity, 10–11
Lande, Russell, 227
Land use, biodiversity and, 224–226, 229–234
La Niña, impact on global weather, 35
"Last straw" theory, 178–180
Latin America:
   deforestation and, 165
   fertility profiles of, 70, 76, 79–80
Latitude, effect on biodiversity, 216
Law of diminishing returns:
   Malthus and, 7–11
   New Growth Theory and, 13–14
Lawrence Berkeley National Laboratory, 142–143
Lead pollution, 309–310
Lee, Dwight, 14
Lee, Thomas, 125, 154
Lifeboat ethics, explained, 9
Life expectancy:
   estimated, 246–247
   impact on world population, 65–66

Life expectancy (*Cont.*):
  increasing, 171
  in twenty-first century, 81
Lightning. *See* Weather
Lightweighting:
  as counterproductive to recycling, 58–59
  defined, 56
Limits to Growth report (Club of Rome):
  on consumption controls, 43
  economic gloom-and-doom projections, 6, 11, 173
  Forrester and, 6, 9
  on pollution, 17
"Little Ice Age," 32–33
Lobster fishermen, harbor gangs of, 104
Longevity. *See* Life expectancy
Lovins, Amory:
  on energy payback horizons, 127–128
  on investing in energy technologies, 143
  on "pocket change" problem, 130
  on profitability of energy efficiency, 146
Low-variant fertility projections, 81–83
Lyme disease, as example of law of diminishing returns, 13–14

MacArthur, R. H., 218, 221
Mace, Georgina M., 227
Major, Philip, 99
Malaria:
  climate changes and, 176, 179–180
  eradicating, 187
Malaysian Land Acquisition Act, 111
Malenbaum, W., 49
Male reproductive problems. *See* Endocrine disruptors
Malthus, Thomas Robert:
  and consumption conundrum, 43
  hypotheses of, 3–4
  law of diminishing returns and, 7–8, 10, 18
  New Growth theorists refuting, 12–21
  supporters of, 5–11
Malthusian trap:
  escaping, 19–21
  law of diminishing returns and, 7–8, 10, 18
  Malthus' theory defined, 3–4
  neo-Malthusians and, 5–6, 9, 15, 18, 20, 182
  New Growth Theory and, 12–21
  overview, 2–3
Mangrove Action Project, 112

Marginal returns, diminishing. *See* Law of diminishing returns
Marine life. *See* Fishing industry
Marine Stewardship Council, 112
Market failure, defined, 119
May, Robert M., 207, 208, 213, 224
Mazola Corn Oil, 55
McKean, Margaret, 94
McNeely, Jeffrey, 208, 225, 233
Mechanical era, 44
Media bias, regarding global warming, 36–37
Median-variant fertility projections, 80–81
Meffe, Gary K., 219, 224
Metals, recycling of. *See* Recycling
Metals and minerals, World Commodity Index, 274–275
Methanol-fueled cars, 129
Middle East:
  defense of, 134–135
  fertility profiles of, 76–78, 79–80
Migratory Bird Treaty Act, 138
Military expenditures, energy-related, 134–135
Million Solar Roof Initiative, 147–148
Mills, L. Scott, 218
Minimum Viable Population (MVP), 211–212
MIT:
  fish research at, 108
  Limits to Growth report, 6, 11
Mobil, 136
Moral restraint, as population control, 4
Mortality:
  breast cancer rates of, 199
  cancer rates of, 286–287
  controls, 9
  weather-related events and, 166–169
MSW. *See* Municipal solid waste
Municipal solid waste (MSW):
  decline in rate of growth of, 55–56
  grocery packaging as a percentage of, 52–53
Muslim societies, and falling fertility levels, 74
Myers, Norman, 208

National Academy of Sciences (NAS), 144, 198, 200
National Audubon Society, 138
National Marine Fisheries Service, 90, 104
National Renewable Energy Laboratory, 144
Native Americans, fishery management and, 101

Natural greenhouse effect. *See* Global warming
Natural selection, theory of, 5
Nature preserves, 224–226
Negative feedback. *See* Feedbacks, climatic
Negative population growth. *See* Zero population growth
Negawatts, 139–140
Neoclassical model of economic growth, explained, 10–11
Neo-Malthusians. *See* Malthusian trap
Net-replacement fertility level, defined, 66
Neurological disorders, chemical-induced. *See* Endocrine disruptors
New England Fishery Management Council, 90
New Growth Theory of economics, 12–21
New Zealand, conservation of marine resources in, 96–99, 101–102, 105
Nichols, Albert, 130
NIMBY, renewable energy and, 136, 139
Nitrogen emissions, 302–305
Noll, Roger, 147
Nonrival goods, explained, 12
Nortel, 45
Novak, Michael, xvii–xix
Nuclear power, 119–120, 134
Nurses Health Study, 200

Oak Ridge National Laboratory, 213
Oceans, climate-related effects of, 29–30
OECD. *See* Organization for Economic Cooperation and Development
Office of Technology Assessment, 144
Oil. *See* Fossil fuels
Oil depletion allowance, 132–133
OPEC, 124, 125
Open-access fishing, defined, 89
Organization for Economic Cooperation and Development (OECD), 68
Organization of Petroleum Exporting Countries. *See* OPEC
Organochlorines. *See* Endocrine disruptors
Orimulsion, 121
Ostrom, Elinor, 94
Our Stolen Future, 195
Oyster depletion. *See* Fishing industry
Ozone:
    concentrations, 308
    depletion, 34

Packaging innovations, 45, 52–53
Paddock, William and Paul, 6
Parasitic diseases. *See* Diseases
PCBs:
    impact on breast cancer, 199–200
    impact on reproduction, 191–195
Peña, Federico, 146
Persian Gulf:
    defense of, 134–135
    oil reserves, 122
Pesticides. *See* Endocrine disruptors
Petroleum. *See* Fossil fuels
Phosphorous loading to Great Lakes, 284–285
Photovoltaic systems. *See* Energy, renewable
Phylogenetic tree:
    chart of organisms, 206
    defined, 213
Plastics, dematerialization and, 54, 58
"Pocket change" problem of consumer behavior, 130–131
Politicization. *See* Government control
Pollution:
    air quality trends and, 290–310
    from aquaculture, 110–112
    control by 3M Company, 61
    energy-related, 125–127, 140
    population growth and, 17
    See also Global warming
Population:
    consumption conundrum and, 43
    and food security, 160–164
    Malthus on, 4–5
    projection of global, 183, 242–243
    See also World population
Population Bomb, The (Ehrlich), 5, 19
Population Explosion, The (Ehrlich), 6
Positive checks on population, 4
Positive feedback. *See* Feedbacks, climatic
Poverty, land use issues and, 229–234. *See also* Famine
Power. *See* Energy, renewable; Fossil fuels
PPP. *See* Purchasing power parity
Preventive checks on population, 4
Privatization:
    of land for biodiversity conservation, 233–234
    of marine resources, 93–107

Productivity:
  economic theory and, 10–11
  impact of democracy on, 18–19
Program for the Human Environment at Rockefeller University, 45, 62
Property loss, weather-related, 166–169
Property rights:
  biodiversity issues and, 224–226, 229–234
  fishing-related, 88–89
Protected wildlife areas, 224–226, 229–234
Proxmire, William, 147
Public goods, defined, 119
Public health. *See* Diseases; Health issues
Purchasing power parity (PPP), 74

Quagga, extinction of, 210
Quahog fishing, as example of ITQ program, 104
Quarto, Alfredo, 112
Quota management system (QMS), New Zealand Fisheries and, 96–99

Radiosondes, for temperature measurement, 33–35
Reason Public Policy Institute, 59
Rebound effect, 140
Recycling:
  dematerialization and, 44–46, 56–59
  of metals, 57–58
  of selected materials, 57
Red List of Threatened Animals (IUCN), 211
Reichl, Eric, 147
Renewable energy. *See* Energy, renewable
Renewable portfolio standards (RPS), 144
Reproductive behavior. *See* Fertility rates
Reproductive problems. *See* Endocrine disruptors
Research and development:
  agriculture/forest-related, 184
  energy-related, 134, 146–147
Res nullius principle, defined, 232
Resources:
  consumption of, 44–47
  depletion of, 14, 18
Resources for the Future organization, 152
Rival goods, explained, 12
Robo-tuna (MIT research project), 108
Rockefeller University, Program for the Human Environment, 45, 62
Romer, Paul:
  on economic growth, 20

Romer, Paul (*Cont.*):
  on human capital, 19
  on innovation, 59–60
  on New Growth Theory, 11–15
Rubbish. *See* Waste generation; Waste reduction
Ruddle, Kenneth, 100
Ruff, Larry, 141

Salmon:
  farm-raised, 109, 111
  tracking, 108
Satellites:
  deep-layer temperature measurement and, 33–35, 240–241
  for fish tracking, 108
Sea cow, extinction of, 210–211
Sea level, rise in, 172, 176
Second law of thermodynamics:
  related to global warming, 29–30
  related to New Growth Theory of economics, 15–16, 21
Secular fertility decline. *See* Fertility decline, secular
Semen quality. *See* Endocrine disruptors
Sen, Amartya, 19–20
Setchell, B. P., 198
Sharpe, R. M., 195
Shell, 136
Shrimp farming, 110–113
Sierra Club, 138
Simon, Julian, xiii–xvi, 87
Skakkebaek, N. F., 195
Skipjacks, role in oyster conservation, 91, 92
Sklar, Scott, 136–137
Skumatz, Lisa, 60
Slash-and-burn agriculture, impact on deforestation, 16
Smith, Adam, 125–126
Smith, Fred, 232
Smog. *See* Pollution
Snapback effect, 140
Soft energy. *See* Energy, renewable
Sokolov, Vladimir, 211
Solar Industries Association, 136
Solar power. *See* Energy, renewable
Solarex, 137
Solid waste. *See* Waste generation; Waste reduction

Solow, Robert, 11
Soulé, Michael E., 218
Southern African Sustainable Use Specialist Group, 225
South Pacific, communal fishing rights in, 99–100
Soviet Union, and greenhouse gas emissions, 148–149
Species:
    endangered, 211–212
    extinctions of, 208–211
    as measure of biodiversity, 205–208, 213–215
Species/area curves, 218–219
Sperm count, low. *See* Endocrine disruptors
Sprague-Dawley rats, in mammary tumor study, 200
Starr, Chauncey, 59
Starvation. *See* Famine
State of the World, The (Worldwatch Institute), 208
Stavins, Robert, 44
Steel, dematerialization and, 50
Storms. *See* Weather
Structural species, defined, 213–214
Subreplacement fertility levels, 66–73, 79
Substitution, role in recycling, 56
Sulfur emissions, 294–297
Sumpter, J. K., 194
Sun, impact on climate, 33
Sustainable development, livelihood and, 234
Sustainable Use Initiative, 210
Sutherland, Ronald, 141
Synthetic Fuel Corporation, 147

Tabors, Richard, 125, 154
Tasman Institute (Australia), 123
Taxonomists, as species' catalogers, 207–208
Tax subsidies, energy-related, 131–134
Technology:
    agricultural productivity and, 162, 184
    and conservation, 44–46
    as driver for economic growth, 12–17
    fishing-related, 107–109
    history of, 44–46
    impact on global warming, 184–187
Telecommunications, dematerialization and, 51
Temperature anomalies charts, 31, 34
Temperatures, global, 240–241. *See also* Global warming
Temporal variation, biodiversity and, 217

Tenure, land. *See* Communal property
Texas Instruments, 136
Texas oil cartel, 124, 132–133
Texas Railroad Commission, 124, 133
TFRs. *See* Total fertility rates
Thailand, shrimp depletion in, 110–112
Thermometer readings, variability of, 30–31
3M Company, 61
Timber products. *See* Wood products
Tobias, Michael, as neo-Malthusian, 9
Tornados. *See* Weather
Total allowable catch (TAC), 96
Total fertility rates (TFRs):
    defined, 66
    projected, 244–245
    See also Fertility rates
Tower Chemical Company, 193
Toxic chemicals. *See* Endocrine disruptors
Trade winds, impact on global weather, 35
Transferability, communal versus private property and, 94
Trash. *See* Waste generation; Waste reduction
Tremblay, Neil, 193
Tropical rain forests. *See* Deforestation
Troposphere. *See* Free troposphere
"Troubled Water: A Call for Action," 112
Tuxill, John, 208

Ultralight steel auto body (ULSAB), 50
Unilever, 112
United Nations:
    Framework Convention on Climate Change, 148
    IPCC. *See* Intergovernmental Panel on Climate Change
    Population Division, 65, 73–74, 79–82
    Population Fund, 3–4
Urban, Dean L., 219
Urban warming bias, 30–31
U.S. Bureau of the Census:
    on Asian fertility rates, 73
    as demographic agency, 65
    fertility-level projections of, 68–71
U.S. Department of Energy, 136, 137, 138, 144
U.S. Department of Health and Human Services, 197
U.S. Endangered Species Act, 227
U.S. Environmental Protection Agency, 55

U.S. Fish and Wildlife Service, 138
U.S. General Accounting Office, 127, 146
U.S. Geological Survey, 121
U.S. Global Change Research Program, 187
U.S. National Academy of Sciences (NAS), 144, 198, 200

Value added, 45
Values, and conservation, 44, 60
Van der Hammen, Thomas, 225
Vector-borne diseases. *See* Diseases
Vegetation, effect on biodiversity, 216–217
Venezuela, as fuel producer, 121
Video telephony, 51
Vietnam, fertility profiles, 74
Volatile organic compounds, 306–307
Volcanic eruptions, impact on global temperatures, 35

Waggoner, Paul, 17
Walker, Brian, 224
Warming, global. *See* Global warming
Washington Post, 146
Waste generation:
  in early twentieth-century New York, 46
  total tons of U.S., 43
  See also Dematerialization; Municipal solid waste; Waste generation
Waste reduction:
  trash fees and, 60
  See also Dematerialization; Municipal Solid Waste; Waste reduction
Water quality, 282–285
Water vapor response, and global warming, 29–30. *See* also Oceans
Wealth. *See* Affluence
Wealth of Nations, The (Smith), 125
Weather:
  as cause of mortality and property loss, 166–169
  See also Climate changes; Global warming
Weather balloons. *See* Radiosondes
Wetlands, losses/gains, 248–249
Wilderness Society, 137

Wildlife:
  effect of chemicals on, 191–195
  preserves, 224–226, 229–234
  See also Biodiversity
Wilson, Edward O., 208, 210, 218, 221
Winch, Donald, 7–8
Windows 98, as example of law of diminishing returns, 13–14
Wind power. *See* Energy, renewable
Wood products, dematerialization and, 48
World Bank:
  global population projection, 183
  on literacy rates, 74–76
World Conservation Union, 211
World Dynamics (Forrester), 9
World Health Organization, 171
World population:
  and above-replacement but declining fertility, 73–76
  depopulation and, 81–84
  future projections of, 78–84
  and high fertility levels, 76–78
  life expectancy and, 65–66
  median age of, 83
  overview, 64–65
  secular fertility decline and, 66–67
  and subreplacement fertility, 68–73
Worldwatch Institute:
  on extinction of species, 208
  on global warming, 145
  Malthusian focus of, 6
World Wildlife Fund:
  and ecosystem conservation, 215
  and fishing industry, 87, 99, 112

Xenoestrogens. *See* Endocrine disruptors
Xerox Corporation, 45

Yergin, Daniel, 139

Zero population growth:
  impact of, 83–84
  trend toward, 47
  See also Depopulation

ACKNOWLEDGMENTS

I especially want to thank Susan Barry at McGraw-Hill for taking on this project and pushing me when I needed a good shove to get it done. I also want to thank Griffin Hansbury at McGraw-Hill for his great patience and for bearing with me through the myriad problems of getting this complex book into final form.

I owe a very great debt of gratitude to Paul Georgia, Environmental Research Associate, at the Competitive Enterprise Institute. He was absolutely instrumental in obtaining and analyzing the voluminous material for "Benchmarks" and finding the artwork that appears in this volume.

Finally, this project would not have been possible without the vision and good-humored leadership of the President of the Competitive Enterprise Institute, Fred Smith.

About the Author

Ronald Bailey is the author of ECO-SCAM: *The False Prophets of Ecological Apocalypse* and editor of the acclaimed *True State of the Planet*. Former producer of the PBS television series *Think Tank* as well as numerous documentaries, Bailey is a sought-after lecturer on environmental issues. A journalist as well, his articles have appeared in *Smithsonian* magazine, *Commentary*, *Barron's*, *National Review*, and *The Wilson Quarterly*, among many others.